TRANSNATIONALISM
AND IMPERIALISM

NEW DIRECTIONS IN NATIONAL CINEMAS
Robert Rushing, editor

TRANSNATIONALISM AND IMPERIALISM

Endurance of the Global Western Film

—◠◠◠—

EDITED BY
HERVÉ MAYER AND DAVID ROCHE

INDIANA UNIVERSITY PRESS

This book is a publication of

Indiana University Press
Office of Scholarly Publishing
Herman B Wells Library 350
1320 East 10th Street
Bloomington, Indiana 47405 USA

iupress.org

Manufactured in the United States of America

First printing 2022

Cataloging information is available from the Library of Congress.

ISBN 978-0-253-06074-7 (hardback)
ISBN 978-0-253-06075-4 (paperback)
ISBN 978-0-253-06076-1 (ebook)

CONTENTS

ACKNOWLEDGMENTS

WE ARE VERY GRATEFUL TO our editor, Allison Blair Chaplin, whose enthusiasm has carried us through the project from start to finish. Thanks are due to the team at Indiana University Press (Sophia Hebert, David Hulsey) and to Jamie Armstrong for her editorial work.

This project originally started as a two-day conference held in Montpellier, France, in November 2018; it was co-organized with Marianne Kac-Vergne and received funding from three laboratories (EMMA in Montpellier, CAS in Toulouse, and CORPUS in Amiens) as well as from SERCIA, the European society for the study of English-language cinema and television. Additional providing for the cover image was provided for by the laboratory RiRRa21 in Montpellier. We thank Marianne and the PhD candidates (Manon Lefebvre, Katia Marcellin, and Laura Lainvaë) for their help, the heads of the three laboratories (Christine Reynier, Nathalie Cochoy, and Frédérique Spill), and, of course, our keynote speakers, Matthew Carter and Andrew Patrick Nelson, who supported the project from the start. We are also very much indebted to the fantastic group of scholars who helped us review all the material submitted for this volume: Jean-François Baillon, Zachary Baqué, Simon Daniellou, Xavier Daverat, Celestino Deleyto, Alessandro Faccioli, Pietsie Feenstra, Dina Iordanova, Mélanie Joseph-Vilain, Marianne Kac-Vergne, Anne-Marie Paquet-Deyris, Vincent Souladié, Clémentine Tholas-Disset, and Johannes von Molke. Given the wide range of cinemas covered, we never could have done this book without you.

Last but not least, we thank our magnificent contributors, who made this project so easy for us and who devoted much time and effort to produce excellent work for this collection. It was an immense pleasure working with you on this book.

On a more personal note, Hervé thanks his awesome wife, the writer Claire Musiol. And David thanks his awesome partner, Virginie Iché, and their equally awesome children, Lisa and Tim.

TRANSNATIONALISM AND IMPERIALISM

—⚎—

INTRODUCTION

HERVÉ MAYER AND DAVID ROCHE

BONE TOMAHAWK (USA/UK, S. CRAIG Zahler, 2015), *The Hateful Eight* (USA, Quentin Tarantino, 2015), *The Revenant* (USA/Hong Kong/Taiwan, Alejandro G. Iñárritu, 2015), *Slow West* (UK/New Zealand, John Maclean, 2015), *The Magnificent Seven* (USA/Australia, Antoine Fuqua, 2016), *The Ballad of Buster Scruggs* (USA, Ethan and Joel Coen, 2018). And in 2017 alone: *Five Fingers for Marseilles* (South Africa, Michael Matthews), *Godless* (USA, Netflix), *Hostiles* (USA, Scott Cooper), *The Rider* (USA, Chloé Zhao), *The Sisters Brothers* (France/Spain/Romania/Belgium/USA, Jacques Audiard), *The Son* (USA, AMC), and *Sweet Country* (Australia, Warwick Thornton). Judging by the list above, the Western is alive and kicking, and it is everywhere. After hibernating in the 1980s following the *Heaven's Gate* debacle (Michael Cimino, 1980) and the waning of the Spaghetti Western cycle in the 1970s, it found a second wind in the 1990s and has been thriving ever since (Nelson xv–xvii). With movies and series being produced worldwide, it is more than ever a global phenomenon. But it is important to remember that the frontier myth has almost always been just that, at least since the invention of cinema. This book aims to account not so much for the Western's lasting popularity (that would require a reception studies approach), but for its continued relevance as a form and discourse. It posits that part of this relevance—exactly how much remains to be seen—is political. As a master narrative of Western imperialism, the Western exceeds the bounds of US cultural and national identity, and resonates across a wide (and sometimes even wild) range of contexts. In short, the narrative's ideological underpinning might very well explain what makes the genre eminently transnational.

TRANSNATIONALISM, IMPERIALISM,
AND WESTERN STUDIES

This book inherits from the so-called transnational turn in the humanities that developed in the 1990s as an attempt to grapple with the origins and implications of late twentieth-century globalization. In various disciplines, transnationalism as a concept and as a theory renewed scientific perspectives by shifting focus from nation-centered concerns and interpretations to notions of hybridity, exchange, or articulation that appear when looking across borders, revealing contrasting points and common threads, and redefining notions of identity and power. In film studies, in particular, since the late 1990s, an interest in transnationalism developed into the field of transnational cinema. Transnational cinema generally refers to films that cross national borders, as stories, as productions, and sometimes as both. But the concept of transnationalism can be interpreted more widely as a repositioning of film studies, in which the "study of *national* cinemas must then transform into *transnational* film studies" (Lu 25). This "critical transnationalism" approaches film from the viewpoint of international networks of production and reception rather than from national film traditions, exploring questions of "postcoloniality, politics and power" (Higbee and Lim 18) that are manifest in the complex economic, political, and cultural negotiations between transnational and national.

At the heart of a transnational approach to film lies the question of Western imperialism and its cultural and political legacy, which structures global film industries as well as academic film studies. Definitions of imperialism vary among historians and political scientists—from restricted perspectives on specific policies and historical developments to inclusive generalizations about forms of domination (Kettel and Sutton 244–46)—but they generally revolve around the idea of an extension of sovereignty beyond national boundaries (Hardt and Negri xii). As such, imperialism must be distinguished from settler colonialism, which characterized the history of both British colonies of white settlement and US-American continental expansion. Whereas imperialism relies on the population and structures of the societies it seeks to control, settler colonialism presupposes the elimination of indigeneity and its replacement by a new social and political order (Wolfe 2). Yet the distinction between imperialism and settler colonialism is much slimmer when it comes to their cultural expressions. Both modes of domination produced similar discourses (such as Manifest Destiny in the US or the "civilizing mission" in France) and fed on a common transnational ideology of white male supremacy, teleological progress, and Eurocentric binaries of savagery and civilization (Said xi–xiv).

Although the cultural products of settler colonial and imperial nations (captivity narratives, colonial novels, Western films, etc.) may explore the specificities of each political context, they also circulate globally and participate in a transnational conversation on the common discourses and ideologies of Euro-American expansion. The global Westerns discussed in this book engage with this conversation, thereby assessing the endurance of imperial and/or colonial histories and cultures in the present.

Exploring the common threads that connect Euro-American histories of expansion, the transnational turn in the humanities affected the historiography of the West and genre film studies of the Western alike, two fields that had been especially concerned with defining the US-American historical experience and its cultural representations as national exceptions. Following Frederick Jackson Turner's frontier thesis of 1893, the historiography of the US-American West presented the history of US-American settler colonialism as the genesis of the US-American nation. Turner and his followers (Webb; Billington) identified in the metaphor of the frontier the singular, exceptional dynamics that spawned the most powerful, productive, and democratic nation. Inaugurating a "tendency towards exceptionalism that has traditionally shaped much of American historical thinking" (Lahti 4), early historians of the West helped the US find its place among imperial nations at the turn of the twentieth century even as their work contributed to set the nation apart from other empires. As Stephanie LeMenager has noted, the widespread focus on the frontier, among historians and in US-American culture at large at the turn of the twentieth century and since, "functioned to separate the USA from global imperial history, marking it as an exceptional national experiment" (qtd. in Kollin, *Captivating Westerns* 15). Research perspectives on the frontier and the history of the West dramatically changed in the 1980s, when a generation of New Western Historians (Cronon; Limerick; White) rewrote the historical West as a diverse and contended place rather than a linear process of national formation. Following Gloria Anzaldúa's hybrid literary exploration of *la frontera*, borderland studies also contributed to redefine national borders in the US-American West, especially the US-Mexico border, as hybrid zones rather than lines of separation (Welchman; Vila). Starting in the 1990s, the historiography of the West also benefited from the growing interest of historians in transnational histories of empires. New studies (Bender; Tyrrell) looked to recast US-American settler colonization within a global imperial movement, rewriting the US historical experience as part of global processes of expansion and exploitation. Historian Robert J. C. Young, for instance, foregrounded the "global dimension" of the history of colonization (qtd. in Paryż 5), while Tony Ballantine and Antoinette Burton argued that empires and colonies "were never fully self-contained or hermetically sealed systems" (qtd. in Lahti 7). Historians now tend to regard the West as "always already transnational," to use Neil Campbell's expression (4), and, to extend Emily Burns's remark about the material culture of the US-American West in late nineteenth-century France, as a cultural construct that was never "a fixed concept but rather a transnational discourse" (3).

Like the mythical West, the Western was transnational from the start. It is only recently, however, that this view has been developed in film genre studies. Foundational scholarship on the Western produced in the 1970s and 1980s tended to follow André Bazin's famous remark of 1953 that the Western was US-American cinema par excellence, identifying the genre with a "national world-view: underlying the whole complex is the grave problem of identity that has special meaning for Americans" (Kitses 12). Subsequent studies of the Western have largely focused on the genre's intimate connections with national identity (Schatz; Buscombe et al.; Coyne). They approached the Western as a US-American exception, a genre intimately tied to US history and bent to explore the formation of a US-American brand of democracy and capitalism. In doing so, these seminal studies participated in fueling a sense of national exception that the genre was originally designed to promote. But Western film studies gradually moved away from the national framework by reframing the genre's origins, development, and circulation within a transnational culture of imperialism. Cultural historians Richard Slotkin and Denise Mary MacNeil identified a Native American influence in the formation of a national mythology of the frontier. In a 2001 article on writer Cormac McCarthy, Susan Kollin famously called on researchers to recognize that the Western's "sensibilities have been shaped by a larger history of imperialism" and to acknowledge the role of a transnational culture of empire in its emergence; and in her 2015 book *Captivating Westerns*, she located the origins of typical Western tropes such as captivity narratives in European Orientalism, notably in the writings of an author often considered to be one of the genre's forefathers, James Fenimore Cooper. The Western's role as a genre with a "colonial past and a postcolonial significance" (Paryż) also came to the fore of Western film studies in the wake of Richard Slotkin's frontier trilogy (1973–1992), many scholars recognizing with Peter Limbrick that "the Western is, at heart, a form of settler-colonial cinema that connects national histories of colonialism to a broader transnational narrative of imperialism, violent dispossession, and its ongoing impacts on national and global identities" (qtd. in Hamilton, 68–69).

The Western genre is now increasingly considered as a US-American version of colonial cinema that has conversed with non-US-American spectacles and narratives of empire since its inception, and that has a long-standing, transnational history of appropriations and articulations with local histories of empire. The production of Western films outside the US originated contemporaneously with the US-American Western at the beginning of the twentieth century, and the questions the genre addressed then—issues of national and racial identity, and the long-lasting effects of colonization on societies and the environment— "remain painfully current" (Spurgeon 5) as the bulk of Westerns are now produced outside the US. Some of the ideological tenets of empire that structure the genre, such as the opposition of civilization and savagery, still power Euro-American foreign policies in the age of counterterrorism (Gregory), promising the Western a bright future as a critical platform to explore the history and politics of imperialism. In such a context, further research on the transnational dimensions of the Western genre is as crucial for understanding the cultural developments of imperialism in the global present as the transnational history of empire is for understanding the historical roots of contemporary globalization (Lahti 7). The Western has always been, and remains, a powerful narrative and aesthetic framework to explore, negotiate, and critique the local operations of global imperial policies, and filmmakers and audiences throughout the world turn to it for reflection and participation.

This collected volume comes in the wake of several publications that studied the Western genre from a more or less explicitly transnational perspective. These studies built both on the transnational turn in film studies and earlier studies of non-US-American, often Italian, Westerns, the latest of which, Austin Fisher's *Radical Frontiers in the Spaghetti Western: Politics, Violence, and Popular Italian Cinema*, explored radical trends in the Italian Western that were specifically European. Thomas Klein, Ivo Ritzer, and Peter W. Schulze's 2012 volume *Crossing Frontiers: Intercultural Perspectives on the Western*, and Cynthia Miller and A. Bowdoin Van Riper's 2014 *International Westerns: Re-locating the Frontier* focused on appropriations of the Western by filmmakers and film industries outside the US, and studied the articulation of a US-American genre with local contexts. *The Post-2000 Film Western: Contexts, Transnationality, Hybridity* (2015), edited by Marek Paryż, expanded on Neil Campbell's work on the *Rhizomatic West* (2008) to analyze border- and genre-crossings as a characteristic development of contemporary Western productions. MaryEllen Higgins, Rita Keresztesi, and Danya Oscherwitz's 2015 collection *The Western in the Global South* focused on how the appropriations of US-American and Italian Westerns by filmmakers in the Global South served a criticism of coloniality. Emma Hamilton and Alistair Rolls's 2018 volume *Unbridling the Western Film Auteur: Contemporary, Transnational and Intertextual Explorations* blended a transnational perspective on the Western with a critical exploration of auteurship in genre films. Together these studies provide a rich and complex picture of the Western as a transnational genre at the crossroads of global dynamics and local contexts, but they also leave room for additional perspectives.

Transnationalism and Imperialism: Endurance of the Global Western Film pursues and complements existing research by bridging transnational film studies with the historical and political concerns of transnational histories of empire. It considers the Western as the product of a transnational culture of imperialism and focuses on the political dimensions of its transnational production, circulation, and appropriations. It embraces the entire history of the Western from the silent era to contemporary productions and applies a transnational approach to the study of US-American productions, thus building the case that the Western is a transnational genre. It also seeks to contribute to ongoing discussions concerning many of the assumptions early writings on the genre took for granted, regarding the genre's simplicity, conservative politics, and US-Americanness (a stereotype which, in some discourses, implicitly or explicitly combines the first two qualities).

NEW PERSPECTIVES ON THE WESTERN

The Western is no longer seen as "the American film genre *par excellence*" (Bazin), the cinematic equivalent of jazz. The myth of the West and the cultural products that gave it expression had circulated before the invention of cinema and continued to do so during the early years of the medium's development. Contemporary historians point to the popularity of the Wild West Show and Western themes already on display at the International Exposition of 1867 in Paris as an explanation for the production of Indian pictures by Pathé in France and Western-themed pictures in Italy in the late 1900s and early 1910s (Burns; Lottini; Wong; see also Magrin Haas's contribution in this volume). Such studies reveal that the history of the Western was transnational from the start, that it was not a simple expansion from Hollywood Westerns to international Westerns triggered, notably, by the success of the Spaghetti Western cycle, as we once believed. Instead, they insist on the transnational history of the West as an imaginary domain and seek to contextualize them within specific regions or nations.

Nor is the Western seen as an obvious or pure genre anymore, the exemplar for any theory of film genre that it once was (Schatz). The classical Hollywood era abounded in generically hybrid Westerns: Western gangster movies (*High Sierra*, Raoul Walsh, 1941), Western melodramas (*Duel in the Sun*, King Vidor,

1946), Western noir (*Pursued*, Raoul Walsh, 1947), Western musicals (*Oklahoma!*, Fred Zinnemann, 1955). With its bandits, Indian wars, and nineteenth-century time setting, the Western is, more fundamentally, perhaps, a generic sibling of the crime film, the war movie, and the costume drama. Slotkin argues that, after World War II, "the cavalry Western provided a way to merge the language and concerns of the war film and the Western" (352), a commonality highlighted by the presence of John Wayne, whose star image was associated at the time more with his roles as a soldier/officer than as a cowboy (243). The integration of noir aesthetics—the use of flashbacks and chiaroscuro lighting, a general sense of oppressiveness—in Hollywood Westerns from the 1940s on (*The Ox-bow Incident*, William Wellman, 1942; *Rancho Notorious*, Fritz Lang, 1952; *High Noon*, Fred Zinnemann, 1953; *The Man Who Shot Liberty Valance*, John Ford, 1962) has been explored by David Meuel in particular. And the US-American road movie has often been seen as the late twentieth-century descendant of the Western (Cohan and Hark 1). This book takes the impurity of the Western for granted, but seeks to account for it because of the genre's transnational history and ideological foundations. The genre's mutations are, of course, closely entwined with its circulations. The classical Hollywood Western influenced the European Westerns produced in France, Germany, and Italy as well as Akira Kurosawa's samurai films or Rocha's Nordesterns (see Lee's and Phillips's contributions to this volume), and the impact of the Spaghetti Western cycle on US-American, European, and East Asian cinema is well documented (see contributions to parts III and IV in Fisher, *Spaghetti Westerns*; Teo 1–2).

Recent scholarship has replaced the genre in a global context and described it as the US-American variant of the colonial/imperialist narrative: such narratives all have in common that they are centered on the conflict between civilization and wilderness, settlers and Indigenous peoples, and on the colonization of the latter by the former. Slotkin had specifically noted the similarities between the Hollywood and British Empire films of the 1930s and the progressive Westerns of the late 1930s–early 1940s, which the casting of Errol Flynn and Olivia de Havilland, stars of *The Charge of the Light Brigade* (Michael Curtiz, 1936) and in *Santa Fe Trail* (Curtiz, 1940) and *They Died with Their Boots On* (Raoul Walsh, 1941), played up (292). The Western and the film of empire share certain themes, narrative tropes, and visual and aural motifs: "The narrative of expansion, the taming of the frontier, the clash between civilization and savagery" (Chapman and Cull 7), the confrontation with another race more attuned to that environment, the relationship between the individual and the collective, the cavalry (Chapman and Cull 44), the lone hero, the last stand, the horse, the rifle or gun, the flag, the savage chants, and triumphant horns. The last stand trope alone—present as it is in the Custer or Alamo movies as well as in the South African–set *Zulu* (UK, Cy Enfield, 1964)—begs for a transnational study of the representations of Western conquest and white male heroism. Many non-US-American Westerns or Western-influenced films draw attention to the similarities and differences between US imperialism and domestic colonial and postcolonial experiences in Australia, France, Korea, and Ireland by citing, alluding to, or even remaking classics like *Shane* (virtually all the town-tamer stories, including those that remake Kurosawa's 1961 *Yojimbo*), *High Noon* (*Calvary*, John Michael McDonagh, 2014), *The Searchers* (*The Tracker*, Rolfe de Heer, 2002; *Jauja*, Lisandro Alonso, 2014; *Les Cowboys*, Thomas Bidegain, 2015; *Sweet Country*), *The Good, The Bad and the Ugly* (*The Good, the Bad, the Weird*, Jee-woon Kim, 2008), *For a Few Dollars More* and *Once Upon a Time in the West* (*Sholay*, Ramesh Sippy, 1975), and *Django* (*Sukiyaki Western Django*, Takashi Miike, 2007).

Finally, although they are still widespread among critics and scholars alike, notions that the politics of the Western are essentially conservative or imperialist have recently been challenged, with calls for more nuanced analyses of classical Hollywood productions. In 1986, Tag Gallagher exposed the limits of an evolutionist reading of the genre's history from conservative classicism to progressive revisionism. More recently, Matthew Carter argued that "Westerns are contradictory in their narrative meanings, existing as platforms for debating the impact and scope of the myth of the West on US culture, rather than acting as a mouthpiece which univocally celebrates a particular version of US-American history—that is to say, 'the white man's story'" (194–95). Viewing the Western as a conservative or imperialist genre amounts to disregarding the ways cultural products not simply reflect but respond to dominant narratives of national identity. Framing the history of the Western in terms of evolution both downplays the revisionist and anti-imperialist work of classical films, and overrates the political progress achieved by revisionist films. When read in context, Western classics like John Ford's *The Iron Horse* are much bolder in rewriting the history of the West and challenging national politics than many recent productions. What Richard Slotkin identified as the scapegoating of frontier mythology in the late 1960s (556–58) can often be applied to the Western's critical and academic reception, whereby a specific genre was made to bear the racist and imperial ideology of a national culture.

Here, too, a transnational perspective on the Western proves fruitful for documenting the genre's critical reevaluation of US-American imperial mythology by allowing scholars to point to complex influences, connections, circulations, and appropriations that participated in the revisionist work of the genre. It could, for instance, clarify how the Western used decentered cultural and geographic perspectives to question and contrast histories and mythologies of empire. International casts, crews, and locations as well as narratives of border crossing and forms of generic hybridization have contributed to cast US-American colonization and imperial myth as local installments in a global story of Western imperialism (as suggested in Slotkin; Miller and Bowdoin Van Riper; Higgins et al.; Hamilton and Rolls). Reading the genre across borders is also necessary to grasp the complexity of marketing, circulation, and reception patterns and the ways the politics of the films can be reframed by producers and appropriated by audiences (Bloom; see Adamson in this volume).

Transnationalism and Imperialism: Endurance of the Global Western Film participates in a move of Western film studies away from the evolutionist, purist, and exceptionalist interpretations of the genre's history—claiming instead that it has always been revisionist, hybrid, and transnational—and complements earlier transnational studies of the Western. It argues that a significant reason for the genre's transnational success is to be found in its exploration of a transnational ideology of imperialism. The Western is easily and widely appropriated in a multiplicity of contexts—whether international, national, or regional—because its ideological structures were shaped by transnational histories of empire that still frame much of the cultural exchanges in the global present. The Western is particularly suited to transnational circulation and cocreation because its imperial language of oppression and emancipation is global, its premises and arguments shared and felt everywhere. Filmmakers around the world can mobilize the Western to comment on the structuring persistence of imperial history in contemporary globalized culture and raise questions of responsibility and continued oppression. This book also argues that transnational perspectives of the Western inform the genre's reflection on its own imperial politics and role within a larger culture of imperialism. Westerns articulate the global operations of imperialism to local historical contexts, but they also build on local histories to expose and often critique the persistence of coloniality in the global present. It remains to be seen whether much can be added to the discussion of US-American identity as reflected in the Western,[1] but it is certain that a lot more remains to be said about the place of the Western as a form of colonial cinema within a transnational culture of imperialism and how the genre responds to the global and local operations of imperialism.

HOLLYWOOD, THE UGLY, THE WEIRD

An account of transnationalism in the Western genre starts with a consideration of US-American films whose narratives, production patterns, and market circulation cross national borders. This broad approach to transnationalism in Westerns virtually encompasses every Western produced in the US. If not all Westerns are transnational from the point of view of production (although individual trajectories of cosmopolitan and international casts and crews could serve such argument), they are so from the point of view of circulation and reception, and often from the point of view of their narratives. If one accepts the common premise that Westerns focus on the frontier, then all Westerns are about what Mary Louise Pratt called the "contact zone" where cultural and racial borders are constantly crossed (6). Embodied in the frontier hero and the networks of affects and exchanges that characterize such a zone, cultural hybridity is at the heart of the genre and, thus, complexifies the notion of a distinctly white Anglo-Saxon national identity. Westerns like *The Searchers* have famously explored this hybridity in critical ways, blurring the core binaries of imperial culture and exposing the savagery at the heart of civilization; Ford's 1956 film remains a primary reference for many transnational Westerns investigating the psychological and political manifestations of colonization (see, e.g., Barrett, Fontanaud, González, and Roche in this volume).

The crossing of strictly *national* borders in US-American Westerns is manifested at the level of production, with foreign writers, directors, producers, or stars having infused the genre's construction and development with their own transnational perspectives. Christopher Frayling remarked, for instance, that "three of the founding fathers of the modern Western—John Ford, Fritz Lang, Fred Zinnemann—were Irish, German and Austrian by origin" (qtd. in Miller and Bowdoin Van Riper). Scholars have since explored the European influence these filmmakers brought to bear on Hollywood productions; for instance, Heike Endter's contribution to *International Westerns* analyzes how Fritz Lang's German origins influenced his Hollywood-produced Westerns (Miller and Bowdoin van Riper), while Costanza Salvi explores how Ford's Irishness informs his "Cavalry Trilogy" in this present volume. Hollywood has also constantly borrowed from foreign cinematic styles and stories to fuel its productions, and the Western is no exception. The influence of Japanese cinema on the genre since *The Magnificent Seven* has been well documented (Teo), while the Italian Westerns of the 1960s influenced US-American productions at the turn of the 1970s (Slotkin 628), but such transnational exchanges date back to the silent era when the pro-Indian films of Pathé and Gaumont influenced

US-American productions and eventually pushed the latter toward large-scale historical dramas on the prairie (Abel).

The transnational dimension of US-American Westerns is also manifest in the genre's global circulation and reception. Researchers have focused on the ways in which Westerns could be marketed differently depending on the regions, shifting the focus of promotion to maximize audience interest in politically charged ways. Russell Meeuf analyzed how the promotion of John Wayne's Westerns focused on the star and emphasized the image of conquering masculinity in France, while it highlighted romance and a multiple cast in the US. Similarly, in this volume, Patrick Adamson discusses the different cuts and promotion materials of a Hollywood silent era epic as the film was sold in Europe or in the US. US-American Westerns were also received and appropriated differently in Australia by international audiences, sometimes with surprising emancipatory effects. Peter Bloom has shown how 1930s Westerns of the populist variety such as *Jesse James* (Henry King, 1939) were so popular among the colonized subjects of the French Empire as to be considered a threat and regulated accordingly by authorities in French Algeria. In his 1967 interview with Peter Bogdanovich, John Ford said the pro-Indian perspective of *Cheyenne Autumn* partly came from a desire to meet the demands of European audiences for such representations (104). Celebrated by the critics of the influential *Cahiers du Cinéma*, Ford was certainly more revered in France than Raoul Walsh, for instance, and the more critical perspective of *Cheyenne Autumn* compared with *A Distant Trumpet*, both focused on the Indian wars in the Southwest, shot mostly in Arizona and released in 1964, may partly result from that.

Finally, in terms of content, many US-American Westerns, especially from the 1950s on, tell stories of border crossings or Western-like stories in foreign contexts. Western tropes and visuals have been employed to represent Mexico in films about the Mexican Revolution since Raoul Walsh's semidocumentary *The Life of General Villa* (1914). Other Latin American countries have been subjected to the same association with the Western in their Hollywood treatment, for instance, Argentina in *Way of a Gaucho* (Jacques Tourneur, 1952), in which the Western provides viewers with a recognizable framework to access Argentine characters and history. Following *Vera Cruz* (Robert Aldrich, 1954), a cycle of US-American films focused more explicitly on US-American cowboys crossing into Mexico and exploited the Mexico setting to critically reflect back on US mythology (see Mayer in this volume). The tendency of US-American cowboys to go south when the western frontier is closed was eventually parodied in *Butch Cassidy and the Sundance Kid* (George Roy Hill, 1969), in which the southern Promised Land—this time Bolivia—is revealed as a mistake and an illusion. The Western has also been an ideal framework for representing Canadian history, sometimes with US-American cowboys crossing the border (Gary Cooper in Cecil B. DeMille's 1940 *North West Mounted Police*) or more often with Canadian characters played by US-American Western stars (William S. Hart in Lambert Hillyer's 1921 *O'Malley of the Mounted*, Alan Ladd in Raoul Walsh's 1954 *Saskatchewan*). *Saskatchewan* is especially harsh in its comparison of US-American and Canadian policies regarding Native Americans, indicting the former for a particularly violent treatment of (particularly violent) Indigenous peoples (the Sioux in the film), as opposed to the pacified relationship of Canadians with the (more pacific) Cree (and Ladd's character with a Cree scout played by Jay Silverheels, who was famous for playing Tonto in *The Lone Ranger* [ABC, 1949–1957]). All in all, the conflation of Western tropes and characters with non-US-American contexts and histories in these films works to dissociate the Western from US-American identity and comment on US history and mythology from a distance.

Non-US-American Westerns can be divided into two groups based on the spatial/historical criteria that have been used to define the US-American genre. There are those set in the US-American West and those that take place in locations and periods that resemble the US-American West because of their history, topography, and geology; a subgroup of the latter category would include stories that adapt Western conventions to a contemporary and sometimes even urban world (*Calvary* and *Les Cowboys* again, but also Australian director Ivan Sen's *Mystery Road* [2013] and *Goldstone* [2016], and the follow-up series *Mystery Road* [Australian Broadcasting Company, 2018–]). Generally speaking, European and Japanese Westerns tend by and large to belong to the first group, those produced in former colonies or occupied areas (the USSR, Australia and New Zealand, Korea, and Latin America) to the second. In a sense, the first group of films merely pursues the Hollywood Western's own attempt to interrogate the complex intertwining of the historical reality of the West and its myth, but they posit that, although the historical reality of the West may be specific to the US and Mexico, the myth—and especially its core ideology—is not. Ideologically speaking, the genre's relevance would, then, lie in the narrative of US imperialism itself, which acquires "universal" and/or local relevance through allegory; when deterritorialized, the Western's political relevance would stem from the "universality" of imperialism. If this distinction is both evident and useful, we would argue that it is actually a matter of degree. Indeed, the indigenous Western immediately invites comparisons between a local situation and the US context, and they do so mainly by reprising generic narratives, figures, motifs, and tropes (e.g., the captivity narrative, the outlaw, the last stand) and often by highlighting such similarities through citation or allusion. The relevance of non-US-American US-American-set Westerns might, in this sense, be more difficult to decipher because, unless the narrative is decentered through the perspective of an immigrant—as in movies like *The Salvation* (Denmark/UK/ South Africa/Sweden/Belgium, Kristian Levring, 2014) and *Slow West*—they do not immediately invite such comparisons; in most cases, the relationship with the local context is a matter of subtext and sometimes even an effect of a context-based analysis adopting a reflectionist approach.

The Spaghetti Western has largely been interpreted in this light. The cycle began as an attempt to channel US-American funding to the Italian film industry, imitate the success of the German Winettou Westerns (Hughes xvi), make up for the decrease in the production of Hollywood Westerns, and, basically, exploit a local audience still in love with the genre (Bondanella 338). And yet it took an explicitly political turn following *A Bullet for the General* (Damiano Damiani, 1967), cowritten by the politically committed author Franco Solinas, and the spawn of Zapata Spaghetti Westerns that followed (Bondanella 359–66). Many Spaghetti Westerns expressed both local and global concerns: the violence and sadism evoking the specter of a return of Fascism in Italy (Hughes 179–80); the cynical and greedy gunmen, the ruthlessness of Western capitalism (McClain). The fact that most directors and screenwriters had experienced Mussolini and World War II and adhered to Socialist, Marxist, or even anarchist views lends weight to such interpretations (Frayling 206–7).

Although Leone's films are generally considered to be less political than those of the other Sergios (Corbucci and Sollima), the US-American West is portrayed as a space where action, movement, and human relations are primarily dependent on capital. This view reaches its apex in *The Good, the Bad, and the Ugly* (1966), heightened as it is by the contrast between the economics of the West—dramatized through a plot centered on three treasure-seeking individuals—and the political strife between North and South. Leone saw the Civil War as a means not so much to engage with the complexities of a specific historical event as to reveal the inhumanity of war and—more implicitly and from a more historiographical perspective—its subsequent rewriting from the victors' point of view (Frayling 205). The film thus insists on the interchangeability between Northern and Southern forces: first, with light irony when Blondie and Tuco mistake a group of Union soldiers for Confederates, later with the bridge sequence in which a drunk colonel rants on about the absurdity of war, and, more provocatively perhaps, by the alteration of a historical fact: the Confederate concentration camp of Andersonville is reimagined as a Union camp. The contrast between two contexts and two modes of violence—one more individual, the other more collective—collapses when Angel Eyes appears in the guise of a Union sergeant, in the scene where Tuco gets tortured, proving that institutionalized violence is a breeding ground for deviant behaviors and for those who are driven by economic and libidinous interests (the plot itself is based on this idea since the treasure is a soldier's war looting).

The concentration camp scenes, thus, epitomize the ambiguity of many non-US-American US-American-set Westerns, notably their attempt to re-create the US-American West, and sometimes even get it right—Leone and his production designer carried out extensive research on costumes, weaponry, and such (Frayling 206–10)—and yet turn it into a universal parable by mixing in elements of twentieth-century European history. The presence of the war also contributes to a critique of the violence of capitalism as an ideology: the nation was born not of the ashes of a conflict in which brother fought against brother (as per Benedict Anderson's famous theory of nationhood) but from an economic drive that, like the film's eponymous characters, preexisted the conflict, managed to negotiate the war, and pursued its course in the aftermath. The force of US-American/Western capitalism is further redoubled by the allegory, since the cemetery and the ghost town before it stand not just for the ruins left in the wake of the Civil War, but also for those in Europe and elsewhere who were profited from, ultimately, by US interests.

Another famous example of a European Western that was well received on the international scene—and that has received much critical attention since—is the Czechoslovakian film *Lemonade Joe* (Oldrich Lipský, 1964). A musical parody of the town-tamer Western, it pits a white-clad gunslinger who promotes Kolaloka lemonade against the Badmans, Doug, the owner of the Trigger Whisky Saloon, and his shapeshifting brother Hogofogo. If parody has generally been described as a mode (Hutcheon), scholars of Czech/Czechoslovakian cinema (Mléčková; Mareš) treat it like a subgenre of comedy that was quite common in domestic cultural productions of the time. Few Western movies had been screened in the country in the years before *Lemonade Joe*'s release (one exception being the anti-HUAC *High Noon*), so domestic audiences would not have picked up the visual allusions to *My Darling Clementine* (Ford, 1946), and the like. But the Wild West had a long history in Czechoslovakian popular culture—a Country and Western group even organized activities in secret (Mléčková 35–36, 50)—and screenwriter Jiri Brdecka had originally created the character in textual form and for the stage (1944–1946) (Mareš 19). So, unlike the Spaghetti Western, *Lemonade Joe* testifies not to the popularity of the Hollywood Western but, much like the French and Italian Westerns of the early silent era, to the power of the frontier myth and Western iconography in Czech/Czechoslovakian culture.

The politics of this delightful film are more ambiguous than a cursory glance would suggest. On the one hand, *Lemonade Joe* is a straightforward satire of US capitalism (Mléčková 55–56; Costanzo 47), drawing a parallel between Western expansion in the nineteenth century on the one hand, and economic and cultural imperialism in the twentieth on the other (Kolaloka, an obvious play on Coca-Cola, means "Crazy Cola" in Spanish). The Westerner as a peddler of soft drinks and good manners is, in effect, a synecdoche of the genre itself: a consumer product (cynically produced as such) and a righteous purveyor of a given ideology in which religion and capitalism collude (drinking lemonade encourages abstinence, which also sharpens one's aim) (fig. I.1). In this respect, *Lemonade Joe* rejoins the combination of love and critique of the genre at the heart of the Spaghetti Western that was emerging at the same time. Aniko Imre has also made a case for a subtextual interpretation of the film's politics, one whereby the "foregrounding of binary symbolism"—notably, the "rigid racist and sexist framework of the Western genre"—functions "as a comedic effort to demystify the rigid framework of official Soviet ideology in the 1960s" (164), that is, the opposition between good/communist and evil/capitalist. From a Cold War perspective, then, this Western parody would tend to show what the opposing ideologies have in common: a drive for profit (Miller 118), a binary worldview, a sense of moral/political righteousness, and a penchant for propaganda. Perhaps this is the political implication of the last-minute reveal that the good guys and bad guys are actually from the same family and manage to get over their differences quite easily to produce the ideal synthesis: Whiskola! Significantly, one of the few political comments made in the film occurs when the sheriff, shocked by Hogofogo's stating his dislike for the lemonade, calls the miscreant "an anarchist," a term that would have been a negative in both the US and Czechoslovakia. If the film overtly critiques the US-American way of life, it also testifies to a love of the genre (and, more generally, to a love of cinema). Indeed, the Western parody delights us because of the inventiveness of its visuals, which, like *The Poacher's Foster-Daughter* (Martin Fric, 1949), a film that no doubt influenced its aesthetics and approach to parody (Mareš 19), tap into techniques borrowed from different periods and forms of silent cinema (tinting, Dutch angles, burlesque accelerated fights, vanishing tricks à la Méliès).

Many national cinemas have a history of indigenous Westerns: the Red/Soviet Westerns, Korea's Manchurian Westerns of the late 1960s and early 1970s, the Brazilian *nordeste* discussed by Phillips in this volume. Australia, in particular, has been producing Westerns since the mid-1900s, and New Zealand, more modestly, since the 1920s, when Rudall Hayward directed several movies

Fig. I.1 The Westerner as a peddler of soft drinks and good manners in *Lemonade Joe* (Oldrich Lipský, 1964) [14:45].

centered on Mahori-Kahera relations, the best known of which is *The Te Kooti Trail* (1927). The most ambitious New Zealand film ever made upon its release (Harris 38), *Utu* (Geoff Murphy, 1983), is exemplary because of the way it taps into the "international generic conventions" of the Western that it "accept[s]" (Margolis 85) to relate the history of colonialism in Aotearoa New Zealand. The story of the pursuit of a Maori Scout turned outlaw (Te Wheke), *Utu* reprises Western tropes and motifs (ambushes, last stands, fetishized weapons, establishing shots of riders crossing prairie country [fig. I.2]), cites classical Westerns like *Winchester '73* (Anthony Mann, 1950) (when Wimeru raises the Stetson rifle over his head), and is heavily influenced by the revisionist Westerns of the 1970s (the Maori village massacre scene, with its emphasis on the murder of women and children, recalls the Washita River and Sand Creek massacre scenes in *Little Big Man* [Arthur Penn, 1970] and *Soldier Blue* [Ralph Nelson, 1970] [Reid 86–87]). Dialogues highlight the underlying ideological structure opposing a wilderness inhabited by "brown bastards" and civilization, metonymically represented by a woman like Emily Williamson who plays Beethoven on the piano moments before being murdered.

Utu engages with Western imperialism on two levels and between three groups: Maori and Pakeha (white settlers), Great Britain and its colony within the diegesis, the US and New Zealand on a cinematic level. If Kenneth Marc Harris's and Harriet Margolis's appreciations of the film's representation of race differ—Margolis sees it as a welcome change in New Zealand film history (94), while Harris insists on how Te Wheke and Miremu ultimately fall into the stereotypical categories of the fetishized Other as theorized by Homi K. Bhabha (51–52)—both scholars agree that the film is (and was intended as)

Fig. I.2 The establishing shots of riders crossing prairie country in *Utu* (Geoff Murphy, 1983), a classic Western trope [66:35].

an expression of New Zealand national identity (Harris 38; Margolis 96). The opening massacre, which causes Te Wheke's desertion from the army and the Maori uprising he will lead, immediately places responsibility squarely on the British; the collusion between church and empire is also underlined when Te Wheke asks whether the vicar, whom he has just killed, "has other Lords than God." The revision of nineteenth-century history—the settlers were prone to seize Maori land while British troops tended to respect the Maori as worthy opponents (Margolis 93)—enables the construction of a national narrative across racial and cultural lines; pointedly, all the characters speak in English and Maori except the British. *Utu*, Harris reveals in his psychoanalytical analysis of the film, dramatizes the Pakeha characters' (Scott's and Williamson's) failure to "measure up to standards imposed by the British colonial father" (represented by Elliot) as well as those set by the Western hero (47). Williamson, the cinematic equivalent of Ford's Ethan Edwards and theoretical equivalent of Slotkin's Man Who Knows Indians, turns out to be quite inept in spite of his impressive four-barrel rifle. Resolution, ultimately, comes from the Maori scout, Wiremu, who executes Te Wheke (his brother) because, unlike others, he is not motivated by payback ("utu" in Maori). Wiremu, Harris concludes, saves the day, ideologically speaking, because he embodies the New Zealand ideal of the 1980s, "a European who is a Maori and a Maori who is a European" (51), but also, cinematically speaking, because his intervention makes Scott's and Williamson's attempts to embody the Western cowboy beside the point—"in New Zealand you don't have to be a 'good cowboy' because the 'Indians' obligingly kill each other" (48). Harris's conclusion, ultimately, suggests that *Utu*'s ideological project is, above all, in the interest of "New Zealand's semi-official ideology" of interracial reconciliation. Although an indigenous New Zealand Western, *Utu*, as a revisionist narrative that nonetheless upholds the national myth, is fodder for Slotkin's argument about the capacity of myth to adapt in revised form and survive as countermyth (654–56).

Yet if *Utu* supports this national myth, it nonetheless acknowledges ongoing racial strife and, thus, the rift between myth and reality—Te Wheke's comment about "warriors in the streets of Aukland" echoes the upheavals in urban areas in 1981 (Harris 49; Margolis 94). Furthermore, unlike the Hollywood pro-Indian Westerns of the 1950s, *Utu* complicates the question of national identity by refusing to align it with a lone hero figure. Taking its cue from *Heaven's Gate*, perhaps, *Utu* adopts a multiprotagonist narrative centered on six characters (three Maoris, two white Kiwis, one British officer), an approach taken up more recently in the Australian Western *Sweet Country*. That a "brown bastard" would potentially emerge as a sort of national ideal—instead of a white Man Who Knows Maoris—is by no means a given, especially for non-Kiwi audiences. So there is something to be said for the film's ending. Not only does it end on a celebration of racial and cultural hybridity, in an attempt, in Margolis's words, to "satisf[y] both Maori *tikanga* and Pakeha law" (94), but the characters repeatedly voice their doubts regarding the superiority of Western civilization over Maori civilization (Williamson) or that the conflict makes it difficult to tell the "right side" apart from the "wrong side" (Wimeru, Scott). Aesthetically speaking, the almost theatrical succession of speeches and chants that prelude Te Wheke's execution (the film cites *MacBeth* on three occasions) maintain the ritual quality of the Western ending but reject the habitual tone: the resolution is not violently brutal, but quietly respectful. Harris's comparison to Leone's musical duels (52–53) thus falls entirely beside the mark in all but one respect: *Utu*'s ending is, in effect, a subversion of the classical Western, a sort of happy reimagining of *The Ox-Bow Incident*, one in which the proponent of justice, the body and voice of the character of color, takes center stage.

A more recent example of a non-US-American indigenous Western that has received much critical attention is the Korean production, *The Good, the Bad, the Weird* (Jee-woon Kim, 2008). For Joyleen Christensen, the film seeks to revive the genre by resorting to characters and aesthetics more characteristic of Korean and Hong Kong martial arts cinema (185–86). If Vivian Lee contends that the film positions itself as a "transnational blockbuster" whose "calculated tactics" aim "to defamiliarize the familiar in the production of 'desirable otherness'" (157), Christensen argues that the film "re-allegorizes [classical Western tropes] as narratives of oppression, dispossession and inevitable resistance" (194), the characters evolving against "a background of nationalist sentiment" that recalls not only the source film but also the Hong Kong production *Once upon a Time in China* (Hark Tsui, 1991) (195). By reallegorizing what was already an allegory in the first place—Leone's use of the US Civil War—*The Good, the Bad, the Weird* asserts the continued relevance of the Western as a transnational allegory of territorial conquest that can reflect similar yet nonetheless culturally specific concerns in various contexts, and engage with national and transnational histories and film histories, notably via intertextuality. The allegorical potential of the Western is, thus, asserted through the reference to Leone, but the film distances itself from its source by insisting on the possibility of relocating the genre. A "weird" rather than an "ugly" Western, the 2008 film assumes its status as a delocalized remake of Leone's 1966 film via its title, and contains scenes that echo Hollywood Westerns—such as the conversation scenes inspired from *The Wild Bunch* (Peckinpah, 1969) (Teo 70)—but also allude to a contemporary British and Italian empire movie set in China, *The Last Emperor* (Bernardo Bertolucci, 1987; the opium den scene) (Teo 62), neatly pointing to the common basis of both genres.

The 2008 film also seeks to revive a national genre—the Manchurian Western—which, like the Spaghetti Western, could appear as an illegitimate bastard of the US-American genre, while distancing itself from its ideological ambiguities. The Manchurian Western cycle of the 1960s and 1970s, with its dramatizations of heroic guerrilla resistance against Japanese military force in a vast desert (Teo 55), has been analyzed (An) as an expression of Korean nationalism closely tied to anti-Japanese sentiment (Teo 57). The 2008 film opposes the nationalist view, first, by depicting Manchuria as a "pan-Asian environment" and, in the director's own words, "a melting pot of race and cultures" (Teo 62)—unlike their models, all three characters (and not just Tuco) are, as members of the Korean diaspora, figures of otherness (Teo 56). Furthermore, by toning up the characters' indifference to history, *The Good, the Bad, the Weird* could "perhaps reflect present-day Asian materialism at its apex" (Teo 73), or else the denial of a period of "increased Korean militarization" (Christensen 196). Yet, as Teo brilliantly demonstrates, not only does the narrative end with the characters' discovering that oil—the treasure the map was pointing— had political and personal significance, implying, as it does, their "uprootedness" (Teo 72), but the characters' comments and motives ultimately betray a discreet form of nationalist sentiment: the Bad wants to be the best, the Bad and the Weird are driven by a symbol of geopolitics and of the transnational

Fig. I.3 The Bad and the Weird are driven by a symbol of geopolitics and of the transnational genre itself, a map, in *The Good, the Bad, the Weird* (Jee-woon Kim, 2008).

genre itself—a map (fig. I.3)—and the Good is not allowed time to share his political views with the Weird (69–71).

Much of the interest of *The Good, the Bad, the Weird* lies in the very ambiguity manifested in its tweaking of the 1966 title. The film may confirm the hypothesis at the core of this book—that the transnational relevance of the genre lies in its imperialist ideology—but it also provides a counterargument, that the genre's power lies above all in the pleasure provided by its aesthetics: "It is action and movement that is the Western's universal form and meaning, not its manifest destiny, or binary oppositions of good/bad, civilisation/ wilderness, inside/outside" (Teo 74). Clearly, the relevance of the Western— and, more largely, of the frontier myth—lies not exclusively in the imperialist ideology that underlies its narrative; it derives much of its power to please, to blind but maybe also to critique from an iconography that had been shaped by representations of the US West and yet found resonance abroad even before the invention of film. The question remains whether the spectacle provided by Western iconography can ever be completely separated from its ideological underpinning: that it is a spectacle of territorial and human conquest.

A TRANSNATIONAL CINEMATIC JOURNEY INTO THE HISTORY OF EMPIRE

Part I of this book proposes several approaches for reading US-American Westerns from the silent era to the twenty-first century through a transnational lens. Contributions in this section adopt different perspectives on

US-American productions that map the broad variety of ways (content analysis, studies of production and distribution) the concept of transnationalism can be applied to a domestic industry. In the opening chapter, Patrick Adamson studies the promotional material and critical reception of *The Iron Horse* in the UK, Australia, and the US with a view to highlighting how marketing strategies mobilized local histories of empire to create the sense of a globalized, yet US/Western-centered, historical understanding; such an approach maximized interest among foreign audiences but also fed on, and cemented, the common ideological and historical features of Western imperial histories. Costanza Salvi's chapter approaches the transnationalism of Hollywood Westerns from the perspective of its most important filmmaker, exploring how the Irish origins of John Ford and his sympathies for Irish nationalism have influenced the politics of his "Cavalry Trilogy" (1948–1950); Salvi shows that Irishness is used to complicate the imperialistic premises of the narrative and fuel Ford's reflection on the Western's historiographical function. Both Mayer and Soubeille's contributions then discuss the transnational dimensions of US-American Westerns from a formal perspective, analyzing how narrative and generic border crossings affect the politics of the genre. In chapter 3, Hervé Mayer looks at *Vera Cruz*, the first film of a cycle of Westerns that articulated the mythology of the US-American West to the historical context of Mexico; Mayer argues that *Vera Cruz*'s Mexico setting mobilizes comparative histories and generic hybridity to provide a decentered perspective on the ideological framework of the Western and US national mythology. Part I concludes with a chapter focused on *Tejano* (David Blue Garcia, 2018), in which Marine Soubeille analyzes the contemporary borderland post-Western as a filmic manifestation of Gloria Anzaldúa's *frontera*; using parody and various formal strategies, *Tejano*, Soubeille argues, recontextualizes the borderland as an always already transnational region.

The films studied in Part II, interestingly enough, are all set in Europe, its colonies, or its former colonies, and they are all generically hybrid, incorporating elements of the war movie, the empire film, the biopic, the Heimat film, or the French *film de banlieue*. In chapter 5, Dragan Batančev analyzes *Kapetan Leši* (Živorad Mitrović, 1960), a Yugoslav production that focuses on the National Liberation War, a conflict between Partisans and Kosovar Quislings that occurred during World War II; the film employs the Western, a genre that initially symbolized the threat of US imperialism, as a framework to celebrate a multinational identity and proposes to integrate Kosovar Albanians by portraying them as brothers, in a perfect illustration of Benedict Anderson's theory of nationhood. Hadrien Fontanaud's chapter deals with a very famous but perhaps less obvious example in the scope of this book, the British-US-American production *Lawrence of Arabia* (1962); by evoking the Western's motifs and tropes in a British empire film, David Lean's epic highlights the imperialist ideology that is at the core of both genres, which it dramatizes and, ultimately, deconstructs through the portrayal of its ambiguous hero. The Orientalist fantasy of the desert and its inhabitants at the heart of the film also points back to the Orientalism of nineteenth-century representations of the US-American West as revealed by Kollin. Marek Paryż's chapter then analyzes *The Dark Valley* (Andreas Prochaska, 2014), an Austrian film that reprises the white savior narrative but replaces the usual racial issues with national concerns, and manifests a certain unease concerning US interventionism, as embodied by its avenging hero. In chapter 8, Jesús Ángel González focuses on *Adieu Gary* (Nassim Amaouche, 2009) and *Les Cowboys*, two films set in contemporary France that explore the nation's troubled relationship to its colonial past and foreground the cracks in its model of social republicanism; the films call on the Western's allegorical potential, notably the cowboy-Indian metaphor, not by respecting the genre's time setting but by revisiting its imagery and narrative.

In the first chapter of the Spotlight on the Italian Western, Alessandra Magrin Haas does more than just remind us of the genre's long history in Italian cinema; films like the Cines production *The Human Bridge* (1913) testify to the presence and the power of the frontier myth in the Italian imagination (Magrin Haas's work on Italy echoes Burns's on France, in this respect), and implicitly fostered national interests by promoting Italian colonialism, notably in Libya, and conservative values (family, community) back home. In chapter 10, Lee Broughton then takes a fifty-year leap to a more familiar period but focuses on a lesser-known work among the five hundred or so Spaghetti Westerns produced: *Matalo!* (Italy/Spain, Cesare Canevari, 1970), an Acid Western that anticipates the cult films *El Topo* (Mexico, Alejandro Jodorowsky, 1970) and *The Last Movie* (USA, Dennis Hopper, 1971). The film's generic instability, Broughton argues, is instrumental in its subversion of imperialism; the transnational history of colonialism is, thus, played out in the hazy background the landscapes provide.

Part III opens with Mike Phillips's study of *Black God, White Devil* (Brazil, 1964) and *Antônio das Mortes* (France/Brazil/West Germany/USA, 1969) by Glauber Rocha, a leader of the highly political Cinema Novo movement; Rocha's ventures into the domestic equivalent of the US-American Western, the Nordestern—set in an arid region of northeastern Brazil populated with outlaws and ranchers—evince a love of Hollywood films (and notably of John Ford) and a wariness of US imperialism, and endeavor to decolonize the genre's spectatorial terms and tap into the revolutionary potential of an aesthetics of violence. Chapter 12 focuses on a more recent Latin American Western, the transnational production *Jauja* (Argentina/Denmark/France/Mexico/USA/Germany/Brazil/Netherlands, 2014), directed by Lisandro Alonso; Jenny Barrett shows how the film's aesthetics, which combine devices typical of New Independent Argentine Cinema with intertextual references to classical Hollywood cinema, develops an anticolonial discourse involving both Argentine history and US cultural imperialism as manifested through Hollywood cinema. In chapter 13, Vivian Lee analyzes the relationship between the Western and the *chanbara* in three recent Japanese "Eastern Westerns": *East Meets West* (Kihachi Okamoto, 1995), *Sukiyaki Western Django* (Takashi Miike, 2007), and *Unforgiven* (Sang-il Lee, 2013); the three films mobilize the Western genre in ways ranging from parody to tribute and self-reflexive critique to explore the connections between US and Japanese cinema and histories of empire. Claire Dutriaux and Annael Le Poullennec's chapter 14 analyzes *Five Fingers for Marseilles* (Michael Matthews, 2017), a South African production that reprises the domestic Boerewor Western, but is above all characteristic of postapartheid cinema in that it seeks to attract an international audience while speaking to national concerns; in particular, it explores the persistence of colonial violence in the postapartheid era and imagines a more utopian national model that would cease to reproduce the cycle of violence.

The Spotlight on the Australian Western starts with Emma Hamilton's historical study of the emergence of the genre in the early 1900s, more specifically, the cycle of bushranging films that culminated with Australia's first feature film, *The Story of the Kelly Gang* (Charles Tait, 1906), and is followed by David Roche's analysis of two twenty-first-century Westerns that endeavor to express a multiracial perspective on the Anglo-Aboriginal relations in the outback, *The Tracker* and *Sweet Country*. Hamilton sees the genre as a site of the entangledness of Australian history (its inscription in the history of Aboriginal peoples and of the British Empire) and film history (notably in relation to US-American cinema); rather than the push-and-pull dynamic foregrounded by Stefan Zimmermann, the cycle ultimately deconstructs such binaries to value cultural and historical exchange. Evincing an awareness of the ideological implications of the Western narrative and motifs, both *The Tracker* and *Sweet Country* deploy a variety of formal strategies in an attempt to decenter the genre and destabilize its imperialist foundations; it is, thus, by interrogating the Western that the films confirm its relevance as a form and discourse with the historiographical potential to address its own history.

Bringing together researchers from France, Great Britain, Spain, Italy, Poland, Australia, Hong Kong, Canada, and the US, this collection offers a transnational perspective on the genre's critical position as a site for the negotiation of issues of power and coloniality within a transnational culture of imperialism. By focusing on the transnational aspects of US-American productions, the contributors to Part I explore the notion that the Western was always already transnational (Adamson) and that US-American Westerns often exploited transnational elements to unpack national myths of empire (Mayer, Salvi, Soubeille). The second and third sections analyze how, throughout the world and since the advent of narrative cinema, filmmakers have mobilized the tropes and visuals of the Western to comment on the past histories and present operations of empire, and the ways in which the global reach of imperial policies and culture has shaped, and been transformed by, local contexts. The Spotlights on the Italian and Australian Western aim not only to give due attention to the countries that have produced the most Westerns outside the US (and that have been doing so since the early silent era), but also to illustrate the two main approaches of the global Western film depending on whether it is set in the US (or Mexico) or indigenized. Non-US-American Westerns that situate their narratives in the late nineteenth-century US and its territories often exploit the allegorical potential of the genre with critical intent, sometimes bringing in elements foreign to the US-American context to expose the contradictions of US-American liberal/imperial identity (Broughton, Lee, Magrin Haas). Non-US-American Westerns set in colonized nations often draw on the populist or pro-Indian Western and use the genre as an emancipative framework for colonized characters in local imperial power relations (Batančev, Dutriaux and Le Poullennec, Phillips, Roche). When Westerns are produced by, or set in, colonizing nations, or when the protagonist is a white colonizer, they often draw on the more critical or revisionist trend of US-American Westerns and tend to exploit their transnational perspective to compare and contrast national histories of empire (Barrett, Fontanaud, González, Lee, Paryż). Westerns set outside the US can also exploit the association of the Western genre with the US to comment on US-American cultural and/or economic imperialism (Barrett, Dutriaux and Le Poullennec, Gonzalez, Phillips). Some contributions even suggest that the Western was the result of a transnational cocreation (Magrin Haas, Phillips) or that it existed as a native genre outside the US (Hamilton). The various films discussed in this collection show that the power of the Western lies not only in its ideology, but in the plasticity of the myth itself, of its narratives, figures, tropes, and iconography, and of the spectacular pleasures they provide.

The chapters in this collection reevaluate the notion that the Western is a US-American creation and a genre tied primarily to US national identity and, instead, purport to rewrite its history as a transnational form that was born in, and shaped by, a transnational history and culture of empire. Many of the chapters also highlight the importance of generic hybridity in the genre's articulation of local contexts and global histories. The Western as a transnational genre is either fused or contrasted with local genres and forms in ways that speak to, and shape the development of, both generic frameworks. This also adds to the notion that the histories of genres, in general, and the Western, in particular, have always been fluid and relational. Finally, many of the contributions to this book reveal anti-imperialist subtexts and revisionist work as essential features of the genre at any given period as they study how transnational appropriations of the Western channel their critical perspectives through references to classical Hollywood. The contributions collected here illustrate that a transnational approach to film does not preclude the category of the national, but rather invites a dialectical articulation of trans- and national perspectives, as they repeatedly discuss how the Western genre is both adapted to national contexts and cultures and transformed by such adaptations. They demonstrate the Western's past and continued relevance as a metanarrative articulating imperialism and revisionism, myth and history, global and local. Together, these contributions redefine the Western genre as an expression of a transnational ideology and culture of imperialism, and refine our understanding of the Western as colonial cinema, driven by the exploration of racial and gender hierarchies, and of issues of progress and violence inherited from, and shaped by, a history of imperialism.

NOTE

1. There may be room for a book-length study on the ways in which the genre has continually confronted and exposed the contradiction at the heart of US-American political mythology—a civilized nation born out of an act of savagery, or how can liberalism originate in imperialism?—but even that would only be discussing the common contradiction of nineteenth- and twentieth-century liberal justifications of empire in the context of the US.

WORKS CITED

Abel, Richard. *The Red Rooster Scare: Making Cinema American, 1900–1910.* University of California Press, 1999.
An, Jinsoon. "The Ambivalence of the Nationalist Struggle in Deterritorialized Space: The Case of South Korean's Manchurian Action Film." *China Review,* vol. 10, no. 2, 2010, pp. 37–61.

Anzaldúa, Gloria. *Borderlands/la Frontera: The New Mestiza*. Spinsters/Aunt Lute, 1987.

Bazin, André. Preface. *Le Western : ou le cinéma américain par excellence*, edited by Jean-Louis Rieupeyrout and André Bazin, Les Éditions du Cerf, 1953.

———. *Qu'est-ce que le cinéma ?. III . Cinéma et sociologie*. Les Éditions du Cerf, 1961.

Bender, Thomas, editor. *Rethinking American History in a Global Age*. University of California Press, 2002.

Billington, Ray Allen. *Westward Expansion: A History of the American Frontier*. Macmillan, 1949.

Bloom, Peter J. "Beyond the Western Frontier: Reappropriations of the 'Good Bad-man' in France, the French Colonies, and Contemporary Algeria." *Westerns: Films through History*, edited by Janet Walker, Routledge, 2001, pp. 197–218.

Bogdanovich, Peter. *John Ford*. Studio Vista, 1967.

Bondanella, Peter. *A History of Italian Cinema*. Continuum, 2009.

Broughton, Lee, editor. *Critical Perspectives on the Western: From "A Fistful of Dollars" to "Django Unchained."* Rowman and Littlefield, 2016.

Burns, Emily C. *Transnational Frontiers: The American West in France*. University of Oklahoma Press, 2018.

Buscombe, Edward, Christopher Brookeman, Edward Countryman, and Christopher Frayling, editors. *The BFI Companion to the Western*. Atheneum, 1993.

Campbell, Neil. *Rhizomatic West: Representing the American West in a Transnational, Global, Media Age*. University of Nebraska Press, 2008.

Carter, Matthew. *Myth of the Western: New Perspectives on Hollywood's Frontier Narrative*. Edinburgh University Press, 2014.

Chapman, James, and Nichol J. Cull. *Projecting Empire: Imperialism and Popular Cinema*. I. B. Tauris, 2009.

Christensen, Joyleen. "'East Meets West Meets East Again': *The Good, The Bad, and the Weird* and the Transnational Dialogue of Auteurs." *Unbridling the Western Film Auteur: Contemporary, Transnational and Intertextual Explorations*, edited by Emma Hamilton and Alistair Rolls, Peter Lang, 2018, pp. 183–202.

Cohan, Steven, and Ina Rae Hark, editors. *The Road Movie Book*. Routledge, 1997.

Costanzo, William V. *When the Word Laughs: Film Comedy East and West*. Oxford University Press, 2020.

Coyne, Michael. *The Crowded Prairie: American National Identity in the Hollywood Western*. I. B. Tauris, 1997.

Cronon, William. *Changes in the Land: Indians, Colonists and the Ecology of New England*. Hill and Wang, 1983.

Fisher, Austin. *Radical Frontiers in the Spaghetti Western: Politics, Violence, and Popular Italian Cinema*. I. B. Tauris, 2011.

————, editor. *Spaghetti Westerns at the Crossroads: Studies in Relocation, Transition and Appropriation*. Edinburgh University Press, 2016.

Frayling, Christopher. *Spaghetti Westerns: Cowboys and Europeans from Karl May to Sergio Leone*. 1981. I. B. Tauris, 2006.

Gallagher, Tag. "Shootout at the Genre Corral: Problems in the 'Evolution' of the Western." *Film Genre Reader*, edited by Barry Keith Grant, University of Texas Press, 1986, pp. 202–16.

Gregory, Derek J. *The Colonial Present: Afghanistan, Palestine, Iraq*. Wiley Blackwell, 2004.

Hamilton, Emma. "'Probably a White Fella': Rolf de Heer, *The Tracker* and the Limits of Auteurism." *Unbridling the Western Film Auteur: Contemporary, Transnational and Intertextual Explorations*, edited by Emma Hamilton and Alistair Rolls, Peter Lang, 2018, pp. 65–84.

Hamilton, Emma, and Alistair Rolls, editors. *Unbridling the Western Film Auteur: Contemporary, Transnational and Intertextual Explorations*. Peter Lang, 2018.

Hardt, Michael, and Antonio Negri. *Empire*. Harvard University Press, 2000.

Harris, Kenneth Marc. "American Film Genres and Non-American Films: A Case Study of *Utu*." *Cinema Journal*, vol. 29, no. 2, Winter 1990, pp. 36–59.

Higbee, Will, and Song Hwee Lim. "Concepts of Transnational Cinema: Towards a Critical Transnationalism in Film Studies." *Transnational Cinemas*, vol. 1, no. 1, 2010, pp. 7–21.

Higgins, MaryEllen, Rita Keresztesi, and Dayna Oscherwitz, editors. *The Western in the Global South*. Routledge, 2015.

Hughes, Howard. *Once upon a Time in the Italian Western: The Filmgoers' Guide to Spaghetti Westerns*. I. B. Tauris, 2004.

Hutcheon, Linda. *A Theory of Parody: The Teachings of Twentieth-Century Artforms*. Routledge, 1985.

Imre, Aniko. "Eastern Westerns: Enlightened Edutainment and National Transvestism." *New Review of Film and Television Studies*, vol. 9, no. 2, 2011, pp. 152–69.

Kettel, Steven, and Alex Sutton. "New Imperialism: Toward a Holistic Approach." *International Studies Review*, vol. 15, no. 2, June 2013, pp. 243–58.

Kitses, Jim. *Horizons West: Anthony Mann, Budd Boetticher, Sam Peckinpah—Studies of Authorship within the Western*. Thames and Hudson, 1969.

Klein, Thomas, Ivo Ritzer, and Peter W. Schulze, editors. *Crossing Frontiers: Intercultural Perspectives on the Western*. Schüren, 2012.

Kollin, Susan. *Captivating Westerns: The Middle East in the American West*. University of Nebraska Press, 2015.

————. "Genre and the Geographies of Violence: Cormac McCarthy and the Contemporary Western." *Contemporary Literature*, vol. 42, no. 3, 2001, pp. 557–88.

Lahti, Janne. *The American West and the World: Transnational and Comparative Perspectives*. Routledge, 2019.

Lee, Vivian. "Staging the 'Wild Wild East': Decoding the Western in East Asian Films." *The Post-2000 Film Western: Contexts, Transnationality, Hybridity*, edited by Marek Paryż, Palgrave Macmillan, 2015, pp. 147–64.

Limerick, Patricia Nelson. *The Legacy of Conquest: The Unbroken Past of the American West*. W. W. Norton, 1987.

Lottini, Irene. "When Buffalo Bill Crossed the Ocean: Native American Scenes in Early Twentieth Century European Culture." *European Journal of American Culture*, vol. 31, no. 3, Oct. 2012, pp. 187–203.

Lu, Sheldon Hsiao-peng. "Historical Introduction: Chinese Cinemas (1896–1996) and Transnational Film Studies." *Transnational Chinese Cinema: Identity Nationhood, Gender*, edited by Sheldon Hsiao-peng Lu, University of Hawai'i Press, 1997, pp. 1–31.

MacNeil, Denise Mary. *The Emergence of the American Frontier Hero 1682–1826: Gender, Action, and Emotion*. Palgrave Macmillan, 2009.

Mareš, Petr. "The Kind Millionaire, Lemonade Joe and Superman. On Czech Film Parodies." *Images*, vol. 14, no. 23, 2014, pp. 15–24.

Margolis, Harriet. "The Western, New Zealand History and Commercial Exploitation: *The Te Kooti Trail*, *Utu* and *Crooked Earth*." In *New Zealand Cinema: Interpreting the Past*, edited by Alistair Fox, Barry Keith Grant, and Hilary Radner, Intellect Books, 2011, pp. 83–97.

McClain, William. "Western, Go Home! Sergio Leone and the 'Death of the Western' in American Film Criticism." *Journal of Film and Video*, vol. 62, nos. 1–2, 2010, pp. 52–66.

Meeuf, Russell. *John Wayne's World: Transnational Masculinity in the Fifties*. University of Texas Press, 2013.

Meuel, David. *The Noir Western: Darkness on the Range*. 1943–1962, McFarland, 2015.

Miller, Cynthia J. "Comedy, Capitalism, and Kolaloka: Adapting the American West in Lemonade Joe (1954)." *International Westerns: Re-locating the Frontier*, edited by Cynthia J. Miller and A. Bowdoin Van Riper, Scarecrow, 2014, pp. 104–20.

Miller, Cynthia J., and A. Bowdoin Van Riper, editors. *International Westerns: Re-Locating the Frontier*. Scarecrow, 2014.

Mléčková, Kateřina. *Western Goes East: Limonádový Joe and Its Possible Interpretations*. Thesis. Masarykovy Univerzity, 2006.

Nelson, Andrew Patrick, editor. *Contemporary Westerns: Film and Television since 1990*. Scarecrow, 2013.

Paryż, Marek, editor. *The Post-2000 Film Western: Contexts, Transnationality, Hybridity*. Palgrave Macmillan, 2015.

Pratt, Mary Louise. *Imperial Eyes: Travel Writing and Transculturation.* Routledge, 1992.

Said, Edward. *Culture and Imperialism.* Vintage Books, 1994.

Schatz, Thomas G. *Hollywood Genres: Formulas, Filmmaking, and the Studio System.* McGraw-Hill, 1981.

Slotkin, Richard. *Gunfighter Nation: The Myth of the Frontier in Twentieth-Century America.* 1992. University of Oklahoma Press, 1998.

Spurgeon, Sara Louise. *Exploding the Western: Myths of Empire on the Postmodern Frontier.* Texas A&M University Press, 2005.

Teo, Stephen. *Eastern Westerns: Film and Genre outside and inside Hollywood.* Routledge, 2017.

Turner, Frederick Jackson. *The Frontier in American History.* 1921. Holt, Rinehart and Winston, 1962.

Tyrrell, Ian. *Transnational Nation: United States History in Global Perspective since 1789.* Palgrave Macmillan, 2007.

Vila, Pablo. *Crossing Borders: Social Categories, Metaphors, and Narratives Identities on the U.S.-Mexico Frontier.* University of Texas Press, 2000.

Webb, Walter Prescott. *The Great Plains: A Study in Institutions and Environment.* Ginn, 1931.

Welchman, John, editor. *Rethinking Borders.* University of Minnesota Press, 1996.

White, Richard. *"It's Your Misfortune and None of My Own": A History of the American West.* University of Oklahoma Press, 1991.

Wolfe, Patrick. *Settler Colonialism and the Transformation of Anthropology: The Politics and Poetics of an Ethnographic Event.* Cassell, 1999.

Wong, Aliza S. "Italian D.O.C.: American Cowboys, Malaysian Pirates, and the Italian Construction of Other-ed Adventurers in Film." *International Westerns: Re-locating the Frontier,* edited by Cynthia J. Miller and A. Bowdoin Van Riper, Scarecrow, 2014, pp. 301–25.

Zimmermann, Stefan. "I Suppose It Had to Come to This . . . How a Western Shaped Australia's Identity." *Crossing Frontiers: Intercultural Perspectives on the Western,* edited by Thomas Klein, Ivo Ritzer, and Peter W. Schulze, Schuren, 2012, pp. 134–48.

HERVÉ MAYER is Assistant Professor of American Studies at Université Paul Valéry Montpellier 3. He is author of *Guerre sauvage & empire de la liberté* and *La Construction de l'Ouest américain dans le cinéma hollywoodien.*

DAVID ROCHE is Professor of Film Studies at Université Paul Valéry Montpellier 3. He is author of *Making and Remaking Horror in the 1970s and 2000s: Why Don't They Do It Like They Used To?* and of *Quentin Tarantino: Poetics and Politics of Cinematic Metafiction.*

PART I

US-AMERICAN WESTERNS FROM A
TRANSNATIONAL PERSPECTIVE

OUR JOURNEY BEGINS IN THE US-American West. It begins where it appears
to have all started—the frontier myth, the Western. A logical beginning, but
one that the following chapters mean to contest or at least qualify by demonstrating that the national myth and the genre it spawned were transnational
from the start.

The journey will take us from the conquest of the West, the US-Mexico border and the Mexican Revolution of the nineteenth century to the twenty-first
century borderlands of Mexico and Texas; from the silent epics of the 1920s on
through the classical and contemporary era; from Hollywood to independent
cinema; from the Western to the post-Western; from John Ford, the man who
"ma[de] Westerns," to a young Tejano director whose first feature film was
screened in festivals, then released on Amazon Prime.

Chapters 1, 2, and 3 demonstrate how a transnational approach can shed
new light on famous works—how the international marketing of a film celebrating US nationhood (*The Iron Horse* of 1924) complicates our understanding of it as engaging exclusively with national concerns; how foreign politics
can creep into what is sometimes considered to be John Ford's most patriotic
work (the "Cavalry Trilogy" of 1948–1950); and how a 1950s Mexico Western
that seems like a textbook example of Cold War interventionist propaganda

(*Vera Cruz*, 1953) actually situates liberalism on the side of Mexican revolutionaries and, thus, raises troubling questions concerning the status of US democracy. Chapter 4 then dwells on a film (*Tejano*, 2018) that was released well after the transnational turn and presents an exemplary case of contemporary notions of *frontera* and hybrid identity. Each chapter insists on the notion of circulation—of goods, vehicles, people (characters), ideas, movies, ideology, and identities; on the dynamic relationship between national (and even regional) and international stakes; and on the imperialist foundations of the genre that endure in spite of its mutations, allowing it to resonate in various contexts and be packaged and marketed as such, and constituting a framework through which the representation of colonial histories can be interrogated.

Our transnational journey into the US-American Western is facilitated by the stories of characters who cross or have crossed these borders themselves; it begins, paradoxically perhaps, along the transcontinental railroad, aboard that symbol of conquest and US-American national identity that is the iron horse.

ONE

—꙳—

TRANSNATIONALISM ON THE TRANSCONTINENTAL RAILROAD

John Ford's *The Iron Horse* (1924)

PATRICK ADAMSON

IN THE 1949 EDITION OF his *The Film Till Now: A Survey of the Cinema*, British film critic and documentary pioneer Paul Rotha recalls John Ford's epic of the US-American transcontinental railroad, *The Iron Horse* (1924), as a film "fit to rank with any in the class of reconstructed fact": "I remember with feeling the long line of railwaymen's camps on the progressing track; the spirit and adventure of the pioneers; the clever rendering of the manoeuvres of the encircling Indians; and above all, the far-stretching landscape across which the steel track was to run" (Rotha, *The Film Till Now* 198–99). As personal as his response might be, Rotha's emphasis on mass movement, scale, and an overall impression of "spirit" aligns it with what was then the dominant interpretation of the film—one advanced with regularity by his contemporaries in the documentary film movement. As he put it, this "naturalist" Western offered rare "edification" by presenting a "theme of grand endeavour . . . to greater purpose than mere fiction" (*Documentary Film* 80). The "father of documentary," John Grierson, was likewise taken with this inspiring and instructive case of "national projection" and adopted the film as an often cited exemplar for his own ambitions: the conveyance of "fundamental and universal themes" to the "common people" (qtd. in I. Aitken 85). *The Iron Horse* left a noteworthy impression on the pair for the force with which it was seen to take the defining nineteenth-century ambitions and achievements of the United States and project them not only for a new generation of US-Americans but for the world.

Projecting images of national life overseas became Grierson's stated occupation in the late 1920s, when he established a film unit at the Empire Marketing Board. Rotha soon joined him there. Tasked with using film to promote the

interests of the British Empire, the officers of the unit "made their first begin-
nings by an analysis of what had been done in the way of national projection
in other countries": *Berlin: Symphony of a Great City* (Walter Ruttmann, 1927);
The Covered Wagon (James Cruze, 1923), another landmark epic Western that
strongly influenced Ford's *The Iron Horse* itself; "and sundry Soviet pictures"
such as *Battleship Potemkin* (Sergei Eisenstein, 1925) (*Documentary Film* 97). In
Grierson's words, these represented "all the documentaries and epics worth a
damn" ("E.M.B. Film Unit" 49). Whether they embedded fictional melodrama
within their "authentic" frontier settings or served overtly propagandistic ends,
their mass reach and concomitant influence over popular understandings of
their subjects proved to him that cinema "could be an adult and positive force
in the world" (qtd. in Deacon 151)—in short, the instrument of uplift and even
enlightenment that would form the basis of his documentary ideal.

This chapter is occupied with the genealogy of such sentiments, examining
Ford's film through what was, by this stage, already a long-standing intellectual
tradition: that cinema, as a universal language with international distribution
networks, might be used to effect globalized historical understanding, self-
visualization, and even harmony.[1] As we shall see, however, these democratizing pretensions served ends at once internationalist and imperialist, whereby
"understanding," in this prominent reading, frequently entailed a standardization of knowledge and the promotion of a hegemonic perspective on history
and humanity. What proponents cast as a laudable undertaking—overcoming
and supplanting the parochial obstacles to communication hitherto posed by
the world's multiplicities of language, tradition, and culture—can today be
identified as cultural imperialism.

The Iron Horse, the story of the building of the transcontinental railroad
in the 1860s, is today the best remembered of a silent-era cycle of epic Westerns that procinema writers singled out as heralding such an educative and
prosocial future for their medium. Indeed, it was in reference to this emergent cycle that, in 1923, Edward S. Van Zile effused: "To-day I find the screen
achieving wonders in conserving, for the sake of posterity, the memory of epic,
epoch-making deeds of derring-do that not only glorify our past but inspire us
with hope and ambition for the future" (196–97). Because they narrated key
nation-building episodes and visualized central aspects of the frontier experience, productions like *The Covered Wagon*, *The Pony Express* (James Cruze,
1925), and *The Vanishing American* (George B. Seitz, 1925) were credited with
reviving and bringing newfound legitimacy to a genre that many critics had
already deemed passé and stagnant because of excessive violence and scenario recycling (Hampton 339–40). In contrast to the lowbrow programs and

serials that had begun to dominate Western production, these were distinctly middlebrow spectacles—including road shows and lavish in their production and promotion. Above all, these prestige efforts apparently offered credible interpretations of an instructive history, their viewing being deemed a matter of civic education. Unlike most Hollywood films, they were seen to exemplify the industry's capacity for mass edification, purveying knowledge about the past—or, at least, familiarizing audiences with the nation's foundational myths.

Given its evident nation-building and community-forging capacities, it is unsurprising that scholars have tended to frame this mode of filmmaking in terms of its exploitation of contemporary nativist sentiment (Kenaga 9, 25–26). It was certainly the case that Hollywood studios were, at this point, engaged in a concerted attempt to appease suspicious morality critics, whose attacks on the film capital's "foreign" power brokers had intensified following a spate of star scandals in the early 1920s. Moreover, this was a decade marked by mounting ethnic nationalism and anti-immigration policy. US-American identity was increasingly defined in terms of inherited and historically established hegemony. In privileging key moments of nineteenth-century westward incursion, films like *The Iron Horse* echoed their day's dominant interpretation of this heritage: heroes push "civilization" across a continent and overcome human and environmental obstacles to birth a modern nation, the experience thereby conferring its people's exceptional qualities.

And yet, this chapter demonstrates that the focus on domestic audiences favored in most analyses of the film elides a key context for its production, promotion, and reception: the popular historical Western of the period was cultivated with cosmopolitan, internationalist identifications and regularly positioned by film writers and intellectuals as a force for democratic social progress on the world stage. The advancement of the epic Western as a vehicle for spreading understanding and, in turn, democracy returns us to *The Iron Horse*'s significance for key figures of the documentary film movement. As foundational as the language of national projection and cultural development was to their enterprise, Grierson and Rotha, in particular, identified a close affinity between post–World War I efforts in international reconstruction and film—a medium with a unique capacity for linking humanity across distance and difference (R. Aitken 658). Grierson rejected the idea of "foisting" an introspective national myth on others, favoring the projection of a "larger international self" that dramatizes "international relationships and dependencies" (qtd. in R. Aitken 655): "It is the only genuinely democratic institution that has ever appeared on a world wide scale" ("Parting of the Ways" 1843). Rotha argued similarly that having "democratic" films "shown here and abroad" would foster "in the long run... a universal acceptance of the democratic philosophy" (qtd. in R. Aitken 655). *The Iron Horse* became a core work for the pair because it represents an interpretation of the US's past as its "larger international self," implicated within a larger ideal of democratic advancement—one inspiring and enlightening for domestic and overseas audiences alike. Its sweeping images of human movement and endeavor unify heterogeneous crowds—Union, Confederate, Irish, Chinese, Italian, and so forth—reflecting and encouraging self-visualization within a narrative that is both national *and* transnational: that of the railroad tracks, cutting across ethnic and sovereign divisions to emphasize common values and shared progress. As a model of historical process, it is one that is in line with a tendency typified by contemporary intellectuals such as Randolph Bourne, who called for the diminution of nationalized perspectives in favor of a "trans-national" understanding of the singularity of the US: that its diverse population and ever-growing global connections would make it the "first international nation" (156).

The global use for cinema imagined here indicates why Ford's film figured so regularly in what Ryan Jay Friedman calls the "utopian-universalist" discourse on cinema, which reached a crescendo in the mid-1920s (1). The proponents of this popular interpretation asserted that the motion picture is the ultimate educational instrument: industrially efficient, singularly impactful, and, above all, universally understandable. By democratizing knowledge and foreshortening disparities on a global level, it could act as a force for harmonious social progress. The rest of this chapter examines how a utopian-universalist notion of uninhibited and democratic communication underscores Ford's first Western epic and the discourse that surrounded it. It is shown that international considerations were an imperative of both the film's recurring collective images and its commercial exploitation: the vision of historical process presented is one drawn beyond the confines of the world's singular nation; and the strategies used to further its reach into global markets reflect the significant impact that the conception of Hollywood cinema as a force for world harmony had on this landmark Western epic.

Finally, I contend that to consider *The Iron Horse* as a transnational historical film is to confront it at its most contradictory: as an imperial narrative paradoxically endowed with democratic potential. The championing of Hollywood cinema as a force for global cooperation betrays some fundamental conceits of the rhetoric of progressive universalism within which it is couched. First, the conflation of national and universal history is shown to perpetuate a developmentalist worldview that centers US-American perspectives on human relations. And, second, what is today identifiable as cultural imperialism is advanced as a benign process: the world's histories and languages being reconciled through Hollywood's "universal" alternative, a sharing of knowledge effecting cultural and social uniformity. A universalized language might serve the interests of future global cohesion, but only by extending an imperial perspective on the meaning and direction of history, along with its attendant ideologies and stereotypes.

FRONTIER HISTORY AND THE "MOVING PICTURE"

The incursion of settlers along the Oregon Trail, the meeting of the rails in Utah—histories of US-American migration and expansion have long been readily translated into the generic iconography of the Western because of their essentially visual dimensions. When he first presented his famous frontier thesis in Chicago in 1893, Frederick Jackson Turner was able to draw on an established pictorial tradition that linked national progress in spatial and temporal terms—mass progression across the continent—to the teleological advancement of democracy over time (Walsh 3). Specifically, his influential distillation of the era's prevalent cultural attitudes toward the frontier identified the process of migration away from Eastern civilization—penetrating and negotiating the untamed western wilderness—as the frontiersperson's legacy, the source of the US's distinctive national character and identity.

Early cinematic representations would depict the progress of the nation thus: as the movement of people across identifiable landscapes, right to left, East to West, Old World civilization to New World. The Covered Wagon was clearly positioned within this tradition in 1923 when its director James Cruze identified "the wagon train itself" as its star (Best Moving Pictures 75)—meaning its continual movement across the frame, often seemingly endless, as it winds into the dusty terrain.

"What The Covered Wagon does for the wagon train," David Lusted writes, "The Iron Horse does for the locomotive by placing the railroad within the foundation myth" (136). Ford's approach to historicizing also involves the crossing of a vast natural landscape by a symbol of US-American progress that was familiar from landscape painting and photography; Frederic Remington and Charles M. Russell were both noted influences on him (McBride 147). Like the westering caravan, the railroad brings a material impetus to the colonizer's iconography, connecting hitherto disparate-seeming territories and leaving a trail in its wake—in this case, one of permanence and technological sophistication. The heroes are the masses of workers, whose physical endeavor in advancing the tracks ensures the establishment and survival of US democracy. The meeting of the Union and Central Pacific lines is not only inflated into a constitutive moment in the national story; it is integrated in a melodramatic narrative. The rival visions for the railroad favored by the hero, frontiersman Davy Brandon (George O'Brien), and the traitorous renegade, Deroux (Fred Kohler), are mirrored in a romantic rivalry for the hand of Miriam (Madge Bellamy), whose father is financing the final stretch of tracks. The villainous half-breed insists that the track pass through territory in which he owns property, and tries to prevent the hero from locating a more direct route his father had once shown him. The film's final scene—the driving of the last spike at Promontory Summit, Utah, in 1869—marks not only the celebration of the "wedding of the rails" as a new symbol of national unity, but also the eventual marriage of Davy and Miriam, linking the overcoming of natural obstacles to the establishment of social harmony.

The crowd, the choreography of collective heroes working to unite the nation, drives this screen history and gives primary expression to the theme identified, and so valued, by the likes of Grierson: the courage and suffering of the many presents an inspiring ideal—the rebuilding of a fractured nation. Their efforts make a reality of an ambition closely associated with Abraham Lincoln, the icon effecting social cohesion through the founding of modern transport links. "Abe" features briefly in an early scene set in the protagonist's youth, but he first appears in the opening dedication:

> To the ever-living memory of Abraham Lincoln, the Builder—and those of dauntless engineers and toilers who fulfilled his dream of a greater nation....
>
> During the Civil War the United States was divided not only into North and South—but also into East and West, by a seemingly impassable barrier of prairie, desert and mountain.
>
> More than to any other man the Nation owes gratitude to Abraham Lincoln, whose vision and resolution held the North and the South, while moulding with blood and with iron the East and the West.

The face of Lincoln immediately follows these titles, lit alone against a black background. Through his guidance and intervention, the bonding of East and West is paralleled with that of North and South. As he later states, without the railroad, "we will have fought in vain" [21:28]. The railroad heralds a peaceful future not merely by virtue of its speed and significance, but by the unifying and character-forming frontier experience of the many contributing to it through the spending of "blood and iron" and the collective ordeal of forging a union across the post–Civil War nation's many divisions.

For many procinema writers of the period, the inspiring scenes of collective enterprise were an important means of encouraging uplift. The sums lavished on staging and promoting epic films were not mere market investments; they were culturally transformative. Encoded in the marvel of films such as *The Iron Horse*—its crowds, vistas, and evident expense—was an impression of historical significance, of empire building, that could inspire future progress along the trail to utopia.

For Vachel Lindsay (1915), expansion and migration make US history inherently cinematic. The motion picture and the nation share a common principle of movement. Inspired by the large-form Westerns' panoramas and their evocation of human movement, he would conclude: "American history, past, present, and to come, is a gigantic movie" (qtd. in Friedman 56). It is on this basis that *The Iron Horse* and its precursor, *The Covered Wagon*, figure prominently in Lindsay's unpublished second book on film. Friedman notes that, together, the two texts privilege "the 'epic' historical film, with its extensive crowd spectacles" as "the one that best illustrates the medium's properties and potentialities," foremost among these being the heralding of a "reign of peace" (48). At the basis of this idea is his understanding of cinema as a "mirror screen," which is to say the motion picture is conducive to social inclusion, for its group images show the "entire population . . . its own face" (Lindsay 65). The medium offers depictions *of* the masses—in the form of crowds—*for* the masses, granting its viewing an important civic function. Watching the progress of civilization reenacted in the vistas of *The Iron Horse* would, per this reading, not only familiarize viewers with their respective pasts; it would engender a type of self-visualization, a recognition and realization of their most admirable collective qualities, historically embedded but with future significance—an inspiring reminder of the US's exceptional national purpose. It is hardly surprising that Grierson would later highlight Lindsay's influence on his entry into the film industry (Marcus 190).

The synchronous movements of humanity depicted en masse would, it was supposed, cultivate among viewers an awareness of essential human unity, even in the case of *The Iron Horse*, where the markers of social and ethnic division are clearly displayed. Early scenes of the Central Pacific show Chinese workers—apparently imported due to a shortage of "white labor"—clearing a route through the Sierra Nevada mountains, tunneling through rock, and even pushing a stuck locomotive (fig. 1.1) [26:39–28:05]. In Nebraska, Irish laborers on the Union Pacific sing together and hammer the tracks into place in rhythm, only briefly halting to fend off an Indian ambush [28:22–29:52]. In short, aside from the film's stars, the workers are presented most often in long shots that emphasize crowd dynamics and choreography against sweeping backdrops.

Fig. 1.1 Chinese workers on the Central Pacific, clearing a route and pushing a locomotive.

Frequently intercut with these are images of individual worker types, toiling and sweating, illustrating the common endeavor that impels these human waves and the tracks laid beneath them.

As Warren Susman suggests, "John Ford is perhaps the most influential *historian* of the United States in the twentieth century" because his films articulate "a philosophy of history, a vision of the process and its meaning" (31). This process and meaning stress the nation's heterogeneity. Indeed, the film's narrative is driven by conflicts between different demographic elements. East is juxtaposed with West, North with South. Even the central, and notably inclusive by 1920s standards, Irish-Chinese-Italian coalition proves distinctly schismatic when it is tasked with overcoming the resistance brought by the one predictably excluded grouping, the Deroux-led Native Americans. Despite the growing popular sympathy for their predicament and their receiving US citizenship in 1924, these movie Indians function primarily as a familiar obstacle to progress here, though their aggression seems to arise more from desperation and deception than innate villainy.

The coalition's internal tensions are channeled most visibly through the figure of Tony (Colin Chase), an Italian stereotype whose atypicality is made apparent through the persistence of Southern European terms, such as *signorina*, in his naturalized English vocabulary. He is the most prominent of the "Eyetalians" and speaks on behalf of a group dismissed in the titles as "foreign laborers making trouble," against whom the dominant grouping determines to "stick together." Tensions peak when Deroux-led Cheyenne forces besiege a train of white settlers and, rather than joining the rescue party, Tony pronounces: "Let 'em send soldiers" [118:30–119:40]. "Saint Columbus found this country—but it's our Saint Patrick who has made it go," is the telling retort that greets the disloyalty of "foreign laborers." Nevertheless, in yet another wedding near the end of the film, Tony marries an Irish woman, heralding reconciliation for the schismatic factions [142:07]. In this context, the Irish can be read as what Charles Ramirez Berg calls "Ford's Ur-ethnics" (75–76). Ultimately, the film's key divisions—white-otherwise, North-South, primitive-progressive—are resolved into an essential unity through: (1) mass labor, (2) marriage, and (3) a shared goal to span the continent.

With the telling exception of Native Americans, the mirror screen of *The Iron Horse* fuses the many peoples or "nations" within the US borders into one totality. Scarce is this more apparent than in the frenetic movement of the citizens of North Platte, Nebraska, the "capital of the Union Pacific," when they load their town onto a locomotive, intending to set up a new base in Cheyenne, Wyoming [70:17–71:05]. Social types intermingle, ready to carry their civilization further across the landscape. Such a conception of US-American community is firmly in accord with noteworthy contemporary writings by the likes of Randolph Bourne. In his influential 1916 essay, "Trans-national America," Bourne espouses the fallacy of a purely national culture, arguing that "the first international nation" is exceptional *because of* its global connections: "America is already the world-federation in miniature, the continent where for the first time in history has been achieved that miracle of hope, the peaceful living side by side, with character substantially preserved, of the most heterogeneous peoples under the sun" (156).

Lindsay's earlier "mirror" model is built on a similarly idealized version of the US melting pot. In this case, however, its principles are developed less introspectively. For an audience that transcended sovereign borders, Hollywood historical films visualize a trail that, if embraced, could lead to an *international* utopia founded on the basis of a shared cultural understanding. Rotha's later linkage of film and the "universal acceptance of the democratic philosophy" is presaged here. According to Lindsay, watching mechanically reproduced images would bind the audiences into one single body, engaged in a shared, transnational act of attention, a nominal "World State": "The World State is indeed far away. But as we peer into the Mirror Screen some of us dare to look forward to the time when the pouring streets of men will become sacred in each other's eyes, in pictures and in fact" (50). Assemblages of people *and* groups sharing modern experiences are deemed essential to the "moving picture" of industrial democracy, with the writer's preference for the term *moving* implicating the movement-based characteristics of US-American history. He concludes that films made in the "spirit" of understanding, both national and international, would help "make world-voters of us all" (50).

The imagery, here, is strikingly hyperbolic. Diverse yet unified by being swept up in the drama of the railroads, the viewers of *The Iron Horse* embark on a shared ritual journey. Mass participants are enlightened; democracy is advanced. The realization of this collective uplift hinges on the assumption that motion pictures enable uninhibited global communication—a claim central to the pervasive utopian-universalist discourse then linking screen culture and social progress. For our purposes, it is important to note this claim's internationalist contingency: Hollywood films being consumed outside of their domestic market were expected to effect a worldwide democratization—or, perhaps more accurately, standardization—of knowledge. The direction of human history could be made explicit, the lessons of a past taught, ultimately suggesting, as it invariably did, the exceptional ideals of the US national project. Disparate peoples would be united in a shared understanding. Social cohesion would be instilled. And the polyglot messages of cinema would usher in an age of cultural democracy.

"The motion picture can do more, I believe, than any other existing agency to *unite the peoples of the world*," wrote Will H. Hays, president of the Motion Picture Producers and Distributors of America, in 1924 (341). "Wars—and other lesser conflicts—are caused because groups and people do not understand each other's ideas and beliefs," he elaborated in an interview the following year (qtd. in Friedman 12). In a period during which suspicion over cinema's social influence animated a number of figures to press for censorship and reform, this made for a powerful rhetorical maneuver—one that cast censorship as a threat to the world's greatest instrument for achieving mutual understanding, uplift, and, in its boldest imaginings, peace. In historical Westerns, such as *The Iron Horse*, the indexical intelligibility of still photography was considered to have been increased by motion to articulate an inspiring human theme. Witnessing foundational national myths evoked in this manner, concluded Van Zile, was to see the "Esperanto of the Eye" put to one of its most compelling uses (189). The impression of movement over time—settlers progressing west across a continent or tracks meeting to bond its coasts—advanced a vision of historical process that was innately polyglot and would travel freely. The promise of cinema, per this popular interpretation, was that humanity could now represent and understand itself as a totality or, to borrow Friedman's phrase, "a single empire that could span the globe" (6).

US-AMERICANIZED WORLD HISTORY

The (re)unification of the US by the heroes of *The Iron Horse* marks another point of "birth" in the nation's master narrative: once threatened, the community and its continuity are established on a yet greater scale. But it simultaneously represents the culmination of a principle that transcends the notion of nation. Even though its overt US-Americanness remained central to promotion, when Ford's film traveled overseas, this transnational understanding of the railroad's significance took on an expanded role.

Scarce is this more apparent than in the version of the film prepared for release in the United Kingdom, where the dominance of Hollywood products and US-American popular culture was increasingly considered a threat to Britain's supposed "national culture" (Higson 242). In this export cut, the opening Lincoln dedication is replaced with the following: "To the honour and memory of GEORGE STEPHENSON, the Scottish engineer, and the men of every nationality who have followed in his footsteps since England led the way by opening the first railway in 1825."[2] The export *Iron Horse* is presented not as the story of Lincoln's national vision reified, but instead as a tribute to the human endeavor "of every nationality," mobilized in the pursuit of a unifying, transnational vision of high-speed transportation.

Compared to its domestic counterpart, the version distributed abroad continually nullifies Lincoln's agency. No room is found for the view: "The farseeing wisdom of the great rail-splitter president is the beginning of the Empire of the West." Even after the president's death is declared via an intertitle, the export cut continues to marginalize the North-South axis of union as a concern [22:50]. Instead, several unique references are made that valorize the spanning of the continent as the height of modern progress: "a shiny path from sea to sea." The subjugation of a US-American national icon, Lincoln, to the British "Father of the Railways," Stephenson, points to how the film's reworking for export distribution reframed New World achievements as the culmination of a globally construed drive for "civilization."

This revised treatment is evinced in the routine elision of historical specificity, which not only detaches the images from the dates, details, and locations associated with historical cinema, but arguably aids their "mirroring" of world audiences. Without specific markers, progress—whether geographic or democratic—can function as a universal desire. "From Sacramento in 1863, the Central Pacific has started with a rush—and after fourteen weeks scorn turns to wonder," becomes: "Men and horses strain every nerve, hauling loco- motives and supplies over the mountains" [25:04 (domestic), 20:18 (export)]. References beyond "the West" are few in the British print, compared to the rich local color of its domestic equivalent. Characters returning "back East [to] Kansas" in one simply go "home" in the other [54:30 (domestic), 44:44 (export)]. Union Pacific crews seen in US-American cinemas are identified as hailing "from Omaha," whereas those shown on British screens are simply "ex-soldiers working peacefully side by side" [28:22 (domestic), 22:50 (export)]. As a reviewer for the *Manchester Guardian* remarked, "It is the railway's film, from first to last; the dream of a railway, and the railway born; the railway's long struggle against nature; the railway's costly triumph" ("Week on the Screen" 9). Lincoln, in this reading, is secondary; he "comes, does his work for the railway, passes" (9). Rather, it is declared a "rather splendid film" for its adherence to the central theme: it "honours the railroad, . . . loves the railroad" and valorizes the "soldiers of the North and South, the Chinese, the Italians, the Irishmen, who worked side by side" (9).

In Sydney, Australia, where *The Iron Horse* completed a record-breaking run of over ten weeks at the Prince Edward Theatre, screenings were accompanied by a short "scenic" entitled *Iron Trail around the World* (1925), detailing the development of railroads worldwide ("Newsy Notes" 31). A Melbourne-based critic suggested that "Romance of the Railway" would have made for a more fitting title for Ford's film and queried why it was "left to an American to sing the epic of the railway": "What picture would be of greater interest in Great Britain and in the Dominions beyond the seas than, for instance, one of George Stephenson's first railway accomplishments?" ("The Pictures" 5).

For its release in Canada, images of the Countess of Dufferin—the Can- adian Pacific's first locomotive, "The Iron Horse of Canada"—were added to promotional one-sheets, alongside stills from the film itself; these were distrib- uted in every station between the two oceans ("Ties Iron Horse to Canadian Road" 817). A review featured in the *Winnipeg Tribune* after the film's premiere there—which was accompanied by a prologue and "views of the first C.P.R. engine of the west, the Countess of Dufferin"—similarly highlighted the film's "mammoth" theme and how it might be extended: "this pretentious battle to lay a pathway of steel across *our continent*" ("'The Iron Horse' Inspires and Thrills" 17, my italics) (fig. 1.2).

The Iron Horse of Canada—the "Countess of Dufferin," first locomotive to make the trip across the Dominion, which takes the place of "Jupiter" in the Canadian version of "The Iron Horse" (Fox), opening there soon.

Fig. 1.2 The Countess of Dufferin, as it appeared in *Motion Picture News,* June 6, 1925. (Courtesy of Media History Digital Library.)

In this manner, the overseas promotion for Western epics routinely worked to frame frontier history within local ideas of empire and human progress. Among the most effective mechanisms for this was the prologue. Introduced alongside screenings of early imported epics in the 1910s, these were, by the early 1920s, an established aspect of film exhibition—albeit one that some regarded as a "bloat" on the program (Altman 385). Beyond their mere entertainment value, these fulfilled an important unifying and contextualizing function, rendering unfamiliar concepts comprehensible by "providing information essential to the entire audience" (Altman 385). It was with this stated intention, ensuring that the film could be "put over" abroad, that, in 1924, Paramount sent Tim McCoy—Native American culture expert and future Western star—and a cast of Shoshone and Arapaho performers to London and Paris on *The Covered Wagon's* "international tour" (Ponicsan 59–60).

It is here, however, that the utopian-universalist concept of global historical understanding is at its most overtly contradictory. First, studio concerns with how US-American historical cinema might be received abroad betray a fundamental conceit: contrary to the rhetoric of procinema writers, silent film was not freely passed around the world's nations and received alike by all their respective peoples. In the case of *The Iron Horse*, it has already been shown how changes in intertitling reframed its narrative and constructed its impression of universal legibility. The fundamental translatability of silent films might have made them highly portable, but they were not innately polyglot.

Second, the attachment of the prologue reveals how established colonial epistemologies informed the promotion and reception of purportedly universal and democratic displays. At the London Pavilion, an appearance by the "20 Living North American Indians from U.S.A. Now Encamped in the Crystal Palace Grounds" was promised before each screening of *The Covered Wagon* ("Film World" 8), recalling the "actual participant" involvement that had legitimized Wild West shows in the late nineteenth and early twentieth centuries. Onstage, McCoy asked the Native Americans about their personal histories, interpreting their sign language for the audience throughout. Several could, in fact, speak English, and the insistence on sign language was likely intended to bolster the impression of cultural disparity and primitive novelty. "The Days of 1863–1869," a forty-three-minute contextualizing introduction overseen once more by McCoy and again featuring Shoshone and Arapaho performers, likewise preceded early screenings of *The Iron Horse*. Although this version— described in McCoy's autobiography, cowritten with son Ronald, as "almost identical to the one for *The Covered Wagon*" (24)—is not recorded as having traveled abroad, *Variety*'s coverage of *The Iron Horse*'s release in Australia gives some sense of how these practices were adapted elsewhere: "The American idea of presentation is being combined with the film and a brilliant prolog is well received" ("Presentation in Australia" 35). McCoy's prologues connect to a larger tradition of Native Americans being expected to enact their "Indianness" for entertainment—usually in invented or spectacularized scenes of "primitive" life and aggression—that stretches back to Buffalo Bill's Wild West shows and the display of imported "exotic" peoples in European ethnographic shows (Lottini 190–94). Stressing the foreignness of its performers through the fulfillment of preexisting audience expectations provided what Irene Lottini describes as "a codified authenticity": the restatement of audience preconceptions about Indianness, usually predicated on the idea of white superiority and their civilizing mission (188).

Recently, Sarina Pearson has made similar arguments on the promotion of Paramount's *The Vanishing American* in Australia and New Zealand. Embarking on a tour of the two countries in the summer of 1926, a hired party of

Hopi and Navajo partook in "cultural demonstrations in the foyers of movie palaces... live prologues before several screenings daily," as well as in a publicly orchestrated meeting with local Maori (Pearson 88). This staged encounter served—in a quite telling fashion—to imbricate both groups in the progressive Darwinian discourse writ large in the film's export title, *The Vanishing Race*: "expanding the film's registers of sentiment, [it] effectively transform[ed] the film from the exceptionally American *Vanishing American* to a universal saga of 'human progress'" (Pearson 90).

CONCLUSION

Like the later *The Vanishing American*, *The Iron Horse* is a paean to the Western world's collective moral purpose and the power of enlightened action to drive human progress. Its concluding "wedding of the rails" binds the heroes of the transcontinental railroad together and makes visible the impetus of US-American democracy. Divisions between racial groups and ethnicities, workers and power brokers, nature and technology—all are subsumed by the newly interlinked tracks, a potent symbol of "the world federation in miniature." But in containing multitudes, with all the hyperbole that moved procinema writers, the mirror screen also served to reify the social and national relations it depicts.

To view *The Iron Horse* in its international contingency is to see it as at once progressive and contradictory. Its narrative celebrates a diverse collective and the overcoming of that which divides them, while its global promotion strategies articulate a clear faith in the film's capacity for instilling shared historical knowledge. However, its conflation of national and universal history is founded on a set of imperial tropes commonplace in the most self-congratulatory treatments of the US's past—something particularly evident in the promotional and retitling strategies that supported its international distribution.

Expanding the story of the US-transcontinental railroad to a more generalized treatment reminiscent of Friedman's "single empire that could span the globe" promotes, on the one hand, transnational cohesion by soliciting audiences to imagine themselves as a totality. On the other, it also advances a soft imperialism by encouraging conformity with the then dominant US-American perspective on the meaning and direction of history. Subsumed into a greater metanarrative, local frames of reference are supplanted or embellished by one ostensibly universal in both scope and meaning.

Of course, this is not to reduce silent cinema's most expressly "democratic" usages to cases of cultural imposition and cultural loss. The strategies outlined here give at least some sense of the complex negotiation involved in the presentation, promotion, and reception of films on export release—even those with famed polyglot appeal, such as Ford's railroad epic.

According to procinema writers, the people of the world would be able to ascend to the next stage of idealized democratic life by embracing US-American norms, encoded in the ostensibly universal language of Hollywood cinema. With this claim, a developmentalist worldview is perpetuated, in which the extension of the cosmopolitan world of the West is deemed utopian. *The Iron Horse* can thus be read as a transnational history with an imperial rationale. The universal meanings expressed through its "moving pictures" are activated only by a reading of the past that enshrines the westward movement of US-American "civilization" as virtuous, inevitable, and the ultimate end of world history.

NOTES

Author's Note: Some of the research/material in this chapter has been published previously in *Film History: An International Journal* (vol. 31, no. 2, 2019) as "American History at the Foreign Office: Exporting the Silent Epic Western."

1. The understanding of cinema as a "universal language" conducive to world peace was both commonplace in silent-era Hollywood discourse and routinely invoked in industry promotion. Its outspoken advocates included D. W. Griffith, Carl Laemmle, Will H. Hays, Walter Wanger, and Douglas Fairbanks (Deacon 139–56; Friedman 6–9).

2. Stephenson is erroneously identified as Scottish when he was, in fact, from Wylam, England.

WORKS CITED

Advertisement for *The Covered Wagon* at the London Pavilion. *The Times*, 4 Sept. 1923, p. 8.

Aitken, Ian. *Film and Reform: John Grierson and the Documentary Film Movement.* Routledge, 1992.

Aitken, Rob. "A 'World without End': Post-War Reconstruction and Everyday Internationalism in Documentary Film." *International History Review*, vol. 35, no. 4, 2013, pp. 657–80.

Altman, Rick. *Silent Film Sound.* Columbia University Press, 2007.

Berg, Charles Ramirez. "The Margin as Center: The Multicultural Dynamics of John Ford's Westerns." *John Ford Made Westerns: Filming the Legend in the Sound Era,* edited by Gaylyn Studlar and Matthew Bernstein, Indiana University Press, 2001, pp. 75–101.

The Best Moving Pictures of 1922–23, edited by Robert E. Sherwood, Small, Maynard, 1923.

Bourne, Randolph. "Trans-National America." 1916. *The American Studies Anthology*, edited by Richard P. Horowitz, S. R. Books, 2001, pp. 146–62.

The Covered Wagon. Directed by James Cruze, performances by J. Warren Kerrigan and Lois Wilson, Paramount Pictures, 1923.

"'The Covered Wagon' Wins Gold Medal as the Best Picture Released during 1923." *Photoplay*, Dec. 1924, p. 42.

Deacon, Desley. "'Films as Foreign Offices': Transnationalism at Paramount in the Twenties and Early Thirties." *Connected Worlds: History in Transnational Perspective*, edited by Ann Curthoys and Marilyn Lake, Australian National University Press, 2005, pp. 139–56.

"The Film World." *The Times*, 29 Aug. 1923, p. 8.

Friedman, Ryan Jay. *The Movies as a World Force: American Silent Cinema and the Utopian Imagination*. Rutgers University Press, 2019.

Grierson, John. "The E.M.B. Film Unit." *Grierson on Documentary*, edited by Forsyth Hardy, Faber and Faber, 1979, pp. 47–51.

———. "The Industry at a Parting of the Ways." *Motion Picture News*, 13 Nov. 1926, pp. 1842–43.

Hampton, Benjamin. *A History of the Movies*. Covici-Friede, 1931.

Hays, Will H. "Today and Tomorrow in the Motion Picture Industry." *The Blue Book of the Screen*, edited by Ruth Wing, Blue Book of the Screen, 1924, pp. 341–42.

Higson, Andrew. "Great Britain." *The International Movie Industry*, edited by Gorham Kindem, Southern Illinois University Press, 2000, pp. 234–37.

The Iron Horse. Directed by John Ford, performances by Madge Bellamy and George O'Brien, Fox Film, 1924.

"'The Iron Horse' Inspires and Thrills at Capitol." *Winnipeg Tribune*, 26 Oct. 1925, p. 17.

Kenaga, Heidi. "'The West before Cinema Invaded It': Famous Players-Lasky's 'Epic' Westerns, 1923–25." Dissertation, University of Wisconsin–Madison, 1999.

Lindsay, Vachel. *The Art of the Moving Picture*. Macmillan, 1915.

Lottini, Irene. "When Buffalo Bill Crossed the Ocean: Native American Scenes in Early Twentieth Century European Culture." *European Journal of American Culture*, vol. 31, no. 3, 2012, pp. 187–203.

Lusted, David. *The Western*. Routledge, 2014.

Marcus, Laura. "'The Creative Treatment of Actuality': John Grierson, Documentary Cinema, and 'Fact' in the 1930s." *Intermodernism*, edited by Kristin Bluemel, Edinburgh University Press, 2011, pp. 189–207.

McBride, Joseph. *Searching for John Ford*. University Press of Mississippi, 2011.

McCoy, Tim, and Ronald McCoy. *Tim McCoy Remembers the West*. Doubleday, 1977.

"Newsy Notes of Fox Folks Far and Near." *Fox Folks*, July 1926, p. 31.

Pearson, Sarina. "Reel to Real: Mimesis, Playing Indian, and Touring with *The Vanishing Race* in New Zealand 1927." *Mimesis and Pacific Cultural Encounters: Making Likenesses in Time, Trade, and Ritual Reconfigurations*, edited by Jeannette Mageo and Elfriede Hermann, Berghahn Books, 2017, pp. 79–110.

"The Pictures." *The Argus* (Melbourne), 27 Aug. 1925, p. 5.

"Pictures and People." *Motion Picture News*, 6 June 1925, p. 2751.

Ponicsan, Darryl. "High Eagle: The Many Lives of Colonel Tim McCoy." *American Heritage*, vol. 28, no. 4, 1977, pp. 52–62.

"Presentation in Australia for Fox Film." *Variety*, 7 Apr. 1926. p. 35.

Rotha, Paul. *The Film Till Now: A Survey of the Cinema*. With an additional section by and Richard Griffith. Vision, 1949.

Rotha, Paul, et al. *Documentary Film*. 3rd ed., Faber and Faber, 1963.

"Short Features." *Exhibitor's Trade Review*, 19 Dec. 1925, p. 27.

Susman, Warren I. "Film and History: Artifact and Experience." *Film and History: An Interdisciplinary Journal of Film and Television Studies*, vol. 15, no. 2, 1985, pp. 26–36.

"Ties Iron Horse to Canadian Road." *Moving Picture World*, 22 Aug. 1925, p. 817.

Van Zile, Edward S. *That Marvel—The Movie: A Glance at Its Reckless Past, Its Promising Present, and Its Significant Future*. G. P. Putnam's Sons, 1923.

The Vanishing American. Directed by George B. Seitz, performances by Richard Dix, Lois Wilson, and Noah Beery, Paramount Pictures, 1925.

Walsh, Margaret. *The American West: Visions and Revisions*. Cambridge University Press, 2005.

"The Week on the Screen." *Manchester Guardian*, 14 Nov. 1925, p. 9.

PATRICK ADAMSON is a film researcher based at the University of St Andrews who received his PhD there.

TWO

—ᗕ—

JOHN FORD'S "CAVALRY TRILOGY" (1948–1950)

Caught between US-American Imperialism and Irish Republicanism

COSTANZA SALVI

NEIL CAMPBELL OPENS HIS PREFACE to *The Western in the Global South* writing that the "oblique, referential manifestation that we might term the post-Western" uses tropes derived from classical Westerns, "whilst never simply repeating them, but instead adapting them for new cultural, political and social commentaries" (xiii). Post-Westerns basically transplant old conventions into global settings, producing a cultural and ideological reappropriation of previous national assumptions about US-American exceptionalism. Campbell emphasizes the genre's survival and complexity across its transnational journeys outside the US, not only by showing how new films utilize and expand old things—they "interact, overlap and inter-relate" with the classical Western (xiv)—but also by proposing new theoretical ideas through which old films can be reassessed; he states that to examine the West is "to think of it as *always already* transnational, a more routed and complex rendition, a traveling concept whose meanings move between cultures, crossing, bridging, and intruding simultaneously" (*The Rhizomatic West* 4, my italics). In *What Is a Western?*, Josh Garrett-Davis adopts a similar retrospective perspective in order to bring old Westerns into conversation with present times—"now even the most classic Western seems more international, sexually ambiguous, and stylized than it once may have appeared"—and he cites the opening ballad from *High Noon* (1952) as an example of a transnational and multilayered product (Garrett-Davis loc. 279). Matthew Carter has interpreted the need to scrutinize the assumption that classical Westerns "*always* promoted a specious myth-historical memory aimed at Anglo-American self-definition" (4). I am particularly interested in the thesis that a transnational analysis of past cultural products allows us to revise our opinions on classical Hollywood cinema, a particularly challenging goal when we are dealing with such a complex and canonical director as John Ford. His films of the late 1940s—*My Darling Clementine,* and the "Cavalry Trilogy" of *Fort Apache* (1948), *She Wore a Yellow Ribbon* (1949), and *Rio Grande* (1950)—are rife with exceptionalist tendencies and use the frontier's mythical experience to respond to postwar ideology; a commitment to national defense against foreign threats coexists alongside an approval of the inevitability of US expansion or the strategy to maintain its political hegemony abroad (most obviously, in the propaganda documentary *This Is Korea!* released in 1951) (Slotkin, *Gunfighter Nation* 334, 355–65; Corkin 235–49, 955–61). However, I aim to examine the trilogy from a different perspective.

Charles J. Maland argued that the terms of Ford appreciation were set through an essay titled "Hollywood's Favorite Rebel," published in the *Saturday Evening Post* in 1949 (220–52). Its author, Frank Nugent, intended to draw a vivid portrait of Ford's individualism that would be widely reproduced in subsequent years through countless articles and books of film criticism (Mitry; Bogdanovich; Baxter; Sarris; McBride and Wilmington). Nugent particularly emphasizes two qualities of John Ford's character: on the one hand, his visual rendition of the immense spaces of the frontier and, on the other, his cantankerous personality, which was said to originate in his Irish descent. As a half-Irish, half-Jewish political liberal, Nugent was particularly clear on this second point, proposing a twofold vision that accounts for the ambiguity and complexity foregrounded in Ford's work. According to Joseph McBride and Michael Wilmington, Ford possesses the quality of standing midway between two types of epic, the pure and the impure. If the former emphasizes the noble characters within the community, the latter evinces a mistrust of heroic deeds and delights in "reversals, perversity, and double meanings" (19). "Ford was a paradox" (19), the authors declare, implying that his work's position on either side of the epic had something to do with his Irish parentage. In *Searching for John Ford,* McBride adds that the filmmaker approaches the "Western genre's puritanical and imperialistic foundations with the subversive, or at least deeply ambivalent, attitude of an unreconstructed Irish rebel" (54).

In this chapter, I consider the attributes and qualities of Ford's Irishness in broader detail. More precisely, I explore this territory from two standpoints: cultural identity and geopolitics. The trilogy depicts a clash of identities between Irish Catholics and white Anglo-Saxon Protestants that implicitly associates the Irish with the Native Americans. In *Fort Apache,* for instance, Colonel Thursday's animosity toward Irish soldiers and the Apache is at odds with the sympathy the film invites us to feel for the Irish lieutenants, suggesting a possible alignment with the position of the indigenous peoples. Second, there are hints of a national pride running through the trilogy and a political support for the formation of an independent and proud Ireland, free from enemy occupation and separated from the British government.

FROM GARRYOWEN IN GLORY

Several Ford scholars have viewed the trilogy's allegiance to Ireland as a desire to gain official recognition of the contribution of Irish soldiers in the construction of the US (Kalinak 157; Morgan 33–45; Coyne 60–62; Corkin 929–53). I would like to qualify this view by arguing that, rather than the imperialist ideology of Western conquest, Ford's Irish soldiers embody a historical tradition of guerrilla warfare that is distinct and separate from the latter. Their presence conjures up symbols that belong to a different nation, as well as values that had great importance to Irish immigrants and descendants living in the US in the late 1940s. A consideration of Ireland's fierce and proud diplomatic strategy during World War II is necessary to understand this particular allegiance within the films and helps illuminate Ford's cultural sensitivity to the land of his ancestors.

In his survey of the construction of Irish identity during World War II, cultural historian John Day Tully explains that, within the growing European crisis, "Irish leaders used neutrality to forge a distinctly national identity" (1). Even though this neutrality was extremely beneficial to the Allies, Prime Minister Éamon de Valera remained inflexible and refused to compromise on many issues, such as British access to the so-called treaty ports or to air facilities in southern and western Ireland (57–59, 93–96). He insisted on neutrality as a method to safeguard Ireland, affirming an Irish identity "separated from the British, sovereign, independent and united under one single nation, rural and Catholic" (120). His project of ending the partition became part of the ongoing construction of identity within and without the nation's borders. Not surprisingly, given the high level of emigration from Ireland toward the US, a series of press campaigns began in 1939 in many US-American cities, during which the prime minister tried to raise the interest of Irish Americans in the fate of their homeland (12–14). The position of Irishmen and -women within US-American society was, in fact, connected to the establishment of an Irish national identity fostered through specific policies and government campaigns in their mother country.[1] The political and social relationship that Irish Americans had with their current country of residence was intertwined with the creation of a mature identity in Ireland. The end of the partition was delayed till November 1948 when the government introduced the Republic of Ireland Act, which was approved by the British Parliament the next year.[2] The law was, to some extent, a culmination of years of struggle to find an Irish identity that would be available to citizens living inside the Emerald Isle, as well as to immigrants living outside the national borders.

The years of production and release of the "Cavalry Trilogy" coincided with these events and probably led Ford and Nugent to emphasize a strong ethnic coding. Moreover, Ford was no doubt aware of the problems linked to the triangular relationship between the US, England, and Ireland during the war. But when the troubles were smoothed over after the armistice of August 14, 1945, he might have felt free to declare personal involvement in Irish economic development, endorsing the cause of Ireland as a proud, independent, and sovereign nation. Such a desire would explain why, throughout the 1950s, Ford tried to promote filmmaking in Ireland. He was involved in the foundation of an Irish company, Four Provinces, with his friend Michael Morris, the Third Baron Killanin, and provided jobs for many Irish actors. He also made a series of movies—*The Quiet Man* (1952), *The Long Grey Line* (1955), *The Rising of the Moon* (1957), and *The Last Hurrah* (1958)—involving Irish content, locations, and distribution (McBride 575).

What we may call the revolutionary, proindependence, anti-imperialist moral center of the trilogy reflects the historical details that brought on the modern Republic of Ireland and emerges through subtle cinematic elements. First, in *Fort Apache* and *She Wore a Yellow Ribbon*, the ideological opposition between characters often discloses proud resistance or rebellious attitudes within the Irishmen, who try to speak their minds beyond the outward display of integration. Second, in *Fort Apache* and *Rio Grande*, the music often taps into the memory and tradition of rebel songs in Irish lore. Each of these two aspects is examined in the following pages.

IRISH RESISTANCE

The Irish soldiers in *Fort Apache* always appear as the preferred target of Colonel Thursday's snobbish distaste when he is not involved in his mission to eradicate the Apache. Thursday, a bloodthirsty and arrogant man, is ashamed that he has been ordered to fight against savages in one of the forgotten outposts of the frontier.[3] He despises the supposedly inferior classes as much as he hates ethnic minorities, whether Irish or Apache, in short all those who are not white Anglo-Saxon Protestants. He cannot disguise his incredulity when he learns that an Irishman, Michael Shannon O'Rourke (John Agar), graduated from West Point, an institution that, in his opinion, should refuse men of such "inferior" origins [26:00–26:44]. He never remembers the name of the lieutenant, calling him "O'Brian" or "Murphy" interchangeably, and, later, he makes a contemptuous remark against the annoying throng of Irish people in the regiment: "Place seems to be full of O'Rourkes" [20:35]. He obstinately refuses to accept the invitation to dance with Mary (Irene Rich) during the Grand March, and he certainly does not view a possible marriage between his daughter and the Irish lieutenant favorably. Yet when Thursday barges into the O'Rourkes' quarters to demand that Philadelphia return home, the Irish character's rebellious temperament erupts abruptly in the major's (Ward Bond) soul (fig. 2.1). Confronted with Thursday's harshness and his request of formality, the O'Rourkes' sense of duty and moral commitment yields to different regulations and conducts—a set of principles ruling over the scene that is linked, I dare say, to another land:

> LT. O'ROURKE: Colonel Thursday, sir, I would like . . .
> THURSDAY: Mr. O'Rourke, I want no words with you at this time.
> LT. O'ROURKE: But, Colonel, sir . . .
> THURSDAY: You heard me, sir. [to Philadelphia:] Now get out of here
>   before I say something I may regret!
> MAJOR O'ROURKE: This is my home, Colonel Owen Thursday, and in my
>   home, I will say who is to get out and who is to stay! [78:50–79:05]

The dialogue is shot in a manner that encourages sympathy for the major and his wife Mary, with the two positioned to the extreme left of the frame beyond the dinner table, while Thursday remains on the right near the threshold, isolated in his extremist position and incapable of movement, an indication that he is unable to think in a flexible way. By contrast, Major O'Rourke expresses the position of an Irish American who is able to change his mind according to different circumstances: he knows the US Army Regulation book by heart, but—at the same time and on a different level—he is also an Irishman who demands respect for the sovereignty of his *home* (a word that is repeated twice), whose rules and orders are written in a different "book of manners." We are, thus, invited to interpret the sentence, "In my home, I will say who is to get out and who is to stay" [79:03], uttered as it is by a character presented as an Irish and a Catholic in a movie released in March 1948, in the light of the Republic of Ireland Act, introduced in the very same year. Facing this new set of values, the high respect for rank and breeding required by Thursday is thoroughly overshadowed. Michael Coyne writes that "this is the precise moment when Irish Catholicism becomes the dominant culture of *Fort Apache*" (61). The Irish lieutenants live up to their national promises even when this legacy expresses a

Fig. 2.1 *Fort Apache*: "This is my home, Colonel Owen Thursday, and in my home, I will say who is to get out and who is to stay." The Irish lieutenant (Ward Bond, *left*) and his family undertake a national promise even when this legacy expresses an anti-imperialist obligation incompatible with the values of their country of residence.

revolutionary and anti-imperialist condition, an obligation incompatible with the values of their country of residence. Reading between the lines of Major O'Rourke's utterance, a firm support for the Irish cause seems to emerge, as well as a blessing for its quest for identity.

Ford's support of Ireland is sometimes mingled with a strong criticism of the destructive circulation of money behind the expansion of the frontier.[4] *Fort Apache*, for instance, suggests that the relocation of Indians to social and geographic margins has terrible consequences on both the property and the sense of security within families: the conquest of the frontier is only beneficial to the dominant group that has the power to drive all the others onto poorer places. It is not incidental that a situation experienced on the nineteenth-century frontier presents many similarities with that of the Irishwomen and -men who were both forced to emigrate because of the famine (1845–1849) and spurned and banished from the dominant group at their arrival in the US.

Two similar characters—Kirby York (*Fort Apache*) and Captain Nathan Brittles (*She Wore a Yellow Ribbon*), played by Ford regular John Wayne—act as mediators to explain the motives and behaviors of both the Irish and the Apache. York and Brittles socialize and bond with the Irish characters (the O'Rourkes and Sergeant Quincannon), who display the same loyalty and friendship with their white Anglo-Saxon Protestant friends. York and Brittles are also the characters most easily inclined to find peaceful alternatives to violence in their relations with the Natives. No other aspect expressing Ford's Irishness is more significant than the unruly and subversive soul of a man-with-an-Irish-temperament, an attitude that might even be attributed to men who have Anglo-Saxon origins but are ready to bravely resist the official line. Consider, for instance, the lecture given by Brittles during his meeting with Pony That Walks (Chief John Big Tree) about the importance of curbing bellicose threats and bloody impulses [88:55–90:30]. His view might have had a particular resonance with Ireland's situation in the postwar years, when playing the neutrality card was a method to create a national identity that gathered the diasporic people of Ireland and the Irish at home within a communal sense of belonging. Brittles rejects the inherent brutality of war and the impulse to destroy the opponent, while remaining, at the same time, proudly steadfast in his position. Through him, *She Wore a Yellow Ribbon* not only offers a view on violence that is completely different from what we might expect in a movie that supposedly upholds the national sense of a mission to rescue and defend the US against utterly inhuman and appalling enemies; it obliquely confirms the proud neutrality of Ireland during World War II. In so doing, it suggests that it is necessary to find a different form of resistance, an alternative to violence, to secure peace.[5]

THE IRISH MUSICAL SPIRIT

The most explicit elements evoking Ireland, I would argue, are the songs and music. In adapting James Warner Bellah's stories for the trilogy, Ford and Nugent added two crucial ingredients that were absent in the source: first, strong allusions to Ireland and Irishmen in the regiment, and, second, references to singing and dancing.[6] These additions are profoundly intertwined, obliquely demonstrating, with their presence, the degree and extent of influence the Irish musical tradition has on US-American culture.

In ethnomusicology, folk songs are represented as the repository of traditions and lores (Leydi 1991; Stokes 1994), a relationship that is clearly manifest in Ford's films, mainly within the theory of Noel Purcell in *The Rising of the Moon* (1957): the old songs enclose "the secrets," a subtle and sinewy truth tied to cultural and ethnic identity [10:50–11:33]. Through songs, we learn about the legends of a mythical past, as well as the emotional and psychological price Irishmen pay when violent foreigners occupy their lands. Many instrumental versions of Irish folk tunes reinforce the strong ethnic coding that characterizes the trilogy: "All Praise to St. Patrick" [*Fort Apache*, 88:04–89:36]; "Garryowen" [*Fort Apache*, 95:44–96:03]; "Fiddler's Green" [*Fort Apache*, 00:23–00:45 and *She Wore a Yellow Ribbon*, 06:05–06:25]; "The Son of a Gambolier" [*She Wore a Yellow Ribbon*, 25:20–26:50]; "Oh, the Days of the Kerry Dancing" [*Rio Grande*, 49:50–50:23]; and one diegetic version of a traditional Irish song, "Bold Fenian Men" a.k.a. "Down by the Glenside" heard in *Rio Grande* [64:56–67:00]. Featured alongside these traditional songs/tunes are at least two relatively recent songs recounting stories of Irishmen and -women: "The Regular Army O!" [*Fort Apache*, 34:00–34:35] and "The Irish Washerwoman" [*Rio Grande*, 49:30–49:50]. The former was written in 1874 by the songwriting team of Ned Harrigan and David Braham, and is sung by the army recruits, while the latter is derived from a traditional jig and used by Victor Young in an instrumental arrangement in connection with Kathleen—a Southern woman of Irish descent—while she is washing the troopers' uniforms.[7]

Let us examine, in particular, two songs that claim the republican tradition of the Irish fighters against British rule. The first song is "Garryowen," which occurs in an exclusively instrumental version in *Fort Apache* as a nondiegetic accompaniment. The title comes from two Gaelic words: *garrai* meaning garden and *Eoin* meaning John. It refers to the area around King John's Castle in Limerick, a big garden that was a favorite holiday resort for people in the area, but it was expanded to connote the whole country, like the shamrock, the color green, shenanigans and leprechauns, and the harp (Boudreau; on Irish symbols, see Eagleton). Later, it became the marching tune of the Seventh Cavalry, and the lyrics were modified accordingly, replacing the Irish strong character with the glory and heroism of the US Army. Legend has it that the song was introduced to the US Cavalry by Major Miles Keogh, who was born not far from Limerick (Kalinak 134). Ford knew the major from the pages of history. Keogh is, in fact, remembered in *She Wore a Yellow Ribbon* by Captain Brittle during one of the graveyard soliloquies in front of his dead wife's tomb, when the jovial mood and musical talent of Keogh is highlighted:

> BRITTLE: We had some sad news today, Mary. George Custer was killed, his whole command. Miles Keogh, you remember Miles? Happy-go-lucky Irishman! He used to waltz so well with you. I guess I was a little jealous. Never could waltz myself. [13:47–14:13]

The connection between this song and the Seventh Cavalry had already been established by the score Max Steiner wrote for *They Died with Their Boots On* (Raoul Walsh, 1941), a romanticized Custer biopic that Richard Slotkin includes in the imperialist Westerns influenced by a progressive ideology (*Gunfighter* 266–67, 288). However, the 1941 movie fully ignores the association with Miles Keogh and Irish history. Custer (Errol Flynn) hears the song for the first time when it is played on the piano by Lieutenant "Queen's Own" Butler (George Huntley Jr.) in a saloon in Monroe, Michigan. According to Paul Andrew Hutton, this character is based on Custer's real-life adjutant, William W. Cooke, who was a Canadian known as "Queen's Own," the same nickname given to the character (41), but who did not have any documented musical talent. There is a lilt of brogue in Butler's voice, and he presents himself as a former officer of the Fifth Royal Irish Lancers, which was not the case of his supposed real-life model. Judging from these elements, Butler seems to be an Irish soldier, but, at the end of the movie, he is openly described by Custer as an Englishman. Shortly before the last stand, Custer calls for Butler and asks him to go back to Fort Lincoln with his letter:

BUTLER: Why are you asking me to go back with it?
CUSTER: Well, for one thing, you're an Englishman, not an American.
BUTLER: Not an American! What do you Yankees think you are? The only
real Americans in this merry old parish are on the other side of the hill
with feathers in their hair. [126:06–126:36]

Butler refuses to go back ("Get somebody else to post your blinking letter!"), and he is killed with the others. Furthermore, the actor himself, George Huntley Jr., son of G. P. Huntley, an Irish actor popular for his comic parts of idle genteel Englishmen from the city, combined with elements of performance, costumes, and props (the monocle, his physiognomy, the comic undertones of his playacting) suggests that, in effect, Huntley was offering another version of the traditional comic parts his father played throughout his career.[8] The strongest evidence of his Englishness is the emphasis on Butler's courage (he decides to stay and help Custer) imposed by the desire to reinforce the film's interventionist subtext and the possible alliance between US-American and British forces in World War II—particularly highlighted by the use of Max Steiner's arrangement of "My Country 'Tis of Thee," a theme that is quite similar to the British national anthem (Coyne 28). *They Died with Their Boots On* completely denies the song's Irish origin and carefully discourages any allusion to the nonbelligerent nation.

Kalinak argues that Ford in two cases—*The Informer* (1935) and *Four Men and a Prayer* (1938)—used Irish songs ("The Minstrel Boy" and "Londonderry Air") in an effort to express the multilayered complexity of controversial historical events (135). This also seems to be the case of "Garryowen" in *Fort Apache*. Ford uses the song for just a few seconds to conjure up the idea of Irishness. The song is heard when the troops are leaving the fort shortly before the last stand, omitting references to the lofty lyrics added when the cavalry inherited the song.[9] Mainly because of *They Died with Their Boots On*, mainstream audiences were already used to linking the myth of the US Cavalry to "Garryowen," so that choosing this song might have been almost inevitable; still, in a movie interested in manifesting what should be concealed under a facade of heroism, we might expect that the soundtrack would serve the same purpose. Despite the importance of claiming the bravery of indomitable men—"The myth is good for the country," Ford once said (*Directed by John Ford* [63:22])—*Fort Apache* highlights the mistakes and dishonesty at the heart of US conquest. "Garryowen" participates in the revelation. A song of resistance stolen from the Emerald Isle and brought across the ocean to be integrated into an imperialist narrative, it is well suited to evoke the radical relativism behind an ostensible truth. Every winner hides a loser who sees the same historical fact from the other side and winds up completely forgotten, whereas the winner conveys the image of an invulnerable self even when he has irreparably failed. This might explain why "Garryowen" is used as a brief ironic comment on the injustice that Thursday is about to commit—a mistake that will be covered up at the end of the movie. Whereas *They Died with Their Boots On* sets the last stand in the context of the Western mythology enfolding the tragedy in a crust of heroism, *Fort Apache* emphasizes failure and weakness: its heroism is much more ambiguous and shaded with complexity and internecine destructiveness.

The song "Bold Fenian Men" (Peadar Kearney, 1916) occurs in *Rio Grande*. It is performed by the Sons of the Pioneers during the dinner of General Sheridan (J. Carrol Naish) and the officers, in the presence of Kathleen Yorke (Maureen O'Hara). The use of this song is very different from that of "Garryowen," mainly because of the lyrics and the presence of performers.[10] It is Quincannon (Victor McLaglen) who interrupts the dinner to introduce the song and, after that, wipes his tears with a large handkerchief adding a lick of comedy in the emotionally charged sequence. The narration establishes the characters' positions in eleven shots. The Sons of the Pioneers stand in a straight line, cutting the frame obliquely from left to right—forming three silhouettes lined up in perfect symmetry. The song lasts no more than two minutes, and the rhythm of the sequence is attuned to its soft melody. The wide shots alternate with close-ups of four members of the audience (Sheridan, Quincannon, Kathleen, and Kirby Yorke) expressing their sense of duty. The first three, all of Irish descent, were led to sacrifice affections and love to an abstract principle, so "Bold Fenian Men" is a very appropriate comment on their abnegation, recounting the losses and sacrifices suffered by Irish fighters. Written during the Easter Rebellion, this song commemorates an earlier failed riot organized by the Fenian movement in 1867 when the Fenians bombed Clerkenwell, a prison in London, where one of them was incarcerated. To the general US-American audience of 1950, "Bold Fenian Men" was no doubt received as a melancholy song relating obscure events out of a forgotten past. But it is safe to assume that Irish Americans and Irishmen and -women perceived much more. For them, the song conjured up the memory of their cause and a moment of heroic loss mentioned quite explicitly in the lyrics:

Some died on the Glenside / some died near a stranger,
And wise men have told us / that their cause was a failure.
They fought for old Ireland / and they never feared danger,
Glory O, glory O, to the Bold Fenian Men.

By thus establishing a direct link to the historical phase of Fenianism, the first important episode of the Irish rebellion against the settlement of the British in the northern part of the country, the sequence emphasizes a peculiar ethnic coding that invites the diasporic Irish people present in the audience to feel a sense of community. Irish spectators would have been able to accurately discern and interpret the ethnic references of the song and receive a precise message; as George Martin eloquently writes, "The scene is a lyrical statement worthy of an Irish bard" (163).

When the regimental singers start to sing the song, they basically serenade Philip Sheridan, an homage emphasized by Quincannon's gesture toward the general. He listens to the song with a pensive mood and a serious attitude (fig. 2.2). Even though the US-American audience knew Sheridan for his great ferocity against the Natives, the general was also an essential figure in the Irish context. His family moved from Ireland to the US in 1830, the year before Sheridan was born, and he later became a Fenian sympathizer. The US-American Fenian Brotherhood offered the position of secretary of war to him in connection with their ill-fated plan to invade Canada and attack the British, a plan that, if Sheridan had accepted it, would have occurred in the same decade that was remembered in the song, the 1860s, when the Clerkenwell prison was bombed. Ford was knowledgeable and passionate about history, and there is little doubt he was aware of these details.[11] If we compare Sheridan to the equivalent

Fig. 2.2 *Rio Grande*: Four frames of the first close-up shot of General Philip Sheridan (J. Carrol Naish) listening to "Bold Fenian Men." Two shots of Sheridan are inserted during a song that lasts no more than two minutes.

figure in *They Died with Their Boots On*, the Irishness of the former distinctly appears. In the 1941 film, Sheridan (John Litel) is a reliable but cold and inflexible figure, with a strict conception of US Army protocol and legal formalities. The 1950 Sheridan is quite different: he is more spontaneous, showing unceremonious manners, and characterized by practical, realistic, and down-to-earth strategies that are absent in his predecessor. The difference is emphasized by the two actors' performance styles. While Litel often embodied robust and hard-nosed authoritative figures, Naish was frequently employed in ethnic parts because of his gift for languages and dialects, and his black hair and swarthy complexion. Moreover, he was of Irish descent and a Catholic, aspects that may have informed his rendition of Sheridan as an ethnic figure, very different from the straight US-American hero that the audience expected him to be. Finally, even if less popular than the very famous "All Praise to St. Patrick," "Bold Fenian Men" is more openly associated with the kind of guerrilla warfare that brought on the modern republic.

CONCLUSION

I am perfectly aware that, if we were to take the rationale proposed herein one step too far, we might end up reducing the Native American characters (especially in *Fort Apache* and *She Wore a Yellow Ribbon*) to the status of mere stand-ins for another nation's political battle, making my analysis just another distortion of Native American experiences. Edward Buscombe has said that "we see in Indians what we want to see, what we need to see" (Buscombe loc. 152). Yet perhaps we can acknowledge that those wants and needs are not just various in kind but change over time, and a possible shift occurs when a third point is brought into the initial dualism. Introducing a different tradition and society within a conflict between two groups might offer a new look on familiar images and issues. I am convinced that an extended comprehension of Ford's complex sensibility toward Native Americans in the trilogy would benefit from the triangular view offered in this chapter. Indeed, Scott Simmon argues that cavalry films produced from the late 1910s to the late 1940s—including Ford's—were seldom a vehicle for justifying the massacre of Indians but presented narratives centered on the relationship between individual heroics and communal obligations. Simmon also describes Ford's skepticism regarding cavalry high-rank commands as a "long-standing" attitude "among Irish Americans," one that was unequivocally endorsed by late nineteenth-century Irish newspapers published in the US, such as the *Irish World* and the Boston *Pilot* (Simmon 71–73, 283; Slotkin, *Fatal Environment* 475–76; Foner 157–69). Ford's Irish ethnicity would, then, represent one of the most interesting keys to understanding his work, and not least his attitude toward minority groups.

The trilogy is not interested in using Irishness as a mere comic counterpoint to drama (Morgan 33–35) nor in showing the legacy of Irish soldiers in building an imperialist America; rather, it uses strong ethnic coding to express proud dissimilarity and contrast. Ireland in Ford's trilogy appears through subtle forms of fierce resistance and criticism. At times, this sentiment was intermeshed with the need for peace and quiet; at others, it was proudly militaristic. The ambiguity that in many cases was considered a constitutive part of Ford's filmic world coincides with the director's tendency to complicate the standard reading of history through constant questioning. If classical Westerns were based on norms and conventions—rugged individualism, masculine violence, and the Anglo-Saxon alliance for the conquest and control of the savage world—Ford often upheld the reverse: communal loyalty, feminine sensibility, and ethnic pride. If this may sound familiar, what warrants deeper observation and scrutiny is how much the disruptive oppositions of the films' contents and forms depend, in effect, on Ford's Irish roots. His homage to Ireland and to the Irish Republican spirit is a subject that should be further analyzed as the seed of what tempers the US imperialist narrative of the trilogy, revealing the flipside of a partial truth.

NOTES

1. Benedict Anderson argues that a nation is an imagined political community based on social structures and cultural patterns that affected, in the case of Ireland, both Irish and Irish Americans.

2. The Republic of Ireland Act, sanctioned by the British Parliament, "declared that Ireland ceased to be part of the Crown's dominions" (Tully 156).

3. Thursday is partly inspired by General Custer, and his flaws work to demythologize the heroic figure. As Hutton points out in his remarkable essay on the perception of Custer in US-American popular culture, *Fort Apache* paved the way for a different understanding of the past, profoundly modern in its capacity to denounce guilt and self-doubt instead of pride and optimism (40–47, 53–54).

4. Peter Lehman points to Ford's and Nugent's inclinations to express a populist vision of the myth of the frontier (141–45).

5. Brittle's position is quite similar to that of Sean Thornton in *The Quiet Man* (1952). Refusing to fight until the last scene, Thornton shows the ability to discriminate between different forms of violence: the fatal and disruptive violent behavior versus the playful fisticuffs that unite men together into a masculine, perhaps even homoerotic, bond.

6. Apart from "Mission with No Record," the source of *Rio Grande*, which briefly mentions the violin played by the colonel, there is no other reference to music in Bellah's stories (Kalinak 219). According to McBride, Bellah's stories are "unreadable" today because of their racist invective against Native Americans; it is likely that the same treatment would have been reserved to Irishmen. McBride writes, in fact, that Bellah was described by his son James as a "fascist, a racist, and a world-class bigot" who viewed Ford as a "shanty Irishman." Yet there are no allusions to Irishmen in Bellah's stories (449).

7. "The Regular Army O!" is an excellent example of how two Irish American entertainers such as Harrigan and Braham, who were very popular in the late nineteenth century, updated and redefined the ethnic stereotype of hard-drinking and unruly Irishmen into something positive (Kalinak 131–33).

8. Literary critic Vivian Mercier argues that, in the Irish theater, a long tradition of satire and parody often leans toward the comedy of manners and

mostly directed against the fashionable world of the British (237–48). Butler appears to be, thus, a friendly caricature of a hedonist British gentleman with an addition of a lick of bravery.

9. "Garryowen" is mixed at the end of the sequence with the lyrics of "The Girl I Left Behind Me."

10. Ford's desire to manifest emotional aspects connected to ethnicity is more evident when he uses folk songs sung by performers from beginning to end as an alternative to less obvious comments given by nondiegetic folk tunes. According to Kalinak, folk songs exalt ethnic lore or revolutionary fervors, especially of minor characters who can express aspects that would remain otherwise remote (83–84).

11. Many aspects of Ford's childhood attest to the filmmaker's in-depth knowledge of Ireland's history and of political events connected with the Troubles (McBride, 20, 47–51, 136–44).

WORKS CITED

Anderson, Benedict. *Imagined Communities: Reflections on the Origin and Spread of Nationalism*. Verso, 1991.

Baxter, John. *The Cinema of John Ford*. Barnes, 1971.

Bogdanovich, Peter. *John Ford*. University of California Press, 1968.

Boudreau, William H. "Garryowen—Regimental Song." First Cavalry Division Association, https://1cda.org/history/garryowen/. Accessed 1 Feb. 2020.

Buscombe, Edward. *'Injuns!' Native Americans in the Movies*. Reaktion Books, 2006. Kindle Edition.

Campbell, Neil. Preface. "'Coming Back to Bad It Up': The Posthumous and the Post-Western." *The Western in the Global South*, edited by Mary Ellen Higgins, Rita Keresztesi, and Dayna Oscherwitz, Routledge, 2015, pp. xiii–xx.

———. *The Rhizomatic West: Representing the American West in a Transnational, Global, Media Age*. Nebraska University Press, 2008.

Carter, Matthew. *Myth of the Western: New Perspectives on Hollywood's Frontier Narrative*. Edinburgh University Press, 2015.

Corkin, Stanley. *Cowboys as Cold Warriors: The Western and U.S. History*. Temple University Press, 2004. Kindle version.

Coyne, Michael. *The Crowded Prairie: American National Identity in the Hollywood Western*. St. Martin's, 1997.

Directed by John Ford. Directed by Peter Bogdanovich, American Film Institute, 1971.

Eagleton, Terry. *The Truth about the Irish*. St. Martin's, 1999.

Foner, Eric. *Politics and Ideology in the Age of the Civil War*. Oxford University Press, 1981.

Fort Apache. Directed by John Ford, performances by John Wayne, Henry Fonda, and Shirley Temple, RKO, 1948.

Garrett-Davis, Josh. *What Is a Western? Region, Genre, Imagination.* University of Oklahoma Press, 2015.

Hutton, Paul Andrew. "'Correct in Every Detail': General Custer in Hollywood." *Montana: Magazine of Western History*, vol. 41, no. 1, Winter 1991, pp. 28–57.

Kalinak, Kathryn. *How the West Was Sung: Music in the Westerns of John Ford.* University of California Press, 2007.

Lehman, Peter. "How the West Wasn't Won: The Repression of Capitalism in John Ford's Westerns." *John Ford Made Westerns: Filming the Legend in the Sound Era*, edited by Gaylyn Studlar and Matthew Bernstein, Indiana University Press, 2001, pp. 132–54.

Leydi, Roberto. *L'altra musica. Etnomusicologia. Come abbiamo incontrato e creduto di conoscere le musiche delle tradizioni popolari ed etniche.* Giunti-Ricordi, 1991.

Maland, Charles J. "From Aesthete to Pappy: The Evolution of John Ford's Public Reputation." *John Ford Made Westerns: Filming the Legend in the Sound Era*, edited by Gaylyn Studlar and Matthew Bernstein, Indiana University Press, 2001, pp. 220–52.

Martin, George R., Jr. "Making a Community: Irish Americans in the Films of John Ford." *Harp: Journal of Irish Studies*, vol. 12, 1997, pp. 159–63.

McBride, Joseph. *Searching for John Ford: A Life.* St. Martin's, 2001.

McBride, Joseph, and Michael Wilmington. *John Ford.* Da Capo Press, 1975.

Mercier, Vivian. *The Irish Comic Tradition: The Key Book of Irish Literary Criticism.* Oxford University Press, 1962.

Mitry, Jean. *John Ford.* Editions Universitaires, 1954.

Morgan, Jack. "The Irish in John Ford's Seventh Cavalry Trilogy: Victor McLaglen's Stooge-Irish Caricature." *MELUS: Multi-Ethnic Literature of the United States*, vol. 22, no. 2, Summer 1997, pp. 33–45.

Rising of the Moon, The. Directed by John Ford, performances by Cyril Cusack and Jimmy O'Dea, Warner Bros., 1957.

Sarris, Andrew. *The John Ford Movie Mystery.* Indiana University Press, 1975.

She Wore a Yellow Ribbon. Directed by John Ford, performances by John Wayne and Joanne Dru, RKO, 1949.

Simmon, Scott. *The Invention of the Western Film: A Cultural History of the Genre's First Half-Century.* Cambridge University Press, 2003.

Slotkin, Richard. *The Fatal Environment: The Myth of the Frontier in the Age of Industrialization, 1800–1890.* University of Oklahoma Press, 1994.

———. *Gunfighter Nation: The Myth of the Frontier in Twentieth-Century America.* University of Oklahoma Press, 1998.

Stokes, Martin, editor. *Ethnicity, Identity, and Music: The Musical Construction of Place.* Berg, 1994.

They Died with Their Boots On. Directed by Raoul Walsh, performances by Errol Flynn and Olivia de Havilland, Warner Bros., 1941.

Tully, John Day. *Ireland and Irish Americans: The Search for Identity*. Irish Academic Press, 2010.

COSTANZA SALVI is PhD student of English Studies at the University of Zaragoza.

THREE

—ഝ—

DECENTERING THE NATIONAL IN HOLLYWOOD

Transnational Storytelling in the Mexico Western
Vera Cruz (Robert Aldrich, 1954)

HERVÉ MAYER

THE TRANSNATIONAL DIMENSION OF HOLLYWOOD Westerns can be approached from multiple standpoints. If the fields of distribution and reception systematically involve the crossing of national borders, this is not true of the fields of narrative and production. Yet, in the history of classical Hollywood Westerns, one cycle of films stands out as a narrative exploration of border crossing that shifted the genre's focus from the exploration of US-American history and mythology to its critical articulation with foreign contexts and perspectives. That cycle of films was labeled the "Mexico Western" and identified as a "subtype of the Western" by cultural historian Richard Slotkin (410). It comprises films of the 1950s and 1960s that were produced by US-American studios, often involved location shooting with local crews in Mexico, and focused on white male characters of the late nineteenth- or early twentieth-century US-American West crossing to Mexico and meddling in Mexican history. Usually, these characters bring US technological and military superiority into a local political struggle (the Second Mexican Empire of 1864–1867 or the Mexican Revolution of 1910–1920), with their support to one side or the other of the conflict determining the course of national history.

Because of their setting and plot structures, Mexico Westerns are not so much concerned with the history of US settler colonialism as they are with US imperialism. According to Slotkin, the cycle developed in parallel with the increased international activity of the US after World War II and was specifically concerned with exploring the conditions and consequences of US interference in Third World nations. As the setting of numerous historical dramas since the silent period, Mexico was the most well known of Third World countries in Hollywood. For some of these films that focused on the Second

Mexican Empire, the post–US-American Civil War setting also conveniently reflected the post–World War II context of their production. For those reasons, the Mexico Westerns provided fertile ground for an evaluation of US foreign policy in the years of the Cold War and decolonization (434). Complementing such readings of the cycle in terms of its relation to US foreign policy, this chapter highlights the impact of the cycle's transnational dimension on Western genre conventions and on the representations of US-American imperial myth and history.

Bringing together elements of the historical drama set in Mexico and the pro-Indian Western of the early 1950s, *Vera Cruz* (1954) was the first film of the cycle and set the course for later productions (Slotkin 410). As the opening titles indicate, the film is set in Mexico after the US-American Civil War and follows US-American mercenaries looking for fortune in the conflict between Benito Juárez and the Mexican people and the Austrian-born, French-supported emperor Maximilian. The story focuses on two US-American characters (Joe Erin [Burt Lancaster] and Ben Trane [Gary Cooper]) who sell their fighting skills to the wealthier emperor, until one of them (Trane) eventually recognizes the liberal ideals of the Juarista resistance as a higher political cause.

Vera Cruz was "one of the first Hollywood films set and filmed entirely in Mexico" (Fojas 68), a decision the producers turned into a promotional argument. The US-American crew of a hundred people lived and worked in the Cuernavaca valley near Mexico City during the two-and-a-half-month shoot in the spring of 1954, alongside two hundred Mexican crew members and uncounted extras who were hired locally. Filmed in Technicolor and SuperScope for a total budget of $3 million, *Vera Cruz* was director Robert Aldrich's and independent production company Hecht-Lancaster's most ambitious film to date. It was also a popular success, earning $9 million in its initial theatrical release (Fuller 28). It is likely that the film was conceived as a political project as much as a big budget production. The emphasis on the Mexico setting in the promotional material capitalized on Mexico's significance in the US-American imagination as "a radical, left-wing and even subversive space" (Fuller 22). Mexico also occupied a specific place for postwar liberal writers, artists, and filmmakers as a site of exile from the investigations of the HUAC and the Hollywood blacklist. In the late 1940s and early 1950s, the largest number of exiles found refuge in Mexico City and the Cuernavaca valley where *Vera Cruz* was shot, and their creative activity gained a "distinctly transnational mode of production [that] contributed to a deliberate aesthetic and political critique of US racism, nationalism, and imperialism" (Schreiber xii). The filmmakers of *Vera Cruz* were not among those US exiles, but most were known liberals who had been directly or indirectly targeted by HUAC investigations, including producer Harold Hecht, actor and producer Burt Lancaster, director Robert Aldrich, and scriptwriter Roland Kilbee (Fuller 28). As a result, their film, as I argue, partakes in what Schreiber identified as the "aesthetic and political critique" produced by the left-wing exiles in Mexico.

Building on existing research on *Vera Cruz*, this chapter seeks to contribute to the discussion of transnationalism within Western films and the ways in which transnational perspectives consolidate the critical work of the genre in exposing the imperial myths and history of the US. It draws both on Richard Slotkin's analysis of the ways in which the Mexican setting of *Vera Cruz* fosters a redefinition of the Western formula and on Stephanie Fuller's conclusion that border crossing into Mexico "enables *Vera Cruz* to explore and critique the concepts of US expansionism and capitalism from without" (Fuller 28). Its specific contribution is to consider how the film's generic hybridity and construction of Mexico as a historical space are exploited in *Vera Cruz* to reflect on the US's history and mythology of colonization.

Complementing and qualifying some of the earlier scholarly studies of the film, I argue that *Vera Cruz* introduces a decentered perspective within the Western genre by using a non-US-American historical setting to redefine and invigorate the genre's reevaluation of frontier mythology. The transnational narrative and production of *Vera Cruz* thus serve to expand and enrich the genre's critique of US-American imperialism. I first focus on the ways in which the Mexican setting of *Vera Cruz* supports an anti-imperialist redefinition of Western generic conventions, casting the native Juaristas as a regenerative force against imperial savagery. I then discuss how the construction of Mexico as a historical space of colonialism serves to highlight the contradiction between US-American liberal mythology and imperial history. Finally, I analyze the relationship between genre and national identity within the film and the ways in which generic hybridity aesthetically serves the criticism of US-American imperialism.

REDEFINING THE WESTERN FROM MEXICO

Vera Cruz's Mexican setting introduces an unfamiliar element in the Western that troubles genre expectations and opens up a creative space for the redefinition of generic conventions. Preceding the opening titles that set the story's time and place to Mexico after the US-American Civil War, the first shot of the film frames the main street of a small town with arid mountains in the background and two characters on horseback approaching the camera [00:10–00:19]. This shot would suffice to firmly establish the film within the Western genre if not

Fig. 3.1 The presence of a Spanish colonial church in the opening shot introduces an unfamiliar element within the Western genre.

for one strange element: the towering presence, center frame and sunlit, of a Spanish colonial church that indicates the setting is not exactly the usual movie West (fig. 3.1). The presence of Spanish colonial architecture, rare though not uncommon in Westerns before 1954, connects *Vera Cruz* to an alternative narrative of the West, one that acknowledges the transnational history of the border region and points to non-US-American perspectives on the colonization of North America. The opening shot also subtly introduces a tension between the US-American and the Mexican elements in the frame, as the approaching US-American Westerners gradually replace and conceal the church as the center of composition. The exaggerated depth of field, combined with frame-within-the-frame composition created by the wall corner in the left foreground, invites viewers to adopt a reflexive position on such transnational negotiations within the Western rather than customarily siding with the US-American element.

Vera Cruz furthers the opening shot's suggestion of alternative perspectives by embracing the point of view of the Mexican Juaristas rather than the US-American protagonists. This perspectival decentering is partially mediated through conventional elements of the Western formula but in ways that revise the mythical story of westward expansion. Indeed, *Vera Cruz* takes its cue from a cycle of Westerns of the early 1950s that sought to adopt an indigenous perspective on the history of US-American settler colonization. This cycle of Westerns, labeled the "Cult of the Indian" Western by Slotkin (366), comprises films such as *Broken Arrow* (Delmer Daves, 1950), *Devil's Doorway* (Anthony Mann,

1950), and *Apache* (Robert Aldrich, 1954), in which an Apache warrior continues to resist US-American colonialism after the surrender of Geronimo.[1] In *Vera Cruz*, the pro-Indian narrative is, in effect, displaced onto the historical conflict in Mexico. As native people resisting imperial rule and as a people of mixed Indigenous descent opposing Euro-American colonization, the Juaristas are aligned with movie Indians. This association is reinforced by the visuals: the Juaristas are identified with the wilderness, emerging from and disappearing into it at will; and apart from their leader General Ramirez (Morris Ankrum) and his lieutenant Pedro (Mexican actor Juan García), they are characterized collectively. Fuller has noted that the Juaristas in *Vera Cruz* are associated with high-angle shots and that the repetition of such shots serves to invite viewer identification with them (25–26); if such high-angle perspective in representations of Mexicans or Latinos usually signifies banditry (26), it is also the favored perspective of movie Indians on white intruders, further associating the Juaristas with Native Americans and repositioning the US-American and European imperial presence as an invasion of Indigenous Mexican territory.[2] In representing the Juaristas as a people of mixed descent, the film resonates with the myth of a mestizo nation, which dominated the construction of Mexican identity after the Mexican Revolution.[3] Yet the film resists the racialist subtext of the mestizo narrative as the association of Juaristas with movie Indians emphasizes indigeneity rather than the European input as the active principle of political liberalism.

In keeping with the narrative structure of the pro-Indian Western, the adoption of an indigenous perspective serves to reverse the conventional distribution of civilization and savagery. Instead of identifying the Juaristas with violence, *Vera Cruz* positions them on a higher moral ground in the defense of civilization. As General Ramirez says to the US-Americans right after Joe Erin shot two challenging mercenaries dead, "We are not savages, señor. We do not kill in cold blood" [19:30]. In the preceding scene, the US-American preference for the rule of force had been emphasized in a low-angle shot foregrounding the corpses of Charlie and his friend after Joe Erin asked, "Anybody else string with Charlie?" [17:20]. Savagery is on the side of the US-Americans who molest children [20:00–21:33] and rape women [50:00–51:05], whose only law is violence and sole motivation is money.[4] Savagery is also on the side of the empire, which, despite its aristocratic outlook and mannered speech, not only grounds its power exclusively in force but draws pleasure from gratuitous assaults on the bodies of the Mexican people; one scene shows imperial lancers laughingly playing with a prisoner's life before killing him [56:35–57:25]. The brutal execution of the anonymous Juarista and the inhumanity of imperial rule are rendered through a POV shot of the fatal spear from the victim's perspective at the moment before death [57:20], the death itself being mediated through the proud posture and sad face of the Juarista spy Nina (Spanish actress Sarita Montiel) in medium shot [57:20–57:25]. Both the POV and reaction shots align viewers with the plight of the natives. The reversal of civilized and savage is also, as Slotkin noted, played out in the characterization of the female protagonists, with the dark woman Nina embodying virtue and redemption for Ben Trane and the blonde Countess Marie Duvarre (French actress Denise Darcel) embodying and inspiring corruption (437). As in the pro-Indian Western that would bloom in later years, whiteness, technological progress, and Americanness are, because of the Mexican setting, dissociated from moral superiority, and the more primitive Juaristas, although they wear sandals and wield "ancient weapons" [19:25] against the US-Americans' Winchester repeating rifles, are the more civilized. If anything, US-American technological superiority endangers the values of civilization and the establishment of democratic governments in the less developed countries in which it is projected. The film thus openly belies the liberal rhetoric of US-American Cold War policy and exposes instead its imperial operations.

Vera Cruz, however, also shares in the political pitfalls of pro-Indian Westerns as the dominant figures in the story remain white, US-American, and male, while the representations of Mexico and the Indigenous perspective are US-American constructions. This can be more largely attributable to the film's reliance on the Western formula and its focus on individual heroes, which Fuller sees as the limit in the film's progressive agenda; several shots literally turn the Juaristas into a mere background for the Hollywood stars (26). While such choral use of the Juaristas is undeniable, the film's focus on the US-American protagonists actually serves to highlight their numerous flaws. Joe Erin is a cynical and cold-blooded mercenary who resorts to lying and killing to get his way and fortune; his character arc reveals the moral depths to which he is ready to sink in the service of his material ambitions. Ben Trane is the more heroic protagonist, his arc leading to redemption as he eventually supports the cause of the Juaristas. In spite of Gary Cooper's alleged efforts to tone down any line or gesture that might tarnish his persona (Williams 35), his character is a slaveholder and ex-Confederate from Louisiana who needs money to rebuild his plantation. Although Trane's Lost Cause is identified with that of the Juaristas, with General Ramirez even congratulating Trane for a "brave struggle" [18:06], his Southern identity primarily strengthens his association with the empire: he is the only US-American at ease in the emperor's palace, speaking French to the countess and boasting of the South's "one or two homes that once might have stood beside all this" [23:38]. The un-Americanness of a Confederate hero could not have been lost on director Aldrich and producers Hecht and Lancaster, whose progressive racial views at the time are manifest in the sympathetic portrayal of black characters both in *Apache* and *Vera Cruz*.[5] Trane can negotiate on an equal footing with the Mexican and European imperialists, not by using force as Erin does, but because they are culturally alike.

While *Vera Cruz* is structured by the individualist thrust of Western narratives, it also tempers it. Not only does the film tarnish the image of the mythic US-American Westerner but it either holds it at a distance or works to erase it from the screen. The introducing shots of Trane are quite telling in this respect. The opening credits [00:40–02:32] feature a series of extreme long shots framing a minuscule rider in wide-open spaces whose figure is consistently concealed by the huge bloodred lettering of the credits. The distance with Trane and Erin is maintained in early scenes through recurrent long shots with deep focus composition, the protagonists positioned in the background while an element of the set (tree trunk, cactus, wall, boulder, etc.) occupies the foreground (for instance, when Trane arrives at the trading post [03:17–03:49] or Trane and the group of mercenaries travel through the country [13:36]). Similar shots are later used to depict the column of US-American mercenaries and Mexican lancers, as they ride through the wilderness [33:45] or when they reach and then leave the convent [36:10, 43:55]. These shots suggest the presence of a hidden observer that later materializes as the Juaristas, but they also maintain a distance between viewers and characters that troubles identification. The concealment of characters within the frame is again performed when Trane arrives at the cantina, where he meets the US-American mercenaries; his progression and arrival is blocked from view by a wall [10:10–10:17]. The film thus challenges and undermines the visual centrality of its US-American protagonists, furthering identification with the Mexican collective. By focusing on antiheroes, foregrounding the savagery of imperialism, and embracing the indigenous perspective of the Juaristas, *Vera Cruz* redefines Western conventions from a Mexican standpoint to critically evaluate the values the genre traditionally associates with national identity. In doing so, the film treats Mexico not as the source of an alternative mythology but rather as an alternative historical space of colonization in North America.

MEXICO AS HISTORICAL SPACE

As the presence of a colonial church in the opening shot suggests, the Mexican setting of *Vera Cruz* introduces a competing set of historical referents that the film articulates with the history of US-American colonization. Certainly, Mexico had been constructed by Hollywood as a "mythic space" since the 1910s (Slotkin 411), and *Vera Cruz* merely followed suit in this respect, using architecture to "creat[e] a Mexican mythology evoking an ancient lineage and epic beauty" able to vie with the grandeur of the movie West (Fuller 24). That said, the Western remains essentially a historical genre with "profound and multi-faceted historical and historiographic functions" (Walker 7) and demands to be evaluated as such. The function of the Mexican setting and architecture in *Vera Cruz* is, thus, to introduce within the Western a non-US colonial history that can be compared to, and contrasted with, US colonization. The opening titles inform us that the story takes place at the end of the US-American Civil War during the Second Mexican Empire, which corresponds to the years 1865–1866. In 1867, under US pressure, France withdrew its military support to emperor Maximilian, and Mexico fell back into the hands of Juárez and the Liberals. The figure of Benito Juárez, a rural man of Indigenous descent, and his struggle for liberalism and independence against European rule are remembered in Mexican memory as a foundational symbol for the modern and democratic Mexican nation (Weeks 12–14). During the empire, the city of Veracruz was the stronghold of Juárez and the Liberals, with the pro-Maximilian Conservatives holding Mexico City. In the 1954 film, the Western's conventional focus on national birth is displaced onto Mexican history, while the title asserts, for those with a sense of the history, its indigenous and anti-imperialist perspective. The impact of such displacement is to steer the Western away from the imperial narrative of national birth through colonization—the frontier myth (Slotkin 10)—and emphasize instead a liberal narrative of national birth through decolonization. Articulating Mexican and US-American historical experiences, the film then uncovers an alternative master narrative of US genesis: the nation was not born out of the frontier, the Indian wars, and territorial expansion, as the Western routinely shows, but out of the Enlightenment, the American Revolution, and the struggle against British imperialism. The Juaristas are associated with Native Americans resisting US-American imperialism, but they are also the Mexican equivalent of the Patriots fighting for freedom and independence against European imperialism. The parallel is made explicit by General Ramirez in an attempt to win over the mercenaries: "Certainly as US-Americans you can appreciate our fight for independence" [17:53]. The Mexican setting here allows the film to contrast antithetical myths of US origins. The fact that the mercenaries would renege on such a historical legacy of revolutionary independence and accept imperial money over a liberal cause only demonstrates the practical malleability of US-American ideals, especially when tested in foreign contexts.

The film's visual treatment of architecture is especially important for developing a historical discourse on colonialism and decolonization. This discourse stems from the different characterizations of Spanish colonial and pre-Columbian architecture, which is associated with differing regimes of power. Spanish colonial architecture evokes the oppressive power of imperial rule and the US-American presence in Mexico. The film multiplies low-angle shots of characters wielding power over others against a background of monumental arches and bell towers. When Erin, in the opening scene, sells a bad horse to Trane for $100, a clear abuse of power, the shot/reverse shot of the transaction shows Erin in low angle backed by the flat bell tower of a mission church [05:36]. Similarly, when the US-Americans later escort the imperial caravan to a convent, the captain of the lancers (Henry Brandon) [36:00], then Trane [37:05], are shot in low angle with the high bell tower of the church.[6] The film also frames colonial architecture to convey shifting power dynamics. When the mercenaries meet the emperor's aide (Cesar Romero) and General Ramirez, the same building corner (with a second-story arcade) in low angle is associated with a succession of characters, as power changes hands within the scene: Little Bit (James McCallion) on horseback molesting a Mexican woman [14:00], Trane on horseback humiliating Little Bit [14:34], and, finally, the Juaristas taking everyone prisoner [19:18]. Whereas Little Bit and Trane were shot in the foreground with the building above them, the Juaristas are lined up on its top, appropriating the material expression of colonial rule.

If Spanish architecture is associated with US-Americans and colonialism, pre-Columbian architecture is identified with indigenous power and resistance to colonization. One scene of the film is shot in the site of Teotihuacán and features the eighteen-century-old Pyramid of the Sun and the two-mile-long Avenue of the Dead. The sequence opens with a full frontal shot of the massive pyramid [53:28], followed by a medium shot of the pyramid that dwarfs the imperial caravan and their US-American escorts as they progress around its base in a very slow pan [53:32–54:09]. The frailty of the caravan is then underlined in a high angle from the side of the pyramid embracing the perspective of a Juarista scout [54:10–54:24] (fig. 3.2). These opening shots use architecture to construct a striking image of indigenous power over Euro-American imperialism. Such power is brutally challenged later in the sequence when the imperial lancers capture and execute a Juarista in a series of shots whose composition is organized around the now distant pyramid [56:36–57:09]. *Vera Cruz* thus uses architecture to distinguish between two regimes of power in Mexican history: Spanish colonialism and pre-Columbian native society. By aligning the empire and the US-Americans with colonialism, and the Juaristas with

Fig. 3.2 Pre-Columbian architecture is identified with indigenous power and resistance to the imperial presence in Mexico.

political autonomy, the film further suggests the likeness of US-American and European imperialism as common enemies of indigenous peoples in a long-lasting struggle for decolonization.

Mexican history is evoked not only through architecture but also through music. Although *Vera Cruz* may be accused of dishing out the exotic image of Mexico for US-American audiences, it also foregrounds a form of syncretic culture known as "fandango," which is explicitly referred to in the film [66:19]. Originally, fandango is a Spanish dance that became popular across Europe in the late eighteenth century but gained a more specific meaning in the state of Veracruz, where it developed as a popular celebration mixing various cultures of colonial society. This specific folklore is celebrated in the fiesta scene at the fictional town of Las Palmas [59:52–64:30] and is used both to construct the image of a unified and inclusive Mexican people (accommodating US-American folk dance as well as the harmonica) and to further establish the empire as an alien element (the arrival of the caravan interrupts the fiesta [60:32]). The Spanish guitar, an instrument that had been appropriated in the popular music of rural Mexico since the eighteenth century, is also prominently featured in the film as an attribute of the Juaristas. Its soft melody, played on screen by Pedro, gives a gentle and humane touch to the assertion of Juarista power when General Ramirez takes the emperor's aide and the US-Americans prisoners [18:20–19:45]. The same melody is reprised on the eve of the final battle, in an evening scene at the Juarista village, where the anonymous peasants rest with their families and quietly prepare for the morning assault [82:40–84:50]. In both instances, long takes and slow panning or tracking movements emphasize gentleness and mastery. More than a mere mythical backdrop or a new frontier for US-American expansion, Mexico in *Vera Cruz* is a distinct historical and cultural space, whose specificity and complexity is exploited to identify US-American actions with European imperialism and establish the Juaristas as the heirs and representatives of a liberal, popular, and native history.

GENRE HYBRIDITY AND FORMAL TENSION

The setting of *Vera Cruz*—Mexico during the Second Empire—seems to have incited the filmmakers to hybridize the Western with another genre or, more specifically, a subgenre of the Hollywood costume drama: period pieces about the aristocracy of early modern Europe. Hybridity is not an unknown phenomenon in the history of Hollywood genres or the Western; in fact, many contemporary researchers in genre theory tend to think that hybridity is the norm rather than the exception in the history of filmic genres (Carter 87). Although the phenomenon has been especially noted since the 1980s in discussions involving postmodernity, hybridity in the Western is a constant feature of the genre's developments. The Western has borrowed from and influenced almost every other Hollywood genre, the most conspicuous exchanges concerning war and empire films (Abel 161; Chapman and Cull 7), science fiction (Mogen 3), and noir (Simmon 207). *Vera Cruz*, for instance, features an interracial group of mercenaries inspired from World War II films, a motif that became a staple of the Mexico Western in the 1960s from *The Magnificent Seven* (John Sturges, 1960) to *The Wild Bunch* (Sam Peckinpah, 1969). The most conspicuous instance of hybridization in *Vera Cruz*, however, is to be found in the articulation of two subgenres of the historical costume drama and their very distinct filmic imaginaries: on the one hand, the Western and its images of late nineteenth-century US-American colonization; on the other hand, films focusing on the imperial courts of early modern Europe. *Vera Cruz* features six-guns and Stetsons, desert landscapes, horseback chases, and the final showdown of black hat versus white hat. But it also features a French marquess and countess, lancers in metal armors, and court ladies in colorful dresses as well as a ten-minute scene in an imperial palace, complete with banquet and ball [22:41–33:10]. The introduction of early modern Europe into the Western comes with the first appearance of the imperial lancers chasing the US-American Westerners [6:25–6:32]. The disruption in shot size, from an extreme long shot framing a cloud of dust on the horizon of a Western landscape to a full shot of a group of shiny-armored lancers who would look at home in a royal drama, suggests that the two imaginaries will be contrasted rather than merged. This is confirmed by the rest of the film. Into the visual contrast is weaved an aural one when, a few moments before Pedro plays his gentle melody on the guitar, the marquess is introduced by a blaring fanfare [15:26]—repeated in the introduction of the imperial palace [22:40] and the emperor [27:20]—displaying imperial regalia. Genre hybridity in Vera Cruz is exploited in such confrontational fashion to suggest the tension and incompatibility of both historical imaginaries.

Vera Cruz's oppositional approach to genre crossing reflects back on both the Western and the imperial costume drama in ways that strengthen their distinct national identities. Vera Cruz mobilizes the association of the Western with the agrarian and liberal ideals of Americanness, while the imperial costume drama in the film is characterized by elements that are more typically associated with Europe: class difference and autocratic rule. Interestingly, Vera Cruz, in doing so, underlines the un-Americanness of the US-American Westerners and establishes the Mexican people and the Juarista cause as the true representatives of US-American liberal mythology. Indeed, the elements in the film consistently identified with the Western are the Mexican landscape, which very much resembles the movie West, and the Juaristas, visually treated as movie Indians.[7] Also Western-like are the Mexican people and their rural towns, whose ruggedness, communal life, and inclusiveness evoke the pioneer communities celebrated in John Ford's films. Because the Western remains the dominant genre, and the Mexican setting is identified with it, all the elements associated with the imperial costume drama appear out of place, aesthetically conveying the invasive presence of the empire/Europe in Mexico/the West. The point where both subgenres meet and collide is in the characterization of the US-American protagonists. As riders in cowboy garb, and as actors and stars associated with the genre, they are immediately identified with the Western. Although most of the mercenaries are little more than white savages, the main characters Ben Trane and Joe Erin are heirs to recognizable Western types: respectively, the Virginian and the gunfighter. And yet, they are narratively associated with the empire, which they serve up until the last fifteen minutes of the film [79:58]. The film's contrasting of both genres amplifies the tension between the visual and the narrative allegiances of the US-American characters and underlines the contradiction between the liberal image of Americanness and the imperialist actions of US-Americans. Through the articulation and confrontation of distinct historical imaginaries in the conflation of US-American Westerners and European aristocrats in Mexico, Vera Cruz formally unfolds its scathing indictment of US-American imperial history and policy.

CONCLUSION

The transnational narrative of *Vera Cruz* decenters the Western's perspective on the history of US-American imperialism by introducing the specificities and similarities of a non-US-American colonial context within the genre. The Mexican setting operates on different levels, all of which contribute to cultivate the anti-imperialist discourse in the Western genre. The unfamiliar visual and narrative elements open up a space for the critical rewriting of generic conventions along the lines of the more liberal productions released in the early 1950s. *Vera Cruz* converges with the pro-Indian Western in its dignified depiction of noble Juaristas fighting for freedom, and the film exploits the narrative distance with US-American history to approach colonization from an indigenous perspective. Although it partakes in the genre's individualist and racist drive when contrasting Euro-American protagonists with a background of Mexican extras, it also works against that very drive by erasing or marginalizing its white heroes in ways that, ultimately, foreground collective values at the expense of individual interests. The Mexican setting also provides the Western with a competing historical perspective that displaces the Western's structural focus on the US frontier and Indian wars to mobilize another (and earlier) foundational episode of US-American history, the American Revolution. The Juaristas are Mexican equivalents to the US-American Patriots of old, calling on US-Americans to remain true to their original myth of liberation. The legitimacy of the Juaristas' struggle against European imperialism is even greater than that of the Patriots, as they are characterized as the genuine heirs of pre-Columbian peoples. Indeed, the colonial dynamics of Mexican history are played out through the visual treatment of architecture, identifying the empire and the US-Americans with Spanish colonization, whereas the Juaristas embody the powerful and inclusive culture of a popular and more Indigenous Mexico. Finally, the Mexican setting offers a possibility for generic hybridization, the political implications of the narrative being played out in the conflicting articulation of different imaginaries. *Vera Cruz* emphasizes the association of the Western with US-American identity and treats the European costume drama as an alien intruder in an otherwise coherent genre to formally express the imperial invasion of Mexico by a foreign power and condemn the actions of its US-American gunfighters. The Mexican perspective eventually exposes the gap between the liberal myth of Americanness, expressed through the Western and projected onto the Juaristas, and the imperial policies of the US, stifling democracy and independence abroad in the name of power and profit. In articulating histories and imaginaries across national and generic borders in ways that reflect back on the Western and its construction of national identity, *Vera Cruz* exploits transnational perspectives within the Hollywood Western to expand the genre's critical reevaluation of US-American imperial mythology and policies, both in the past and in the present.

Vera Cruz inspired some later Mexico Westerns to reprise its decentered criticism of US imperial myth and history. *The Wild Bunch* (Sam Peckinpah, 1969) and, to a lesser extent, *The Professionals* (Richard Brooks, 1966) expanded on some of the narrative and visual themes condemning US-American political choices abroad, while *Major Dundee* (Sam Peckinpah, 1965) further explored the problematic implications of post–Civil War divisions. Other Mexico Westerns instead took a less critical turn, celebrating the liberating use of US-American force abroad (in John Sturges's *The Magnificent Seven*, 1960, and its three sequels) or using Mexico as a foil against which divided US-Americans can regain unity (in Andrew V. McLaglen's *The Undefeated*, 1969).

NOTES

1. Directed by Robert Aldrich, *Apache* starred Burt Lancaster and was produced by Hecht-Lancaster Productions. The action takes place in the late 1880s, strictly on US soil, between Arizona and Indian Territory (present-day Oklahoma). The film was released in early 1954 and, in addition to its star, shares some of its cast with *Vera Cruz*: Morris Ankrum plays an assimilated Cherokee farmer in Indian Territory, and Charles Bronson plays an accommodationist Apache warrior and the protagonist's rival.

2. The high-angle shot of a Juarista overlooking the stagecoach and imperial caravan at the foot of a pyramid [54:12] is reminiscent of Geronimo (Chief White Horse) overlooking the stage crossing Monument Valley in *Stagecoach* (John Ford, 1939) [69:14]. Another example would be Lance Poole (Robert Taylor) watching the sheepherders trespassing on his land in *Devil's Doorway* [56:40]. Such staple shots in Westerns (see D. W. Griffith's *The Massacre*, 1912 [16:18] or, later, John Ford's *The Iron Horse*, 1924 [10:27]) reposition US-American westward expansion as a territorial invasion and colonization.

3. According to Armida de la Garza, the mestizo narrative that dominated the discourses of Mexican national identity from the 1920s to the 1990s celebrated cultural and racial hybridization, but it was embedded in a racialist subtext that relegated indigeneity to the past and privileged the European element as the source of progress (6–8).

4. In favoring collective causes over individual greed as a legitimate basis for action, the film also develops a scathing critique of US-American capitalism as predatory and socially harmful (see Fuller 26).

5.   In Apache, two black Union soldiers are more sympathetic to the Apache than their white officers. In Vera Cruz, the character of the African American Union veteran Ballard (played by famous dancer and choreographer Archie Savage) is interestingly fleshed out as the better end of the bunch of mercenaries. His actions serve to debunk racist stereotypes—when he rescues Nina from rape at the hands of white mercenaries [51:08–51:26] or when he fights imperial troops bravely [88:55–89:10] and dies betrayed by Joe [89:50]—or to evoke Savage's artistic career through dance performances fusing American and Mexican folklore [62:30–62:55; 64:12–64:23].

6.   The association of Trane with religion also evokes his redemptive path, as shown toward the end of the film when US-Americans finally side with the Juaristas, and Trane is repeatedly shot with a conspicuous cross in the background [78:30; 78:46].

7.   The Western genre has overwhelmingly favored the desert landscapes of Southern California, Utah, or Arizona where most films were shot, even when the action was set in other areas of the historical West (Simmon 53; Henriet and Mauduit).

WORKS CITED

Abel, Richard. Americanizing the Movies and "Movie-mad" Audiences, 1910–1914. University of California Press, 2006.

Apache. Directed by Robert Aldrich, performances by Burt Lancaster, Jean Peters, John McIntire, Charles Bronson, and Morris Ankrum, United Artists, 1954.

Carter, Matthew. "The Post-apocalyptic Frontier: Reappropriating Western Violence for Feminism in Mad Max: Fury Road." Unbridling the Western Film Auteur: Contemporary, Transnational and Intertextual Explorations, edited by Emma Hamilton and Alistair Rolls, 2018, pp. 85–104.

Chapman, James, and Nicholas John Cull. Projecting Empire: Imperialism and Popular Cinema. I. B. Tauris, 2009.

de la Garza, Armida. "Diversity, Difference and Nation: Indigenous Peoples on Screen in Mexico." National Identities, vol. 12, no. 4, 2010, pp. 413–24.

Fojas, Camille. Border Bandits: Hollywood on the Southern Frontier. University of Texas Press, 2008.

Fuller, Stephanie. "'Filmed Entirely in Mexico': Vera Cruz and the Politics of Mexico in American Cinema." Journal of Popular Film and Television, vol. 41, no. 1, 2013, pp. 20–30.

Henriet, Gérard, and Jacques Mauduit. Géographie du western : Une nation en marche [Geography of the Western: The March of a Nation]. Nathan Université, 1989.

Mogen, David. Wilderness Visions: Science Fiction Westerns. Vol. 1, Borgo, 1982.

Schreiber, Rebecca M. *Cold War Exiles in Mexico: U.S. Dissidents and the Culture of Resistance*. University of Minneapolis Press, 2008.

Simmon, Scott. *The Invention of the Western Film: A Cultural History of the Genre's First Half-Century*. Cambridge University Press, 2003.

Slotkin, Richard. *Gunfighter Nation: The Myth of the Frontier in Twentieth-Century America*. University of Oklahoma Press, 1998.

Vera Cruz. Directed by Robert Aldrich, performances by Gary Cooper, Burt Lancaster, Denise Darcel, Cesar Romero, Sarita Montiel, Morris Ankrum, and Charles Bronson, United Artists, 1954.

Walker, Janet, editor. *Westerns: Films through History*, Routledge, 2001.

Weeks, Charles A. *The Juarez Myth in Mexico*. University of Alabama Press, 1987.

Williams, Tony. "Some Further Thoughts on *Vera Cruz*." *Film International*, vol. 13, no. 2, 1 June 2015, pp. 30–40.

HERVÉ MAYER is Assistant Professor of American Studies at Université Paul Valéry Montpellier 3. He is author of *Guerre sauvage & empire de la liberté* and *La Construction de l'Ouest américain dans le cinéma hollywoodien*.

FOUR

—◊◊◊—

TRANSNATIONAL IDENTITY ON THE CONTEMPORARY TEXAS-MEXICO BORDER IN *TEJANO* (DAVID BLUE GARCIA, 2018)

MARINE SOUBEILLE

THE US-MEXICO BORDER IN TEXAS is an agitated place of cultural hybridity and conflict, and has been ever since the territory seceded from Mexico. While some movies about the border—*The Golden Dream* (Quemada-Díez, 2013), *Sicario* (Villeneuve, 2015)—seem to propose a simplified generic perspective, picturing flows of Mexican migrants struggling to cross the river and the border, focusing on the difference and separation between the two sides rather than their possible connection, other movies that are set in the area endeavor to reflect the hybrid nature of its landscape, culture, and language, and give pride of place to minorities and notions of transidentity. The profound and harrowing social gap, materialized between Texas and Mexico by the Rio Grande, is, indeed, one of the main subjects of these films.[1]

The southern border states of the US (California, Arizona, New Mexico, and Texas) have historically been the privileged locations for many classical Westerns and have come to signify "the West," even though the story was supposedly taking place in Utah, Colorado, or even the Oklahoma Territory.[2] In films displaying the great red canyons of Arizona and Utah or the stark desert of southern Texas—*Red River* (Hawks, 1948), *The Searchers* (Ford, 1956)—the border with Mexico is seen as another frontier where Mexicans stand for savagery in their Turnerian opposition to Anglo-American civilization, albeit to a lesser extent than indigenous peoples. While the preconceived opposition symbolized by the frontier appears to have dominated the classical Western scene and participated in the construction of the US-American idea of nation, the rewriting of such a simplistic view—as Neil Campbell and Stephen Tatum have argued when discussing the post-Western[3]—practically dates back to the inception of the genre, which regularly challenged its own role in both national and transnational history. This particular (mis)representation of the Mexican border and culture has been recognized and dealt with by a series of transnational Westerns that deliberately displace the idea of the frontier and its narrative and visual codes in other contexts, and particularly onto the US-Mexico border, in order to question the place of Mexican culture in the southernmost parts of the nation and to criticize the all-white tale explored by the classical Western. *Lone Star* (John Sayles, 1996), *Three Burials* (Tommy Lee Jones, 2005), and *No Country for Old Men* (the Coen brothers, 2007) are three such examples. Through this change of scenery—and, therefore, perspective—the imperialist "legacy of conquest" (in Patricia Limerick's words) becomes more blatant. Here, on the Texas-Mexico frontier, US imperialism and its confrontation with the Mexican presence appear as a defining and scarring foundation, tackled by these films' complex depictions of an ambiguous space.

An heir to the abovementioned contemporary border Westerns, the independent production *Tejano* (David Blue Garcia, 2018) reflects on the social and cultural specificity of the Mexican border by tackling the issue of identity in the borderland. Shot in the Rio Grande Valley on both sides of the official border, the film tells the story of a young Tejano[4] farmer who decides in an act of desperation to smuggle drugs from Mexico to Texas. After almost getting caught when going through customs, he flees and decides to cross the river and border illegally, becoming the hunted migrant he himself used to chase out of his grandfather's ranch. This reversal of both roles and identities mirrors his Tejano background and offers a point of entry into the criticism of the very existence of the border, as well as a reevaluation of the opposition between the Anglo-American "us" and the ethnic minority "them," which has long been dramatized and sometimes even challenged in classical Westerns like *The Big Trail* (Walsh, 1930) and *The Ox-Bow Incident* (Wellman, 1942). Building on previous analyses of border Westerns (Fojas) and on the theories of the border as *frontera*, "a vague and undetermined place" (Anzaldúa 25) whose complexity resides in the legacy of conquest (Limerick, *Something in the Soil* 88), this chapter offers a detailed analysis of *Tejano* as a contemporary transnational Western that not only deconstructs the generic and cultural conventions associated with the Western, but goes further than its predecessors by parodying these conventions in the service of political satire. In doing so, *Tejano* evidences the absurdity of a white and imperialist understanding of the southern Texas border space by reminding us of its shared history with Mexico and its people. Adopting a transnational perspective on this movie ultimately leads to a reinterpretation of the figure of the cowboy in the contemporary US.

A CHANGE IN PERSPECTIVE: FROM THE
FRONTIER TO *LA FRONTERA*

The frontier theory as outlined by Frederick Jackson Turner constructs a clear oppositional space between the forces of civilization, which are white, Anglo-Saxon, and mostly male, and the untamed wilderness, metonymically represented by the rugged landscape, savage animals, and/or Native American tribes encountered by the settlers during Western expansion. Generally speaking, it is the place of an encounter between the anthropological Self and the ethnographic Other, of the classical opposition between "us" and "them," and it is viewed from an Anglo-American point of view (Kearney 117). By opposing otherness, the US-American pioneer, as a cultural representation, is defined in a specific place and time by what he is not in terms of values, culture, and social organization; by extension, he embodies and encapsulates the entire nation. Cultural historians such as Richard Slotkin have generally distinguished classical Westerns, which followed this conception of the frontier and participated in the elaboration and circulation of the national myth based on a simplified version of frontier history, from revisionist Westerns of the 1960s onward, which offer a more reflexive and critical view of the myth.

More recently, Matthew Carter has considered Westerns as works that have both questioned and conveyed the national myth regardless of their epoch, causing repercussions on Western culture and identity (*Myth of the Western* 4). For Patricia Nelson Limerick, Western popular culture—including productions in the twentieth century that try to revise it (*Legacy of Conquest* 222)— has failed to convey anything other than the national ideology as exposed by Turner. When revisionist movies side with the Indians, they still tend to represent history as two sided, switching the good and the bad sides instead of complexifying the story (John Ford's 1964 *Cheyenne Autumn* is a case in point). Limerick and the New Western History have thus endeavored to shed light on the breadth of intercultural relations on the frontier, rejecting the simplistic idea of a two-sided confrontation and reflecting on the imperialist nature of the trope. The concept of *frontera*, a response to Turner's frontier that Limerick borrows from Gloria Anzaldúa, appears more fluid, more hybrid than the former; it is also deliberately transnational, since she uses the Spanish term to point to the fact that Latino, Chicano, and Native cultures coexist in these border spaces and tint the newly settled Anglo-American civilization with various colors.[5] This theory transforms the geographically vague but ideologically straight line of the frontier, whereby one side opposes the other, into a borderland, an ideological in-between space where exchanges of gunshots, culture, and blood thicken and blur the relationships between existing cultural entities, creating yet another indeterminate space. In this sense, Limerick understands the US-American Southwest as a perfect representation of the *frontera*, a borderland where the line exists geographically (as a border) but where centuries of exchanges have proven the Anglo-American identity to be a cultural construct rather than historical reality. Limerick remarks that "it is one thing to draw an arbitrary geographical line between two spheres of sovereignty, it is another to persuade people to respect it" (*Legacy of Conquest* 222). Indeed, on the Mexican border, the legal separation might exist physically, but laws and separations fail to make sense, and the boundless region becomes a kind of no man's land where cultural considerations and personal interests stand above the official text. The border is in the middle of the space, not around it; it does not define but splits.

Movies like *Lone Star*, *Three Burials*, and, more recently, *Tejano*, all belong to a trend of contemporary Westerns that describe the borderlands between Mexico and South Texas as a *frontera*. In South Texas, the frontier still exists physically, materialized by the hard US-Mexico border, and metaphorically by the political and social struggles the crossing of this line generates. Interethnic tensions and troubled coexistence are features of frontier life that can still be found on the southern border and its representation in these films, but, instead of picturing the nonwhite character as alien, these films set out to belie Limerick's remark that "Hispanic history remained on the edges of Western American history" (*Legacy of Conquest* 253) by making nonwhite identity a central issue of the film. Although it relies on a classical Western revenge narrative, *Three Burials*, as Matthew Carter "Cowboy" has shown, resonates as a *frontera* movie aiming to place the Mexican character at the center of the plot. By having the character played by Tommy Lee Jones transport the lifeless and gradually decomposing body of Melquiades Estrada, a Mexican farmer, the movie exposes the pestilent injustice of his murder in plain sight until it becomes unbearable. In *Lone Star*, the official frontier myth around Sheriff Buddy Deeds is disrupted by his son's excavation of the past and the revelation that he might have shot a Mexican migrant, Eladio Cruz. By revealing the truth behind the story, the official myth is challenged and, ultimately, overthrown. In so doing, the "true" story unearthed by Sam Deeds reintroduces the Mexican character in the narrative by allowing him to function not as a mere victim but also as a historical agent. Yet, if both *Three Burials* and *Lone Star* successfully center southern Texas history on Mexican characters, the rewriting of history is nonetheless performed by an Anglo-American figure trying to right his fellow citizens' wrongs. It is in this respect that *Tejano* goes much further.

Tejano, like *Three Burials*, is set in the *frontera*, on either side of the Mexican border. Apart from the first images showing the main character crossing the river at night (an event explained later on in the narrative), the film's opening is grounded in the classical opposition of the frontier movie, transposed onto the contemporary Mexican border. A young Texas rancher, Javi, can be seen chasing Spanish-speaking illegals from his family's land, "border jumpers" who have made a hole in the fence [3:50]. From this moment on, however, the story and the character's identity are increasingly blurred and complexified, as though the hole in the fence had caused a breach in people's identity and characterization. A Tejano raised by his Mexican grandfather in the Rio Grande Valley, Javi is at a crossroads between two cultures; he has Mexican blood in his veins, speaks Spanish and English with ease, and has a Mexican girlfriend, Lorena, on the other side. With the exception of his friend, a young customs officer named Duke (John Wayne's nickname), every other character in the film as well as a majority of the film's cast and crew is either Mexican or Latino. From the start, the inadequacy between the ambiguity of this border culture and the Manichaean opposition underlying frontier ideology is foregrounded, challenging a reading of the film as a Western. Indeed, *Tejano* first appears as a contemporary Mexican gangster movie, dealing with issues including the drug cartels, the thinning out of grazing fields, and the migration policies to control immigration flows. Yet many of its visuals are borrowed from the Western, and it is they that shed light on the region's imperialist legacy today and, inevitably, question the place and origin of these conventions in the cultural imagination.

WESTERN CONVENTIONS IN THE SERVICE OF SATIRE

The historical and cultural relations developed over the years transpire through ambiguous characterization, rendering moot any clear-cut opposition between ethnic groups (here Mexican, Tejano, and Anglo-American). The series of recent US-Mexico border films dramatize, exaggerate, and criticize the persistence of conflicts between North and South of the border, the constant living "on this thin edge of barbwire" (Anzaldúa 25). In *Tejano*, this constant questioning of codes could be considered as a satirical rewriting of the Western's most popular tropes.[6] If, at first glance, *Tejano* resembles a modern thriller, hints of the film's Western legacy immediately appear, in costumes, landscapes, and specific compositions. The classical epic Western landscape of the arid plains and red mountains is reinvented, here, to match the reality of modern border life; the plains are cultivated, but they are desiccated lands, increasingly barren due to the lack of water and funding. They become a kind of "new" wilderness where there is nothing left to reap. Establishing tracking shots of the desolate land seem to comment in silence on the lies that sold Texas as the "Magic Valley" in the early twentieth century.[7] Modern wind turbines, crushing symbols of technological progress, have replaced the traditional windmill looming over the ranchers' fields and come to replace cattle. The figure of the cowboy on horseback, the first scenes indicate, has been replaced by Javi riding a four-wheeler among these peaceful metal giants. Noticing the lack of rain, and thus the likely failure to grow crops in the future, Javi's boss professes: "I guess the future is these damned ugly windmills," evidencing the reality of today's life and rejecting, in the process, the old model of the livestock farmer that cannot be upheld anymore [26:46]. Although the overbearing presence of technological progress crushing an earlier model echoes many classical Westerns, it also signifies the end of the Western model as pictured in the popular imagination and proves that contemporary Texas can no longer represent the traditional Western.[8]

The film reenvisions the Western landscape in a striking fashion during a Hollywoodian chase scene that occurs halfway through the movie [59:38–62:36]. The hero finds himself climbing gigantic piles of clothes in a recycling factory. Revealed by a boom shot panning left as he enters the building, the piles of clothes resemble an unlikely version of the great mountains of the West, an arduous and labyrinthine terrain, in short, the characteristic setting of the chase between lethal enemies in Westerns like *Devil's Doorway* and *Winchester '73* (both directed by Anthony Mann in 1950). Using the landscape to his advantage, Javi escapes by hiding under a mound of clothes, closely followed by his rival, Adelio (his brother-in-law), thus rewriting the trope in a comical and modern way. If used clothes are unlikely to inspire a sense of the Burkean sublime, the scene, which refuses the frontier myth's romanticizing of the chase, offers a commentary on the dire reality of border life, the economic arrangement ruling maquiladoras, and the social inequalities they maintain.

Tejano initially seems to recycle classical stock characters that verge on parody: with his white hat, jeans, and boots, the grandfather is dressed like a typical Western cowboy, while the woman running the cartel is dressed in black leather and wears a black hat. Here, the typical Western iconography distinguishing good from evil, notably the white hat/black hat, seems to provide a clear indication as to which side we should choose. Yet what remains of the Western soon rings out of tune, with Javi, the modern cowboy, wearing a cap instead of a Stetson and riding a quad instead of a horse. *Tejano* even seems to mock the low-angle shots of Western heroes meant to convey their moral superiority by picturing its hero standing on the roof of his shabby house, holding a gun in his cast arm [79:58]. The parody reaches its peak in the final showdown of the film staged as a Mexican standoff, incidentally executed by Mexican or Tejano characters only [77:12–86:13].[9] Here, a series of extreme long shots in which characters appear as mere silhouettes on the deserted plain, interspersed with extreme close-ups of the protagonists' faces and their meaningful hats, can probably be considered as the most "Western" scene of the film, but paradoxically, it is, in effect, one of the most revealing moments of the absurdity of the conflict itself. Indeed, in order to get Javi to hand back the drugs he ran away with, the cartel leader has decided to attack his family's farm and kidnap his girlfriend, Lorena, following the advice of the latter's own brother. The brother himself is kidnapped by Javi's grandfather, and both sides threaten to eliminate their sibling hostages. The finale, quite literally, proposes a Mexican standoff, in which members of a same family will most likely die no matter the outcome, thereby illustrating the internal war waged in the borderland. *Tejano* thus encourages us to reflect on the legitimacy of the border, the only thing that separates these groups being the side of the border they live on. The real antagonist exposed by the film is neither the outlaw nor the illegal migrant who was born "on the wrong side" of the fence, but the physical border itself and, more profoundly, the geopolitics it embodies. The fence, the river, and the customs office, all physical signifiers of the border, are ultimately the real triggers of conflict; their only justification is the historical legacy of conquest and political arm wrestling, made irrelevant by years of living next to each other and sharing a culture.

Violence is everywhere in *Tejano*, and it is depicted to the point of excess. A joyful soundtrack accompanies a man whom we can see washing the blood off the street of Matamoros, as if his actions were as mundane and meaningless as sweeping dust or buying groceries [8:15]. The cartel leader explains to Javi that in order to have him carry drugs in his cast, his arm must be broken [33:48], and it must not only look real; it has to be real, even if it verges on cruelty. The graphic violence with which Javi's arm is fractured on screen [35:09] echoes the gratuitous violence with which the border fractures the region. Similarly, however mingled and mangled the culture might be on either side of the official border, the latter—like the broken arm that is its metaphor—is painfully forced into existence. Gratuitous violence appears to be the rule in this lawless space.

The parody of the Western genre also questions the existence and efficiency of the hard border. Projected at the Dallas Film Festival of 2018, the movie was not, according to Garcia, meant as a criticism of Donald Trump's ambition to build a wall between the US and Mexico. Yet border policy and migration

Fig. 4.1 Silhouettes in the sunset: Adelio and Arturo (*left*) versus Javi and Lorena (*right*) [84:35].

control are central issues in the film. The iron fence on the northern shore of the Rio Grande, which existed long before Trump's inauguration, is depicted in *Tejano* as yet another trial the hero has to overcome once he has successfully crossed the river. Standing in front of it, Javi realizes by observing some border jumpers that the fence simply comes to an end a few yards away [53:45]. This ironic and absurd moment is, no doubt, meant to remind us that, even though border policies are getting tougher, the border remains porous, and many illegal immigrants still make it to the other side and even find work.

The film combines and contrasts the basic genre tropes that it parodies with more complex characterization. Toward the end of the standoff, four silhouettes stand against the dying light of the sunset, representing the two sides of border relations: on the left, Adelio is kneeling in front of the grandfather, begging for his death, while, on the right side, Lorena and Javi's figures are enlaced (fig. 4.1). Although the composition is based on a simple scheme opposing love and conflict, it bears a much deeper significance. This moment is a paradigmatic example of the film's "shadow theater" aesthetics. By using backlighting in the most iconic scenes, Garcia highlights the stock characters as such, endowing them with no distinguishable trait but only a recognizable contour. Reducing them to the status of iconic figures thereby rings as a warning against the simplifying power of popular myths and films. Yet this is countered by the aesthetics of the rest of the movie, which is shot in natural light. In doing so, backlighting aesthetics prove their impossibility to capture the reality of border life, which is much more ambiguous, both politically and ideologically. Rejecting years of borderland culture, it is the simple Manichaean view, projected in

Fig. 4.2 Arturo's grave among the windmills [87:28].

popular consciousness, that keeps tensions alive and contributes to reinforcing prejudices regarding the myth of a "foreign invasion" from Latin America.

In *Tejano*, the demise of the Western model in this region of Texas is suggested by the death of Arthuro, Javi's grandfather. Not only did he embody the epitome of the filmic cowboy; he also represented the economic model of the small independent rancher as professed by Thomas Jefferson. His grave—a pile of dirt with just his Stetson and rifle on top—works as a symbol of the death of the cowboy [87:28]; above it, a humble wooden cross stands among slowly rotating electric windmills, which embody the new model—that of ecological awakening and the end of a careless harvesting of natural resources that was at the core of westward expansion (fig. 4.2).

While it has become clear that Western conventions can no longer make sense of the reality of the Texas-Mexico border today, the reason behind this change of model warrants further analysis. Why should this border space be read as a *frontera* rather than a frontier? How can a Tejano movie, hybrid to the core, challenge the way the region is represented on-screen and thought about in ideological terms?

TEJANO CULTURE AND IMPERIALIST HISTORY

Centuries of common history and endless fights over territory and property have left their marks on the landscape and in the cultures on either side of the border, creating yet another hybrid geographic and cultural space. The annexation of the territory by Mexico and the US, its brief existence as a republic, the presence of Native American tribes and their assimilation, and also the battle of the Alamo are testimonies and landmarks of the winding history of the region and its complex myth of origins. *Tejano* illustrates this hybridity in terms of both narrative and narration.

In the 2018 film, everybody is or was connected to both sides of the frontier and is thus culturally hybrid. As a Tejano, with ties to the Mexican side that are familial (and thus historical) and emotional, Javi embodies a culturally hybrid identity specific to the area. Kimberly Sultze's remarks about *Lone Star* are equally relevant for *Tejano*, a film that pictures characters for whom personal and common history "is intermixed—and often in conflict with—'official' history" (265). Javi's grandfather speaks Spanish at home, and, when he falls ill, asks for a Chicano shaman to cure him with rites. Though he is proud of his Latino background, he is the character of the story who best resembles the Anglo-American hero of the Western, embodying the archetypal cowboy. Yet this hybrid figure only seems surprising if one ignores the origins of the figure. Originating in the northern Mexican "vaquero," the cowboy was reappropriated by Western US-American culture in the nineteenth century as a symbol of a hardworking man, who tamed cattle on horseback for a living, always asserted his independence, and, ultimately, became the embodiment of the frontier hero.[10] In *Tejano*, the cowboy is returned to his rightful Mexican origins, reminding the audience that, like the state of Texas, the character of the cowboy was Mexican before it was US-American—even though years of US-American imperialism, through soft and hard power, have striven to erase it. This reflection on the cowboy also illustrates the cultural and historical palimpsest that was built over the years on the borderland. What first appears as a parodic reversal could, therefore, be interpreted as a way to reinstate the truth about the region and its Mexican history.

Even the white US customs officers, who seem to embody US-American culture and values, have a troubled relation to law and morality. Aptly called Duke, Javi's best friend operates as a smuggler for the Mexican drug cartel, while monitoring the border all day long. Although his moral duality might remind one of some of John Wayne's greatest roles (Ringo Kid in *Stagecoach* and Ethan in *The Searchers*, 1939 and 1956, respectively, directed by Ford), here he only holds a secondary part in the story. The officer who arrests Javi plays with the legislative loophole represented by the border space where his office is situated, thus taking the law into his own hands like a perverted marshal. He explains: "See, son, we haven't let you back in yet. You're in no man's land. You aren't a citizen and you haven't got any rights until you cross that little yellow line over there" [47:30]. As the embodiment of the law in a lawless and violent frontier space, it is natural that his character should reflect its contradictions. In ideological terms, the reminiscence of the Western marshal, and the fact that such behavior still occurs today, offers a commentary on the legal status of the frontier and of those who choose to cross it. The film not only questions the characters' identities, but, through them, seems to be contributing to the construction of the identity of a place: a borderland community trying to build its own history on a heap of contradictions. This borderland culture, born of conflict and ethnic mix, is revealed to be fundamentally transnational.

The endless physical and metaphorical crossings of borders reflect not only on the characters' intricate relations to history, but also on the porous nature of a barrier arbitrarily established by national entities; this is achieved through the foregrounding of the region's transnational dimension. In *Tejano*, as in *Three Burials*, the language barrier is constantly crossed and blurred (Carter 7). Both films can, therefore, be compared since both main characters reveal the fluidity of their cultural identity by switching from one language to the other, bridging the two worlds. Javi's speaking English to his grandfather, who always answers in Spanish, is like a never-ending arm wrestling match between two cultures. And yet Javi speaks perfect Spanish with the guardian of the customs bridge and with the migrants he meets when crossing the river. His fluidity is what makes him a *frontera* hero, and his crossing the river becomes a rewriting of the frontier hero's capacity to navigate between civilization and savagery, not justified by his wisdom or knowledge of the "other" but by his mixed origins.

The crossing of the border, for Anzaldúa, is only a perilous trial because the frontier line was drawn in the middle of a territory that should not have been split; her statement, "The border that divides the Mexican people was born on February 2, 1848," is a reminder that the cultures on either side are very similar and the border was created quite recently (29). The first conversation staged between Javi and Lorena's brother Adelio [09:02] shows how fluid language can be in the border region, and how mastering one or both idioms can become a display of power (depending on which side you are standing on) and an instrument of inclusion, exclusion, or even submission. While Javi is speaking Spanish with Lorena in the pharmacy she works in, Adelio, in an attempt to fit in (he is capable of switching from one language to the other with ease), interrupts and asks Javi, "No pharmacies in Texas?" in English. It is a way for him to reject Javi's attempt at inclusion and to put him down as nothing more than a "gringo." Adelio ends the conversation by saying "Hasta luego, Tejano, I'll see you later"—as though Javi could not understand Spanish without a translation—in order to signify that he, too, can master both languages and adapt to both worlds. This evidences the double standards imposed on Latinos in the US: being Tejano and speaking both languages allows Javi, as a US-American citizen, to manage easily in each world, communicate, and cross the border, but Adelio, as a Mexican who lives on the border, does not enjoy such privileges; for him, language is not so much a bridge as a weapon. Because Javi was born in Texas he is considered "white," while Adelio, born a few kilometers south, is not.

Javi crosses the actual border almost as often as he is seen switching from one language to another. He goes to Matamoros twice [8:04; 27:30], comes back to Texas thrice [12:00; 40:52; 51:42], with his final crossing of the Rio Grande appearing in the opening flash-forward [0:48]. When doing so, Javi benefits from his mixed "Tejano" identity—or from his being a "gringo;" Mexicans (such as Lorena's brother) look at him in defiance, while US border officers are affable with him. All this changes when he crosses it illegally. Once he is sent across to smuggle drugs in his arm cast, he immediately becomes suspect and is thus treated like a Mexican or a white ethnic. Border officers detain him and make him understand that he has no rights in this legal no man's land, while Mexican crossers help him find the gap in the wall as one of their own. The film's opening scene echoes Anzaldúa's description of the "mojados" (those who cross), as they "wade or swim across [the Rio Grande] naked, clutching their clothes over their heads" (33). This reversal emphasizes the sense that identity is not a given or a fixed thing, that it can, in the borderland, evolve quickly and become, in Anzaldúa's words, a "crossroads," thereby weakening both the actual and the metaphorical border.[11]

Later on, after double-crossing the drug cartel who forced him to be their mule, Javi tries to reprise his role as the "Anglo" cowboy defending his family and land; he attempts to save both his grandfather and girlfriend (both Mexican) from the assault of the "Mexican others," his brother-in-law and the cartel leader, villains who have kidnapped a member of their own family as leverage. It is this level of moral, physical and iconographic crossing that reveals how difficult it is to take sides in the borderland, even when one is forced to do so. This paradox not only allows the film to comment once again on the absurdity of the border; it also evokes the region's history. The film's climax—the Mexican standoff scene with the house serving as a fort—can be analyzed as a re-enactment of the battle of the Alamo, an event that is central to Texan culture and the construction of the region's identity in popular memory, and that has become both a myth and a motif that is a variation on the last stand. As during the battle of the Alamo, the conflicts waged in the name of a national ideal actually oppose people who shared common origins and who just had, at some point, to pick a side and defend it. Indeed, if US history has mainly retained the names of the white US-Americans there (James Bowie and Davy Crockett), the majority of the rebels were actually Mexican farmers living in Texas who fought and fell against the Mexican army. A similar logic is reprised in *Tejano* and its internal dispute. And just as contemporary historians have undertaken the task to reinstate Mexican people on the heroic side of the Alamo, *Tejano* sets out to revise Mexican history and recognize its legacy and complexity.[12] In the end, identity, like the border between two spaces, is no longer—or never was—either hard or definite.

CONCLUSION

The point *Tejano* seems to be making through its parody of Western tropes is that, although the frontier "closed" in 1890, border troubles are far from over and the dynamics of the *frontera* remain highly charged in terms of culture, economics, and identity. If the frontier myth and the Westerns it has inspired seemed to oppose recognizable entities, the people living in the Mexican borderland offer a narrative in which cultural or ideological sides cannot be so easily defined as "Mexican," "Latino" and/or "American." By constantly contesting the simplicity with which lines are drawn and stock characters fashioned, the film offers a transnational reflection on the borderland's present and past. Of course, the opposition never was clear-cut in the first place. By transforming the frontier into a *frontera*, scholars such as Anzaldúa and Limerick, or filmmakers such as John Sayles, Tommy Lee Jones, and David Blue Garcia, challenge US-American identity as pictured by popular culture. It is particularly true of southern Texas, where professing the existence of a US-American identity, as opposed to Hispanic people and culture, entails a fundamental denial and misinterpretation of the region's history. The ideological shift, which led New Western historians and scholars to reconsider identity in the region as a complex construction pairs with the gradual acknowledgment that Westerns (in particular, contemporary ones) retain a transnational consideration. This realization jeopardizes the relevance of the Western genre, as traditionally perceived by popular culture, in its capacity to make sense of an evolving world. This is why *Tejano* might be viewed as a Western on the wane: the satirical tone with which simple Western motifs are used and remodeled in a dirtier, less grandiloquent fashion emphasizes the impossibility for a contemporary production to limit itself to such a schematic or fantasized representation. In a place where cultural, social, and linguistic barriers never really existed in the first place, Western stock characters can only be disincarnate silhouettes. Thus, the hard border the Trump administration is promoting—and which would split wide open what has been described as an "unnatural boundary" (Anzaldúa 25)—could be understood as another form of Western illusion that hardly corresponds to the world we live in. By (re)claiming the border space as a *frontera*, *Tejano* contributes by reminding contemporary decision makers that the US is no longer—or hardly ever was—a Western scenery, where righteous cowboys defend their hard-fought territory.

NOTES

1. Gloria Anzaldúa calls the border a "1950 mile-long open wound" (24) and Guillermo Gomez Peña calls it "the geopolitical wound"; both use the metaphor of the injured body to denounce the unnatural quality of the border.

2. Rollins states about Western filmic landscapes that "almost every recognizable Western trait is more truly SouthWestern [than Western]" (488).

3. While Neil Campbell questions the recent emergence of post-Western criticism in the history of the genre, Stephen Tatum addresses its historiographical counterpart, the New Western History, arguing that the "popular" conception of the West it claims to deconstruct might be a misleadingly monolithic view.

4. Someone living in Texas who is a descendant of the Mexicans living there before Texas became a republic and a US state.

5. The term *Latino* designates a person living in a Spanish-speaking American country or sharing such culture by descent; *Native* refers to people whose ancestors were born on the American continent; and *Chicano* indicates people whose mixed origins, Native and Latino, give them a particular claim to South Texas as the place of their birth nation, Aztlan. Limerick lengthily discusses the difference between Turner's frontier and her concept of *frontera*, which can be summarized in this sentence: "[L]a *frontera* is less ethnocentric than the 'frontier,' acknowledging that the West was and is multicultural" (*Adventures* 72).

6. Although there is a long history of Western parodies playing on the genre's conventions since the 1920s, *Tejano* is, here, considered as a satire, a darker, more serious version of parody that uses the codes of the genre to craft a political criticism. See Matthew R. Turner's article on parodies (219).

7. This myth of the Magic Valley is explained by Brannstrom and Neuman: "In the first decade of the twentieth century land developers and boosters promoted the Lower Rio Grande of Texas as the 'Magic Valley,' a place for Anglo farmers to obtain water for irrigating vegetables and citrus crops and to exploit Hispanic labor" (2).

8. Sam Peckinpah's Westerns picture the fateful presence of technological modernity over older Jeffersonian models.

9. Though its origin is disputed, the term *Mexican standoff* allegedly originated from nineteenth-century Mexican conflicts between Vaqueros and

Bandidos, but has been used extensively as a narrative trope of the Western. Here, the film gives back its true origin to the scene, by staging latino vaqueros (Javi and his grandpa) and bandidos (the drug cartel) as characters of the standoff.

10. The transformation of the cowboy from poor farmer to US-American hero can be attributed to T. Roosevelt who selected the cowboy as a national symbol in his 1888 pamphlet called "Ranch life and the Hunting Trail."

11. Judith Butler, in *Bodies That Matter*, cites Anzaldúa's "crossroads of cultural and political discursive forces" to replace the fixity of the notion of "subject" (124).

12. Holly Beachley Brear asks: "How [to] change an entire mythology of the struggle between the good Anglo and the evil Hispanic portrayed in most Alamo films?" (3).

WORKS CITED

Anzaldúa, Gloria. *Borderlands—La Frontera*. Aunt Lute Books, 2007.

Barrera, Cordelia. "Border Theory and the Politics of Place, Space and Memory in John Sayles's *Lone Star*." *Quarterly Review of Film and Video*, vol. 27, no. 3, 2010, pp. 210–18.

Brannstrom, Christian, and Matthew Neuman. "Inventing the 'Magic Valley' of South Texas, 1905–1941." *Geographical Review*, vol. 99, no. 2, 2009, pp. 123–45.

Brear, Holly B. *Inherit the Alamo: Myth and Ritual at an American Shrine*. University of Texas Press, 2010.

Butler, Judith. *Bodies That Matter: On the Discursive Limits of "Sex."* Routledge, 1993.

Campbell, Neil. *Post-Westerns: Cinema, Region, West*. University of Nebraska Press, 2013.

Carter, Matthew. "'I'm Just a Cowboy': Transnational Identities of the Borderlands in Tommy Lee Jones' *Three Burials of Melquiades Estrada*." *European Journal of American Studies*, vol. 7, no. 1, 2012, document 4, https://doi.org/10.4000/ejas.9845. Accessed 1 Mar. 2020.

———. *Myth of the Western: New Perspectives on Hollywood's Frontier Narrative*. Edinburgh University Press, 2014.

Fojas, Camilla. *Border Bandits: Hollywood on the Southern Frontier*. University of Texas Press, 2008.

Kearney, Michael. "Transnationalism in California and Mexico at the End of the Empire." *Border Identities, Nation and State*, edited by Thomas M. Wilson and Hastings Donnan, Cambridge University Press, 1998, pp. 117–41.

Limerick, Patricia N. "The Adventures of the Frontier in the Twentieth Century." *The Frontier in American Culture*, edited by James R. Grossman and Richard White, University of California Press, 1994, pp. 67–102.

———. *The Legacy of Conquest: The Unbroken Past of the American West.* 1987. W. W. Norton, 2011.

———. *Something in the Soil: Legacies and Reckoning in the New West.* W. W. Norton, 2001.

Pratt, Marie Louise. *Imperial Eyes: Travel Writing and Transculturation.* Routledge, 1992.

Rollins, Peter. *The Columbia Companion to American History on Film.* Columbia University Press, 2003.

Slotkin, Richard. *Gunfighter Nation: The Myth of the Frontier in Twentieth-Century America.* University of Oklahoma Press, 1998.

Sultze, Kimberly. "Challenging Legends, Complicating Border Lines: The Concept of Frontera in John Sayles's *Lone Star.*" *Hollywood's West: the American Frontier in Film*, edited by Peter Rollins, University Press of Kentucky, 2005, pp. 261–80.

Tatum, Stephen. "The Problem of the Popular." *The New Western History: The Territory Ahead*, edited by Forrest G. Robinson, University of Arizona Press, 1998.

Turner, Frederick J. "The Significance of the Frontier in American History." *Annual Report of the American Historical Association*, 1893, pp. 197–227.

Turner, Matthew R. "Cowboys and Comedy: The Simultaneous Deconstruction and Reinforcement of Generic Conventions in the Western Parody." *Hollywood's West: The American Frontier in Film*, edited by Peter Rollins, University Press of Kentucky, 2005, pp. 218–35.

MARINE SOUBEILLE is PhD candidate at Université Paul Valéry Montpellier 3.

PART II

EUROPEAN WESTERNS AND THE CRITIQUE OF IMPERIALISM

OUR JOURNEY NOW TAKES US out of the plains of the US-American West-ern to the shores of Europe, whose history gave birth to a variety of colonial stories, and where the fascination for US frontier narratives predates even the invention of cinema. France, Italy, and Great Britain, among others, have all had long-standing love affairs with Western-themed pictures, producing them even before they had become a recognizable Hollywood genre and conversing with the genre in countless productions since. Other nations shared in the enthusiasm of their more productive cultural neighbors (such is the case of Austria in regard to the German tradition of Western productions), and oth-ers still developed a taste for the material for more political reasons (such as Yugoslavia during the Cold War). Italy, of course, stands out, alongside France, as one of the earliest European producers of Westerns and as the country that single-handedly reinvented the genre in the 1960s.

Part II takes us from the British Empire at the time of decolonization to contemporary France and the problems inherited from a troubled colonial past, from the construction of a national memory in post–World War II Yugoslavia to the exhuming of its darkest blind spots in contemporary Austria. While survey-ing the genre at the crossroads of the 1960s and its contemporary neoclassical or post-Western reinventions, each chapter explores the Western's hybridization with other genres, whether transnational (the war film, the empire film) or of a more local variety (the Heimat film, the French *film de banlieue*). Most of the films contemplated here are historical dramas reenacting foundational or more intimate moments in the construction of the nations that produced them, while the French films relate contemporary stories on the legacy of empire. All these films, quite surprisingly, situate their narratives in their countries of production, thus articulating the Western genre to local settings and histories (the World War II front in Yugoslavia, Jordan's desert soon to be placed under British mandate, the nineteenth-century Austrian Alps, a French postindustrial town, and the contemporary Middle East).

Our journey through Europe concludes with a visit to Italy, charting two locales ignored by most surveyors: the earliest moments of the Western when Italian cinema imprinted its mark on the budding genre, and the later phase of the Spaghetti Western when it was infused with acid flavors.

Next stop: Yugoslavia, 1960.

FIVE

—ℳ—

A YUGOSLAV "LEMON TREE IN SIBERIA"

The Partisan Western *Kapetan Leši*
(Živorad Mitrović, 1960)

DRAGAN BATANČEV

THE PARTISAN WESTERN WAS A hybrid of the most emblematic genres of socialist Yugoslavia, the war film (popularly known as the Partisan film) and the Western. In postwar Yugoslavia, the National Liberation War was represented as a threefold "founding myth" (Goulding 11): a resistance against the Axis powers, a Communist revolution, and a civil war fought between the Communist-led Partisans and various Quislings. Unsurprisingly, the goal of the multifaceted Yugoslav war remembrance culture was teaching younger generations about the legacy of the National Liberation War and preserving "the brotherhood and unity" of Yugoslav nations.

The topos of civil war emerges as a link between the Partisan film and the Western. Building on Will Wright's well-known, if reductive, structuralist approach to the Western, Peter Stanković discerns three principal characters of the 1970s Partisan Westerns—the Partisans, the Germans, and *narod* (people/nation)—which resemble Wright's types of the gunman, ranchers, and homesteaders, the main difference being that, in the Partisan Western, the characters are mostly collective (253). Accordingly, "the representation of Quislings as utterly incompetent soldiers appears to be primarily in the function of systematic discrediting of the Partisans' ideological opponents" (Stanković 254). A Yugoslav edition of Jean-Louis Rieupeyrout's book *Le Western, ou le cinéma américain par excellence*, prefaced by André Bazin, was published in 1960 and provided a timely definition of the Western as "any movie of action-based, adventurous, military character with a plot set in the Western areas of the United States" that focused on the conflicts between the wilderness and civilization, settlers and Native Americans, and representatives of the law and violent men (Vučetić, *Coca-Cola Socialism* 64). Rieupeyrout's definition of the Western emphasized the genre's military dimension, which was particularly important for the then emerging Partisan Western.

This chapter investigates how the Partisan Western *Kapetan Leši* (*Captain Leši*) adapts US-American cultural imperialism and approaches the World War II conflict between the Partisans and Kosovar Quislings in order to symbolically absorb Kosovar Albanians into the postwar supranational Yugoslav project. My overview of the Americanization of Yugoslav culture and the historical background of nationalism in Kosovo and Metohija (henceforth Kosovo) sets the stage for the narrative, iconographic, and production analysis of the film, coupled with the juxtaposition of *Kapetan Leši* and related Hollywood and Eastern European Westerns. In conceptualizing the key terms of this volume, I follow Chapman and Cull's dictum that "the American empire is not a formal empire of territorial acquisition but an informal empire of political and economic influence" (17). Furthermore, although it would be questionable to describe *Kapetan Leši* as a post-Western because of its enthusiastic and unquestioning appropriation of the genre, Jesús Ángel González's understanding of the transnational dimension of post-Westerns is applicable to *Kapetan Leši* insofar as the film "use[s] features from the Hollywood Western genre and establish[es] a political relationship between space and national identity, by using locations situated in cardinal points different from the West precisely to question the identities and foundation myths of the countries where they are made" (5).

BETTER PARTISANS AND BALLISTS
THAN COWBOYS AND INDIANS

The 1948 Tito-Stalin Split was the crucial turning point in postwar Yugoslav history, ushering in the country's self-management doctrine combining elements of market-driven economy and socialist ideals of equality, as well as the establishment of the Non-Aligned Movement as an alternative to Cold War polarization. Josip Broz Tito's government went through different periods of proximity to the USSR and US, which, in turn, resulted in different forms of political, economic, and cultural cooperation with both superpowers.

In her investigation of the Americanization of 1960s Yugoslav culture, Radina Vučetić supplements Tomlinson's conceptualization of US-American cultural imperialism with her own view of Americanization as "a phenomenon that with the help of nonpolitical symbols and stereotypes, and by its own insistence on its nonpolitical nature, carries out US-American political plans and achieves its objectives" (*Coca-Cola Socialism* 8). Vučetić adds that the Americanization of

Yugoslavia was by no means a linear transfer but a complex process involving adaptation and hybridization of US-American cultural forms. This is also the case of Partisan Westerns. Indeed, the wide popularity of US-American cultural products in post-1948 Yugoslavia included the domination of Hollywood films. Both Tito and the ordinary moviegoer favored Westerns—*Rio Grande* (1950), *High Noon* (1952), and *Shane* (1953), in particular, were big hits. Numerous Western coproductions were shot in Yugoslavia, leading a Yugoslav stunt double, Gojko Mitić, to become a major transnational star of East German *Indianerfilme* (a Western subgenre featuring Native Americans as protagonists and white settlers as antagonists). The Yugoslav press reported on the activities of the John Wayne fan club in Zagreb, the popularity of Karl May's *Winnetou* novels among Yugoslav youth, local impersonators of cowboys and sheriffs, and other Western-inspired phenomena (Vučetić, *Coca-Cola Socialism* 64–68).

It is in this context that the writer/director of *Kapetan Leši*, Živorad "Žika" Mitrović (1921–2005), came to the fore. Born in Belgrade, Mitrović published original Western comics in the interwar period to pay for English lessons and a subscription to *American Cinematographer* and *The Hollywood Reporter* (Crnjanski). Having directed a few documentaries about the postwar modernization of Kosovo, Mitrović made his feature debut with a Partisan Western set in World War II Kosovo, entitled *Ešalon doktora M.* (1955). This story about the combat between the Partisans and the Kosovar Ballists was a box office success, and the critical acclaim Mitrović received for "replacing the tired, pathetic Partisan epic with a lively and attractive action-filled spectacle" (Ranko Munitić, qtd. in Vučetić, *Coca-Cola Socialism* 69) enabled him to direct Partisan Westerns such as *Obračun* (1962), the sequel to *Kapetan Leši*, and *Brat doktora Homera* (1969), which combined the iconography and the final showdown from Sergio Leone's *A Fistful of Dollars* (1964) and *The Good, the Bad, and the Ugly* (1966) (Vučetić, "Kauboji" 144).

Mitrović's model for producing attractive films about the ideals of the freedom fight and revolution demonstrated how to transform bureaucrat-run Yugoslav cinema into a network of profit-oriented production units—a self-declared objective of the Yugoslav government since the mid-1950s (Miloradović 90–91). The influence of Mitrović's production model is visible in Partisan Westerns like *Diverzanti* (1967), *Most* (1969), *Valter brani Sarajevo* (1972), and *Partizanska eskadrila* (1979), all directed by Hajrudin "Šiba" Krvavac (Vučetić, "Kauboji" 144–46), as well as Predrag Golubović's *Bombaši* (1973) and *Crveni udar* (1974). More importantly, "[Mitrović's] 'imported' poetics with local themes had a pedagogical role, as film magazines of the day reported. It would guide children toward playing Partisans and Ballists instead of the traditional cowboys and

Indians, and it was also thought that films like *Kapetan Leši* would lead young people to share the ideals represented by the captain rather than those of Tarzan" (Vučetić, *Coca-Cola Socialism* 71).

Mitrović himself argued in 1982 that the goal of his films was to compete as much as possible with the most popular foreign films (Kurjak-Pavićević)—in other words, to compete with the products of US-American cultural imperialism. This, however, does not mean that Mitrović's approach to the genre was the result of his being a party member, for "we need to get rid of the binary logic of 'either party hack, or dissident master,' and permit the possibility that party members were also capable of criticizing their society" (Jovanović 288). In fact, Mitrović's early career focus on Kosovo gave him an opportunity to bring a fresh perspective on the province's nationalisms.

The 1389 Battle of Kosovo is an ideal event for studying the complicated history of ethnic nationalism in Kosovo evoked in *Kapetan Leši*. The battle has been mythologized by Serbian nationalists as the collapse of the medieval Serbian Empire (Čolović). During the five-hundred-year Ottoman yoke in the wake of the battle, a growing number of mostly Muslim Albanians had populated Kosovo, to the point that the Serbianization of the province became a virtually impossible mission in the interwar Kingdom of Serbs, Croats, and Slovenes (from 1929 known as the Kingdom of Yugoslavia), whose creation in 1918 marked the definite end of Ottoman imperial rule of the province. The effort to establish Serbian domination in Kosovo led to the World War II backlash spearheaded by the abovementioned anti-Communist, anti-Yugoslav, and anti-Greek Albanian collaborationists, the Ballists. After the Yugoslav Partisans finally received the support of the Allied forces, an increased number of Kosovar Albanians joined the Partisans when the new Communist government promised Kosovo the right to secession in a new Yugoslav federation (Vickers 137). But when the Yugoslav leadership remained unwilling to press Serbian Communists to give up on Kosovo, Kosovar Albanians focused on limiting Serbian migration to Kosovo and gaining cultural autonomy.

The mythology of the Battle of Kosovo echoes the Western mythology analyzed by Richard Slotkin, particularly in terms of framing the 1389 battle as the last stand of Serbian Christendom against the Ottoman invasion. The myth of Kosovo as the cradle of Serbian national identity was utilized by the turn-of-the-century Kingdom of Serbia to expand its southern frontier at the expense of the weakened Ottoman Empire, and thus effectively oppose similar territorial ambitions of the Austro-Hungarian Empire in the lead-up to World War I. It should be stressed, however, that the impact of the Battle of Kosovo and its US-American counterpart, Custer's Last Stand, differ insofar as the latter, albeit a resounding defeat of the US Army, could not fundamentally hinder the project of closing the US-American frontier. In contrast, the conflict between Serbs and Albanians in Kosovo remains unresolved to this day. Whereas the US-American Western, even in its revisionist iterations, continuously demonstrates the dominance of the colonizers, *Kapetan Leši* moves away from the mythology of the Battle of Kosovo and its attempt to incorporate Kosovar Albanians into the supranational Yugoslav state. Put differently, the Western comes into being as the US-American genre par excellence precisely because there is no doubt regarding the triumph of the white settlers, while Mitrović's film can only emulate its US-American generic model without presenting a universally agreed-on resolution of the Kosovar national conflict. In 1960, the year of *Kapetan Leši*'s premiere, Kosovar Albanian nationalism was still far from its culmination, but it seems the film identified its disintegrative power. With the exception of a deserter named Helmut, *Kapetan Leši* does not feature Germans as the Partisans' archenemies, which is all the more reason to conclude that the film recognized Kosovar Albanian nationalism as a foundational threat to Yugoslav federalism.

A HERO FROM DOWN SOUTH

The story of *Kapetan Leši* starts at the end of World War II, with an ethnic Kosovar Albanian Partisan captain, Ramiz Leši, seeking to destroy the remnants of a Ballist squad led by the notorious Kosta and Leši's brother Ahmet, whom Leši considers a traitor. Upon learning his brother had refused to kill anyone, Leši saves his brother who reveals he was forced to join the Ballists to protect the Leši bey family. In the end, Ahmet helps his brother who is posing as an undercover Ballist, shoots Kosta, and returns with Leši to their family estate.

Early Yugoslav Partisan films, including *Kapetan Leši*, share a common feature with the national cosmogony of early Westerns, for, in the world of the Western, "from the groups of different nationalities, languages, religions and ethical systems . . . an integrated society was supposed to be created, a new nation, a new setup" (Turković 140). An important aspect of the Western's national cosmogony is the harmonization of an individual and a collective, through which the hero finds his place in society and acquires meaning for his personal sacrifice. As Benedict Anderson remarks, "The nation is always conceived as a deep, horizontal comradeship. Ultimately, it is this fraternity that makes it possible . . . for so many millions of people, not so much to kill, as willingly to die for such limited imaginings" (7). The notion of horizontal comradeship is particularly relevant for the history of conflicts such as the US-American Civil War represented in Hollywood Westerns and the civil war in occupied World War II Yugoslavia represented in Partisan Westerns. The process of national cosmogony, marked by a socialist prefix, takes place in *Kapetan Leši* as well, with the new Yugoslav state relying on the ideological conversion of masculine heroes in trying to reconcile different nations, religions, and cultures.

Moreover, the Yugoslav state is ready to forgive the heroic comrade his crudeness, as in the scene when Leši attempts to seduce a teacher and one of the few Serbian characters in the film, Vida [13:00–13:13]. Coming from Belgrade and looking like a typical blonde schoolmarm, Vida reminds Leši of his duty toward collectivism by asking him to lend the family piano to a local school, but, at that stage, Leši is still not politically "mature" enough to give up on his brother's aristocratic inheritance. Representing the nation that claimed a historical right to Kosovo since the Middle Ages, Vida bears semblance to the Native Americans retreating in front of the colonizers of the Wild West. At the same time, the Serbian teacher is more akin to the colonizers from Hollywood Westerns in that she comes from the capital to educate a provincial soldier (Leši) on how to organize a new government, which means that, in *Kapetan Leši* at least, Serbs are ready to construct a supranational identity with Kosovar Albanian Communists.

Similarly, the strong state in Mitrović's film appears ready to forgive the repenting Ballists, such as Leši's brother Ahmet, for passively supporting the nationalists. Although Ahmet's main excuse for joining the Ballists was his family's safety, his social status is very close to the pro-Islamic Kosovar Albanian beys, who backed the Ballists to preserve their land ownership. The beys had dominated both Albanian lower classes and the oppressed Christian population, and remained by and large loyal to the Ottoman Empire during its multicentury occupation of Kosovo, which only ended after the First Balkan War (Vickers 44–67). In *Kapetan Leši*, Mitrović essentially transposes the archetypal Western conflict between the rich landowners and poor farmers into the Balkan context, the difference being that the land in Kosovo (and the rest of Yugoslavia) was to be collectivized. In other words, *Kapetan Leši* strives to transform the national conflict between Kosovar Serbs and Albanians into an act of emancipatory class struggle by the Kosovar Albanian peasantry against their beys, the last representatives of ancient forms of economic exploitation associated with Ottoman imperialism. *Kapetan Leši* thus transforms World War II nationalist strife into a socialist revolution that seeks to integrate Kosovar Albanians into a supranational Yugoslav federation.

The symbolic thrust of the outlined generic transposition depends on the configuration of national representation. Nikica Gilić suggests that "Kosovar Albanians and other minorities were sometimes treated in Yugoslav films in the nationalist manner similar to the treatment of US-American minorities in the Western genre," emphasizing the fact that, in *Kapetan Leši*, an ethnic Serb (Mitrović), working for a Belgrade company (Slavija Film), directed a predominantly Serbian and Macedonian cast, with some Kosovar Albanian actors (240–41). Transnational (and transethnic) cooperation was a staple of Yugoslav cinema in which, for instance, a Serbian director would be hired by a Slovenian studio to direct a Croatian star. However, Gilić's conflation of national and racial minorities in Yugoslav and US-American cinema notwithstanding, it should be noted that, in the first postwar decades, there was a short supply of skilled actors and technical personnel in Kosovo. And even though the charge of linguistic hegemony could not be entirely discarded, given that Albanian characters in *Kapetan Leši* speak Serbian, the situation changed in the 1970s and 1980s when the first productions in Albanian began to appear as a result of Kosovar political autonomy.

Another set of Western conventions pursued in *Kapetan Leši* concerns the genre's iconography. For example, the smoky and noisy tavern frequented by Leši and his friends is reminiscent of the saloon in *Rio Bravo* (1959) (Vučetić, "Kauboji" 138). After defending his Walter Brennan–like sidekick Šok in a customary fistfight, Leši follows the curvaceous red-headed tavern singer and hooker with a heart of gold, Lola, for a one-night stand in her room on the tavern's upper floor [18:32–21:42]. Hurt that Leši does not return her love, Lola falls for his enemy, Kosta, only to sacrifice herself in the end and help Leši capture Kosta's squad, thereby fulfilling her destiny in the well-known Western trope of the saloon B-girl (Bazin qtd. in Vučetić, "Kauboji" 139) (figs. 5.1 and 5.2). The film's rendition of Prizren, Leši's hometown, combines visual traits of old Oriental towns, on the one hand, and settlements on the Mexico-US border, on the other. Long shots, in turn, reveal characters who "ride on horses through canyons and gulches, attack one another from behind boulders, and gallop through landscapes identical to the prairies in the Wild West" (Vučetić, *Coca-Cola Socialism* 70), all captured in Kosovo and central Serbia. The rocky hideouts used by Ballists and the eerie earth pyramids of Đavolja varoš—the setting of the final showdown—bear a strong resemblance to picturesque landscapes from *Broken Arrow* (Delmer Daves, 1950) and *Naked Spur* (Anthony Mann, 1953). Costume design is another prominent feature of *Kapetan Leši*, as Partisans in spotless military uniforms fight against filthy and merciless Ballists, wearing Albanian folk costumes that highlight their conservatism.

Fig. 5.1 The hooker with a heart of gold, Lola (Selma Karlovac, *left*) and the schoolmarm Vida (Marija Tocinoski, *right*) in Vida's apartment.

Fig. 5.2 Captain Leši (Aleksandar Gavrić, *right*) and his sidekick Šok (Petre Prličko, *left*) in the Ballists' mountain hideout.

Thus, the Ballists' opposition to the Partisans' integrationist and federalist political agenda echoes the conflict between the South and the North in the US-American Civil War. Last, Leši's protagonism is underscored by his skillful gunplay and riding a white horse.

Interestingly, film color played a significant role in *Kapetan Leši*'s transnational reach.[1] Mitrović and his colleagues must have been attracted to the colorful 1950s Hollywood Westerns they saw in Yugoslavia, but it is possible they could not afford the kind of film stock favored by Hollywood, so they opted for the more available alternative. Shot in vivid and optimistic Agfacolor, *Kapetan Leši* was clearly meant to appear in stark contrast to the more dramatic black-and-white 1950s Partisan films. Only three Yugoslav films, including *Kapetan Leši* and its sequel, were made with Agfacolor (Koshofer 3–4), which was first produced in Nazi Germany, and then in West and East Germanies, as an alternative to Kodak and the like (Diecke 211–14). According to a Yugoslav journalist (Jajčanin) irritated by the film's international commodification, *Kapetan Leši* had an unidentified West German coproducer negotiating a larger role for a Yugoslav turned West German actress Selma Karlovac a.k.a. Elma Karlowa. It is very likely that the same producer secured Agfacolor stock from the Leverkusen factory, along with the participation of another West German actor, Rainer Penkert, who played a key role as Leši's brother, as well as in the distribution of the film in West Germany under the title *Auf der Spur der Verräter*. The film was actually presold to the West German company for DM 170,000, with an option for the global distribution to be bought by MGM for $400,000, meaning that *Kapetan Leši* alone was worth almost the entire yearly export of all Yugoslav films to West Germany (Batančev 372). *Kapetan Leši* thus contributed to building a transnational cultural bridge between socialist Yugoslavia and capitalist West Germany, which is striking because of the way in which the film quite literally rendered the socialist Yugoslav revolution more colorful and appealing to the Western European audience.

Ideologically speaking, *Kapetan Leši* lacks the characters of political commissars, as well as images or slogans related to the Yugoslav leader Tito, so it could be argued that the director wanted to avoid propaganda. That said, the Yugoslav army plays an important role in the film, much like in the partisan spectacles from the 1970s and 1980s, when it was positioned as one of the three pillars of Tito's Yugoslavia, together with the Communist Party and Tito himself (Zvijer 85–103). Consequently, Leši stands for a soldier of the people's Partisan army who, despite his larger-than-life proportions, remains uninterested in the world of high politics; the idea of Yugoslavism in *Kapetan Leši* comes from below (the hero who is close to the people and rejects his family wealth), not from above (Tito or the party representatives). In Mitrović's film, Kosovar Albanians organically accept the ideology of supranational socialism, which effectively neutralizes the aforementioned Kosovar Albanian nationalist backlash against perceived Serbian domination. This assumption is reflected in the film's popularity among the audience and film critics alike, with only occasional complaints that Mitrović's generic hybridization was a "lemon tree in Siberia" (Lisinski qtd. in Vučetić, *Coca-Cola Socialism* 71). Captain Leši became "the Yugoslav Flash Gordon or Tom Mix" (Deneš qtd. in Vučetić, *Coca-Cola Socialism* 72), spawning one of the first Yugoslav sequels as well as a comic book series and popular song (Batančev 377). Having been compared to Gary

Cooper for his portrayal of Leši, Aleksandar Gavrić "attained the status of one of Yugoslavia's first film stars" and "was the first Yugoslav actor to appear on the cover of the magazine *Filmski svet*, heretofore 'reserved' only for the stars from the West" (Vučetić, *Coca-Cola Socialism* 70). *Kapetan Leši* was popular not only in West Germany but also in Algeria (Batančev 373). Overall, Mitrović successfully adapted the Western topoi of US-American imperialism for his contribution to the Yugoslav national debate. A more elaborate comparison of *Kapetan Leši* with its Hollywood predecessors and Eastern European analogues in the next section amplifies the film's specificity in the genre's transnational milieu.

MARX AND MAY

While there seem to be no explicit sources on *Kapetan Leši*'s role models, it would be hard to overlook the influence of John Ford's oeuvre on Mitrović (Vučetić, *Coca-Cola Socialism* 69), especially the emphasis on the military dimension of state building in the "Cavalry Trilogy" (1948–1950), embodied in the strong and righteous officers played by John Wayne. It is important, though, to keep in mind that the "Cavalry Trilogy" takes on the clash of the US state and Native American tribes, a racially charged conflict decided long before its cinematic rendition, whereas *Kapetan Leši* presents an ideologically imbued civil war between Communist and nationalist Kosovar Albanians as reflecting the undecided confrontation between Kosovar Albanians and their Yugoslav and Serbian opponents. Moreover, *Kapetan Leši*'s plot recalls, in some respects at least, that of *The Searchers* (1956) inasmuch as Leši's anxiety about his brother's joining the ideologically impure Ballists parallels Ethan Edwards's obsession with his niece's abduction by the Comanche. There are also telling differences between the two films. The protagonist of *The Searchers* is a defeated Confederate soldier who arguably seeks to return to the fold of his white settler identity; by comparison, Captain Leši is a war victor who does not hesitate to cooperate with other nations in building postwar Yugoslavia.

It is tempting to note that *Kapetan Leši* was not tailored to the pattern of postwar Hollywood Westerns, in which "a confident vision of the grand sweep of American history as an inevitable, onward march of progress is lost" (White 23). However, as Matthew Carter has convincingly demonstrated in his critique of the sharp division between "classic" and "revisionist" Westerns, "the cinematic Western metamorphoses according to the exigencies of a given time and the visions of individual artists, but as a whole it has refused any defined pattern of continuous development" (224). Moreover, Janet Staiger posits, "The argument that earlier Westerns—c. 1930–60—are instances of a somehow more 'pure classical genre,' is to suggest narrative simplicity and even mono-ideological naivety" (qtd. in Carter 34). Clearly, there is no need for a strict classification of *Kapetan Leši* when its main antecedents resist falling into categories such as strictly "optimistic" or "pessimistic" Westerns. This rings even more true when comparing the Partisan Western to other Eastern European forays into the genre.

Unlike the DEFA-*Indianerfilme*—*Spur des Falken* (Gottfried Kolditz, 1968), *Osceola* (Konrad Petzold, 1971), *Tecumseh* (Hans Kratzert, 1972)—*Kapetan Leši* is not an ironic modification of the Western. In East German films, inspired by the writings of Karl May, Native Americans were given a leading role in the struggle against the settlers. Tim Bergfelder contends that "Karl Marx rather than May, the international solidarity of the oppressed, and anti-imperialist sentiments provided the answer to the quest for identity," even if some of these films represented "resistance against socialism as 'a form of alien domination,'" with the implication being that they "may have been open to multiple and even resistant, ideological readings" (203). By contrast, *Kapetan Leši* did not play on anti-imperialist and anti-US-American sentiments. When Mitrović claimed he wanted to compete with Hollywood Westerns, it was only because he saw a way of using the genre's popularity to promote rather than contest socialist Yugoslavism.

Writing about other subgeneric cognates of the Partisan Western, Vincent Bohlinger labels the classic *White Sun of the Desert* (Vladimir Motyl, 1970), set in Turkmenistan, a Soviet Western "to distinguish [it] from the European Red Westerns that predated, rather than influenced the film" (307). There are numerous connections between *Kapetan Leši* and *White Sun of the Desert*, including a focus on the revolution and civil war in an "underdeveloped" province, gunfighting and a soldier as the main character. The protagonist of the Soviet film is Russian by origin, and thus a representative of the majoritarian part of Soviet identity; his rivals are the Basmachi guerrillas, whom the film situates "in the place of the Indians, as the darker-skinned Other representing savagery and wilderness, and positions the burgeoning Soviet state as 'civilization'" (Bohlinger 310). Historically, the Basmachi stood up to the Russians as imperial oppressors, but "such objections are, unsurprisingly, not given voice in the film, in ways similar to the indigenous tribes of American Westerns" (Bohlinger 311). Crucially, "the choice of the Basmachi as enemies reflects an attempt at strategic sensitivity toward non-Russian Soviet cultures; they were used because they were a *political* group, not an ethnic group. The Basmachi, in fact, comprised various ethnicities, but any mention of specific Muslim groups was written out of the script in order to avoid complications" (Bohlinger 313).

This mirrors Mitrović's decision to avoid any emphatic reference to the Ballists' nationality, framing them instead as collaborators and bandits. The reluctance to name and potentially stigmatize recalcitrant nations evinces the desire of socialist states to incorporate these national minorities into their supranational cultures and efface an imperial and colonial legacy, thus running counter to the tendencies of many US-American Westerns.

In her analysis of 1970s Hungarian Westerns about pre-twentieth-century roving bandits fighting against the Hapsburg and Ottoman Empires, Sonja Simonyi identifies the idiosyncrasy of the region where these outlaws operated: "The *puszta*, a large stretch of flatland spreading across eastern Hungary, fulfills an important role in the national imaginary, celebrated as the site where nomadic Hungarians are thought to have settled in the ninth century, a physical space designated as the birthplace of the Hungarian nation" (223). To a varying degree, Hungarian Westerns demythologize the romantic, nationalist image of the Hungarian outlaw, thereby correlating with the similar treatment of Kosovar Albanian nationalists in *Kapetan Leši*, not to mention the Yugoslav film's deconstruction of Kosovo as the hotbed of Serbian and Albanian national myths.

All in all, while there is no evidence that *Kapetan Leši* directly influenced subsequent Eastern European Westerns, there is an obvious likeness of generic structures transferred and employed to think through the issues of imperialism and national integration. Additionally, the regional Westerns benefited greatly from transnational cultural exchanges within Europe, further exemplified by Simonyi's mention of Yugoslav-born Bulgarian Djoko Rosic, the star of Hungarian Westerns.

CONCLUSION

As Vučetić argued, "Attractive American forms, especially in terms of mass culture, were the ideal frameworks for 'packaging' content that suited [Yugoslav] authorities," while, in terms of consumerist culture, "Americanization and the orientation toward the West were used as 'shock absorbers' for problems facing Yugoslav society, and above all it was nascent nationalism that needed to be 'absorbed'" (*Coca-Cola Socialism* 304). *Kapetan Leši* appends this conclusion by showing that the US-American cultural imperialism manifested by the Hollywood Western was refashioned from a serious threat to the Partisan film genre to a useful representational form in Yugoslav national debates. Furthermore, certain facets of *Kapetan Leši*'s narrative and reception suggest that a danger greater than US-American cultural imports came from the feudal and bourgeois subjugation of Kosovar Albanian peasants in the Ottoman Empire and Kingdom of Yugoslavia. *Kapetan Leši* also offers historical initiative to Kosovar Albanians in building a socialist society in which Serbs would be their partners rather than their masters, even if this proposition comes with a note of cultural condescension toward the province.

In the complex world of Yugoslav supra- and transnational cinema, *Kapetan Leši* appeared too early to effectively dispute the representation of Kosovar Albanians by non-Albanian filmmakers. On the other hand, the transnational coproduction with a West German partner was based on commercial interests, which was yet another indication of the influence of the US-American way of life. In the genre's wider transnational context, *Kapetan Leši* eschewed the anti-imperialist and anti-US-American connotations of the *Indianerfilme*, while sharing its affinity for militaristic state building, its avoidance of political alienation of ethnic minorities, and its repudiation of older national myths with John Ford's classics, Soviet *White Sun of the Desert*, and Hungarian Westerns, respectively. In the end, a concentrated dose of the Western's individualism, embodied in the exceptional Leši, infused the foundational myth of the World War II freedom fight with spectacular entertainment and radiant appeal, but ultimately fell short of establishing a stable historical image of Kosovo.

NOTE

1. I would like to thank Josephine Diecke, a PhD student working on the research project *Film Colors: Technologies, Cultures, Institutions*, funded by the Swiss National Science Foundation, for kindly pointing me to the sources on the color of *Kapetan Leši*.

WORKS CITED

Anderson, Benedict. *Imagined Communities: Reflections on the Origins and Spread of Nationalism*. 1983. Revised, Verso, 2006.

Batančev, Dragan. "Cenzura partizanskog vesterna *Kapetan Leši* (1960)." *Historijski zbornik*, vol. 67, no. 2, 2014, pp. 361–79.

Bergfelder, Tim. *International Adventures: German Popular Cinema and European Co-Productions in the 1960s*. Berghahn Books, 2005.

Bohlinger, Vincent. "'The East Is a Delicate Matter': *White Sun of the Desert* and the Soviet Western." *International Westerns: Re-Locating the Frontier*, edited by Cynthia J. Miller and A. Bowdoin Van Riper, Scarecrow, 2014, pp. 303–19.

Carter, Matthew. *Myth of the Western: New Perspectives on Hollywood's Frontier Narrative*. Edinburgh University Press, 2015.

Chapman, James, and Nicholas J. Cull. *Projecting Empire: Imperialism and Popular Cinema*. I. B. Tauris, 2009.

Čolović, Ivan. *Smrt na Kosovu polju*. Biblioteka XX vek, 2016.

Crnjanski, Vladimir. Interview with Živorad Mitrović. novikadrovi.net/razno/3 -razno.php. Accessed on November 27, 2011.

Diecke, Josephine. "Agfacolor in (Inter)National Competition." *Color Mania: The Material of Color in Photography and Film*, edited by Barbara Flueck-Iger et al., Lars Müller, Fotomuseum Winterthur, 2019, pp. 211–21.

Gilić, Nikica. "Narrative and Genre Influences of the Classical Narrative Cinema in the Partisan Films of Živorad-Žika Mitrović." *Partisans in Yugoslavia: Literature, Film and Visual Culture*, edited by Miranda Jakiša and Nikica Gilić, Transcript, 2015, pp. 227–44.

González, Jesús Ángel. "Transnational Post-Westerns in Irish Cinema." *Journal of Transnational American Studies*, vol. 7, no. 1, 2016, pp. 1–26.

Goulding, Daniel J. *Liberated Cinema: The Yugoslav Experience, 1945–2001*. Indiana University Press, 2002.

Jajčanin, M. "Kapetan Leši." *Slobodna Dalmacija*, 23 Feb. 1961.

Jovanović, Nebojša. "We Need to Talk about Valter: Partisan Film and the Anti-Leftist Odium." *Partisans in Yugoslavia: Literature, Film and Visual Culture*, edited by Miranda Jakiša and Nikica Gilić, Transcript, 2015, pp. 283–313.

Koshofer, Gert. "Agfacolor-Kinofilme International." www.filmportal.de/sites /default/files/Agfacolor-Kinofilme_alphabetisch_0.pdf?fbclid=IwAR3PsEQH H3DUWEhidwawqt94TM9tsznR6ECQ-df9E_zvJgxAiT_ja1rkgOU. Accessed on June 7, 2019.

Kurjak-Pavićević, Olga. "Žika Mitrović: O 'Kapetanu Lešiju,' 'Savamali,' crnom talasu, Makavejevu, psovkama u YU filmu . . ." Yugopapir, www.yugopapir. com/2016/06/zika-mitrovic-o-kapetanu-lesiju.html. Accessed on May 28, 2019.

Miloradović, Goran. "Glas 'likvidirane generacije': Autorizovani intervju s filmskim rediteljem Jovanom Jocom Živanovićem." *Godišnjak za društvenu istoriju*, vol. 17, no. 2, 2010, pp. 74–113.

Simonyi, Sonja. "'They Sing Songs about Us Here': Outlaw Figures in Hungarian Westerns of the 1970s." *International Westerns: Re-Locating the Frontier*, edited by Cynthia J. Miller and A. Bowdoin Van Riper, Scarecrow, 2014, pp. 220–34.

Slotkin, Richard. *Gunfighter Nation: The Myth of the Frontier in Twentieth-Century America*. University of Oklahoma Press, 1992.

Stanković, Peter. "1970s Partisan Epics as Western Films: The Question of Genre and Myth in Yugoslav Partisan Film." *Partisans in Yugoslavia: Literature, Film and Visual Culture*, edited by Miranda Jakiša and Nikica Gilić, Transcript, 2015, pp. 245–64.

Turković, Hrvoje. *Filmska opredjeljenja*. Centar za kulturnu djelatnost, 1985.

Vickers, Miranda. *Between Serb and Albanian: A History of Kosovo*. Hurst, 1998.

Vučetić, Radina. *Coca-Cola Socialism: Americanization of Yugoslav Culture in the Sixties.* Translated by John K. Cox, Central European University Press, 2018.

———. "Kauboji u partizanskoj uniformi: Američki vesterni i partizanski vesterni u Jugoslaviji šezdesetih godina 20. veka." *Tokovi istorije: Časopis Instituta za noviju istoriju Srbije,* no. 2, 2010, pp. 130–51.

White, John. *Westerns.* Routledge, 2011.

Zvijer, Nemanja. *Ideologija filmske slike: Sociološka analiza partizanskog ratnog spektakla.* Filozofski fakultet, 2011.

DRAGAN BATANČEV is PhD Candidate in Film and Moving Image Studies at Concordia University.

SIX

LAWRENCE OF ARABIA (DAVID LEAN, 1962) AND THE WESTERN

Reframing the Imperialist Hero

HADRIEN FONTANAUD

UPON ITS RELEASE IN 1962, *Lawrence of Arabia* was the long-awaited concretization of years of failed attempts to bring Thomas Edward Lawrence's (1888–1935) story to the big screen. As a transnational effort produced by the London-based US-American producer Sam Spiegel, directed by the British director David Lean, and written successively by the US-American screenwriter Michael Wilson and the British playwright Robert Bolt, it reflected a long-term interest for the story of Lawrence on both sides of the Atlantic. A British officer and writer, Lawrence became famous for his participation in the Arab revolt against the Turks during World War I. Nicholas J. Cull and James Chapman describe him as "the first celebrity whose image was created by the mass media" (Cull and Chapman 5); his legend was, indeed, forged by the US-American journalist Lowell Thomas. As early as 1925, Hollywood director Rex Ingram tried to make a film out of the Arab Revolt but was discouraged by Lawrence himself. The British producer Alexander Korda then tried to make a film out of the Lawrence story during the 1930s. After World War II, other such projects were envisaged in the US (by Columbia) and in Britain (by Terence Rattigan and the Rank Organization), but none came to fruition.[1]

These US-American and British film projects testify to the appeal of Lawrence and more generally the British Empire. The empire film was a prominent genre in both the US and Great Britain. Alexander Korda produced a cycle of empire films, often directed by his brother Zoltan Korda, including *Sanders of the Rivers* (1935), *The Drum* (1938), and *The Four Feathers* (1939). At the same time, Hollywood was making its own brand of empire films, such as *Lives of a Bengal Lancer* (Henry Hathaway, 1935), *The Charge of the Light Brigade* (Michael Curtiz, 1936), and *Gunga Din* (Georges Stevens, 1939). Although the two genres reflect the different historical and national contexts of Great Britain and the US—the latter being a colony of settlement that sought to build a new political order through migration and conquest, and thus required its own distinct narrative[2]—Hollywood's interest in British imperialism has led to comparisons with the US-American Western. Commenting on the decline of A-list Westerns in the 1930s, Richard Slotkin suggests that new genres like the empire film had taken over some of the Westerns' "mythographic functions" (259); he points to a continuity between the politics of the frontier and the way Hollywood viewed British imperialism: "In a sense, these movies merely flesh out in fiction the Roosevelt thesis which envisioned the transformation of the racial energies that won the West into the basis of an Anglo-Saxon alliance for the conquest and control of the undeveloped world" (267). At the end of the decade, the Western returned to the front stage, and Hollywood empire films declined, but "the new Western drew on and modified the mythographic and iconographic achievements of the major genres of the 1930s" (Slotkin 271). The 1941 Western, *They Died with Their Boots On* (Raoul Walsh) echoed *The Charge of the Light Brigade* in many ways: both films star Errol Flynn and end with a sacrificial cavalry charge against natives, the last stand trope providing a heroic rationale for a military blunder. These narrative similarities, and the circulation of actors and directors from one genre to another, suggest that the empire film and the Western were sibling genres in the minds of the producers and audience.

The connection between the British Empire film and the Western is less evident, yet both genres fulfill a similar symbolic function within their national mythology and share common narrative tropes. As Marcia Landy observes, "The closest counterpart to the Western genre and its celebration of American myths is the film of empire, . . . which, with its own set of equally potent cultural myths celebrates the triumph of British law, order and civilization over barbarism" (97). While the empire film declined in Hollywood after the 1930s, it remained an important feature of British cinema during the 1940s and 1950s. Just as Hollywood used British colonial history and literature to renew its own imperial imagery, post–World War II British films of empire drew from the Western to capitalize on its popularity with the audience and modernize the genre. As Wendy Webster has noted, "By drawing on the Western the empire film could offer an image that by the mid-1950s was the most common visual image of adventure consumed in Britain, as cinema attendance declined and Westerns were imported by the new commercial television companies" (97).

A film like *North West Frontier* (Jack Lee Thompson, 1959) featuring Lauren Bacall, a prominent Hollywood star, exemplifies the bridges between

US-American and British cinema. It "drew heavily on the western with the train occupying the place of the stagecoach, as hordes of Indians descended to attack it and were successfully beaten off" (Webster 98).

Lawrence of Arabia belongs to this transnational history of cinematic imperialism. Its title alone harks back to the 1930s biopics centered on British imperial figures produced on either side of the Atlantic, such as 20th Century's *Clive of India* (Richard Boleslawski, 1935) and Gaumont British's *Rhodes of Africa* (Berthold Viertel, 1936). The 1962 film stands at the crossroads of British and US-American cinema, and draws on both traditions of the empire film. The tangled history of the empire film and the Western suggest that the mythology of western conquest and British imperialism have a common ideological background and belong to a wider ensemble of imperialist narratives. This chapter endeavors to explore how *Lawrence of Arabia* positions itself in relation to such narratives and engages with the two genres' visual and thematic similarities as well as their differences. The objective is not just to point out overt or implicit references to the Western, but to analyze how they work within the film, how they are transposed in the framework of the empire film, and how they shape the film's discourse on imperialism, especially through the character of Lawrence.

IMPERIALISM AS PERSONAL FANTASY

By 1962, Britain's credibility as an imperial power had been shaken by the loss of the Suez Canal in 1957, and most of its colonies had followed India's lead in 1947 and were gaining independence. *Lawrence of Arabia* reflects this wider context of decolonization: Arab nationalism is portrayed sympathetically, and the title character stands by the colonized people. Significantly, Lawrence (Peter O'Toole) is made unaware of the Sykes-Picot Agreement (1916), in which the French and the British decided their respective areas of influence in the Middle East, and this ignorance contributes to a critique of the cynicism of colonial politics. Yet Lawrence's charismatic personality is also a vehicle of nostalgia, with the title itself reclaiming the popular legend by placing him "in the lineage of great imperial heroes who also included Clive of India, Rhodes of Africa, and Gordon of Khartoum" (Chapman and Cull 6). In his analysis of Lawrence and his autobiographical writings, Edward Said describes the man as an imperial agent whose actions were informed by the tradition of Western Orientalism but also driven by a "new dialectic": "the orient must be made to perform, its power must be enlisted on the side of our value" (238). For Said, "The orientalist has now become a figure of Oriental history, its shaper, its characteristic *sign* for the

West" (238). Lawrence's authority as Oriental expert allows him to "assume the role of oriental prophet giving shape to a movement in 'the new Asia'" (243); he "equates fully with the struggle of the New Asia to be born" (243), and this struggle is reduced to his own experience.

Although Said's analysis focuses on Lawrence's writings and ignores the film, the British officer's 1926 autobiography *Seven Pillars of Wisdom* was the main source for the final version of the script (Jackson 53). The film follows similar patterns as those described by Said: the Arab revolt is reduced to Lawrence's involvement, while Lawrence's Bedouin clothes express his status as an Oriental prophet; he effectively becomes their leader and shapes Arab history by leading them to victory. Near the end of the film, Lawrence presides over the Arab National Council in Damascus [207:42–210:29]. Here, the film contrasts Lawrence's effort to maintain unity and the ineptitude of Arab leaders who are incapable of making basic decisions to fix their electric generators or ensure water supplies as old tribal rivalries are revived; the film, thus, falls back on the stereotype of natives unable to rule themselves without the guidance of a white man. This attempt to propose a more liberal discourse within the empire film suggests a parallel with Hollywood pro-Indian Westerns of the 1950s, pioneered by films like *Broken Arrow* (Delmer Daves, 1950) and *Devil's Doorway* (Anthony Mann, 1950); the former especially offers the prototype of a narrative whereby a white man realizes the wrongs inflicted on Indians and comes to identify with them; the main character Tom Jeffords (James Stewart) is the archetype of the "Indian lover": he befriends the Apache leader Cochise (Jeff Chandler), stands against the bigotry and violence of the white community, and even marries an Indian woman, Sonseeahray (Debra Paget). Her death at the hands of white racists reaffirms the separation of both communities, yet, thanks to his knowledge of Indian culture and language, he is able to act as a bridge between the two cultures and negotiates a peace treaty with Cochise. Ultimately, *Broken Arrow*'s revisionist perspective serves to reaffirm white superiority, as it is the good will and determination of the white hero that shape the destiny of the natives, not their own agency.

Lawrence of Arabia can similarly be understood as an attempt to rescue the imperialist project by giving it a more acceptable face while maintaining a reassuring racial hierarchy. However, if Lawrence's perspective on the events dominates and shapes the narrative, the precise role and place given to his subjectivity calls for closer scrutiny. His subjectivity is mainly expressed through his fascination for the desert, as exemplified in the apparition of the desert landscape [17:39–18:50]: Lawrence's blowing out a lit match in an office in Cairo is followed by an extreme long shot of a desert sunrise. The contrast between the two shots could not be sharper: an indoor space versus an open space, a close-up versus a long shot. Yet the sound of Lawrence's breath overlapping the cut links both events: the character literally blows out a flame and illuminates the sky. The close-up emphasizes Lawrence's white skin and clear blue eyes, staring at the flame. The desert at dawn functions like an epiphany, a mystical revelation of his exceptional destiny. And yet the office is steeped in stereotypical icons of Oriental mysticism: the Egyptian bas-reliefs on the wall and the statue of a sacred cat.

This sequence reinforces the characterization of Lawrence as Oriental prophet while nonetheless hinting at how cliché such imagery is. The emphasis on subjectivity allows the film to distance itself from Lawrence and make room for the perspective of others. The British diplomat Dryden (Claude Rains) warns him: "Only two kinds of creatures have fun in the desert: Bedouins and Gods" [17:17]. Later, Prince Feisal (Alec Guinness) states: "I think you are another of these desert loving English: Doughty, Stanhope, Gordon of Khartoum. No Arab loves the desert. We love water and green trees. There is nothing in the desert and no man needs nothing" [50:33]. Feisal thus contradicts Dryden's statement that Bedouins "have fun in the desert" and places Lawrence in a line of famous Orientalists, suggesting that his perception of Arab culture and fascination for the desert are Western constructs. The implications of Feisal's comment are furthered by Auda Ibu Tayi's ironic question: "The Arabs? The Howeitat, Aegyle, Ruwalla, the Banu Sa'ad, these I know. I have even heard of the Harith. But the Arabs? What tribe is that?" [96:39]. By emphasizing Arab tribalism, Auda Ibu Tayi indicates that Lawrence classifies very different realities under an artificial label. The terms *Arab* or *Bedouin* are both used throughout the film to indifferently qualify diverse peoples; they are, then, the equivalent of *Indian* in the Western.

Interestingly, Auda is interpreted by Anthony Quinn, an actor who had previously played Indian Chiefs in Westerns such as *They Died with Their Boots On* (Raoul Walsh, 1941) and *Buffalo Bill* (William Wellman, 1944). His performance insists on the savage and exotic sides of the character; his Auda is a picturesque bandit, easily handled by Lawrence who appeals to his pride and cupidity. If Feisal is also interpreted by a white actor, the character, however, is far more complex than Auda. At the end of the film, after Lawrence's return to England and the collapse of the Arab Council, Feisal imposes his conditions on General Allenby (Jack Hawkins) and Dryden, both representatives of the British government, by exploiting the popular enthusiasm for the Arab victories evidenced in a variety of press headlines [220:49–221:13]. When Allenby replies that the Arab army was led by a British officer, Feisal answers: "Lawrence is a sword with two edges . . . we are equally glad to be rid of him, are we not?" A cynical but apt and cunning politician, Feisal has not followed Lawrence's vision but has used him to further his own end. Although *Lawrence of Arabia* remains an Anglo-American production made from a Western perspective, with most Arab characters portrayed by British and US-American actors, these dialogues suggest that the Arab characters are nonetheless allowed to voice an alternative view to Lawrence's dominant perspective.

THE DESERT AND THE WESTERN FRONTIER

Introduced as a quasi-mystical vision of Lawrence, the desert crystallizes the hero's dreams and desires; it articulates Lawrence's Oriental fantasy with a popular imagery that recalls the US-American West. Evoking infinity, the barren spaces of the West brought, as Scott Simmon notes, "a disquiet alleviated only when its landscape was filled" (52); its very emptiness seemed to call for a narrative of conquest, "a plot line that sets two races Indian and white, . . . contending for the open space" (53). The desert in *Lawrence of Arabia* is also a space of projection, a blank page on which Lawrence attempts to write his own destiny, most patently when he proclaims, "Nothing is written" [81:47]. Commentators of the film have pointed out the similarities between the Jordanian setting of Wadi Rum, where the film was partly shot, and Monument Valley in John Ford's films (Jackson 68). Both locations are characterized by massive rock formations and red sandstones buttes. While *Stagecoach's* (1939) vision of westward expansion is optimistic as John Ford "fills" the desert and balances the landscape with the characters, *The Searchers* (1956) contrasts the tiny characters against the massive buttes, resorting to the "disquietingly empty space" (Simmon 53) to offer a darker view of Western mythology. In *Lawrence of Arabia*, Wadi Rum brings a sense of the sublime in tune with the epic tone of the film; its immensity exalts Lawrence's heroism. Yet, like Ford's *The Searchers*, the white hero is often filmed in extreme long shots, reduced to a tiny silhouette, overwhelmed by the seemingly infinite desert.

An unspoiled territory for the white Anglo to tame and conquer, the desert stands for the frontier between civilization and savagery; it is here that the white hero encounters otherness and conflicts arise. The British characters define the Bedouins according to their relation with the desert; Lawrence himself states: "The desert is an ocean in which no oar is dipped. On this ocean, the Bedouins go where they please and strike where they please" [48:13]. Like Hollywood movie Indians, Bedouins are closely associated with the wilderness. Recurring shots in *She Wore a Yellow Ribbon* (Ford, 1949) show Cheyenne and Arapaho warriors atop the heights of Monument Valley, silently watching the cavaliers unaware of their menacing presence. These movie Indians are part of the landscape to the point of becoming invisible. Even when portrayed sympathetically, they retain a sense of otherness and menace for the white characters; in *Broken Arrow*, James Stewart's character is suddenly targeted by arrows coming out of nowhere, with the reverse shot only revealing an empty landscape of trees and rocks. Lawrence's first glimpse of the Bedouin in the desert is highly similar [24:03–24:52]: with the help of his Arab guide Taffas, he catches a glimpse of a group of Bedouin. Although Taffas points them out to him, Lawrence—and we the viewers—can only see an empty landscape; his binoculars turn out to be indispensable for him (and us) to make out a column of riders in the far distance. The scene thus establishes a difference between the white man and the native who can spot indigenous peoples at first glance; it also conveys a sense of curiosity and fear, as the two characters crouch to avoid being spotted by the riders.

The Bedouin's intimate relationship with the desert is made clear when Sheriff Ali (Omar Shariff) makes his entrance [28:29–34:48]. In a long shot, Taffas and Lawrence are seen in the foreground standing behind a well, while, in the far distance, a small trembling black spot starts moving along the horizon; the heat blurs the lines between earth and blue sky, which the white sand reflects. The black spot advances, materializing into a black-clothed rider (fig. 6.1). Emerging from the blurred horizon, Ali looks like a "mirage," a word used by David Lean himself to describe the character's entrance (Ehrenstein and Lean 69). Ali's gradual apparition presents him as a creation of the desert, one of its many tricks and dangers. This impression is confirmed when he kills Taffas; it is the first time Lawrence and the spectators experience Bedouin violence. Lawrence sets a moral hierarchy between him and the Arab as he calls out Arab tribalism: "So long as the Arabs fight tribe against tribe, so long will they be a little people, a silly people—greedy, barbarous and cruel, as you are" [33:43].

In his study of the film, Steven C. Caton states that the sequence can be read as "an allusion to the violence and lawlessness of the US-American frontier as depicted in Western film, if, that is, the duel is thought of like a shootout in a Western movie" (189). Caton also points to "the circulation of Lawrence's revolver in crucial scenes, a narrative device that allows the director to refer again and again to the problem of violence as issuing from the hand of the colonizer as much as it does from the colonized" (189); he even sees it as a reference to *Winchester '73* (Anthony Mann, 1950), where a rifle passes "through several hands—young and old, law-abiding citizen and outlaw, white and Indian—suggesting

Fig. 6.1 Sheriff Ali's first appearance, in a still from *Lawrence of Arabia* [29:59].

the spread of violence on the Western frontier" (189). In *Lawrence of Arabia,* the revolver effectively circulates from colonizer to colonized: Lawrence first gives the weapon to Taffas as a gift [22:34]; he tries to use it against Ali before getting shot, and, later, Lawrence takes it from Ali to execute a man, but, as he throws it in disgust, it is seized by a Bedouin [105:45–106:46]. For Caton, such references to the Western enable the film to challenge the racial distribution of violence and suggest that it comes from the "civilized men" as well as the "savages."

The staging of Ali's entrance is also a clear reference to the Western: a cavalier emerging from the horizon is a common way to introduce the hero in the early shots of many Westerns (*Broken Arrow, Shane* [Georges Stevens, 1953], *The Searchers*). Like the Westerners, Ali is a solitary and mysterious figure characterized by his gun skills. Ali's association with the imagery of the maverick Westerner thus complicates the reading of his violence as a simple expression of Arab barbarity. Yet, whereas Ethan Edwards is brought to the brink of savagery by his wandering life in *The Searchers,* Ali is a "savage" brought closer to civilization. Lawrence's criticism of Arab divisions expresses the colonizer's indifference to the cultural differences and histories of the variety of peoples he previously labeled as Arabs. This sequence paves the way for the subsequent evolution of both Lawrence and Ali: while the imperialist hero is progressively stripped of his prestige, Ali becomes Lawrence's "better conscience" (Jackson 53) and tries to stop him from falling into brutality (pointedly, Ali's violence is justified, and he does not kill Lawrence but offers him water from his well instead).

DECONSTRUCTING THE IMPERIALIST HERO

Lawrence of Arabia's allusions to the Western do more than just point to the similarities between the film of empire and the US-American genre; by evoking a narrative of conquest and settlement distinct from British colonialism, they, ultimately, complicate traditional imperialist representations. The construction of the British imperialist hero also draws on such tensions and resemblances. Discussing the empire film, Landy distinguishes between "the rugged self-made individual" of the Western and the British hero, "the primary agent and administrator of a system of justice that transcends his individualism," and "not the renegade or outlaw fighting against both the oppressive forces of established society and the forces of barbarism" (99). Although the Westerner also protects the civilized community and enables its development, his relation to civilization is more conflicted; Slotkin describes his trajectory as a dialectic whereby "Americans must cross the border into 'Indian Country' and experience 'a regression' to a more primitive and natural condition of life so that the false values of the 'metropolis' can be purged and a new, purified social contract enacted" (14). By crossing the border and experiencing "regression," the hero becomes a "man who knows Indians" (Slotkin 14), who must experience his savage or dark side in order to tame it.

However, the differences between the two genres need to be qualified. Indeed, the empire film evinces a similar theme of the regeneration of civilization through regression. Among British productions, the most striking example is perhaps Zoltan Korda's *The Four Feathers*. In it, the protagonist, Lieutenant Faversham (John Clements), sidelined because of his cowardice after refusing to take part in the Mahdist War in Sudan, decides to take on the identity of a Sangali native and join the troops anonymously to defeat the "barbarian" troops of the Mahdi and restore his reputation. Ideologically speaking, this can be compared to Theodore Roosevelt's interpretation of the conquest of the West as the regeneration of the Anglo-Saxon race, the contact of the wilderness, and the war against the savages favoring the development of a specific "American 'racial' character" (Slotkin 42–51). Like Roosevelt's "frontiersmen," the British imperialist hero must "learn to fight the savages according to savage rules" and find in their fanaticism a "model of nationalist patriotism the Whites will have to relearn" (Slotkin 47); he must tap into a more primitive energy from the passivity of civilization to rescue the imperial project.

They Died with Their Boots On expresses such an admiration for the purity of the savage against the corruption of civilization through the character of the Indian chief Crazy Horse, exalted as a model warrior by the film's hero, General

Custer (Errol Flynn); he describes Crazy Horse as "the only cavalryman I've seen around," contrasting the physical prowess of the native who escaped from his camp on horseback with his drunken men [85:09]. In *Lawrence of Arabia*, the question of the regeneration of white masculinity through the emulation of the "savage" is directly raised by Lawrence's superior, General Murray (Donald Wolfit), who openly questions the protagonist's virility as he sends him to meet Prince Feisal: "Who knows? It might even make a man out of him!" [15:19]. However, unlike Faversham in *The Four Feathers*, Lawrence is not a coward who tried to avoid his duty, and, in many respects, he resembles Custer in *They Died with Their Boots On*. Both are portrayed as independent and undisciplined— Custer, an unruly West Point cadet with the worst record of his class, achieves glory after refusing an order to retreat during the US-American Civil War; Lawrence takes Aqaba, even though his superiors insisted he was not to give any military advice. Both are ultimately betrayed by "the forces of established society" (Landy 99): corrupt politicians and businessmen in *They Died with Their Boots On*, British colonial politics in *Lawrence of Arabia*.

However, although Custer negotiates a peace treaty with the Lakota Indian when it is invalidated by the maneuvers of white businessmen, ultimately, his trajectory conforms to Roosevelt's racial nationalism, as he takes up arms against Crazy Horse and sacrifices his life to protect the white community against the savages. Lawrence, on the other hand, is not a race warrior but an Indian/Arab lover who supports the cause of Arab nationalism, to the point where his commanding officer General Allenby wonders if "he has gone native." His position, however, is fundamentally ambiguous, as, in the end, it appears all he did was serve, albeit unwillingly, the interests of British imperialism. Lawrence's contradictions remain unresolved; he does not die in a sacrificial last stand like Custer, nor does he triumphantly reintegrate British society, as in *The Four Feathers*. England is only shown in the opening sequence relating Lawrence's tragic motorbike accident on a countryside road and funeral at St. Paul's Cathedral [04:33–07:44]. The film ends with Lawrence driving away from the desert in a jeep, as his driver tells him he is "going home"; a motorcycle passes by and vanishes in the distant horizon [223:01–223:23]. England is depicted as a dead end, a tomb almost, as the motorbike echoes Lawrence's tragic accident in the opening. The motorbike disappearing into the horizon recalls the visual cliché of the lone rider leaving into the sunset to "reaffirm the hero's essential individuality" (Schatz 52); here, however, it only foreshadows (on the diegetic level) Lawrence's accident, which had already been depicted in the film's opening scene. The hero's final departure is given a tragic turn by the flashback structure, and a strong sense of failure pervades the ending.

Lawrence's defeat is best exemplified by his capture and the beating he is given by the Turks in the second half of the film [172:14–178:40]; it signals a rupture in the treatment of Lawrence. "Can you pass for an Arab in Arab town?" [170:06] asks one of his companions as he prepares to enter the Turkish-held town of Deraa. Arrested and interrogated by the Turkish bey (José Ferrer), Lawrence is stripped of his Bedouin clothes, revealing his blond hair and pale body. Allusions to his fair skin and blue eyes make clear that the Turks see through his disguise. It is implied that Lawrence is raped as well as beaten; an insistent close-up of the bey's mouth, and his lightly touching Lawrence's chest, do tinge the scene with disquieting sexual undertones. The sequence concludes with Lawrence thrown out, face down on the muddy street; his fall from grace echoes an earlier shot where he mimicked Christ walking on water by treading in a puddle. Although the Turks are treated as a rival imperial power, the sequence exemplifies the film's Orientalist tendency by establishing a contrast between Lawrence's paleness and their brown skin, while hinting at their perversion and brutality and emphasizing their otherness and savagery.

The Deraa sequence prepares the ground for the slaughter, ordered by Lawrence, of a column of retreating and wounded Turkish soldiers. The transformation from idealized hero following his victory in Aqaba to violent war criminal allows Lean and Bolt to offer a critical exploration of the imperialist hero and his values. It is similar to the arc of Ethan Edwards in *The Searchers*. Benefiting from John Wayne's charisma and star persona, Ethan emerges as "a hero of heroes whose character and fate are, therefore, commentaries on American heroism in its historical and its cinematic form" (Slotkin 464); although Ethan's violence is initially justified by the slaughter of his family, his obsessive quest for revenge and extreme hatred eventually come to mirror the brutality of the Comanche. Though not an "Indian hater" like Ethan, Lawrence's personal grudge against the Turks after the Deraa episode hints at revenge being the prime motivation for his drift toward extreme violence.

The main similarity between the two characters, however, lies in their relation to the desert, the wild untouched land they mean to tame and conquer. In *The Searchers*, the opening and closing sequence marks Ethan's affiliation to the wilderness. He emerges from the desert and, in the end, returns to it. His red shirt reflects the colors of the buttes, so that he blends in with his environment. He is dominated by the landscape, framed as a small figure against the backdrop of towering rocks. The rugged environment reflects his violent personality. Lawrence is similarly subjugated by the territory he wished to conquer; it becomes a place where the hero has to face himself and his own potential for savagery. Lawrence's triumph over the desert is given a tragic twist: he has to

Fig. 6.2 Lawrence's face covered in sand, in a still from *Lawrence of Arabia* [119:35].

kill the man he rescued from the Nafud desert, and, as he returns to Cairo after taking Aqaba, one of his two companions dies in quicksand. Lawrence later confesses to having enjoyed the sight of death and the sensation of killing [130:13–131:03], and his sadism ultimately culminates in the massacre of the Turks. He is both unable to fully assimilate in another culture or dominate his own savage side. In Feisal's words, he is just "another of these desert loving English men," at once subjugated to its influence and alienated from himself. After the quicksand episode, Lawrence is shown walking among a whirlwind of sand, disappearing behind it, the ensuing medium close-up of his sand-covered face revealing a broken man, vanquished and irremediably tainted by the surrounding wilderness (fig. 6.2) [116:21–117:21].

CONCLUSION

Analyzing Lawrence and his writings, Edward Said deciphered "an unresolved conflict in Lawrence between the White Man and the Oriental, and although he does not explicitly say so, this conflict essentially restages in his mind the historical conflict between East and West" (242); for Said, Lawrence presents the conflict as "his vision of himself as an unresolved, 'standing civil war'" (242). A similar personalization is at work in *Lawrence of Arabia*. Yet, if the emphasis on Lawrence's subjectivity confiscates the narrative of the revolt from the Arab to the profit of the white hero's personal tragedy, paradoxically, it is also what destabilizes the imperial narrative. *Lawrence of Arabia* proposes an exploration of its ambivalent eponymous protagonist. Lawrence is portrayed as being caught between two cultures, as both a British agent and an Arab leader.

This dual allegiance makes him, as Feisal says, "a sword with two edges." It is Lawrence's conflicted subjectivity that structures the film and shapes its political stance toward imperialism.

The desert serves both as a projection of Lawrence's Oriental fantasy and as the main vehicle for a traditional imperial representation and hierarchy. Through its imagery and visual similarities with cinematic representations of the US-American West, *Lawrence of Arabia* exploits the similarities between the empire film and the Western. The reference to the Western is highly ambivalent, as its popular imagery of adventure and outdoor action contribute to reinforce the visual and narrative appeal of Lawrence's legend, while complicating and challenging imperial representations, and inscribing them within a transnational history of imperialism. As we have seen, *Lawrence of Arabia* shares the ambivalence of many Hollywood pro-Indian Westerns between a liberal/progressive intention and the affirmation of white superiority. However, the introduction of the Western within the framework of the empire film allows *Lawrence of Arabia* to develop a critical exploration of the myth surrounding its hero. Although the film still adheres to a Western perspective and displays the exotic quality of its Orientalist setting, it uses visual and narrative tropes from the Western to expose the contradiction of the myth of British imperialism and present a more realistic representation of its violence and potential destructiveness. Throughout the film, comments on Lawrence made by British and Arab characters (especially by Feisal) shed a critical light on Lawrence's actions and attitudes.

The comparison of the British and the US-American hero underlines the ideological commonality between the empire film and the Western, and their affiliation to a broader, transnational category of imperial narratives. By endowing Lawrence with traits usually associated with the Westerner (his solitude, his drive to violence, his ambivalent identity caught between nature and culture), Lean and Bolt expose the imperialist hero's inner contradictions; as the film advances, the imperialist hero is deconstructed, torn both between British and Arab cultures, and between his public heroic image and the reality of his own cruel actions. Released the same year as *The Man Who Shot Liberty Valence* (Ford, 1962), *Lawrence of Arabia* adopts a similar revisionist approach to confront the legend and the fact, deconstructing the myth to reveal a more ambivalent reality. It emphasizes the proximity of the imperialist hero and the Westerner, as both are attracted to the purity of the savage and the wilderness while being the main agents of their subjugation. As such, the parallels with Hollywood pro-Indian Westerns and contemporary revisionist takes on the conquest of the West inscribe *Lawrence of Arabia* not only in a transnational history of imperialism, but also within a wider context in which the national imperialist mythology was increasingly being questioned and criticized.

NOTES

1. For a detailed account of the various film projects before Spiegel and Lean, see Jackson (26–43).

2. On the distinction between colonialism and settler colonialism, see Veracini (1–15).

WORKS CITED

Caton, Steven C. *Lawrence of Arabia: A Film Anthropology*. University of California Press, 1999.

Chapman, James, and Nicholas J. Cull. *Projecting Empire: Imperialism and Popular Cinema*. I. B. Tauris, 2009.

Ehrenstein, David, and David Lean. "Epic Dialogue." *David Lean Interviews*, edited by Steven Organ, University Press of Mississippi, 2009, pp. 67–76.

Jackson, Kevin. *Lawrence of Arabia*. British Film Institute, 2007.

Landy, Marcia. *British Genres*. Princeton University Press, 1991.

Lawrence of Arabia. Directed by David Lean, performances by Peter O'Toole, Omar Shariff, Alec Guinness, Anthony Quinn, Columbia Picture, 1962. Edition 3 DVD, Sony Picture Home Entertainment, 2009.

Said, Edward. *Orientalism*. Penguin Book, 1985.

Schatz, Thomas. *Hollywood Genres*. McGraw Hill, 1981.

Simmon, Scott. *The Invention of the Western Film: A Cultural History of the Genre's First Half-Century*. Cambridge University Press, 2003.

Slotkin, Richard. *Gunfighter Nation: The Myth of the Frontier in Twentieth-Century America*. University of Oklahoma Press, 1998.

Veracini, Lorenzo. *Settler Colonialism: A Theoretical Overview*. Palgrave Macmillan, 2010.

Webster, Wendy. "Domesticating the Frontier: Gender, Empire and Adventure Landscapes in British Cinema, 1945–59." *Gender and History*, vol. 15, no. 1, 2003, pp. 85–107.

HADRIEN FONTANAUD is PhD candidate at Université Paul Valéry Montpellier 3.

SEVEN

—ഝ—

UNWANTED SALVATION

The Use of the Savior Formula in *The Dark Valley*
(Andreas Prochaska, 2014)

MAREK PARYŻ

THIS CHAPTER FOCUSES ON THE ambivalence of the generic scripts employed in the Austrian Western *The Dark Valley* (2014), directed by Andreas Prochaska and based on a novel by Thomas Willmann, with respect to the moral justification of the protagonist's actions as well as the moral limits of US-American interventionist policies. The film introduces a US-American hero, born of an Austrian mother, who comes to a village in the Austrian Alps to take revenge on the clan that has long oppressed the community; as a result, his intervention will have a liberating effect on the villagers as a collective. The protagonist's motivation remains unknown at the beginning, but, once it has been explained, the plot moves smoothly toward its finale in accordance with the revenge formula.

In accentuating the irreversible—and supposedly positive—consequences of the revenge act for the entire community, *The Dark Valley* adheres to the logic of the savior film. In a US-American context, the savior film features "a white messianic character [who] saves a lower-or working-class, usually urban or isolated, nonwhite character from a sad fate" (Hughey 1). In his study of this film genre, Matthew Hughey writes that the white savior trope "is so widespread that varied intercultural and interracial relations are often guided by a logic that racializes and separates people into those who are redeemers (white) and those who are redeemed or in need of redemption (nonwhites)" (2). Hughey adds that "such imposing patronage enables an interpretation of nonwhite characters and culture as essentially broken, marginalized, and pathological, while whites can emerge as messianic characters that easily fix the nonwhite pariah with their superior moral and mental abilities" (2). In *The Dark Valley*, the racial connotations of the savior film have been replaced by analogous national connotations, and the way in which the Austrian Western constructs cultural difference, especially the opposing hierarchies of values on which this notion is based, mirrors the solutions to be found in this film genre.

What is crucial for the present argument is that, while white savior films "perpetuat[e], in subtle and friendly terms, the archaic paradigm of manifest destiny, the white man's burden, and the great white hope" (Hughey 15), they explicitly project a fantasy of a selfless support of the disenfranchised and the underprivileged. On the other hand, revenge films justify selfish actions that have violent outcomes. The point is that, in *The Dark Valley*, the use of the generic scripts of saviorism and revenge yields a dissonant combination of selflessness and selfishness when the issue of the protagonist's motivation comes up. This dichotomy defines the moral conflict at the heart of the film and relates it to the global dynamics of the genre, attesting to the applicability of the Western formula in the examination of various national contexts, while simultaneously raising questions as to its limits. In a rather critical review of the film, Jessica Kiang has described *The Dark Valley* as "a German movie whose DNA is entirely American." However, in certain ways, the Austrian Western resists US-American conventions. This resistance is signified through elements taken from the culturally specific Heimat film—and notably its classic variant "based on the idea of the Alpine region as a source for physical and mental recovery" (Poole)—which undermines the moral perspective imposed by the US-American Western. Ralph J. Poole[1] writes of the ideology of the Heimat film that it "seems rooted in former and presumably better times. The myth of a better past is played out in safeguarding—freezing—nature against technology and, in analogy, in keeping its inhabitants within a moral system that defies the intrusion of modernizing evils" (Poole). References to this genre in *The Dark Valley*, on the one hand, raise questions about sovereignty and the right of societies to live according to the norms that have evolved in the course of their history, even if those norms appear to be starkly at odds with certain supposedly "universal" normative imaginings. On the other hand, such references problematize the recognition of redemptive action, suggesting that its moral justification is inseparable from specific configurations of power.

Stanley Corkin writes that "the repressed dimension of Westerns is their relationship to imperialism" and that the genre has the "power to graft discussions of imperialism onto assertions of the power and sanctity of the individual" (5). Such meanings are implicit in the Western's symbolic construction of "America" as, in John White's words, "peace-loving and slow to anger but ultimately, if necessary, able to bring down 'fearful consequences' on its enemies" (3). In the course of its development, the Western has time and again proved to be a useful narrative tool in mediating the ways of envisaging and interpreting international tensions and conflicts, as well as of defining the role of the US in them. Arguably, this aspect of the Western first became manifest in the 1950s and 1960s, with the release of a series of films that portrayed small-scale interventions carried out by well-trained US-American gunmen on the territory of Mexico. Richard Slotkin writes that "the evolution of the 'Mexico Western' proceeded in step with the development of American policy in the struggle for hearts and minds in the Third World and reached its height of popularity during the Vietnam War" (410). The tropes of counterinsurgency Westerns, as Slotkin dubs such productions (410), have more recently resurfaced in US-American drug films—perhaps most spectacularly in *Sicario* (Denis Villeneuve, 2015)—with Mexican drug barons as substitutes for manic bandits or crazed revolutionaries. Interventionist scenarios that bring to mind counterinsurgency Westerns also appear in films about the wars in the Middle East.

Interestingly enough, interventionist themes that have clearly been inspired by US-American Westerns can also be found in recent transnational Westerns produced outside the US. For example, the Macedonian *Dust* (Milcho Manchevski, 2001) features two US-American sibling gunmen who, having traveled to the Balkans, become involved in the Macedonian uprising against the Turks. The Bolivian *Blackthorn* (Mateo Gil, 2011) introduces a US-American protagonist who aims to right the wrongs that have been done to a group of Indigenous miners. *Dust* and *Blackthorn* are important analogues for *The Dark Valley* insofar as all three films portray US-American gunfighters who, while abroad, undertake actions whose outcome will permanently change a given local social and/or political order. Despite their personal flaws, these gunfighters ultimately function as paragons of US-American ideals of justice, equality, and democracy. What Slotkin says of Mexico in counterinsurgency Westerns— that it is "Americanizable" (410)—is also true of the Macedonian village in *Dust*, the Bolivian mining community in *Blackthorn*, and the secluded Alpine settlement in *The Dark Valley*, as all three films anticipate some form of democratizing transformation. The Austrian Western, however, differs from the other two films in one respect in particular: by foregrounding a manic revenger, it carries disquieting implications as to the equivocal nature of interventionist scenarios and exemplifies a tendency of contemporary Westerns to convey "how the obsession of 'looking like a hero' exposes a history of violence that has fully realized a self-consuming destructive potential" (Holtz 117). And whereas *Dust* and *Blackthorn* employ utopian scripts to image the far-reaching social, economic, and political advancement of the respective societies or even nations that they depict (Paryż 137–40, 144–53), *The Dark Valley* is devoid of analogous implications and leaves the viewer pondering the very possibility of a painful small-scale transformation.

FRAMING SAVIORISM

The Dark Valley opens with the image of a man on horseback riding into a mountain village (fig. 7.1). The horseman, Greider (Sam Riley), is immediately faced with six Brenner brothers, the sons of the most powerful man in the area. He finds lodging at a house that belongs to an elderly widow and her daughter Luzi (Paula Beer). The young woman is engaged to Lukas (Thomas Schubert), and their wedding day, according to the local rule, is to be decided by old Brenner (Hans-Michael Rehberg). The same rule makes every newlywed woman share Brenner's bed until she gets pregnant. When the Brenner brothers take Luzi after the wedding, Greider confronts them and frees her. Prior to this scene, Greider's identity has been revealed: his mother was the only woman to ever escape from the village, though not without avoiding violation and witnessing the crucifixion of her husband who arranged the escape. After a shoot-out in the woods in which he kills four Brenner brothers—two have been eliminated earlier in the film—Greider goes to meet old Brenner, his biological father.

The Dark Valley portrays an isolated community of people who are victims of oppression and concomitantly share, to a certain extent, the responsibility for the local history of abuse. Their silence sanctions the "tradition" that the Brenner clan has imposed on them; they believe that they ought to be loyal to the Brenners for their protection. Luzi's mother explains the circumstances to Greider: "Brenner decides about what happens in the village, but he also takes care of us" [14:47]. Of course, a number of people in the village are related to the powerful clan by blood, although such family ties remain unacknowledged. It is quite symptomatic that, while the rules observed by the villagers are progressively revealed, the community as such does not really play an important role in the film's action. The opening sequence includes a shot of a group of villagers watching Greider ride in with an expression of puzzlement and uncertainty on their faces, a clear indication that they are not used to the sight of strangers [6:44]. Another situation that can be seen as a glimpse of the community's life is the wedding sequence that attests to the painful public spectacle the newlyweds are subjected to. Participation in wedding ceremonies forces the villagers to relive what they had been through themselves and reminds them of their subordinate status in relation to the Brenner clan.

Apart from the Brenners, Luzi and her mother, and Lukas and his family, the only other members of the community who gain some prominence in the plot

Fig. 7.1 Greider approaching the village [5:12].

are the priest and the married couple who own an inn, and this is because the three directly share the responsibility for the punishment of Greider's mother and her husband. The retrospective scene depicting the crucifixion shows a bunch of agitated men, some of whom must be from outside of the Brenner clan, but none of whom can be identified as an individual [59:15–59:50]. It is only at the end of the film that the faces of some of the villagers can be seen distinctly in a series of shots. Lukas is taking a wounded Greider to Luzi's place and the people witness this, giving the US-American intruder looks that are far from grateful. Luzi says in voice-over: "Nobody said anything, but there were many who wanted to chase him away or even do something worse. Old Brenner left his seed in every family. And freedom is a gift that not everybody is willing to accept" [108:02]. Interestingly, the closing credits are illustrated, in documentary fashion, with shots of the faces of anonymous members of the community, as if their individuality had been established belatedly [110:00–114:00]: however, the blank expressions on these faces do not signify anything hopeful. The film does not really present the villagers in an empathetic light, but stresses, however, their lack of choice; it portrays them as victims who have turned into mute witnesses of other people's suffering and humiliation, and who have indirectly helped sustain the pathological order.

The Brenners exploit every occasion to assert their power, and it is apparent that they want to be feared rather than respected; they are the only ones in the village who own rifles. The six brothers stick together and express extreme self-confidence by being noisy. Old Brenner shows a degree of reticence, but his sons repeatedly manifest their superiority through possessive or humiliating gestures toward others. There are two meaningful situations in which Hans (Tobias Moretti), the eldest brother, grabs Luzi by the back of her neck and directs her steps [11:07; 67:24]; she would have obeyed him anyway, but he evidently wants to make her feel subservient through demeaning treatment. Hans does this because such is his right, a sign of excess that has become normalcy.

The form of patriarchy the Brenner clan has established in the village depends on the strict physical control of female bodies. The image of Hans holding Luzi by the back of her neck symbolically corresponds—through a representation of a possessive male gesture—to that of his father appreciatively looking at Greider's mother when she was still a girl. The latter image is introduced in the flashback sequence, narrated by Luzi in voice-over, that recounts Greider's mother's and her parents' arrival at the village [59:55–60:48]. They were driven out of their former place by hunger, and they headed for the settlement in the mountains, seeing no other way of survival. Brenner allowed them to stay and informed them right away of the condition they resignedly accepted by staying: "That day [Brenner] told her parents what happens to the girls in the valley, and that he decides who stays and who leaves. They talked to him and cried, but the hunger was stronger. They gave Brenner their word and stayed in the valley." Brenner is portrayed, here, as an ominous, shadowy, faceless figure; the camera assumes his point of view in a high-angle shot, in which his hand touches the girl's mouth and forces it open so that he can see her teeth. Such a reductive image emphasizes Brenner's total control over the people he "protects." The Dark Valley thus constructs an image of a pathological patriarchy that takes advantage of those who have experienced extreme economic deprivation and imposes the sexual exploitation of women as an element of the social contract.

In a sense, then, Greider is destined to right the wrongs committed by the Brenners because of his complete isolation from the social circumstances that have allowed abuse to become a norm. This primarily has to do with his status as an outsider and a foreigner, but the fact that he is not defined in any way in reference to family roles—apart from being a loving son—is meaningful in that regard, too.

The patriarchal excesses of the Brenners are sanctioned by religion, and, excepting the men from the clan, it is the priest who most actively defends the order of the settlement. During their wedding ceremony, he makes Luzi and Lukas understand that they must succumb to the divine will of which the local tradition is an emanation [53:32–55:20]. In his sermon, he retells the story of Joseph and Mary in such a way as to give Lukas and Luzi to understand what their respective duties as newlyweds are. His words not only confirm his involvement with the Brenners, but also testify to his own degeneration, resulting from the dictatorial model of a community in which he occupies a privileged position. The priest equals the Brenners in his readiness to resort to physical violence, which is shown in the flashback of the crucifixion of Greider's mother's husband [59:11]; as the Brenners are nailing the man's hands to the cross, his wife is pushed to the ground, and the priest holds her face to one side to make her watch the cruel punishment of her beloved. The scenes of the wedding and the crucifixion appear in the film in close succession and are connected through Greider who comes to the church after Luzi and Lukas's wedding to kill the priest. Before shooting him, he says he wants to take a confession and shows him a medallion with a portrait of his mother. In terms of narrative structure, the confession frames the flashback about Greider's mother. The proximity of the scenes of the wedding and the crucifixion within the film's plot establishes an image of the priest's downright perversion. However, *The Dark Valley* in no way suggests that the role of religion in perpetuating the rituals of abuse boils down to one man's evil nature; religion is part and parcel of the mindset that allowed a form of social pathology to emerge in the first place. This is highlighted through a more general employment of religious symbolism, centered on the cross on which Greider's mother's husband died and that towers over the valley; it is not a sign of Christ's sacrifice but a warning for those who may commit the "sin" of disobedience.

The way *The Dark Valley* constructs the social fabric of its setting is based on an inversion of the tropes of the Heimat film. Andreas Prochaska reiterated in the interviews that what fascinated him about Thomas Willmann's novel was its "mixture of the Western and the homeland novel" (Schiefer). Willmann himself acknowledged two key inspirations for his novel: Sergio Leone and Ludwig Ganghofer ("Interview"), a major German author of Heimat novels from the late nineteenth and early twentieth centuries, whose numerous works were later adapted for the screen. The origins of Heimat literature, from which an analogical film genre subsequently emerged, go back to the last decade of the nineteenth century and are inextricable from the rise of the Heimat movement, which was a "reaction to rapid industrialization and the concomitant shift from rural to urban living" (Kaes 165). Anton Kaes writes that, "in the ideology of this antimodern, antiurban movement, Heimat was precisely that which was abandoned on the way into the cities; from then on the word 'Heimat' began to connote 'region,' 'province' and 'country'" (165). According to Kaes, "German literature has weighted this term with emotional connotations almost to the breaking point: Heimat means the site of one's lost childhood, of family, of identity. It also stands for the possibility of secure human relations . . . and the romantic harmony between the country dweller and nature" (165). The meaning of Heimat had various inflections over the course of history, so that, after Hitler's rise to power, it became "a synonym for race (blood) and territory (soil), a deadly combination that led to the exile or annihilation of anyone who did not 'belong,'" whereas after World War II, "when millions of Germans had lost their homes or were displaced from their homeland," "it signified above all the experience of loss" (166). Kaes adds that, in the 1970s, the Heimat genre underwent a thorough reinvention in a series of films that "presented country life as false idyll, a breeding ground for private and collective neuroses" (166). Johannes von Moltke observes that contemporary German audiences still associate the Heimat film with "a fairly stable set of plots and images, consisting of picturesque Alpine landscapes . . . [and] of morally upstanding men and girlish women clad in traditional dress trying to track down the sinister poacher whose self-serving obsession threatens the fabric of the local community" (23). *The Dark Valley* interrogates the tenets of the Heimat film by aligning its tropes with that of the guilty town, which has been also used in Westerns, perhaps most appealingly in *High Plains Drifter* (Clint Eastwood, 1973), the story of a mysterious rider who comes to a mining town where the sheriff was once killed as a result of the townspeople's conspiracy against him. The Westerns that employ this motif explore the corrupting influence of an unspeakable secret on an entire community and highlight the degeneration of an individual moral sense as a result of a person's immersion in communal life. Relations within the community are determined by the haunting memory of the evil that was once perpetrated.

The conventions of the Heimat film provide a showcase that complicates Greider's function as a savior, defining him in social terms as an antagonist. If his aim is not only to kill the Brenners but also to liberate the villagers, to elicit their agency, and to inspire them to create a new reality, the question remains open whether its achievement is at all possible. Greider actually forces the people to admit their shame or confront their guilt, and, for obvious reasons, this is not an easy process. The villagers have learned to repress what they have been unable to forget, and now all their secrets have come to light; thus, they elicit very little gratitude toward the savior. In a word, he has not given them much choice regarding the way of life they would prefer to pursue as a collective. They are far from taking for granted the ideas and standards that the US-American hero presumably considers to be universal democratic fundamentals. His democratic attitude manifests itself in his respectful treatment of his two hostesses, something that Luzi and her mother perceive as a novelty. However, the villagers have few occasions to appreciate Greider's attitude and the values that inform it, and, even if they did, they would remain blind to such values—or any other alien values—because they have not developed a notion that social relations are shaped in the process of negotiation. It can be said, therefore, that by disrespecting their exclusive rules, Greider infringes on their sovereignty, and his power does not result from his high morality, but—as in the case of the Brenners—from his readiness to commit acts of extreme violence.

REVENGE AND COMMUNITY RENEWAL

Józef Jaskulski, who reads *The Dark Valley* alongside the literary work of Thomas Bernhard and Martin Pollack, describes Greider as a version of the *Nestbeschmutzer*, an archetype that is common in contemporary Austrian literature for addressing the problem of the country's Nazi past. Drawing from the work of Polish sociologist and cultural studies scholar Karol Franczak, Jaskulski writes that a *Nestbeschmutzer* is "a mediator artist who imparts unwanted and repressed knowledge about Austria's Nazi involvement and self-victimization, providing commentary on the working-through of the country's history, denouncing its ostensible and ceremonial character, and nullifying the clear-cut social categories" (63). The writers of *Nestbeschmutzer* literature "reject dominant narratives, . . . brood over the shameful deeds of their community, reject tribal bonds, exclude themselves from the communal experience, renounce proximity in favor of distance, and devise new, alternative dictionaries that inscribe the familiar with alternative, alienating significance" (63). Jaskulski emphasizes the symbolic implications of Greider's activity as a photographer in the light of the *Nestbeschmutzer* archetype: "Wandering around the valley, he takes pictures of its landscape and inhabitants, as if in a dual quest to commemorate the site of past crimes and their perpetrators (and bystanders)" (66). Greider's intervention thus precludes a state of collective amnesia.

The Dark Valley reworks the *Nestbeschmutzer* archetype by placing it in a transnational context. Characters that embody this archetype often look at the culture in which they were raised from the outside, having left their native parts at some point in their lives and then returning home so as to come to terms with their burdensome legacy. In physical terms, Greider, as a foreigner, has been completely separated from the culture of the Austrian mountain village until his arrival there, but, concomitantly, he has been psychologically anchored in this culture through the nightmarish memories that his mother passed on to him. In the village, Greider soon finds out that the nightmare he imagined is true. To some extent, Greider's inability to free himself from the burden of a culture that is essentially alien to him accounts for his radicalism. Having completed his violent actions, he leaves behind the legacy that has tainted him as a human being, even though he never embraced it.

Greider strives to achieve a form of self-redemption, but he can complete the plan that leads to it only if he confronts the killer in himself and embraces

the part of his identity that, perhaps, appalls him as much as his Brenner an-
cestry. This is why he is, as Jaskulski puts it, "a conflicted personality" and "a
bundle of anger, revulsion and compulsive habits which all drive him to return
to his homeland and face his legacy" (67). Slotkin points out that the revenger
Western often puts emphasis on "the neurotic element in the hero's makeup"
(381); "in such a tale, the redemption of the hero from the darker side of his own
nature has little or no meaning for a larger society" (382). Slotkin concludes
that "the revenger Western . . . fetishizes 'psychology,' isolating the private
dimension of the original story and replacing social with exclusively personal
motives, insisting (in effect) that the private dimension determines the whole
significance of the story" (382).

In *The Dark Valley*, the social meaning of Greider's actions is saved by the
employment of the savior script, which collides with the revenger script, and
such collisions become most apparent in a series of scenes featuring mirrors,
suggesting that the hero experiences an increasing internal turmoil. In the first
of these scenes, Greider is shaving before a mirror [18:05]; his focused look and
the precise movement of his hand bespeak composure and confidence. Later
in the film, there is a shot of Greider's reflection briefly—and accidentally—
captured in a mirror on a table [39:26]. He looks anguished, probably tired, and
he opens a medallion with the picture of his mother as if to remind himself of
what he is doing in a cold, uncomfortable room. The third instance with a mirror undermines the implications of the first [42:40]. It follows Greider's killing
of the second Brenner brother, and it begins with a very symptomatic shot of
a bowl of water, with the camera placed underneath the surface and directed
vertically upward; Greider's hands break through the ice on the water, and the
diluted features of his face can be discerned. This image symbolically encapsulates the hero's duality. The film then cuts to a profile close-up of Greider
washing his face, and then to a rear shot of him, as he is staring—hatefully, it
seems—at his mirror reflection, with the camera gently zooming in to draw
the viewer's attention to the importance of this shot. One half of Greider's face
is lit, the other immersed in dimness, while a part of his face remains outside
the mirror frame. His look expresses extreme anguish, and the composition of
the shot signifies his fragmentation. Greider is on the verge of a psychological
eruption, although at this stage in the film, we do not yet know the real cause
of his compulsive behavior.

In the revenge sequence, one scene in particular shows Greider's shock at
his own capacity for cruelty, when he comes to punish the innkeepers, who
took money for hiding his mother and her husband and then betrayed them to
Brenner [77:50–81:00]. Instead of a neat and quick kill, he indulges in torture.

After threatening the innkeeper with a gun, Greider throws a sack of coins toward his wife and tells her to eat them; he even tries to force a coin into her mouth, holding up her head, but he draws back, as if repulsed by her grotesque wrinkled face. It can be assumed that he has suddenly recognized in this ugly and greedy woman a bitter, desperate human being that has been reduced to the basic predatory instincts and deserves pity rather than hate. More importantly, this is also a moment of self-recognition: Greider has reached the limits of his self-control. By inflicting violence on two helpless, if wicked, people, the savior has become indistinguishable from a torturer. Greider's portrayal is in keeping with a more general tendency in contemporary Westerns to bring out the psychological ambivalence of their heroes, which often has to do with their inability to come to terms with their past—Lee Clark Mitchell sees this tendency as a distinguishing feature of newer productions in the genre: "The swerve taken by contemporary Westerns lies in their evocation of an anguished response to the grip of the past, with the hero unable to escape either himself or his history, immured in circumstances where violence offers a mere fleeting respite from conditions that persist nevertheless" (21).

The extent of Greider's control over the situation is reflected not only in his determined adherence to his plan, but also in his ability to provoke other people's reactions and steer their actions. This applies to the Brenners in the first place. When he kills the second Brenner son, he leaves a signature, as it were, that will enable his identification as the killer, thus accelerating the final confrontation [42:00]. His ability to engineer the course of events is symbolically enhanced by his weapon, a repeating rifle, which is juxtaposed with the old breech-loading rifles used by the Brenners. This obviously signifies Greider's technological superiority, which strengthens the moral sanction of his actions (Joyce 116). The Brenners use their rifles to maintain a state of oppression that preserves their privileges; by contrast, Greider uses his to settle a conflict. The exclusive possession of rifles gives the Brenners an illusion of omnipotence, and this ultimately precipitates the destruction of the clan. It is clear that the Brenner brothers disregard the rules of a fair fight; when they surround the shed in the woods where Greider has been hiding, they fire several rounds of shots at the building. They have come to believe that their sheer number is a guarantee of victory. However, as a result of their immersion in the alienating reality of the village, they are completely unprepared to face the kind of force that Greider embodies. This force has a lot to do with technological advancement, a process that the villagers have always been oblivious to. The village's self-containment is contrasted with the expansive tendencies of the modern era, epitomized—even if only implicitly in the film—by US imperialism. In a

Fig. 7.2 Hans Brenner confronting Greider in the final shooting scene [1:31:10].

way, the Brenners' attachment to the old ways accelerates the chain of events that leads to their deaths.

In the memorably choreographed shoot-out scene, Hans Brenner counts the shots Greider has fired, and when he is sure that Greider has no bullets left in his rifle, he steps forward with a victorious smile before raising his rifle [91:10] (fig. 7.2). This medium close-up of Hans en face and is a meaningfully composed shot. The barrel of his gun rises in front of the middle part of his body, suggesting powerful phallic connotations and reminding us of the history of abuse that the Brenners are responsible for. The shot of Hans is followed by a reverse medium shot of Greider who repeats his rifle and shoots, also in slow motion. Hans falls down and Greider walks up to him and finishes him off. This is all extended in time through slow motion and a combination of images of the rifle, the shooter, and the victim. These images suggest that, on the one hand, Greider knows his weapon intimately, but, on the other, he treats it like a tool, uses it when necessary, and handles it with proper skill. Jaskulski describes Greider's pictures as "aseptic" (67), but this word is, perhaps, even more relevant in regard to his way of killing. The meaning of such a depiction of violence is quite unlike the implications of Greider's torture of the innkeepers: interventions can be necessary, and their moral justification depends, not infrequently, on the precision with which they have been executed.

Greider's role as a savior involves his ability to catalyze a change in people's attitudes, foreshadowing a possible renewal of the community as a whole. This is evidenced by the hero's influence on Luzi and Lukas. However, the fact that only these two characters embrace his intervention implies that a positive transformation of the social order cannot be taken for granted. For Luzi, Greider's stay at her house as a tenant provides an opportunity to at least try and assert her female independence by interacting with a man in an unusual way for a local woman. Her initial brusqueness toward him quickly turns into curiosity, and when the stranger has his first dinner with her and her mother, Luzi asks him whether he really comes from the US and whether he saw any Indians there, a degree of spontaneity that her mother can only frown at [13:50]. The film connects Greider's influence on Luzi to the fact that she has the courage to suggest to Lukas that they escape from the village, an idea that terrifies her beloved man. This occurs early on in the film, and, at this point, Lukas is not up to something that would undermine the order of things. Thus, Luzi resignedly accepts her sad fate. She recovers her will to resist the oppressors when she helps Greider disarm the Brenner brothers who are taking her to their place after the wedding. For a short while, she is a woman with a gun, but this does not signify a lasting radical liberation; later on, Greider tells her to hand the gun over to Lukas. *The Dark Valley* is far from redefining the woman's role in the Western, and it ends with a rather conservative image of a healthy family; Luzi says in voice-over: "It was the last time I saw him [Greider]. That day I told Lukas that I was expecting a child. He was very happy and proud because something was finally the right way" [109:03]. The routines of everyday life, reflecting the community's gender hierarchy, will not change, but the women will at least know that some things depend on their actions.

The Dark Valley's relatively conservative agenda in terms of gender politics is confirmed by the film's depiction of Lukas's transformation under Greider's influence from a helpless, cowardly youth into a man who takes decisive action. The initial image of Lukas is established by a series of scenes that strongly suggest his emasculation. On two occasions when they see each other alone, Luzi hints at how little Lukas can do—and he understands the hints immediately. His complete powerlessness is emphasized in the scene of the wedding party during which the Brenner brothers humiliate him [67:00]. His self-esteem cannot be any lower than at this very moment, and this moment paves the way for a profound personal transformation that he will soon undergo. When Greider brings Luzi back to her family, Lukas turns out to be the only person that entertains no doubts as to how to act. He is the only one who is ready to use the rifle that Greider took away from one of the Brenner brothers, and it is with this rifle that he later saves Greider's life. We have not witnessed Lukas's transformation, but we see its undeniable outcome—empowerment. This kind of film ending in which the main hero is saved by another character in a situation when his life is threatened is rather conventional, and it typically attests to the newly discovered agency on the part of the person who kills the hero's powerful enemy. However, this would not have happened had it not been for the hero's prior life-changing influence on the person that later saves him. Symbolically, the killing committed by Lukas is a foundational act of violence as it signifies the beginning of a new era in the community's history, just as Greider's killing of the Brenners marks the end of an era.

CONCLUSION

The Dark Valley ends on a somewhat paradoxical note: a new order can be preserved thanks to the man with a gun—Lukas—a symbolic good father who will ensure that the healthy rules of social life will be observed. The community faces the prospect of a profound change, but one thing remains the same: the one who decides about its way of life is the man with a gun. Hughey writes of white savior films that their "producers, critics, and audiences often present these films as straightforward and impartial narratives about heroic characters, intercultural friendships, and the humanistic struggle to overcome daunting odds"; all analogical issues become "normalized as common sense" (8). What the use of the savior trope in *The Dark Valley* helps normalize is violence that has moral sanction as a basis of social organization. After a spectacle of violence, rooted in the revenge Western and casting doubt on the implications of saviorism, the savior script and the revenger script eventually reach a neat resolution in the film's vision of a new order.

However, on a more general level of political implications, *The Dark Valley* retains its ambivalence about the interventionist policies of modern Western powers. The critique the film conveys in this regard has to do with the definitiveness of interventionist operations and with the likely myopia of those who engineer them. The interventionist scenario that unfolds in *The Dark Valley* leaves no room for a negotiation of values and solutions. Even if Greider is an emanation of the democratic order, the villagers have not learned a lesson in democracy in the course of his actions. This aspect of the film becomes more apparent if we compare *The Dark Valley* with another recent German-language film, *Western* (Valeska Grisebach, 2017), which makes use of Western tropes in far less evident ways than the Austrian production. As a matter of fact, if it were not for the direct reference to the genre in the film's title, such a framework for the interpretation of its tropes would not easily suggest itself. The 2017 film portrays a group of German engineers and workers who are building a power plant in Bulgaria. They embody the expansive economic and technological ambitions of the West, but the film—instead of constructing symbolic references that would exemplify this—examines down-to-earth relations between the presumed invaders and the local population. Various tensions arise, but an open conflict never erupts. *Western*'s counterpart of the Western hero is a worker who develops an interest in the way of life of the Bulgarian countryside and comes to function as an intermediary between two cultures. Thus, *Western*, while admitting the inevitability of a certain course of development in a globalizing world, highlights—in a way that is a far cry from idealization—the importance of dialogue. By contrast, the interventionist subtext of *The Dark Valley* ultimately forecloses the space of dialogue and negotiation.

NOTE

1. I wish to thank Ralph Poole for allowing me to read his manuscript.

WORKS CITED

Corkin, Stanley. *Cowboys as Cold Warriors: The Western and US History*. Temple University Press, 2004.

The Dark Valley. Directed by Andreas Prochaska, performances by Sam Riley, Tobias Moretti, Paula Beer and Thomas Schubert. Allegro Film, 2014.

Holtz, Martin. "The Western and the War Film: Clint Eastwood's *American Sniper* as Genre Hybrid." *Studia Filmoznawcze*, vol. 38, 2017, pp. 105–19.

Hughey, Matthew W. *The White Savior Film: Content, Critics, and Consumption*. Temple University Press, 2014.

"Interview with Director and Screenwriter Andreas Prochaska." Julianwhiting. files.wordpress.com, https://julianwhiting.files.wordpress.com/2015/11/english -language-film-notes2.pdf. Accessed 15 May 2019.

Jaskulski, Józef. "A Contaminated Landscape: Andreas Prochaska's *The Dark Valley* as a *Nestbeschmutzer* Western." *Studia Filmoznawcze*, vol. 38, 2017, pp. 59–73.

Joyce, Justin A. *Gunslinging Justice: The American Culture of Gun Violence in Westerns and the Law*. Manchester University Press, 2018.

Kaes, Anton. *From Hitler to Heimat: The Return of History as Film*. Harvard University Press, 1992.

Kiang, Jessica. "Berlin Review: 'The Dark Valley' Starring Sam Riley Is a Dour, Unoriginal German-Language Western." Indiewire, 10 Feb 2014, https://www .indiewire.com/2014/02/berlin-review-the-dark-valley-starring-sam-riley-is-a -dour-unoriginal-german-language-western-89222/. Accessed 15 May 2019.

Mitchell, Lee Clark. *Late Westerns: The Persistence of a Genre*. University of Nebraska Press, 2018.

Paryż, Marek. "A Map of Longings: Utopian Underpinnings of Contemporary Transnational Westerns." *Studia Filmoznawcze*, vol. 38, 2017, pp. 137–55.

Poole, Ralph J. "The Future Was Dark: *Das finstere Tal* as Alpine Western." *Cultural Politics and Propaganda: Mediated Narratives and Images in Austrian-American Relations*, edited by Waldemar Zacharasiewicz, ÖAW Verlag. Forthcoming.

Schiefer, Karin. "Andreas Prochaska on His New Film *The Dark Valley*." Austrianfilms, Jan. 2014, http://www.austrianfilms.com/news/en/i_wanted _to_take_the_opportunity_to_make_a_genre_film. Accessed 15 May 2019.

Slotkin, Richard. *Gunfighter Nation: The Myth of the Frontier in Twentieth-Century America*. Harper Perennial, 1993.

von Moltke, Johannes. *No Place Like Home: Locations of Heimat in German Cinema*. University of California Press, 2005.

White, John. *The Contemporary Western: An American Genre Post-9/11*. Edinburgh University Press, 2019.

MAREK PARYŻ is Associate Professor at the Institute of English Studies at the University of Warsaw. He is author of *The Postcolonial and Imperial Experience in American Transcendentalism* and editor with John R. Leo of *The Post-2000 Film Western: Contexts, Transnationality, Hybridity*.

EIGHT

—ᵐᵐ—

TRANSNATIONAL POST-WESTERNS IN FRENCH CINEMA

Adieu Gary (Nassim Amaouche, 2009) and
Les Cowboys (Thomas Bidegain, 2015)

JESÚS ÁNGEL GONZÁLEZ

DESPITE THE OMINOUS PREDICTIONS AT the turn of the century, Westerns stubbornly refuse to disappear and continue to fulfill a relevant aesthetic and cultural function not only in the US, but also in many other parts of the world. Whether films like *Lone Star* (John Sayles, 1996) or *No Country for Old Men* (the Coen brothers, 2007) are called "post-Westerns" (Campbell), "late Westerns" (Mitchell), "contemporary Westerns" (Nelson), or simply "Westerns" (Carter) remains less important, in the end, than the quality of the films and their capacity to articulate US-American anxieties and conflicts by referencing the US-American West and the Western. For the transnational versions of the genre, as I have argued elsewhere ("Transnational"; "Foundational"), the term *post-Western* seems to be more appropriate, since it underlines the temporal and spatial displacement. Films like *Into the West* (Ireland, Mike Newell, 1992), *800 Bullets* (Spain, Álex de la Iglesia, 2002), and *Once upon a Time in Anatolia* (Turkey, Nuri Bilge Ceylan, 2011) tell stories in times and places far away from the US-American West, and even from a period of conquest (they usually take place in a contemporary setting and in the country where they are produced), but make references to the Western in order to establish a dialogue with the "deeply haunting assumptions and values" of the genre (Campbell 31).

Interestingly enough, these films, like many US-American Westerns, make semantic and/or syntactic references (Altman) to the genre in order to articulate discourses about the national identity and foundational myths of these countries. For example, *800 Bullets* mimics the syntactic model of some "revisionist Westerns" (the old cowboy trying to resist the passing of time) and adapts it to

148

the situation of a former stuntman in the Almería Western sets used to shoot Spaghetti Westerns; it also adds plenty of semantic references to the genre (specifically about film production), but the biggest difference with Westerns is that it does so in order to articulate a discourse about Spanish national identity, cultural conflicts, and foundational myths (González "Foundational"). Similarly, in a French postcolonial context, screenwriter-director David Oelhoffen's *Far from Men* (2019) adapts Albert Camus's short novel *L'Hôte* and inserts it into a Western framework to tell the story of a French-Algerian schoolteacher (played by Viggo Mortensen) who has to escort a prisoner at the time of the Algerian war for independence; again, the references to the Western are both syntactic (the structure of the tale following the steps of the prisoner and his guard, the hero as "man in the middle" who needs to look at his own conscience) and semantic (the desert, the use of guns, the threat of war), but they are used to articulate a discourse about French imperialism and the French colonial presence in Algeria.

The studies quoted above have shown that most transnational post-Westerns share the following features: (1) clear references to the Western that invite the spectator into a space of dialogue and reflection with the assumptions and values of the genre in a contemporary situation and a new physical context; (2) the choice of a specific landscape and region in this new environment that are reminiscent in different ways of the US-American West; (3) the use of that landscape with a political intention, that is, to probe into the national identity, foundational myths, and contemporary sociocultural contradictions of the country where these films are set and produced; (4) the analysis of the difficulties of integration of racial, ethnic, or social minorities, the "contemporary Others," who are constructed as the equivalent of Native US-Americans in Westerns; (5) the exploration of the conflicts derived from the application of traditional models of masculinity (paradigmatic of the original genre) to contemporary national situations; and, finally (6) the study of the contrast between death and regeneration: the use of the conventions of a supposedly "dead" or "dying" genre (Agresta) to explore the regenerative possibilities of a particular landscape and context. The present chapter uses this paradigm to focus on two French films, *Adieu Gary* (Nassim Amaouche, 2009) and *Les Cowboys* (Thomas Bidegain, 2015), that also use the Western to analyze the problems and contradictions of the French republican model and the integration of the Muslim population in France.

ADIEU GARY (2009)

Adieu Gary is the first feature film directed by Nassim Amaouche, a filmmaker who belongs to the new generation of Maghrebi-French cinema that has been hailed by the critics as a "new 'New Wave' involved with the issue of migration" (Gaertner).[1] These new filmmakers—Amaouche, but also Abdellatif Kechiche (*The Secret of the Grain*, 2007), Rachid Bouchareb (*Days of Glory*, 2006; *Outside the Law*, 2010), and Rabah Ameur-Zaïmeche (*Wesh-Wesh, qu'est-ce qui se passe?* 2002; *Dernier Maquis*, 2008), to name a few—have offered "a new perspective about French society . . . a point of view so far ignored [about] the question of immigration and its consequences for the generations born in France" (Gaertner 15).[2] Of course, we cannot forget the role of other directors who had already dealt with issues of immigration like Karim Dridi, Rachida Krim, and Malik Chabane, or the contribution of filmmakers without an immigrant background (Yves Boisset, Jacques Doillon, Mathieu Kassovitz, Jean-François Richet, Phillippe Faucon), who nonetheless have been making very interesting films about the French suburbs and racism since the 1970s.

The Western references in *Adieu Gary* are explicit from the beginning, since the Gary of the title is, of course, Gary Cooper, and the film actually includes direct citations from two Westerns starring Cooper: *Man of the West* (Anthony Mann, 1958) and *Vera Cruz* (Robert Aldrich, 1954). Gary Cooper has been called the "quintessential American hero" (Meyers 116), but the roles he played changed, in fact, in the last stages of his career to include more complex protagonists. Thus, the characters he plays in these two films are more nuanced than, for example, the straightforward heroes of *The Virginian* (Victor Fleming, 1929) and *Sergeant York* (Howard Hawks, 1941). In *Vera Cruz*, Cooper plays a mercenary hired by Emperor Maximilian during the Mexican Revolution; in *Man of the West*, he plays a redeemed outlaw who must choose between his former partners in crime and a more respectable life in the company of his uncle and cousin, a plot line that, as we shall see, is the inspiration for *Adieu Gary*'s main story line. The Cooper persona as flawless male role model also plays an important part in a subplot with Oedipal connotations: José, the teenager who sees the clips just mentioned on television, seems to be affected by a mental block ever since his father (nicknamed after the US-American actor) left the family; as a consequence, he is continually shown watching Cooper's Westerns on television. Finally, the Western traces include the protagonist's arrival in town in a very unusual "train" (a car using obsolete train tracks) and a most peculiar setting; in place of the open landscapes of other transnational post-Westerns (like Anatolia, the Almería desert, or the Algerian desolate mountains in the films mentioned above), *Adieu Gary* shows us a cityscape that looks just like a Western ghost town, "a main street that," as Amaouche himself has pointed out, "you could swear came from a Western film set" (Goutte 121).[3] However, the location is not a film set but the surreal Cité Blanche du Teil, a company town (*cité ouvrière*) built in 1880 in the South of France to provide housing for the workers of a cement factory owned by the Lafarge Company, which has now been almost completely deserted.

Having established these Western references, *Adieu Gary* tells the story of a mixed-race family and the slightly eccentric surrounding community living in this *cité ouvrière*. The protagonist, Samir, has just left prison and, like Cooper's character in *Man of the West*, needs to decide if he will go back to his criminal life dealing drugs or look for an honest job following his brother's and father's example. His white father, Francis—an allegorical name with a *"connotation nationale"* (Goutte 117)—had lost his Moroccan-born wife some years before and has now lost his job, since the unnamed company has decided to close down the factory. However, out of personal and professional pride, he keeps going to work in order to repair the machine he was working on when he was laid off. Samir's brother, Icham, has a menial job at a supermarket and would like to reconnect his Moroccan roots, although he does not speak Arabic and has never set foot in Africa. Thus, the film shows Icham as an example of the complexities of integration, particularly for mixed-race individuals, and depicts the psychological displacement of these Arab-French teenagers when they play a video game where they need to identify with US-American soldiers whose mission is to kill Muslim terrorists. We can see, then, how, as in other transnational post-Westerns, *Adieu Gary* deals with the difficulties of integration of Muslims as "contemporary Others" equivalent to Native Americans, an analogy that is visually underlined by a poster of a Native American chief (possibly Sitting Bull) that Samir has in his room [11:56].

With this in mind, and although Fareed Ben-Youssef describes a very bleak racial present and future in *Adieu Gary* for "the French-Arab's vexed subject position in the ghost towns of post-9/11 France" (87), I agree with most French reviewers who point out that the racial picture presented in this film is fairly positive. Mauger, for instance, states: "Tolerance, understanding, fraternity, between French and immigrant workers, between men and women, between fathers and sons: in the working world that Nassim Amaouche describes, we can still find some essential ingredients of solidarity" (149).[4] In fact, although the film does not hide the problems of miscegenation, it also presents moments of idyllic republican integration. One scene in particular (filmed in a perfect circular sequence shot [19:42–22:10] to underline the harmony of the moment) shows people of French, Spanish, and Arab origin sharing Spanish food to the Arab-sounding music of the ever-present *oud* (Arab lute) played by the Palestinian Trio Joubran. The only act of rebellion enacted by this group of idle Maghrebi-French unemployed—by comparison with the extreme violence shown in banlieue films like *La Haine* (Mathieu Kassovitz, 1995) or the acts of terrorism shown in *Made in France* (Nicolas Boukhrief, 2015)—is the harmless, playful simulation of a Spanish bullfight pass in front of a French train [22:11–22:54].

In fact, like most contemporary Maghrebi-French filmmakers who "move beyond the migration framework to present a social rather than ethnic point of view" (Gaertner 19), Amaouche's focus seems to be more on social than racial or religious issues in order to deal with his country's national identity and contemporary social contradictions.[5] France's current constitution defines the nation as "an indivisible, secular, democratic, and *social* Republic" (my emphasis), and the construction of a social welfare state has been at the core of the French Republic since early revolutionary times. In fact, Francis still believes in the French dream of *"Liberté, Égalité, Fraternité,"* and his stubborn decision to keep going back to the factory is an example of his refusal to accept the end of this national foundational myth. However, as Amaouche has pointed out, *"Adieu Gary* speaks about the end of a certain age for the working class, and the beginning of another, about a transformation" ("Anecdotes").[6] The traditional French (and European) idea of welfare state or social capitalism (exemplified by a *cité ouvrière* with all sorts of social services for the working class, from health care to trade unions) seems to be disappearing under the pressure of a contemporary form of neoliberal capitalism. An example of this decline in workers' rights are Francis's partner's occupation as a guinea pig for pharmaceutical laboratories (testing the side effects of new drugs), and his sons' jobs at the supermarket where they are forced to wear a mouse hat as a visual symbol of their subjugation. It seems apparent that the French welfare state model embodied by Francis is in danger of disappearing under the dehumanizing pressure of neoliberal forces; Francis's proud and seemingly sterile response is to keep working at the factory that the owners have decided to close down.

It is in this respect that the choice of a Western-like setting seems particularly relevant, since, as in other post-Westerns, we are dealing with a posthumous place, a ghost town like Lassoo in *Man of the West.* In the 1958 film, the outlaw gang that the Gary Cooper character gets involved with are planning to rob a bank in this town, but, when they get there, they find that nobody lives in the town anymore. The only sentence heard in the clip José watches is "Tous tués!" (All of them killed!), a comment that the narration of *Adieu Gary* shows us before presenting the deserted cityscape of La Cité Blanche du Teil [16:45–16:55, 34:16–35:06].[7] Thus, the 2009 film's title can, on the one hand, be related to the Oedipal subplot mentioned above: Francis, disguised as Gary Cooper, rides into the sunset after an intervention designed to help José deal with his

Fig. 8.1 Francis, disguised as Gary Cooper, rides into the night in *Adieu Gary*.

psychological blockage; after this, José "kills the father," learns to accept the situation, and says goodbye to his surrogate father "Gary" [60:56–63:00]. The title seems to imply, then, that the model of masculinity represented by Gary Cooper and the Western is no longer valid. As Tony Soprano says in the first episode of *The Sopranos* (HBO, 1999–2007), "Whatever happened to Gary Cooper? The strong, silent type. That was an American. He wasn't in touch with his feelings. He just did what he had to do." José's mental blockage, like Tony's panic attacks, suggests that the "strong, silent" model of masculinity shown in Westerns is no longer relevant in contemporary societies; the problem is that men have a hard time looking for alternative models of masculinity in a more egalitarian society (fig. 8.1).

On the other hand, the title also seems to imply that the US-American solution to contemporary problems is defunct, as Anthony Palou summarizes: "Goodbye capitalism, goodbye American myth."[8] The French myth of republican solidarity is, likewise, shaking, as shown visually in two scenes. In the first, the town's main drug dealer (a handicapped person in a wheelchair) ironically displays a torn banner with the legend "Tous unis pour la victoire" (All united for victory), a symbol of the French Republic in times of war [53:11–53:24]. The second scene perfectly illustrates a comment made by Amaouche about the relationship between social and religious issues: "In some popular neighborhoods people are more sensitive to religion than to Karl Marx: this is an objective reality" ("Anecdotes").[9] The scene shows the establishment of a Mosque in the building where the Maison du Peuple (the house of the people, a traditional meeting place for trade unions and workers) used to stand [51:22–53:09], as a way of showing that, among the working class at least, the model of secular solidarity of the French welfare state is being replaced by a religious model. In fact, although Amaouche has publicly expressed his distrust of organized religion, the vision of Islam presented in this film is quite positive; Muslim women enjoy a high degree of freedom, sexual and otherwise, and the only "pioneer" who wants to settle back in this Western-looking ghost town is the young religious leader who wants to establish the mosque in order to provide religious and social services for the population.

Martin Goutte has pointed out how the film uses a "miscegenation" (*métissage*) of genres (the Western and French poetic realism of the 1930s) to reflect the film's focus on ethnic miscegenation, and this hybridization (which is, in fact, a common feature of many post-Westerns) helps convey a nostalgic, melancholy tone. As Michel Euvrard has noted, the characters seem to be "hung in a sort of void between two utopias," the utopia of the lost past and a utopia of future hope. Meanwhile, they do not realize that "la Cité Blanche that hosts them ... could be the framework for a contemporary utopia" (263).[10] This "contemporary utopia" is shown in the semihappy, poetic ending provided by the film. Francis (with Samir's help) manages to repair the machine he had been working on, and workers of different ethnic groups smile at the combination of the sound of the factory and the church bells, while Muslims start going to the mosque, which has inherited the social features of the Maison du Peuple [66:02–69:29]. This combination of image and sound helps create a moment of "regeneration *without* violence"—the exact opposite of the imperialist ideology analyzed by Richard Slotkin (1973)—and of temporary collective cohesion that invites us to look forward to a more hopeful future for the French ideal: "The transformation of this building in mosque expresses both a certain sadness and a possible comfort in front of affirming change, mutations, energy and life" ("Anecdotes").[11] Although it does not deny the deep tensions in French society, *Adieu Gary*, notably through its reference to the Western, seems to be presenting a utopian possibility of mixed-race social harmony in this strange microcosm of French society.

LES COWBOYS (2015)

In contrast with *Adieu Gary*, *Les Cowboys* (2015) focuses on the risks of applying the values associated with the Western to a context of Islamic radicalization and terrorism in Europe. It is the first film directed by Thomas Bidegain,

Fig. 8.2 The protagonists of *Les Cowboys* in a door-framed shot reminiscent of *The Searchers*.

a scriptwriter known for his collaborations with director Jacques Audiard on films like *Un prophète* (2009) and *Dheepan* (2015), which also deal with the integration of minorities in France. Both Audiard and Bidegain are well known for sharing an "attraction for Hollywood cinema genres and for narratives that foreground violent masculinity" (Vanderschelden 253), so it seems coherent for Bidegain's first directing venture to bring the Western home and adapt the plot of *The Searchers* (1956) to contemporary France. Ford's 1956 film may, in fact, be one of the most influential Westerns of all times, particularly if we think about the 1970s, when it was called the "Super-Cult Movie of the New Hollywood," the film that "all recent American cinema derives from" (Byron 45). Bidegain has mentioned two 1970s movies in particular that are based on *The Searchers*— Martin Scorsese's *Taxi Driver* (1976) and Paul Schrader's *Hardcore* (1979)—as influences for this story of a father looking for his daughter, whom he believes was kidnapped by her Muslim boyfriend in 1994; in his quest, the father, like Ethan Edwards, displays his blatant racism and hatred for the "dark [Muslim] Others" that end up including the girl herself. As Jonathan Romney has pointed out, *Les Cowboys* includes other overt references to *The Searchers*, like the daughter's red bandana ("a nod to the identifying medal that Ethan gives young Debbie") and an image of the protagonists framed by a door looking out at a gray sea ("a melancholy Europeanization of Ford's iconic door-framed shots of the endless American outdoors") (fig. 8.2).

As in other transnational post-Westerns, the syntactic and semantic references to Westerns are obvious, not only in the title, the narrative structure, and the allusions to *The Searchers*, but also in the rather disconcerting first sequences: the characters are all dressed as cowboys, and the people play,

sing, and dance to country music, but they all speak in French [00:52–01:56].
It is a "disorienting and metaphoric" sequence, "a microcosm of one culture
mushrooming in the heart of another" (Catsoulis). In fact, we are in a country-
and-Western fair in rural France, a good example of the fascination that the
US-American West still holds for people all over the world, including the
French. The film then shows us the father's search and his descent into a spiral
of fear, hatred, and death, but also the contrast with his son, who, after the father's death, takes over the quest in his own terms and develops a much more
understanding attitude toward both Islam and his own sister—in fact, the last
section of the film shows his marriage to a Muslim girl and his respect for his
sister's decision to join Islam.

Of course, most critics have easily identified the Western references, but
they have also noticed the hybridity and generic indeterminacy typical of post-
Westerns, as Nicolas Gendron has pointed out: "The very nature of the Western runs through Les Cowboys, but without anchoring it completely within the
genre" (47).[12] This hybridity is most evident in the first part of the film, where
we can see a mixture of Western and noir conventions that Jean Baulieu has
related to Audiard and the Dardenne brothers, who coproduced the film (21).
The critics have also highlighted Bidegain's excellent use of the ellipsis not
only to tell a complex two-decade-long family story, but also to focus on the
contemporary sociopolitical background, that is, the situation of Muslim immigrants in France and the development of Islamic terrorism both in France
and around the world. In fact, unlike other transnational post-Westerns, Les
Cowboys does not use an easily identifiable region of France as the location
for the story (the beginning is supposed to take place in L'Ain region, but this
is not referenced prominently), but expands it to an international setting, as
we follow the characters from the dark back rooms of poverty and Muslim
immigration in France or Belgium to the Muslim heartland in Syria, Yemen,
and Afghanistan. In Afghanistan in particular, the horse-riding scenes in open
landscapes reinforce the references to Westerns and the analogy between
Muslims and Native Americans, as does the presence of a shady US-American
agent (played by John C. Reilly) who is shown smoking with Afghan chiefs,
just as their Western genre counterparts would have passed along the calumet
[62:10–63:04]. Les Cowboys eventually returns to France, which remains the
main focus of the story. Bidegain himself has stressed the power of the Westerns as a sociocultural framework to assess the "state of the nation": "There
is this idea that every Western shows the state of the nation. So when you
watch a Western, you get to know the world of the farmers, or the world of the

Indians, or the moment of democracy. Every time, it's a state of the nation. All the good Westerns do this. And so I had this idea of showing a certain state of the nation and using this model to talk about us and relate how the situation has progressed" (Talu).

Accordingly, Bidegain shows us the state of the French nation regarding a specific issue: the failed integration and subsequent radicalization of Muslim immigrants, a problem that has been related to French "national identity" (Lichfield), France's "identity crisis" (Gobry), and French exceptionalism.

As Farhad Khosrokhavar has highlighted, "When it comes to Jihad, there is a French exception" in the way that France deals with its immigrant population. The French "model of integration" has often been contrasted to "an Anglo-American 'multicultural' model that celebrates community identities and ethnic difference" (Chabal 90) and is closely tied to France's colonial past and its postcolonial present. According to Weil and Crowley, the French model of integration has its roots in the ancien régime, and it was modified during the Enlightenment and the Revolution, and later implemented by the Third Republic (1870–1940) "through strict separation between individual culture and religion (confined to the private sphere) and the secular state which inculcated in both French and foreign children, via the schools, a common civic culture" (112). This model is intimately tied to the concept of "republican universalism" (Stovall 259), which argues that all citizens of the Republic should be treated as individuals only, without regard to differences based on race, religion, or gender. Republican universalism has its origins in the French Revolution, which "in addition to providing republicanism with a founding myth . . . was the crucible of republican 'values'" (Chabal 12). These values, encapsulated in the French national motto (*Liberté, Égalité, Fraternité*), can also be summarized thus: universal suffrage, a commitment to Enlightenment rationality, secularism, an interest in social conditions, and a civic conception of patriotism (Chabal 12). Secularism (*laïcité*) has become particularly relevant for the model of integration we are dealing with here, since it is tied to the French view of the republican school and has been defined as "the 'cornerstone of the republican pact,' a 'universal principle,' and a 'republican value' that is 'constitutive of [French] collective history'" (Chabal 27). In fact, it is included in the definition of the nation in the current 1958 constitution: "France is an indivisible, secular, democratic, and social Republic . . . without distinction of origin, race, or religion" (Silverstein 11).

However, events like the 2005 riots, the "veil wars" of the past two decades, or the more recent terrorist attacks by Islamist radicals have made different commentators insist on the "failures of the republican model of social integration," since there seems to be a contradiction between the model's theoretical emphasis on equality and the discrimination suffered by ethnic or religious minorities (Stovall 259–60). This contradiction has also been linked to France's colonial history and to the paradoxes of the Third Republic, which managed to blend republican democratic ideology with the creation of a large empire where the colonized were subjugated and left without rights. Since immigration, as Albert Memmi put it, "is the punishment for the colonial sin" (qtd. in Silverstein 16), "the post-colonial predicament [has now] become an integral part of French society"; institutionalized racism blocks access to housing and the labor market, while spatial segregation has turned many French banlieues into areas where unemployment, violence, and social exclusion are the norm (Chabal 80), a situation that has been linked to the radicalization of young Muslims in France in recent French films like *Made in France* and *Disintegration* (Philippe Faucon, 2011).

Bidegain tackles these complex issues by showing the father's prejudices in the first part of the film: he cannot accept his daughter's conversion and "betrayal." The fact that we find out about the girl's disappearance in the "disorienting" first sequence of the film is also metaphorical: the father and all his friends in the country festival identify with US-American values and culture—and not with just any set of US-American values but, more specifically, with the racist discourse transmitted in the classical Hollywood Westerns, where Native Americans were often presented as savages and their views erased. As the son takes over the quest, we see the development of worldwide Islamic terrorism through visual/aural references to the terrorist attacks of New York (2001), Madrid (2004), and London (2005), and we learn that the daughter's former husband Ahmed may have been involved with terrorist groups. Even though the son keeps on looking for his sister, after he experiences firsthand the discourse of Western-like violence in Afghanistan (he shoots Ahmed in self-defense), he learns to accept Islam, ends up marrying a Muslim woman (Ahmed's second wife), and accepts his sister's decision to live within Islam in Belgium. As Bidegain has explained, the son's evolution is also explained indirectly through references to Western conventions, since, rather than teach his own son to shoot a gun, he teaches him to make a bow [90:05–90:57]. "The cowboy/Indian metaphor we're spinning really concerns the father because he sees the world that way—what we used to call the war of civilizations. . . . On the other hand, the son won't see civilizations, he'll see people. . . . So when he's with his own son, he shows him how to make a bow, how to become an Indian, too. He opens up to the world. . . .

At least, the second generation becomes wiser and opens up to the world" (Talu).

Finally, the association between the French assimilationist discourse and the racist message of some US-American Westerns is also made explicit visually in the last section of the film; when he returns to the yearly country music festival, his Muslim fiancée shows her horse-riding abilities, but she is rejected by the Western-loving community because she is wearing a hijab. The scarf, torn off by a French woman wearing a cowboy hat, frames her as both Muslim and Native American [84:40–85:27].

We can see, then, how, as in other transnational post-Westerns, *Les Cowboys* talks about national identity and cultural conflicts using Western-based metaphors, but it also deals with the contradictions of following a traditional mode of masculinity, as shown in the contrasts between fathers and sons. Critics like Gendron and Baulieu have pointed out that the film still lacks the voice of women and Muslims—"The vision is clearly white, Western, and male" (Baulieu 21)—and that we still have to wait for other films that show us the converted girls' points of view.[13] Meanwhile, it seems clear that, in this film, if there is any possibility of regeneration without violence and of a different kind of masculinity, it lies in "becoming an Indian, too," in understanding and accepting the "dark Other's" perspective and embracing a more multicultural model of integration that accepts difference and does not attempt to push minorities into forced assimilation.

CONCLUSION

In *Adieu Gary* and *Les Cowboys*, we can appreciate the contemporary local power of the global Western myth because these films clearly demonstrate that the Western is still a "malleable parable for contemporary political realities" (Bloom 214), even when this parable is told in a transnational context. By making overt references to the Western genre—in the titles of both movies, but also in the deserted cityscape of La Cité Blanche du Teil of *Adieu Gary* and the country-and-Western fair of *Les Cowboys*—and by adapting the plot structure of classical Westerns like *Man of the West* and *The Searchers* to a contemporary French environment, these transnational post-Westerns show that the cowboy-Indian metaphor is still a valid trope for dealing with contemporary problems like the deterioration of the social republic and the integration of Muslim minorities in France.

The republican model based on a social welfare state and racial integration (the "*secular*, democratic, and *social* Republic" heir to the foundational myth of the French Revolution) is shown to be shaking under the attacks of contemporary neoliberalism (which results in unemployment and loss of dignity at the workplace), fundamentalism, and disintegration. Both films show the difficulties inherent in the French model of integration and propose multicultural solutions that respect the rights of the "dark Others" equivalent to Native Americans in the Western genre (Muslim immigrants of North African origin in *Adieu Gary*, Muslim converts in *Les Cowboys*) to show their difference and look for their own personal ways of integration. Both films also propose solutions based on the acceptance of diversity, miscegenation, and hybridization, like the combination of the images of the mosque and the sound of the church bells at the ending of *Adieu Gary*, the son's acceptance of his sister's new life as a convert at the end of *Les Cowboys*, or the mixed-origin couples that we can see in both films (the father in *Adieu Gary*, the son in *Les Cowboys*).

Like other transnational post-Westerns, the two films also deal with the difficulties of adapting the traditional model of masculinity shown in many Westerns to contemporary realities. This is very clearly shown in *Adieu Gary*, where the title itself and the Oedipal subplot show that new realities need new heroes capable of showing their feelings and connecting to their surroundings, but also in *Les Cowboys*, where the new generation is able to overcome the "war of civilizations" by opening up to the world and "becoming an Indian, too." Finally, like other transnational post-Westerns, both films use the conventions of a "posthumous" genre that refuses to die in order to explore the regenerative possibilities of a new social contract that combines a social perspective with tolerance and respect for religious differences.

NOTES

1. Original quote: "Nouvelle 'Nouvelle Vague' attachée à la question migratoire." This and the rest of the translations from French are my own.

2. Original quote: "Un regard neuf sur la société française . . . un angle de prise de vue jusque-là ignoré [sur] la question migratoire et ses conséquences pour les générations nées en France."

3. Original quote: "Sa rue principale qu'on jurerait sortie d'un décor de western."

4. Original quote: "Tolérance, compréhension, fraternité, entre ouvriers français et immigrés, entre hommes et femmes, entre pères et fils: dans le monde ouvrier que décrit Nassim Amaouche, il reste encore quelques ingrédients essentiels de la solidarité."

5. Original quote: "Dépassent le cadre migratoire pour poser un regard non plus ethnique mais social."

6. Original quote: "Parle de la fin d'une certaine époque ouvrière et du début d'une autre, d'une transformation."

7. Campbell relates the prefix post in post-Western to the idea of posthumous, since the films refer to a film genre that lives on beyond its apparent death, and uses the words "ghost Western" for films dealing with the haunting presence of the myth of the West: "The post-Western is an attempt 'to learn to live with ghosts,' so that with greater thought, sense, and understanding, we might also begin 'to live otherwise and better . . . more justly'" (96).

8. Original quote: "Adieu capitalisme, adieu le mythe américain."

9. Original quote: "Que dans certains quartiers populaires on soit plus sensible à la religion qu'à Karl Marx est une réalité objective."

10. Original quote: "Les personnages sont suspendus dans une sorte de vide entre deux utopies," "la Cité blanche qui les héberge . . . pourrait être le cadre d'une utopie d'aujourd'hui."

11. Original quote: "La transformation de ce local en mosquée exprime à la fois une certaine tristesse . . . et un réconfort possible face à un changement, des mutations, de l'énergie, de la vie qui s'affirment."

12. Original quote: "La nature même du film western traverse *Les Cowboys* sans pour autant l'ancrer complètement dans le genre."

13. Original quote: "La vision est nettement blanche, masculine, occidentale."

WORKS CITED

Adieu Gary. Directed by Nassim Amaouche, performances by Jean-Pierre Bacri, Dominique Reymond and Yasmine Belmadi. Les Films A4, Rhône-Alpes Cinéma, Studio Canal, 2009.

Agresta, Michael. "How the Western Was Lost (and Why It Matters)." *The Atlantic*, 24 July 2013, www.theatlantic.com/entertainment/archive/2013/07/how-the -western-was-lost-and-why-it-matters/278057. Accessed 28 Aug. 2021.

Altman, Rick. *Film/Genre*. British Film Institute, 1999.

"Anecdotes du film 'Adieu Gary.'" Allociné, www.allocine.fr/film /fichefilm-138072/secrets-tournage. Accessed 27 Jan. 2018.

Baulieu, Jean. "Les Cowboys : La Poursuite Infernale." *Séquences: La revue de cinéma*, vol. 304, Sept.–Oct. 2016, pp. 20–21.

Ben-Youssef, Fareed. "Disrupted Genre, Disrupted Lives: Adieu Gary and the Post-9/11 Banlieu as Ghost Town." *Studia Filmoznawcze*, vol. 38, 2017, pp. 75–89.

Bloom, Peter J. "Reappropriation of the 'Good Badman' in France, the French Colonies, and Contemporary Algeria." *Westerns: Films through History*, edited by Janet Walker, Routledge, 2001, pp. 197–216.

Byron, Stuart. "The Searchers: Cult Movie of the New Hollywood." *New York Magazine*, 5 Mar. 1979, pp. 45–48.

Campbell, Neil. *Post-Westerns: Cinema, Region, West*. University of Nebraska Press, 2013.

Carter, Matthew. *Myth of the Western: New Perspectives on Hollywood's Frontier Narrative*. Edinburgh University Press, 2015.

Catsoulis, Jeanette. "Review: In 'Les Cowboys,' a Girl Vanishes, and Her Father Can't Bear It." *New York Times*, 23 June 2016, www.nytimes.com/2016/06/24 /movies/les-cowboys-review.html. Accessed 28 Aug. 2021.

Chabal, Emile. *A Divided Republic: Nation, State and Citizenship in Contemporary France*. Cambridge University Press, 2015

Les Cowboys. Directed by Thomas Bidegain, performances by François Damiens, Finnegan Oldfield and Agathe Dronne. Les Productions du Trésor, La Fabrique Films, Lunanime, 2015.

Euvrard, Michel. "Adieu Gary : Vérités et utopies." *Séquences : La revue de cinéma*, vol. 263, Nov.–Dec. 2009, p. 32.

Gaertner, Julien. "Une nouvelle 'Nouvelle Vague' ? Comment l'immigration maghrébine régénère le cinéma français (1970–2012)." *Hommes et migrations: Revue française de référence sur les dynamiques migratoires*, vol. 1297, 2012, pp. 6–19.

Gendron, Nicolas. "Père Courage et le Kid." *Ciné-Bulles*, vol. 34, no. 4, Fall 2016, p. 47.

Gobry, Pascal-Emmanuel. "France Is Having an Identity Crisis." *The Week*, 23 Sept. 2016, theweek.com/articles/650116/france-having-identity-crisis. Accessed 28 Aug. 2021.

González, Jesús Ángel. "Foundational Myths and National Identity in European Transnational Post-Westerns." *Western American Literature*, vol. 54, no. 3, 2019, pp. 257–94.

———. "A Genre Auteur? Enrique Urbizu's Post-Western Films." *Hispanic Research Journal*, vol. 18, no. 1, 2017, pp. 60–73.

———. "Transnational Post-Westerns in Irish Cinema." *Journal of Transnational American Studies*, vol. 7, no. 1, 2016, pp. 1–26.

Goutte, Martin. "Adieu Gary : Du métissage et des moyens d'en rendre compte." *In Praise of Cinematic Bastardy*, edited by Sebastian Lefait and Philippe Ortoli, Cambridge Scholars, 2012, pp. 116–26.

Khosrokhavar, Farhad. "Jihad and the French Exception." *New York Times*, 19 July 2016, www.nytimes.com/2016/07/20/opinion/jihad-and-the-french-exception .html. Accessed 28 Aug. 2021.

Lichfield, John. "France's Crisis of National Identity." *The Independent*, 25 Nov. 2009, www.independent.co.uk/news/world/europe/frances-crisis-of-national -identity-1826942.html. Accessed 28 Aug. 2021.

Mauger, Gérard. "Après 'la classe ouvrière' : À propos de Adieu Gary, un film de Nassim Amaouche, 2009." *Savoir/Agir*, vol. 4, no. 10, 2009, pp. 147–49.

Meyers, Jeffrey. *Gary Cooper: American Hero*. William Morrow, 1998.

Mitchell, Lee Clark. *Late Westerns: The Persistence of a Genre*. University of Nebraska Press, 2018.

Nelson, Andrew Patrick. *Contemporary Westerns: Film and Television since 1990*. Scarecrow, 2013.

Palou, Anthony. "Cow-boys et indiens dans un coin d'Ardèche." *Le Figaro*, 7 July 2009, www.lefigaro.fr/cinema/2009/07/21/03002-20090721ARTFIG00435-cow -boys-et-indiens-dans-un-coin-d-ardeche-.php. Accessed 28 Aug. 2021.

Romney, Jonathan. "Film of the Week: Les Cowboys." *Film Comment*, 24 June 2016, www.filmcomment.com/blog/film-week-les-cowboys. Accessed 28 Aug. 2021.

Silverstein, Paul. *Postcolonial France: Race, Islam, and the Future of the Republic*. Pluto, 2018.

Slotkin, Richard. *Regeneration through Violence: The Mythology of the American Frontier*. University of Oklahoma Press, 1973.

Stovall, Tyler. "Diversity and Difference in Post-colonial France." *Postcolonial Thought in the French-speaking World*, edited by Charles Forsdick and David Murphy, Liverpool University Press, 2013, pp 259–70.

Talu, Yonca. "Interview: Thomas Bidegain and Finnegan Oldfield." *Film Comment*, 24 June 2016, www.filmcomment.com/blog/interview-les-cowboys-thomas -bidegain-finnegan-oldfield. Accessed 28 Aug. 2021.

Vanderschelden, Isabelle. "Screenwriting the Euro-noir Thriller: The Subtext of Jacques Audiard's Artistic Signature." *Studies in French Cinema*, vol. 16, no. 3, 2016, pp. 248–61.

Weil, Patrick, and John Crowley. "Integration in Theory and Practice: A Comparison of France and Britain." *The Politics of Immigration in Western Europe*, edited by Martin Baldwin-Edwards and A. Martin Schain, Routledge, 1994, pp. 110–26.

JESÚS ÁNGEL González is Professor of English at the University of Cantabria. He is author of *La narrativa popular de Dashiell Hammett: 'Pulps,' cine y comics* and editor with Stefania Ciocia of *The Invention of Illusions: International Perspectives on Paul Auster*.

NINE

—〰—

SILENT WESTERNS MADE IN ITALY

The Dawn of a Transnational Genre between US
Imperial Narratives and Nationalistic Appropriations

ALESSANDRA MAGRIN HAAS

WHEN DISCUSSING WESTERNS IN ITALY, scholarly attention has, thus far, been squarely centered on the Spaghetti Western.[1] And yet as silent era histor- ian Riccardo Redi reminds us, "Italian Westerns were not an invention of the 1950s" (*Cinema* 155). The shortage of studies on the early days of this genre begs for further consideration. A survey of cinema catalogs indicates that Italian interest in the Western setting blossomed in the silent era, when foreign films using the US-American West as a backdrop (both European and US-American productions) featured frequently in cinema halls all over the country. As Redi compiled in *Film stranieri sugli schermi italiani*, in 1911 alone, at least twenty-six foreign movies that employed a Western setting were screened everywhere in Italy. As the trend began to develop, at least four Italian Western-themed pic- tures were produced that same year. Italian cinema production in the silent era was, generally, highly sensitive to foreign influences, as Redi has highlighted (*Cinema* 73). Yet it is also evident that, once those foreign trends were recog- nized and understood, Italian directors and production companies were able to appropriate and repurpose them in their own culturally specific ways.

In opposition to the holistic approach that Nanna Verhoeff adopted in her influential study on silent era US-American Westerns, this paper examines the national features of early Italian Westerns to underscore their idiosyncrasies and place boundaries on their non-Americanness. Considering early Western pictures in a culturally specific framework does not necessarily reduce them to a collection of "essentializing features," to use Verhoeff's expression (165). It is, instead, useful to the detection of an imperialist and, at the same time, jingois- tic narrative, which, through the use of Western scenes, imagery, and settings, reached a wide range of audiences in an epoch of aggressive colonial expansion and cultural anxieties. Furthermore, recent scholarship has emphasized how, in the early days of the genre, the Western in Italy amounted to a mere receptacle of foreign-looking allusions devoid of accurate historical characterization.[2] This chapter departs from this view to look specifically at how early Italian Western-themed films employed the Western framework and exotic references to subtly promote Italian colonialism. By employing Western settings and elements, the films analyzed herein reflect the conflict between the Italian government's imperialist aims in Africa during the Libyan campaign and the flow of mass migration to the US. Emigration to America was supported by some government officials as the natural outlet to Italy's overpopulation, yet it was seen by others as a hindrance to Italy's official colonial plans.

The relation between Buffalo Bill's Wild West and Italy was a key element to the popularization of Western-themed films and other popular cultural products. Buffalo Bill (William F. Cody's stage name) visited Italy twice with his show and established a strong bond with Italian audiences. He introduced Western settings and aesthetics on a mass scale, rendering them accessible to, and ultimately fashionable for, Italians for the first time.

Motion pictures used melodrama as a vehicle to render the Western framework more attuned to Italian audiences. Romance and family sagas in the West symbolize a different type of colonialism, a specifically Italian one based on family and community values and opposed to the Anglo-Saxon individualist settler-colonial model. These Western-themed motion pictures, which use the West to promote nationally specific goals, are ample proof of the early transnational dimension of the fledgling genre.

A FATEFUL MEETING BETWEEN PIONEERING ENTREPRENEURS: BUFFALO BILL, FILOTEO ALBERINI, AND THE GENESIS OF ITALIAN SILENT WESTERNS

The birth of Italian Western-themed films appeared to be driven by the imprints and scripts that Buffalo Bill's Wild West show left behind.[3] The liaison between cinema industry and Buffalo Bill began in a very straightforward way. The pioneer of Western entertainment was approached by the Italian pioneer of motion picture technology: Filoteo Alberini, founder of the Cines film studio and a forefather of the Italian cinema industry (Brunetta 6).[4] Alberini was only able to meet Buffalo Bill in 1906, several years after Thomas Edison and the Lumière brothers had this privilege. At this time, Alberini was pursuing cinematography full-time, expanding his business countrywide (Lombardi 82–106).[5]

In March 1906, when Buffalo Bill arrived in Rome for the second time, hoping to repeat the tremendous success his Wild West show had achieved there sixteen years earlier, Alberini was impatiently waiting for him. Through his Masonic affiliations, Alberini struck a deal with Buffalo Bill, who was also a Mason: an agreement of 25,000 liras to be paid by Alberini's motion picture business to Cody's company "in order to secure exclusive [access] and the property rights for the shoots" (Bernardini 64). During the weeklong Roman stay of the Wild West show, Alberini filmed the show's performance in its entirety. The footage was screened immediately in Alberini's Cinematografo Moderno and a couple of days later at the other Roman theater he managed, the Cinematografo Lumière, also known as Gran Salone Lumière (Anon., 1906). The two motion pictures, initially entitled *L'Arrivo di Buffalo Bill a Roma* (*The Arrival of Buffalo Bill in Rome*) and *Rappresentazione completa della troupe di Buffalo Bill* (*The Complete Performance of Buffalo Bill's Troupe*), were subsequently joined together and released in several parts of Italy with the title *Buffalo Bill's Wild West* (Bernardini 65).[6]

While US-American footage of Buffalo Bill's Wild West Show has been preserved, restored, and is now widely available through the Library of Congress, this was, unfortunately, not the case with Alberini's.[7] Nevertheless, the films of Alberini undoubtedly amplified the impact that Buffalo Bill's show exerted on the Italian national cultural debate. Indeed, the imperial metanarrative behind Buffalo Bill's show had tantalized the colonial fantasies and ambitions of early twentieth-century Italy—at the time engaged in negotiations at the Algeciras conference, with high hopes of expansion into Libya (Magrin 34). Although devoid of an exact cultural counterpart, the images of white supremacy that *Buffalo Bill's Wild West* showcased found an echo in Italian nationalist rhetoric, which had remained smoldering with frustration for years and would resurface in the nation-building debate in the advent of the Italo-Turkish War.[8]

Parallel to the nation-building discourse in the first decade of the 1900s, and reinforced by intermedial exchanges, Western topics permeated serial popular literature, theatrical production, and film. Fostering the fascination for the Western were the Buffalo Bill dime novels published by Milan's Casa Editrice Americana as well as the adventure novels written by Verona author Emilio Salgari, which often featured Buffalo Bill among the main characters. Giacomo Puccini's 1910 play *La fanciulla del West* (*The Girl of the Golden West*) stirred further interest in the Western by providing the proof that this genre could adapt well to contexts other than the widely decried *lowbrow*.[9] At the same time, the Italian film industry underwent swift yet profound changes in the years following the passage of Buffalo Bill's show. While the appearance on the market of numerous independent film studios provided rife domestic competition, the arrival of feature films revolutionized the methods of production and distribution (Redi, *Cinema* 69).

Alberini was the first to immortalize "Western Scenes" on Italian silver screens, but Cines (which he had founded in 1906 and whose direction he would leave in 1908) did not produce the first Italian-Western feature film. Instead, Turin's Itala Film held this primacy with the picture *La voce del Sangue* (1910), which was distributed in the US that same year as *The Voice of the Blood* (*Moving Picture World*). 1910 marked a turning point in the history of the distribution of Western-themed motion pictures in Italy, as foreign productions began to appear consistently on the Italian market; material arrived from Pathé, American Kinema, Vitagraph, Bison, and Éclair (Redi *Film*).[10] Prior to that, Western-themed films had not been circulated much and consisted mainly of French productions. Records show that, in 1907, Pathé distributed its *Cowboys et peaux-rouges* (also known as *Les Apaches du Far West*), which was released in Italian with two different titles: *Indiani e Cowboy* and *I predatori del Far West* (Redi, *Film*). In 1909, Éclair distributed Victorin Jasset's *Riffle Bill, le roy de la prairie* (Italian title *Riffle Bill, re della prateria*), and Gaumont distributed the slapstick Western *Calino veut être cowboy*, in Italian *Calino vuole diventare cowboy* (Redi, *Film*). Unfortunately, the films above are all that remain in the archival records about pre-1910 Western-themed motion pictures. It could be argued that the influence of international Westerns galvanized Italian national interest in the crucial years before World War I.

As a first example of an Italian Western feature film, *La voce del sangue*'s story line suggests it only partly differed from US-American productions.[11] The film dramatized a typical conflict between savagery and civilization, in the style of Mary Rowlandson's "captivity narrative."[12] The setting is divided between a farm in an unknown prairie and an Indian settlement; the bucolic family life in the prairie is disrupted by the arrival of Indian pillagers who raid the farm, try to kill its owners, and eventually seize their infant son. Twenty years later, the aging father of the little boy is also taken captive by the same Indian tribe. In the Indian encampment, he recognizes his son, now an adult, and meets his grandson. Together they decide to abandon savagery "to snatch the child from that life of robbery and killing," as the promo boasted (Bernardini and Martinelli, 1910 444). The white settlers are represented as the victims of indigenous ferocity, yet the Indians are not punished with slaughter or removal; civilization is simply chosen as the righteous way of life.

The plot was underlain by a moral message that resonated with sanctimonious ideas linking ethical values with the white man's civilization. Certainly, it struck familiar chords with Italian audiences raised in a culture that glorified "Christian missions." These were celebrated in many aspects of social life such as, for instance, human exhibitions, which were an alternate pastime to cinema for early twentieth-century Italians.[13] Nevertheless, the film appeared perfectly suitable and satisfying for foreign spectators as well, albeit with some reservations. *The New York Dramatic Mirror* lamented that "the story didn't admit of much finesse. The picture of wholesale slaughter in the courtyard is effective but did horse-owners in those days dock the tails of their steeds?" (Bernardini and Martinelli, 1910 444). On the other hand, the *Moving Picture World* declared the film "a real novelty in the line of dramatic productions" (Itala release), "A dramatic picture, affording opportunity for this capable company of actors to present a picture of power. It holds the attention from beginning to end, and whether one agrees with it or not one must admit that the story is well worked out and convincing as shown" (Bernardini and Martinelli, 1910 445). Thus, while a US-American audience was chiefly concerned with historical accuracy, in Italy *La voce del sangue* mainly evoked the struggle to uphold Christian morals.

MELODRAMA IN THE FAR WEST: COLONIAL AMBITIONS AND NATION-BUILDING NARRATIVES

After the release of *La voce del sangue*, other Italian film studios started producing their own Western films. In 1911, Ambrosio released *La Cintura d'oro*, set in California during the gold rush. A gold digger is robbed and held captive by the treacherous owners of an inn, and, after a series of feats, he is finally rescued by his wife. Itala film released the slapstick *Il re dei lanciatori di laccio* starring Cretinetti (played by André Deed) who, along the lines of *Calino veut être cowboy*, attempted to perform cowboy tricks without much success.[14] Cines also realized that it was worth capitalizing on this newly available genre and released *Rivalitá e coraggio*. The film told the story of Antonio, an Italian émigré settled in the Far West, and his struggle to defend his ranch against jealous Anglo-Saxon cowboys (Bernardini and Martinelli, 1911 121). Both la *Cintura d'oro* and *Rivalitá e coraggio* displayed distinctive features that resonated with ideas and situations familiar to twentieth-century Italians. The gold rush setting, for example, was dear to Italians—more so than the wild environments of Wyoming or Colorado—because it evoked one of the most prosperous areas of Italian "indirect colonialism" through migration: California (Choate 65).[15] Furthermore, both films are the antithesis of the celebration of rugged individualism, centered as they are on the importance of a kinship network and widespread

Fig. 9.1 Pinocchio in the Far West and the "Canadian Soldiers" attacking the Indians and wearing the Italian Colonial Uniform, from Giulio Antamoro's *Pinocchio* (1911). (Courtesy of Fondazione Cineteca Italiana, Milano.)

family bonds to overcome adversity—the extended family being one of the pillars of Italian society.

It is evident how, from this moment on, Western-themed pictures proved congenial to Italian directors, who adopted the imagery and appropriated the imperialist narrative to address issues of national identity as well as colonial concerns and aspirations. In 1911, such concerns were to be found not only in canonical Western-themed films but in the most unexpected subjects, such as the quintessential Italian folktale *Pinocchio*. In the first film adaptation of *Pinocchio*, director Giulio Antamoro added an extra scene set in the Far West where the wooden puppet and his father Geppetto are kidnapped and almost cannibalized by a group of Indians (Mazzei). After many twists and turns, the pair is ultimately saved by a troop of soldiers. The scene is set on the border with Canada, and all the Indians are wearing Lakota-style full-feathered regalia, a deliberate reference to Buffalo Bill's Wild West's legacy to the Italian collective imaginary. Worthy of note is that the so-called "Canadian" soldiers that rescue Pinocchio from the Indian attack are wearing not the classic red "Mounties" outfit, but the colonial uniform of the Italian army in Libya, whose invasion had begun earlier in 1911 (De Berti 166; Argiolas 101) (fig. 9.1). Within this atypical Western scene lies, therefore, an understated yet clear message of colonialist propaganda addressed to the nation's youths: the colonial troops are "heroes" who can defeat "Indigenous savages"—with the North American Indians as "alter egos" of the North Africans—and save Pinocchio, a prototype of an Italian in the making, from barbarity. The peculiar ending of this scene proves how, even in a children's film, Italians managed to tweak Western concepts and aesthetics and weave them into their own nation-building narrative.[16]

Between the beginning of the Italo-Turkish War and the years leading up to World War I, this type of colonial suggestion featured frequently in Italian cinema, in all sorts of subjects and not just in the obvious propaganda films or documentary material. As both Denis Lotti and Giorgio Bertellini noted in their respective compelling studies, films with a historical setting, such as *Schiavo di Cartagine* (1910), and dramatizations of epic and classic literary tales, like *Didone Abbandonata* (1910), *Il Cid* (1910), and *Salambó* (1911) concealed messages that alluded to the impending Libyan campaign (Lotti 15; Bertellini 140). A taste for the exotic had been present for decades in Italian *highbrow* culture, while national cultural debate in those years actively fostered the interest in North Africa, represented as a land of opportunity (Schiavulli). In popular culture, *Orientalism* reverberated in multiple mediums: the novels of Emilio Salgari, the short stories of Luigi Motta, or the illustrations of Buffalo Bill's pulp fictions by Nerbini—in which animals of the Sahara sometimes featured in the Mojave Desert.[17] It is, therefore, no wonder that exotic and distinctly African elements appeared in a number of Italian Western-themed films of the 1910s, such as in Pasquali's *Il Supplizio dei Leoni* (1914).[18] Cines's 1912 release *Due vite per un cuore* (*A Sister's Ordeal*) also featured a scene with lions in a cave and exhibited pelts of African animals in the interior setting of the ranch—as did *Sulla via dell'oro* (*The Human Bridge*) in 1913 and *Nel paese dell' oro* in 1914[19] (fig. 9.2). Sometimes exotic references were meant as deliberate allusions to colonialism; at other times they were due to choices dictated by the availability of the decor for the scenery, whereas in some cases they came down to conflations that Western movie scripts inherited from the dime novel stories on which they had been molded.[20]

Due vite per un cuore renewed Cines's "Western fever," which had begun in 1911 and would carry on until the outbreak of World War I. In 1913, *Sulla via dell'oro* was distributed, while the following year saw the release of *Nel Paese dell'oro*. The three movies share many features, notably a strong melodramatic component (though this is not a unique trait of Cines, as melodramatic acting is a feature that unites the majority of Italian silent Westerns of other film studios of the time, such as Ambrosio, Savoia, Pasquali, to name but a few). In these three Cines Westerns, features of the melodramatic tradition are noticeable and consistent: strong emotions, sensational adventures, troubled love stories, deadly perils, group brawls, abductions, and families in need of rescue. The firm rooting in melodrama is also obvious in the films' casts. In particular, *Sulla via dell'oro* featured the iconic melodrama actress Hesperia, in addition

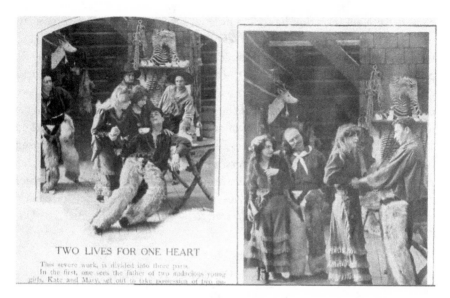

Fig. 9.2 Scenes from *Due vite per un cuore*, with Zebra pelts visible in the background. From the promotional article in *La Cinematografia Artistica*, no. 1, 1 Oct. 1912, p. 29. (Source: Museo Nazionale del Cinema di Torino, online, http://www.rivistecinema .it/catalogs/C5-101401/. Accessed 23 Feb. 2020.)

to Amleto Novelli and Lea Giunchi, with both actors coming from different performing backgrounds (Lea Giunchi was one of the first female comical actresses) but who in those years were also engaged in dramatic acting, for example, in the colossal *Quo Vadis* (Wyke 213). Their interpretations of cowboys and cowgirls are extremely expressive, their countenances, manners, suggestive gestures, and acrobatic feats making up for the lack of speech and emotional dialogue. Consequently, melodrama served the purpose of connecting an Italian audience with a foreign imperialist ideology through the means of an inherently Italian form of expression.

The histrionic scripts and performances of these movies are superimposed on a Western framework and aesthetic, which, however, did not relate to the original themes of the US-American genre—based on the celebration of US founding myths and of "the American Character." The challenge for Italian movie producers like Cines was to appeal to international audiences, while at the same time implementing an Italian nationalist subtext. As a result, Cines strove to make the scenes look authentic, which was a driving factor for the exportation of their films to the US. One of the strong features of *Sulla via dell'oro*, for example, was the staging of the US-American wilderness. In *Nel paese dell'oro,* on the other hand, the hideout scene in the antique ruins shatters the illusion of a US-American scenery. The interior shots attempted to recreate a Western domestic scenario using local items, which did not always produce the desired outcome, as in the case of *Due vite per un cuore* (*A Sister's Ordeal*). Certainly, the costumes are one of the most accomplished aspects of the Westerns produced by Cines. If the cowboys of Pasquali's *Il supplizio dei leoni* were accused by foreign critics of not being credible because they looked too elegant, the costumes of the Cines cowboys were carefully recreated based on those of Buffalo Bill's Rough Riders, while the cowgirls' attire was modeled on the costume of Annie Oakley, the famous Wild West show sharpshooter and rider. Cines exported these movies internationally, where they were fairly well received.[21] *Sulla via dell'oro* appeared to be especially appreciated by US-American audiences.[22]

MASS MIGRATION AND IMPERIALIST GOALS

1913 was one of the most prolific years for Italian-made silent era Westerns. In addition to Cines's *Sulla via dell'oro,* five films were released: *Silenzio eroico* (Savoia), *La vampira indiana* (Aquila), *Il bersaglio vivente* (Ambrosio), *Il circolo nero* (Celio), and *Nel vortice del destino* (*In the Vortex of Fate*) (Savoia). *Silenzio eroico* is a love story amid Far West miners, where Maria, the female protagonist, is fought over by her lover, Ramirez, and the brute Alvaro who wants to have her at any cost, even if that means trying to have Ramirez killed (Bernardini and Martinelli, 1913 2:246). In the case of *La vampira indiana,* which serendipitously featured Sergio Leone's parents, there appears to be a further genre overlapping the Western-dramatic structure (Frayling 15); it is the femme fatale, which added mysterious and supernatural undertones to the film, rendering it a sort of "Weird Western" *ante-litteram.*[23]

Il bersaglio vivente dramatizes the dilemma of a cowboy facing the unstoppable advance of modernization. Becoming indifferent to the anachronistic prospects of a life in the West, he decides to repurpose himself as a sharpshooter in the rising world of urban entertainment. In the metropolitan setting, he faces a series of dramatic events connected to a troubled love story. Loose parallels with Buffalo Bill's life story could be drawn, and, considering the endurance of this character in Italian popular culture, it might have inspired the plot to an extent.[24] *Il circolo nero* is divided between Rome and the West. Count Ruggeri joins the criminal gang the "black circle" to quickly repay his gambling debts. Realizing that organized crime is not for him, he decides to take refuge in the US-American West, where he rebuilds an idyllic life by working as a cowboy on a ranch (Bernardini and Martinelli, 1913 1:116). *Nel vortice del destino* dramatizes the story of an unhappy marriage and its unexpected consequences. Discovering his wife's betrayal, Richard Hoertz leaves the Old World to venture into the Mexican West and start a new beginning, leaving his son Franz with his mother and her new companion Marx. Following the death of his adoptive father, Franz goes to America where he works as a miner in Mexico. Embroiled in a fight at the mine, he ends up killing his attacker and is chased by a lynch mob of miners. He is saved by Sheriff Gutierrez who turns out to be his father Richard under a new identity. Together they leave the violent Mexican West behind and depart quickly for Europe to be finally reunited with, respectively, their mother and dying wife (Bernardini and Martinelli, 1913 2:82). The film envisions the West as a brutal place of failed opportunities, while casting a redeeming light on return migration and family reunification, experiences that considerably affected the phenomenon of Italian emigration.

Indeed, the steady flow of migration, especially to the Americas, was engendering constant demographic anxieties about the success of Italy's colonial goal: securing a "place in the sun" (Veracini). Before the Italo-Turkish War, the national debate on emigration was polarized, with backers of the "demographic empire" believing that "Italy's true colonial possibilities lay in America, where huge Italian populations had settled of their own free will" (Choate 7). On the other hand, Italian nationalists lamented the ignominy of the "free colonies of emigration," which were viewed as "demonstrations of Italy's national oppression and exploitation" (Choate 13).

With the beginning of the Libyan campaign, the revamping of nationalist rhetoric started to vehemently discourage emigration to the US, which was seen as an irreparable loss of resources that needed to be redirected toward Africa. An echo of this discourse can be identified within the context of the silent Western production of those years. Specifically, the Italian Westerns shot during the Libyan campaign represented the West as well as the broader US-American setting (which, given the relevance of Latin America in the framework of Italian immigration, often included Mexico and Argentina) as either a "land of promise," where one is allowed to rebuild one's life (as in *Il circolo nero*), or, rather, as an obsolete setting devoid of resources (*Il bersaglio vivente*) and even as a hostile environment that must be abandoned (*Nel vortice del destino*, *Nel paese dell'oro*). Such allusions, subtle as they might seem, still conveyed polarizing and even dissuasive subtexts against emigration to the New World. The split representation of the Americas dramatized in these movies reflected the conflict in the colonial imagination of Italy and the unresolved dilemma in the direction of its imperialistic aims.

After the beginning of World War I, two further films were distributed, *Il testamento del cercatore d'oro* (Savoia, 1915) and *Amore di Gaucho* (Ambrosio, 1915), a Western set in Argentina. As the war progressed, Europe's film production generally decreased. In Italy, Westerns were replaced with actual war propaganda films (Martinelli 109). The genre would pick up again after the end of the war, with the film *La figlia dell'oro* (Fidia films, 1919) directed by Nino Martinengo, and then with scattered releases that continued into the mid-1920s (Martinelli 110–13).

Without a doubt, these early Westerns with an Italian twist provided an embryonic imprint to the tradition that would eventually lead to the "invention" of the Spaghetti Westerns. Rather than embracing the exceptionalist message heralded by US-American Western-themed motion pictures, which found no viable cultural equivalent in Italy, Italian silent productions interlaced the profitable Western scaffolding with familiar narratives relating to their national identity, and with understated references to their position in the imperialistic scenario of Europe. Furthermore, the transnational circulation of these films, the adaptability of some of the stories to a US-American context, and their fairly positive reception across the Atlantic do not exclude the possibility of an early cross-pollination between the European and the US-American strands of this genre.

NOTES

1. I would like to thank the Eye Film Institute in Amsterdam for kindly allowing me to view the Italian Westerns in the Desmet Collection, and the cinema archive of Milan (Cineteca Milano) for arranging a viewing of Giulio Antamoro's *Pinocchio* for me. I am also grateful to the anonymous reviewers for their suggested improvements on this work.

2. Alovisio 54. In the US, movie Westerns were undergoing fundamental transformations. Early silent Westerns had been shot in the country's eastern woodlands and—following in the tradition of James Fenimore Cooper's tales—told stories of white trappers and Indians. After the industry moved to Hollywood, Westerns focused on the Plains Wars in desertlike settings, and Native Americans were seen, in the words of Scott Simmon, "as essentially one more roadblock thrown by nature against the advance of pioneers" (25).

3. Arguably, the same could be claimed for other European countries with an early interest for Westerns, like France, Germany, Austria, and the Netherlands, which, however, fall outside the narrow scope of this study.

4. For more information on Alberini's engagement in cinema business and in the establishment of Cines, see Redi *La Cines* and Canosa.

5. According to scholar Gabriella Turnaturi, between 1901 and 1907, the number of cinema halls in Rome rose from three to twelve (242).

6. Cinema entrepreneur Ercole Pettini also filmed the Wild West show in the city of Brescia. His documentary was entitled *L'Attendamento di Buffalo Bill in Campo Marte (Brescia)* (Bernardini 64, 80).

7. I would like to thank Dr. Mario Musumeci and Aldo Bernardini for the precious information about Alberini's films they provided in our conversations at Rome's Centro Sperimentale di Cinematografia and in correspondence.

8. In particular, there was a heated debate in national newspapers and illustrated satire. Bountiful examples can be found in the Bologna satirical weekly *La Rana*.

9. "Lowbrow" in the framework of cultural studies refers to what is commonly defined as popular and less sophisticated culture. For more information on the debate on highbrow and lowbrow, see Levine.

10. Beginning in 1908–1909, film studios like Ambrosio, from Turin, started to trade on a regular basis with film studios abroad.

11. Out of the seventy-seven films Itala Film produced, only two have survived (Redi, *Cinema* 32). The advertisement catalog of Itala provided a summary of the plot, and the *Moving Picture World* offered a review of the film.

12. Personal accounts of captivity at the hands of indigenous tribes were among the most popular publications in nineteenth-century Italy and often informed the fictional Western stories of Emilio Salgari and of his epigones (Curreri and Foni 20).

13. For further reading, refer to Abbattista and Turnaturi.

14. Cretinetti was a stock character in Italian silent cinema and represented "the village fool."

15. For further reading, see Rolle.

16. For other perspectives on *Pinocchio* (1911) and the "Western" sequence, see Mazzi and Manzoli-Menarini.

17. Emilio Salgari (1862–1911) often combined Western and South American settings in his novels (such as in *Il re della prateria* and *Duemila leghe sotto l'America*). Luigi Motta (1881–1955) was one of Salgari's ghostwriters who continued his work after Salgari's untimely death. For Buffalo Bill's dime novels, see Maini and Nocentini.

18. Vittorio Martinelli lamented that the screenplay writers were too ignorant (Martinelli 113), although this explanation seems fairly simplistic. The film was produced by Pasquali film studio and was launched in America as *The Mexican Mine Fraud* (Bernardini and Martinelli, *1914* 254).

19. See picture n.3.

20. Emilio Salgari often referred to "American lions" (or cougars) in the novels set in the Americas. It is possible that the intention was to refer to those specific

felines but that screenwriters, unable to find a better fit, fell back on readily available circus animals, like lions.

21. The first two movies had been circulated also in the US, Britain, France, and the Netherlands as well as in German-speaking countries. This is ascertainable from the film's promotional material and billboard that displayed multiple languages, as well as from the fact that an existing copy of the film is held in the Desmet Collection of Amsterdam's Eye Film Institute. As for *Nel paese dell'oro*, there is no available information.

22. A review from *El Paso Herald* described it as an "astonishing picture . . . that will amaze everyone with its daring and sensational feats" ("Astonishing Picture").

23. *Weird Western* is a genre inaugurated by the short stories of Robert E. Howard and by the ensemble of pulp fictions that followed. In film, the genre began at the end of the 1930s and became very popular only by the 1960s, Westerns with occult connotations—such as *Billy the Kid versus Dracula* (William Baudine, 1966)—becoming staples in Hollywood "B-Movies" (Green 2).

24. The film proved a flop and was deprecated by the critics (Bernardini and Martinelli, *1913* 1:74).

WORKS CITED

Abbattista, Guido. *Umanitá in mostra: Esposizioni etniche ed invenzioni esotiche in Italia (1880–1940)*. Edizioni Universitá di Trieste, 2013.

Alovisio, Silvio. "Immaginare un nuovo mondo. Sulle tracce del western nel cinema muto italiano." *Il western in l'Italia: Cinema, musica, letteratura e fumetto*, edited by Matteo Pollone, Graphot, 2020, pp. 49–66.

Argiolas, Pier Paolo. "Il Camerata Pinocchio: Fughe e avventure tra manganelli e cioccolata." *Xenoi: Immagine e parola tra razzismi antichi e moderni, atti del Convegno internazionale di studi, Cagliari, 3–6 febbraio 2010*, edited by Cannas Andrea et al., Liguori Editore, 2012, pp. 93–108.

"L'arrivo a Roma di Buffalo Bill's." *Il Messaggero* [Rome], 26 Mar. 1906, p. 4.

"Astonishing Picture at Bijou." *El Paso Herald*, 28 Oct. 1913, p. 12.

Bernardini, Aldo. *I film dal vero 1895–1914*. La Cineteca del Friuli, 2002.

Bernardini, Aldo, and Vittorio Martinelli. *Il cinema muto italiano 1913*. Vol. 1, Nuova Eri, 1994.

———. *Il cinema muto italiano 1913*. Vol. 2, Nuova Eri, 1994.

———. *Il cinema muto italiano 1914*. Vol. 2, Nuova Eri, 1993.

———. *I film degli anni d' oro 1911*. Vol. 2, Nuova Eri, 1996.

———. *I film dei primi anni 1910*. Nuova Edizioni Rai, 1996. Bertellini, Giorgio.

"Dramatizing the Italian-Turkish War (1911–12): Reports of atrocities, newsreels, and epic films in Italy and the USA." *Early Popular Visual Culture*, vol. 14, no. 2, 2016, pp. 131–54.

Brunetta, Gian Piero. *Il cinema muto italiano*. Laterza, 2008.

Canosa, Michele. *1905: La Presa di Roma*. Le Mani, 2006.

Choate, Mark. "From Territorial to Ethnographic Colonies and Back Again: The Politics of Italy's Demographic Expansion, 1890–1891." *Modern Italy: Journal of the Association for the Study of Modern Italy*, vol. 8, no. 1, 2003, pp. 65–75.

Curreri, Luciano, and Fabrizio Foni. *Un po' prima della fine? Ultimi romanzi di Salgari tra novitá e ripetizione 1908–1915*. Luca Sossella, 2009.

De Berti, Raffaele. "Il Pinocchio cinematografico di Giulio Antamoro." *Le Avventure di Pinocchio: Tra un linguaggio e l'altro*, edited by Isabella Pezzini and Paolo Fabbri, Meltemi Editore, 2002, pp. 157–73.

Frayling, Christopher. *Sergio Leone: Once upon a Time in Italy*. Harry N. Abrams, 2005.

Green, Paul. *Encyclopedia of Weird Westerns*. McFarland, 2016.

"Itala Release." *Moving Picture World*, 9 July 1910, p. 125.

La Rana (Bologna), April 1906.

Le Roy, Eric. "Quando gli Apache percorrevano gli Champs-Elysees." *Bianco and Nero*, vol. 58, no. 3, 1997, pp. 15–24.

Levine, Laurence W. *Highbrow/Lowbrow: The Emergency of Cultural Hierarchy in America*. Harvard University Press, 1988.

Lombardi, Giovanna. *Filoteo Alberini l'inventore del cinema*. Arduino Sacco, 2008.

Lotti, Denis. "La guerra allusa." *Immagine: Note di storia del cinema*, vol. 3, 2011, pp. 11–52.

Magrin, Alessandra. "Rough Riders in the Cradle of Civilization: Buffalo Bill's Wild West Show in Italy and the Challenge of American Cultural Scarcity at the Fin-de-Siècle." *European Journal of American Culture*, vol. 36, no. 1, 2017, pp. 23–38.

Maini, Roberto, and Anna Nocentini. *I fumetti di Nerbini della Marucelliana*. Nerbini, 1994.

Manzoli, Giacomo, and Roy Menarini. "Pinocchio, comico muto." *Fotogenia*, 1999, pp. 211–22.

Martinelli, Vittorio. "Laggiú nell' Arizona." *Bianco and Nero*, vol. 3, 1997, pp. 107–14.

Mazzei, Luca. "L'italiano di legno (o le straordinarie avventure di un burattino chiamato Pinocchio nel primo cinema italiano)." *Bianco and Nero*, no. 579, 2014, pp. 121–35.

Moving Picture World, July 1910, p. 125.

Redi, Riccardo. *Cinema muto italiano*. Marsilio Editori, 1999.

———. *Film stranieri sugli schermi Italiani*. Vol. 1, Giannini, 2003.

———. *La Cines: Storia di una casa di produzione Italiana*. Paolo Emilio Persiani, 2009.

Rolle, Andrew F. *Westward the Immigrants: Italian Adventurers and Colonists in an Expanding America*. University of Colorado Press, 1968.

Schiavulli, Antonio. *La guerra lirica: Il dibattito dei letterati italiani sull' impresa di Libia (1911–1912)*. Giorgio Pozzi Editore, 2009.

Simmon, Scott. *The Invention of the Western Film: A Cultural History of the Genre's First Half-Century*. Cambridge University Press, 2003.

Turnaturi, Gabriella. "Les métamorphoses du divertissement citadin dans l'Italie unifiée (1870–1915)." *L'Avènement des loisirs*, edited by Alain Corbin, Flammarion, 2001, pp. 223–49.

Veracini, Lorenzo. "Italian Colonization through a Settler-Colonial Studies Lens." *Journal of Colonialism and Colonial History*, vol. 19, no. 3, Winter 2018.

Verhoeff, Nanna. *The West in Early Cinema*. Amsterdam University Press, 2006.

Wyke, Maria. *Projecting the Past: Ancient Rome, Cinema and History*. Routledge, 1997.

ALESSANDRA MAGRIN Haas is an early-career researcher at the University of Strathclyde. She is associate editor of the project The Papers of William F. Cody.

TEN

—ɯ—

WHERE THE CLASSICAL, THE TRANSNATIONAL, AND THE ACID WESTERN MEET

Matalo! (Cesare Canevari, 1970), Violence, and Cultural Resistance on the Spaghetti Western Frontier

LEE BROUGHTON

HENRY NASH SMITH'S BOOK *Virgin Land: American West as Symbol and Myth* (1950) has become an indispensable tool for scholars seeking to make critical sense of US-American-made Westerns. The conquest of the West was an imperialist endeavor, and Smith's book provides a cogent account of the political communications and cultural productions that encouraged and ensured that the colonization of America was a success. Artistic license, a desire to justify the horrors of Manifest Destiny, and the need for compelling stories may override historical facts in the majority of Hollywood's Westerns, but Smith's work—particularly the chapter "The Garden and the Desert" (201–13), which articulates a range of contemporary critical thoughts relating to historical conceptions of civilization and savagery on the Western frontier—does allow scholars to find symbolic and even historical pertinence in some of Hollywood's generic output, and serves to enrich and enliven our understanding of those films.

But can H. N. Smith's work be fruitfully employed to interrogate Italian Westerns—films that have traditionally been judged to be historically, culturally, and spatially displaced from the US-American West, and thus dismissed as failed copies of Hollywood films that should, in turn, resist traditional modes of interpretation? The Italian and Spanish coproduction *Matalo!* (Cesare Canevari, 1970) is a transnational Spaghetti Western (a film set in America's past but shot on location in Spain by Italian and Spanish producers and starring actors drawn from around the world) that is also a generically unstable work. Although it has a convincingly articulated Western setting, this particularly idiosyncratic film periodically features tropes and modes that would more usually be associated with Italian *giallo* thrillers, experimental art cinema, exploitation films, and Bollywood romances. *Matalo!* is further distinguished by its status as an "Acid" Western: the film sports a psychedelic-experimental rock soundtrack by Mario Migliardi and features lead characters who are clearly coded as hippies-cum-radical counterculture types.

However, if H. N. Smith's work on the garden and the desert is employed as an optic with which to interrogate the weird narrative developments and gratuitous acts of violence that play out in *Matalo!*, it becomes apparent that Canevari did actually make a Western that was mindful of the historical concepts of civilization and savagery—which were erroneously informed by notions of race and habitat—while also rejecting the ideologically driven narrative scenarios that the majority of Hollywood's classical Westerns had typically included when they sought to utilize those very same concepts to tell stories that justified colonialism.

This chapter thus considers the ways in which *Matalo!* follows some of the recognized symbolic codes of the classical Western, while pointedly rejecting others in favor of alternatives that would perhaps resonate more readily with Italian audiences. The chapter also reflects on the ways in which *Matalo!*'s transnational identity, its status as an Acid Western, and the influence of other film forms might affect our understanding of the film. Ultimately, *Matalo!* is found to be a multilayered film that confronts the ideologies of imperialism in a variety of ways. Indeed, the film's subtle and cryptic symbolic landscape actually makes references to a potted history of transnational colonialism.

THE GARDEN, THE DESERT, AND OTHER
ANTINOMIES OUT WEST

Rainfall and its effect on the land in agricultural terms are key dimensions that inform the historical and metaphorical conceptualizations of the garden and the desert. H. N. Smith notes that the myth of the Great US-American Desert and its sense of "otherness" had been established in 1810 when Zebulon M. Pike likened "the vast treeless" Great Plains to a "sterile waste like the sandy deserts of Africa" (202). Smith adds that this "absence of trees ... was regarded as proof that the area was unsuited to any kind of agriculture and therefore uninhabitable by Anglo-Americans" (203). This, in turn, suggested that "Others" (Native Americans, Mexicans, and other "migratory tribesmen") were the only peoples capable of thriving there (204). As Smith points out, in the imperialist Anglo-American mindset, "such peoples were considered uncivilized. They could not be integrated with American society and were therefore perpetual outlaws" (205).

Even more damning, as Smith observes, was the suggestion that, if US-American frontiersmen were to adopt a pastoral life on the plains, "they would become nomadic brigands, [and] a menace to [the] settled agricultural communities farther to the East" (205). Indeed, Washington Irving noted that life on the plains might encourage the births of "new and mongrel races . . . the amalgamation of the 'debris' and 'abrasions' of former races, civilized and savage" (qtd. in H. N. Smith 205). However, occupation of the plains soon became a necessity due to the pressures of expansion, which, as Smith explains, ultimately led to "the myth of the garden of the world" being "projected out across the plains" (208). This myth served to convince interested parties that rainfall on the plains would increase, resulting in a garden that would support civilized and agrarian-minded Anglo-Americans (211).

While the garden and the desert remain the mythic opposites that loom largest in historical accounts of the settlement of the West, a further overarching antinomy that inevitably involves the enactment of violence can be detected at the heart of most Western narratives: civilization versus the wilderness. The essence of the myth of the Great US-American Desert and of the settler's struggle against the inhospitable desert is often altered for dramatic effect in classical US-American Westerns, becoming instead the ideological battle that is waged between settlers and uncouth villains, Native Americans, and Mexicans. Richard Slotkin observes how every incarnation of the ever-evolving myth of the frontier had "represented the redemption of US-American spirit or fortune as something to be achieved by playing through a scenario of separation, temporary regression to a more primitive or 'natural' state, and *regeneration through violence*" (12). And so, the classical Western hero must defeat those who represent the wilderness, thus allowing the morally sound settlers that he has defended to bring progress and civilization to the frontier. At a symbolic or allegorical level, the hero and the decent folk that he sides with effectively transform a section of the desert into a garden: a place where life, civilization, and the children of the future US-American nation can grow and prosper.

Another antinomy that is relevant to this chapter is the classical Western versus the Acid Western. Rumsey Taylor notes that the term *Acid Western* was first employed by Pauline Kael in her 1971 review of Alejandro Jodorowsky's Mexican production *El Topo* (1970). While there is no single unifying feature that is shared by all Acid Westerns, Kael's following assessment of *El Topo* does serve to broadly describe the content and appeal of some—but not all—such Westerns: they represent "exploitation filmmaking joined to sentimentality—the sentimentality of the counter-culture. They mix frighteningly well: for the counter-culture violence is romantic and shock is beautiful, because extremes of feeling and lack of control are what one takes drugs for . . . the counter-culture has begun to look for the equivalent of a drug trip in its theatrical experiences . . . increasingly movies appear to be valued only for their intensity" (qtd. in Taylor). Rumsey Taylor adds that, "unlike its mainstream counterparts, the acid Western . . . amalgamates the violent with the absurd in such a way that the result, to a specific audience, achieves a certain profundity," while Jonathan Rosenbaum observes that Acid Westerns differ from classical Westerns "in their generational biases, which lead them . . . to overturn or ironically revise . . . generic norms" (51). Inherently countercultural in their outlook, Acid Westerns clearly position themselves in opposition to the classical Western, as is revealed by films such as *El Topo* (Melia 101) and the US-American productions *Zachariah* (George Englund, 1971) and *The Hired Hand* (Peter Fonda, 1971).

MATALO!'S PRODUCTION CONTEXT

Following World War II, the concerns of European intellectuals regarding the US's wide-reaching political and economic influence and the penetrating effects of US-American cultural imperialism were exacerbated by the implementation of the Marshall Plan in 1948; the mass dumping of a huge backlog of Hollywood feature films (including many Westerns) onto European cinema screens; the subsequent adoption of US-American youth culture trends and fashions by European youngsters; and the persistent presence of US-American soldiers on European soil. For many, Europe had become a US-American sphere of influence and that influence was felt particularly strongly in Italy (Fisher 19). As such, the very existence of Spaghetti Westerns has traditionally been seen as an example of the effects of US-American cultural imperialism in action. Indeed, these films were initially dismissed as "cheap, opportunistic imitations" of US-American cultural productions (Frayling, *Spaghetti* 121).

It is then wholly appropriate for Paul Smith to adopt the language of postcolonial studies when he suggests that Spaghetti Westerns should instead be regarded as subaltern ripostes (4). He opines that the Italians seized a dominant model of US-American filmmaking and transformed it into a new genre that possessed "different signifying ends and social functions within . . . [the Italians'] . . . own cultural [system]" (4–5). To this end, Paul Smith's assessment of the cultural tensions and interplay at work here feeds nicely into the theoretical framework that Marwan M. Kraidy dubs "critical transculturalism" (149). Within this framework, cultural exchange can be recognized and, at times, celebrated as a two-way process that can potentially allow those situated at the peripheries of globalization to create meaningful—and empowering— culturally hybrid works without losing sight of the fact that the world is a site of unequal power distribution that brings with it the continued threat of cultural imperialism. Significantly, *Matalo!* is a hybrid film on two counts: it foregrounds genre hybridity while also being culturally hybrid.

Director Cesare Canevari made films in a number of key Italian *filoni* (crime drama, sexploitation, Nazisploitation, etc.), but his Spaghetti Western *Matalo!* is probably his most striking effort. During the early years of the Spaghetti Western boom, most Italian directors were happy to loosely copy the basic themes of whichever Sergio Leone film was topping the box office charts. However, Leone's break from filmmaking in 1967 was followed by the big budget and epic Italian and US-American coproduction *Once Upon a Time in the West* (*C'era una volta il West*, 1968), which proved impossible to imitate. This state of affairs led to the production of several Italian Westerns that featured wholly original—and sometimes obviously political—narrative content. *Matalo!* is one of those films. Its lead actor, the Colombian Lou Castel, had previously starred in the first Zapata Spaghetti Western, *A Bullet for the General* (*Quien Sabe?* 1967). The Zapata Spaghetti Westerns were political films set in Mexico during times of revolution and the majority of them told allegorical tales that criticized the US and the West's contemporary colonialist interference in the affairs of South American and Third World countries, while also arguing that violent resistance was the way to counter such interference (Frayling, "Zapata" 12). As will become apparent, *Matalo!* also has something to say about colonialism, but its criticisms are expressed in a much subtler and more cryptic manner.

MATALO! AND THE ACID WESTERN

The film tells the story of Bart (Corrado Pani) and a hippie-like gang of criminals—Ted (Antonio Salines), Phil (Luis Davila), and Mary (Claudia Gravy)—who hide out in a ghost town in the desert before and after robbing a US Army payroll stagecoach. When three innocent people—Constance Benson (Ana Maria Noe), Ray (Lou Castel), and Bridget (Ana Maria Mendoza)—are found in the town, the paranoid gang amuse themselves by inflicting physical and psychological abuses on the trio. As such, *Matalo!*'s story line is very much concerned with pockets of civilization being breached by symbolic representations of the wilderness and savagery, and vice versa.

Much of *Matalo!*'s status as an Acid Western is dependent on the majority of its main characters being coded as hippies. Ray wears an unusual jacket that features a neat paisley pattern, while Bridget sports a floral-patterned shirt, beads, and a fur-trimmed waistcoat that is a psychedelic patchwork of colored cloth. These two protagonists seem to be aligned with mainstream hippiedom's positive outlook of nonviolence and "peace and love." As the film's antagonists, Bart, Ted, Phil, and Mary seem to represent the darker, violent, and more cult-ish aspects of hippiedom. Their wardrobe includes cheesecloth shirts, head-bands, bell-bottom trousers, fur waistcoats, beads, and psychedelic-colored waistbands. Spaghetti Westerns tend to feature generic and easily recognized music that invariably takes its inspiration from the works that Ennio Morricone composed for the Westerns of Sergio Leone and others. Here, *Matalo!*'s Acid Western credentials are consolidated by an experimental-cum-psychedelic electronic music score that also features Eastern-sounding pieces and an acid rock song that foregrounds blistering fuzz guitar work, driving drums, electronic sound effects, and stoner vocals.

The intensity of many of *Matalo!*'s scenes, particularly those involving torture and violence, chime readily with Kael's understanding of the Acid Western. Interestingly, the pointed way in which the film pits analogues of a contemporary youth-oriented counterculture against each other deviates greatly from the US-American Acid Western model, wherein the hippie analogues usually come into conflict with members of the older generation or the representatives of capitalism. This marked deviation suggests that *Matalo!*'s narrative might serve to remind local viewers of the violent struggle that was being fought between the left- and right-wing factions of a new generation of young political activists on Italy's streets at the time of the film's release (Heath-Kelly 35).

TRANSNATIONALISM AND GENRE HYBRIDITY

Matalo! is distinguished by the way in which it periodically takes on the traits of other film genres. An early example occurs when Mary slowly rides into the ghost town while Bart is bathing in a water trough [18:57–20:04]. It transpires that Mary is actually coupled with Phil, but a series of zoom shots, eyeline matches, and sly facial expressions make it clear that Bart and the approaching Mary are completely enamored with each other. Bart even subconsciously clasps his right hand over his heart (a movement that surely signals his love for Mary), and, in what amounts to an interesting reversal of the gender relations that are usually seen in popular cinema, it is the clothed female (Mary) who watches the naked bathing male (Bart) here (figs. 10.1 and 10.2). With Asian Indian–influenced music underscoring this dialogue-free sequence, the film

Fig. 10.1 As Bart silently stares at the approaching Mary, his right hand subconsciously clasps his heart and signals his secret love for her.

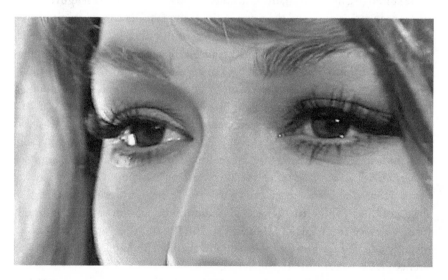

Fig. 10.2 The zoom in on Mary's eyes reveals that she is staring intently at Bart, who she is secretly in love with.

suddenly takes on the generic traits of a scene of romantic intrigue from a Bollywood movie. Phil's suspicions and Ted's confusion with regard to Mary and Bart's open but nonverbal signals of mutual attraction are communicated via a further series of knowing glances and quizzical looks rather than dialogue. All the while the ethnic percussion and the shrill and quickly ascending and descending notes heard on the soundtrack indicate that the four characters are feeling a variety of dangerous emotions. When viewed within the wider context of *Matalo!*'s subtle and cryptic symbolic landscape, this atypical episode's pointed evocation of the Indian subcontinent inevitably leads to thoughts of a land that once suffered greatly under the yoke of Western imperialism. Later on, it is revealed that Mary had once been coupled with Ted, and she takes delight in flirting with him and teasing him. Ted's reactions and his palpable sense of longing, lust, and frustration are reminiscent of the intensely melodramatic and psychosexual shenanigans that are commonly found in the films of Russ Meyer, wherein physically strong and hypersexual women are able to upset patriarchal society's gender-related power relations (Broughton, "Rethinking" 61).

Matalo!'s generic properties deviate even further when darkness falls on the ghost town [21:10–26:18]. Accompanied by strange vocal noises and music more suited to a horror film, the ominous shadow of an unknown figure with a rifle is seen moving around the town. A lightning-fast close-up of an observing eye that is barely a few frames in length is intermittently cut into this sequence. Here, the film takes on the atmosphere of an Italian *giallo* thriller, with emphasis placed on the voyeuristic activities of an unidentified third party, who is eventually revealed to be Mrs. Benson. A similar *giallo*-like trope is employed later in the film [48:30] when a new unidentified third party begins voyeuristically spying on the ghost town's occupants (this turns out to be Bart, who was presumed to be dead following the stagecoach robbery). Its numerous torture sessions lead *Matalo!* further into the realm of the horror genre. One sequence in particular [50:43–52:38] involves Mary placing Ray beneath a child's swing that she then swings on—back and forth—while slowly lowering the knife that she is holding in order to effect a small-scale approximation of the eponymous torture device from Edgar Allan Poe's "The Pit and the Pendulum" (1842), recently adapted for film and television in the US (Roger Corman, 1961) and France (RTF, Alexandre Astruc, 1964).

Matalo!'s torture sequences are employed in further interesting ways. When the gang discovers Mrs. Benson's home, they immediately begin to abuse her, and the film takes on the generic qualities of the home invasion genre for a spell [40:36–44:22]. When the gang captures Ray and Bridget, their immediate reaction to these symbols of civilization is to harshly beat them [45:45–48:28]. At this point, the film takes on the generic qualities of exploitation films from the early 1970s. Indeed, the gang is essentially cast in the mold of the nihilistic and murderous counterculture types that would figure in films such as Wes Craven's *The Last House on the Left* (1972), and they delight in putting the pair through all manner of physical abuses. Ray bears the brunt of the torture, and one lengthy torture sequence [62:16–70:18] is shot in an experimental-cum-art-cinema style that further upsets the film's generic stability: featuring some canted shots, striking editing, and presented in slow motion with discordant-but-ethereal sounds dominating the soundtrack, the sequence takes on a quite surreal quality and evokes the feel of a waking nightmare. If we take Hollywood to be the creator and advocate of distinct and iconic film genres, Canevari's pointed employment of the kind of genre hybridity that I have outlined above plays like a willful act of resistance to US-American cultural imperialism. Indeed, I would argue that Canevari's determined efforts to bend, hybridize, and remold the generic properties of the classical US-American Western in such extreme and startling ways could be understood to be precisely the kind of subaltern riposte that Paul Smith associates with Spaghetti Westerns (4).

CIVILIZATION AND WILDERNESS IN *MATALO!*

Bart is first introduced in a civilized space, a vibrant town—a part of the desert that imperialist endeavors have turned into a garden figuratively speaking—where he is to be hung for some unspecified crime [2:18]. Before Bart's execution can take place, the symbolic representatives of the desert and the wilderness invade the town, and a gang of Mexicans rescues him [3:36–7:46]. To underscore their status as uncivilized and savage Others, Canevari has the Mexicans behave like the Indians found in Hollywood's colonialist Westerns: they ride around the gathered townsfolk in a tight circular formation, shooting dead the representatives of civilization in an indiscriminate manner. As with Hollywood's Indians, the Mexicans' savage nature is symbolically linked to their status as nonwhites. When Bart rides out into the desert with the Mexicans, it is clear that he is at ease with these savage Others and the wilderness in which they operate. So much so that he has taken on their savage ways, and he soon kills them all to retrieve the stolen gold he had used to pay them [9:34–11:02]. Bart and the hippie Westerner gang, thus, can be read as analogues of precisely the kind of formerly civilized but now nomadic desert-dwelling brigands that were a genuine historical concern according to Henry Nash Smith (205).

Bart meets up with Ted and Phil, and the trio head to the ghost town, which is, by its very nature, a former pocket of civilization (a failed garden, figuratively speaking) that has been reclaimed by the wilderness and become a part of the desert again. Mary arrives the next day with the gang's supplies. First, it is signaled that Mary, like the rest of the gang, is at home in the desert since she has safely traveled to the town alone without mishap. Her clothes indicate that she is both a hippie analogue and a child of the wilderness: she sports a variety of Native American–inspired outfits, including one that fuses hot pants with a tasseled skirt. A dusky beauty, her name suggests that she is an Anglo-American woman, but she might well be a representative of the "new and mongrel races," a mixture of the "civilized and the savage," that Washington Irving had historically feared would be the result of a life lived on the plains (qtd. in H. N. Smith 205).

Mary's ability to act like the Other is an important aspect of her devious skill set. Beyond dressing like a Native American, Mary also convincingly disguises herself as a Mexican woman in order to flag down the US Army stagecoach and kill two men during the robbery. Phil even tells Mary that she "play[s] the part of a Mexican girl very well" [33:15–33:18]. The rest of the gang also dresses as Mexicans for the robbery. When Phil and Mary subsequently meet up with Baxter (Miguel del Castillo), the "Mr. Big" who planned the enterprise, we are presented with the kind of finely dressed gentleman who would normally be associated with the East. Significantly, Baxter explains that the brutal killings the gang carried out during the robbery have made it difficult for him to dispose of the stolen gold in the US. He duly advises them that they will have to deliver the gold to his place in Mexico instead [60:52–61:56]. These scenarios—the murderous gang disguising themselves as Mexicans and the dishonest Eastern gentleman Baxter having an abode in Mexico from which his criminal operations are run with ease—equate the Other (the Mexican people and Mexico itself) with savagery and lawlessness.

But while this fits with the US's historical colonialist outlook and the ideologies of classical Hollywood Westerns, it also possesses local significance that is specific to Italy (Broughton, *Euro-Western* 93). When the Northern state of Piedmont's imperialist project to unify Italy by force during the 1860s succeeded, the annexed Southern states were perceived to be lawless lands, and Southern Italians were likened to primitive Africans (Dickie 28–29). The Piedmontese saw Southern Italy as a "dark" territory that needed to be "civilized" (Dunnage 1–2), which essentially led the Northern Italians to Other the South of their country in the same way that Anglo-Americans had initially Othered America's Great Plains by comparing them to African deserts. When Southern rebels rejected the imposition of Piedmont's laws by engaging in acts of banditry, a civil war erupted (from 1861 to 1865), which made a lasting impression on the Italian public and contributed much to the "sense of southern 'difference' which came to dominate historical and contemporary understandings of the South" (Riall 150). Hence, Maggie Gunsberg suggests that echoes of the negative historical attitudes relating to Southern Italy and its people are often symbolically manifested in the Spaghetti Western's representations of Mexico and Mexicans (210). That would certainly appear to be the case with some of the Mexican symbolism that is employed in *Matalo!* However, the Anglo-American Baxter's easy ability to exploit Mexico (taking land and property, and possessing enough influence to dispose of the stolen gold there) can be read as a metaphor for colonialism that might actually view Italy's history from a Southerner's perspective, since Don H. Doyle reports that some Southern Italians still possess a shared public memory that regards Piedmont's historical annexation of Southern Italy as an act of colonialist aggression and theft (5).

Matalo! features three characters who can be read—initially, at least—as representatives of civilization, and two of them (Ray and Bridget) are shown to be completely out of their depth in the desert, while the third (Mrs. Benson, the ghost town's last remaining resident) has adapted to living there. It is the gang's violent treatment of this defenseless old lady that works to establish the full extent of their savage nature. Mrs. Benson has simply refused to give up on the dream of a garden in the desert, and, when the gang finds her, they discover that she has been living in her own secret "oasis"—on the inside, her home is luxurious and offers every comfort of civilization. The emphasis that is placed on Mrs. Benson's love for her material possessions here (her fine ornaments, furnishings, furniture, elegant clothes, etc.)—and the psychological distress the gang causes her when they destroy some of them—plays like a pointed comment on the rampant public obsession with consumerism that had swept through Italy during the 1950s and 1960s, an obsession that, Andrea Bini observes, was intrinsically linked to the "wider process of the 'Americanization' of Italian society" that occurred when Italy became a sphere of US-American influence during the postwar years (94).

When talking about the town, Mrs. Benson tells Ray, "They all deserted the place, even my husband" [70:46–72:24]. Ghost towns (or sparsely occupied towns) appear in a significant number of Spaghetti Westerns, and their presence can be argued to possess a symbolic importance that is local in nature and related directly to the contemporaneous Americanization of Italy. While the US's cultural, economic, and political "colonization" of Italy after World War II led to the rapid modernization of the country's industrial North, it did little to alter the lives of those who lived in the rural South of the country. Indeed, Jonathan Dunnage notes that when Italy's postwar economic miracle came to an end in the early 1960s, it was clear that not all Italians had enjoyed its benefits equally: the country's long-standing North-South economic divide had persisted unchanged (150–52). Consequently, around three million Southern Italians had been forced to migrate North in search of work during the 1950s

(153). Harry Robinson confirms that "Italy offers the classic case of regional imbalance and rural depopulation," while observing that "it is estimated that the
numbers leaving the south during the decade 1960–70 averaged about 130,000
annually" (82). As such, the symbolic image of the ghost town found in Spaghetti Westerns might resonate with the socially unsettling effects that the
depopulation of small rural towns had on Southern Italian communities during
the 1950s and 1960s. The ghost town encountered in *Matalo!* is a particularly
pointed and damning symbol since it resists the ideology of the classical Hollywood Western: any hope of "regeneration through violence" is rejected here,
and the town is without citizens at the film's end.

While Ray can be read as being a representative of civilization, he is also
able to align himself with the skills of the Other in a wholly positive way. John
G. Cawelti observes that, in the imperialist mindset of white Southern popular
mythology, "the black slave or servant is often shown to have a special understanding and skill with horses" (77). Here it is Ray who possesses that special
understanding and skill. When Ray is first introduced in the wilderness [31:32–
33:04], he has collapsed due to dehydration, and it is his horse that rouses and
rescues him. Ray's horse also rescues him later in the film when Ted is merci-
lessly beating him [66:54–68:36]: the horse suddenly appears from nowhere
and, sensing that its master is in danger, rears onto its hind legs and uses the
power of its flailing front hooves to pummel Ted into submission. Later on,
Mrs. Benson tries to set Ray up as a kind of heroic "town tamer" (Slotkin 352),
but it is not to be: Ray is a peace-loving man who does not know how to use the
guns that Mrs. Benson offers him. When Ted attacks him at the film's end, Ray
defends himself by positively embracing the skills of the Other again. Here,
Ray uses a succession of expertly aimed boomerangs to kill Ted [79:32–81.08].
While it has been suggested that some Native American tribes may have used
boomerangs, in the worldwide public's shared consciousness the boomerang
is an instantly recognizable symbol that is most commonly associated with the
Aboriginal peoples of Australia. Taken at face value, this might suggest that
Ray is a transnational extension of Slotkin's "the man who knows Indians" (16),
here reformulated as the man who knows Aborigines. Either way, this atypical
episode cannot help but bring to mind the Aborigines and their plight as the
ongoing victims of historical imperialism.

MATALO!'S FINALE AND FINAL THOUGHTS

In contrast to Ray, it seems that living in the desert alone for countless years
has infused Mrs. Benson with an element of savagery: she arms herself and

enters into a free-for-all gun battle with Ted, Phil, and Mary during the film's finale [76:28–78:19]. While the film's final gun battle rages, Bart is seen comically trying to catch the escaped donkey that the stolen gold has been loaded onto. When the battle is over, Phil and Mary are revealed to be dead. Mrs. Benson promptly shoots Bart in the back, mortally wounding him, before he turns and shoots her dead. This finale is a handy reminder of the many ways in which *Matalo!* finds itself at the meeting point between the classical Western, the transnational Spaghetti Western, and the Acid Western. On the one hand, it obeys the rules of the classical Hollywood Western as far as its female characters and its criminal characters are concerned. E. Ann Kaplan notes that promiscuous female characters in Hollywood films tend to be punished (82), while Jon Tuska observes that punishment equally awaits dishonest female characters and the villains that they consort with (226). With these "rules" in mind, Mary's death—and the deaths of Phil, Ted, and Bart—come as no surprise. In addition, Pam Cook asserts that if a US-American Western's heroine "is allowed to be active, it is in the hero's cause rather than her own" (44). Ray settles his differences with Bart at the film's end and is happy for him to leave with the gold. Thus, the gold-greedy Mrs. Benson breaks this "rule" when she shoots Bart in the back and is doomed to die herself.

But the film breaks with the narrative conventions of the classical Western when it delivers symbols and subnarratives that relate to its status as a transnational Spaghetti Western. The ghost town has been tamed, but the ideological imperatives of the classical US-American "town tamer" Western are noticeably absent, and violence has not led to regeneration. This is because the town's symbolic function appears to relate to the depopulation of rural Southern Italian villages during the 1950s and 1960s rather than the birth of the modern US. There are no decent folks left to assert control and reestablish a pocket of civilization in the wilderness in this instance. In a classical Western, Ray and Bridget would likely have become romantically involved and settled in the town, but, instead, the two characters remain dedicated to reaching whatever unspecified destinations they were heading for at the start of the film, and they part just as they met: traveling in different directions. Again, we might read this need to travel and reach a destination alone as reflecting the hundreds of thousands of similar migratory journeys that Southern Italians in search of work were forced to undertake during the 1950s and 1960s.

In terms of *Matalo!*'s Acid Western properties, Kael's observation that "for the counter-culture violence is romantic and shock is beautiful" (quoted in Taylor 2013) and Taylor's (2013) assertion that such films amalgamate "the violent with the absurd" in order to achieve "a certain profundity" ring true throughout

Matalo! During the finale, we can specifically point to Bart's comedic attempts to catch the donkey being crosscut with the deadly gun battle and Ray's use of the lethal boomerangs to kill Ted. Furthermore, Ray's use of boomerangs represents the kind of ironic and racially centered revisions of "generic norms" that Rosenbaum associates with Acid Westerns (51).

CONCLUSION

This chapter has offered a reading of *Matalo!* that has employed the work of Henry Nash Smith and others in order to argue that, for all of its strangeness and its historical, cultural, and spatial displacement from the US-American West, *Matalo!* does follow some recognized symbolic codes of the classical Western while pointedly rejecting others. In doing so, I have shown that the film's transnational identity, its status as an Acid Western, and the sense of genre hybridity that the influence of other film forms bestow on it have an obvious impact on our understanding of the film. *Matalo!* was made following the Italian Western's adoption of radical political themes via the Mexican Revolution–set Zapata Spaghetti Westerns, but the film's own symbolic and narrative engagements with notions of imperialism and colonialism remain much more subtle, cryptic, and transnational, by comparison. *Matalo!*'s transnational nature does result in the apparent presence of symbols and scenarios that would seem to speak to a local audience about local issues and, as a consequence, deviations from the classical Western's model are evident, most notably in its novel symbolic use of the ghost town and the absence of the ideological imperatives that are usually associated with US-American-made "town tamer" Westerns. The collision between the classical, the transnational, and the Acid Western that unfolds here ultimately results in a multilayered work, whose narrative symbolically resists the influence of US-American cultural imperialism while covertly providing references that amount to a potted history of international colonialism. Paul Smith (4) once likened Spaghetti Westerns to a subaltern riposte. This would, to my mind, be a wholly appropriate way in which to describe *Matalo!*

WORKS CITED

Bini, Andrea. *Male Anxiety and Psychopathology in Film: Comedy Italian Style.* Palgrave Macmillan, 2015.

Broughton, Lee. *The Euro-Western: Reframing Gender, Race and the 'Other' in Film.* I. B. Tauris, 2016.

———. "Rethinking the Representation of Race and Gender in American Exploitation Westerns from the 1960s." *Critical Perspectives on the Western: From A Fistful of Dollars to Django Unchained*, edited by Lee Broughton, Rowman and Littlefield, 2016, pp. 57–72.

Cawelti, John. G. *The Six-Gun Mystique Sequel*. Bowling Green State University Popular Press, 1999.

Cook, Pam. *Screening the Past: Memory and Nostalgia in Cinema*. Routledge, 2005.

Dickie, John. "Imagined Italies." *Italian Cultural Studies*, edited by David Forgacs and Robert Lumley, Oxford University Press, 1996, pp. 19–33.

Doyle, Don H. *Nations Divided: America, Italy, and the Southern Question*. University of Georgia Press, 2002.

Dunnage, Jonathan. *Twentieth Century Italy: A Social History*. Pearson Education, 2002.

Fisher, Austin. *Radical Frontiers in the Spaghetti Western: Politics, Violence and Popular Italian Cinema*. I. B. Tauris, 2011.

Frayling, Christopher. *Spaghetti Westerns: Cowboys and Europeans from Karl May to Sergio Leone*. Routledge and Kegan Paul, 1981.

———. "Zapata Spaghetti: Reflections on the Italian Western and the Mexican Revolution." *Critical Perspectives on the Western: From "A Fistful of Dollars" to "Django Unchained,"* edited by Lee Broughton, Rowman and Littlefield, 2016, pp. 1–25.

Gunsberg, Maggie. *Italian Cinema: Gender and Genre*. Palgrave Macmillan, 2005.

Heath-Kelly, Charlotte. *Politics of Violence*. Routledge, 2013.

Kaplan, E. Ann. *Women and Film: Both Sides of the Camera*. Routledge, 1991.

Kraidy, Marwan M. *Hybridity, or the Cultural Logic of Globalization*. Temple University Press, 2005.

Melia, Matt. "Landscape, Imagery, and Symbolism in Alejandro Jodorowsky's *El Topo*." *Reframing Cult Westerns: From The Magnificent Seven to The Hateful Eight*, edited by Lee Broughton, Bloomsbury Academic, 2020, pp. 93–110.

Riall, Lucy. "Garibaldi and the South." *Italy in the Nineteenth Century*, edited by John A. Davis, Oxford University Press, 2000, pp. 132–51.

Robinson, Harry. *Population and Resources*. Macmillan Education, 1981.

Rosenbaum, Jonathan. *Dead Man*. British Film Institute, 2000.

Slotkin, Richard. *Gunfighter Nation: The Myth of the Frontier in Twentieth-Century America*. Athenium, 1992.

Smith, Henry Nash. *Virgin Land: American West as Symbol and Myth*. Vintage Books, 1957.

Smith, Paul. *Clint Eastwood: A Cultural Production*. University of Minnesota Press, 1993.

Taylor, Rumsey. "Acid Westerns." *Not Coming to a Theatre Near You*, 1 Apr. 2013, http://www.notcoming.com/features/acidwesterns/. Accessed 16 Sept 2019.

Tuska, Jon. *The American West in Film: Critical Approaches to the Western.*
Greenwood, 1985.

LEE BROUGHTON is a freelance writer, critic, film programmer, and lecturer in Film and Cultural Studies. He is author of *The Euro-Western: Reframing Gender, Race and the 'Other' in Film* and editor of *Critical Perspectives on the Western: From* A Fistful of Dollars *to* Django Unchained and of *Reframing Cult Westerns: From* The Magnificent Seven *to* The Hateful Eight.

PART III

WESTERNS IN A POSTCOLONIAL
OR POSTEMPIRE CONTEXT

FROM THE US AND EUROPE, our journey spirals outward to other continents where the Western spawned and has since been leading a colorful life, and, in one case, where it was born in the shadow of its more famous US-American twin.

Part III follows the Western's expansion into South America, with its legacy of Portuguese imperialism in Brazil and Argentine colonization, before taking us across the Pacific to Japan, an understudied East Asian producer of Westerns, and heading on down to South Africa where the Western has always attracted audiences both black and white. Finally, we wind back to Australia, a country in which Western films have been a consistent feature of national production.

Here again, each chapter demonstrates that the Western has been appropriated and articulated to local genres (the *chanbara*) and that, in many cases, it is not an imported good but a native form (the Nordestern, the Boerewor Western, the bushranging picture). In most cases, the films surveyed here still converse with the dominant US-American version of the genre, in its classical (*Black God, White Devil, Jauja*), revisionist (*Unforgiven*), or post-Western (*Five Fingers for Marseilles*) forms as well as with the Italian Western (*Sukiyaki Western Django, Five Fingers for Marseilles*); they often aim to explore local histories of imperialism as much as US-American cultural hegemony.

Focusing on 1960s Brazil, chapter 11 offers a radical exploration of regional poverty, race relations, and US imperialism. Chapter 12 considers a twenty-first century take on Argentina's transnational history of colonialism, mixing classical Hollywood and New Independent Argentine Cinema. Chapter 13 compares three films from the 1990s to the 2010s to get a sense of the variety of Japanese cinema's relations to the Western, and the complicated relationship of a postimperial and post-US-occupied nation to the genre. Finally, chapter 14 contemplates colonial violence in its postapartheid manifestations and how rewriting the Western can help visualize—and hope for—a less violent future for South Africa.

In Australia, our terminus, we uncover the native heroes and themes that excited local audiences in the national productions that emerged in the 1900s, and rediscover the contemporary dynamism of the genre in providing radically new ways to visualize and write the history of Australia and Western colonialism.

Next stop: 1960s Brazil.

ELEVEN

—ɯ—

WEST BY NORTHEAST

The Western in Brazil

MIKE PHILLIPS

THIS CHAPTER EXAMINES THE RELATIONSHIP between US-American Westerns and Brazilian Nordesterns, films set in the arid northeastern region known as the *sertão*. The two national genres display similar geographic terrains and material historical parallels, such as conflicts between social banditry and industrial progress, or between small farmers and cattle barons. Where the mythology of the West revolves around cowboys and frontiersmen, the folklore of the Northeast concerns the exploits of *cangaceiros* (bandits), *jagunços* (hired guns), and *coroneis* (ranchers, sing. *coronel*). Despite the two nations' shared history of settler colonialism, there are stark divergences in their developmental trajectories. US cultural and economic imperialism, in Brazil and throughout Latin America, is both cause and effect of persistent underdevelopment.[1] The northward flow of natural resources has long been accompanied by a southward flood of mass media (Johnson 6–7, 36, 45, 60). US-American cinema thus becomes both an insidious tool of economic subordination and a cherished vehicle for popular entertainment. This apparent paradox animates the dialectical style of Glauber Rocha's *Antônio das Mortes* (*O Dragão da Maldade contra o Santo Guerreiro*, 1969), which juxtaposes Western iconography with Brazilian folklore in a self-consciously hybrid form and through a radical mode of transnational spectatorial address.

Rocha was the leading theoretician of the Cinema Novo movement that emerged in Rio de Janeiro in the late 1950s. Cinema Novo (Portuguese for "New Cinema") aimed to make politically engaged and distinctly Brazilian films, and rejected the aesthetic standards, narrative conventions, and industrial practices of commercial cinema. This school drew inspiration from Italian neorealism and the French New Wave, though its directors were as likely to borrow from

John Ford or Howard Hawks as from Vittorio De Sica or Jean-Luc Godard. In a public discussion of his earlier film *Black God, White Devil* (*Deus e o Diabo na Terra do Sol*, 1964), Rocha teased his fellow leftist Brazilian cineastes on this point: "To the disgust of many of you, this film was greatly influenced by the Western. It has a lot in it of John Ford, whom you don't like but I love." Referring to the gunslinger who becomes the eponymous antihero of the film's sequel, he continued, "Antônio das Mortes is himself a figure of Fordian citation: the way he looks, the way he moves, the use of landscape, the use of ballads" (Rocha, *Deus e o Diabo* 136, my translation). Over the course of both films, Antônio is shown to be an ambiguous character colored by a troubled past but possessing a deep moral sense, in the manner of canonical Western protagonists. Like Akira Kurosawa, Rocha "learned from [the] grammar of the Western" (Richie 147) and "poached" from it rather than simply elaborating on it.[2]

In a 1967 interview, Rocha explained that "one can make a Western or a Nordestern by taking lessons from Hawks or Ford, but inverting content and form: this is aesthetic cannibalism" (*Revolução* 92, my translation). This method derives from the modernist poet Oswald de Andrade's "Cannibalist Manifesto" of 1928, which advocated absorbing European, African, and indigenous influences quite deliberately and self-consciously in order to create a new uniquely Brazilian synthesis. By invoking Andrade, Rocha aligned himself with the emergent movement of Tropicalism.[3] The best-known expression of this aesthetic is in pop music, where artists like Caetano Veloso, Gilberto Gil, and Os Mutantes combined samba, bossa nova, and northeastern folk music with psychedelia and the *Sgt. Pepper*–era Beatles. Where Cannibalism satirized European aesthetic traditions, Tropicalism incorporated global mass culture, much of it imported from the US. Given the global popularity of the Western in this period and the unavoidable visual, characterological, and historical parallels between the West and the Northeast, Cannibalism was an eminently appropriate tactic for combating US cultural imperialism. Antônio is not a transplanted Western gunslinger, but the manifestation of a syncretic process through which Rocha borrows ostensibly colonialist forms to tell his decolonial story.

The stakes of this endeavor are complicated by the need to address film festival and art house audiences in the Global North, in addition to Brazil's radical intelligentsia and its potentially revolutionary underclass. Rocha's innovative mode of transnational spectatorial address and the radical historiography encapsulated in his dialectical approach to form combine to constitute a theory and practice of anti-imperialist generic hybridity. Rocha's hybridizing tactics trouble our understanding of Hollywood hegemony, in accordance with Christina Klein's call "to see Hollywood as an *object* rather than an agent of

Fig. 11.1 The professor's history lesson in *Antônio das Mortes* [1:47].

globalization, a reservoir of symbolic resources from which [non-US] film-makers draw as they navigate their way through their own globalized cultural economy" (873). As we shall see, the specific "symbolic resource" that Rocha poaches from the Western is one of its most enduring icons: the horse.

In the opening sequence of *Antônio das Mortes*, a disheveled professor crouches amid a group of boys, prompting them to repeat important dates in Brazilian history [1:36–2:28]. The list includes "discovery" by Europeans (1500), independence from Portugal (1822), the abolition of slavery (1888), the foundation of the Republic (1889), and the death of Lampião, the most fa-mous cangaceiro of all (1938). The scene takes place in the village square, with the professor and his students clustered in the foreground (fig. 11.1). Above the squat buildings behind them can be seen the mountains that surround the town, echoing the expansive depth of field in John Ford's Monument Valley Westerns. As the lesson progresses, a man on horseback leads a small group of cattle across the square in the middle ground. Behind him follow two more rid-ers, who briefly stop and circle in front of the Sudoeste (Southwest) Bar before moving on. The riders represent in miniature two enduring Western tropes: cattle drives and cowboy partners. Juxtaposed with the history lesson, these generic allusions create a dissonance between history and myth that undoes their frequent conflation in Hollywood Westerns. Far from suggesting the absolute separation of history and myth, however, Rocha's allusive but discordant maneuver prompts a reconsideration of their dialectical imbrication. To understand how this works, it is important to see *Antônio das Mortes* in the context of the Nordestern and its ambivalent relationship to the US-American Western.

TIME VAGUE: *O CANGACEIRO* AND THE EPIC PAST

The ubiquity of US-American cinema in Brazil dates to World War I, when Hollywood took advantage of the halt in European film production to become the undisputed leader in the global cinema market. US-American studios could easily recoup expenses in domestic exhibition, allowing them to spend more on production than foreign competitors and to export their product virtually risk free. During the silent era, Hollywood pictures regularly accounted for 80 percent or more of the total number of films released annually in Brazil (Johnson 36). It is hardly surprising, then, that producer/director Thomas Ince's Westerns inspired the first short film by Humberto Mauro, the most influential Brazilian director of the interwar period. Made in 1925, *Valadião, o Cratera* (*Valadião, the Crater*) "follows a band of desperadoes through the mountains of Minas Gerais," a largely rural interior state north of Rio de Janeiro (Johnson and Stam 25). That same year, a feature entitled *Filho sem Mãe* (*A Son without a Mother*) marked the first appearance on the screen of cangaceiros, the folk heroes of the *sertão* who would soon become fixtures in national popular cinema.

The coming of sound and the consequent language barrier for imported films fostered optimism in the Brazilian film industry, which found popular success with homegrown musical comedies known as *chanchadas*. US-American films were still pervasive, however, maintaining an average annual market share of over 80 percent in the 1940s (Johnson 61). After World War II, while much of Europe instituted protectionist policies to limit US dominance and rejuvenate domestic film production, the floodgates were left open throughout Latin America. For the moment, the fate of Brazilian cinema was left to a group of São Paulo industrialists who founded the Vera Cruz studio in 1949. With disdain for the down-market *chanchada* and fantasies rivaling the likes of MGM, they set out to make a more sophisticated type of film that would be competitive in foreign markets.

The studio's only international success, Lima Barreto's *O Cangaceiro* (1953), would later become a key intertextual foil for *Antônio das Mortes*. While films about the bandits of the *sertão* had proliferated over the previous quarter century, only Vera Cruz's prestige production would inspire the coinage *Nordestern*, a portmanteau combining *nordeste* (northeast) and *Western*. The term sardonically alludes to *O Cangaceiro*'s unabashed mimicry of Hollywood formulas, immediately apparent in its opening scene [1:58–5:27]. In standard Western fashion, the film fades in on a group of anonymous riders traversing a wide shot of open space. These cangaceiros join in a folk song with a call-and-response form, reminiscent of the singing cowboys of the 1930s or the Fordian motif of group singing. The song gives way to an orchestral recapitulation of its theme, which flows into a fluttering, descending musical cue clearly modeled on Hollywood scores. Galdino, the leader of the cangaceiro band, cuts an imposing figure as he rides toward the camera in a low-angle shot, deftly maneuvering his horse into a perfect medium-long shot in profile. The stranger whom he has stopped to confront is a surveyor dispatched from the capital. Galdino forcefully informs him that there will be no roads built through his territory.

The concern with roads is an unconventional reframing of a common motif in Western films: the construction of railroads. In a US-American Western, the encroachment of industry into pastoral lands often provides the central conflict, but here the surveyor is cursorily dismissed and never heard from again. W. D. Phillips notes, "In contrast to the American Western's morality of expansion, the Brazilian Northeastern inherited the local traditions of desperation and contraction ... that resulted from severe drought and rampant poverty" (Phillips 253). This moment thus highlights both Vera Cruz's Western pastiche and the intractable contradictions that arise when the genre is uncritically transplanted to a context of underdevelopment.

The scene's lack of narrative motivation may suggest that its main function is to present the immediately recognizable and popular image of the cangaceiro (Bernardet and Ramalho 36). Yet it can also lead to a misrecognition of the sadistic Galdino as a heroic "social bandit," reminiscent of a Jesse James.[4] This is especially true for audiences who have internalized Western generic expectations through regular consumption. As Rocha acknowledged, "In a US-American Western, there is already an established language. When the hero appears, you already know who he is *because of his horse*, because of what he's wearing. He brings all the necessary information with him. In our case the hero can't bring information with him that way because we don't have a cinematographic or literary tradition that speaks of this. And this may be a limitation of our cinema" (Delahaye, Kast, and Narboni 84, emphasis added).

Vera Cruz refused to recognize, or at least declined to engage, this limitation. This is apparent in the Western tropes that proliferate in the opening scene, but also in the prominence of horses throughout the film. Rocha severely criticized *O Cangaceiro* as a cynical imitation of Hollywood, partly based on the fact that the real Northeastern bandits very rarely went on horseback (Rocha, "Beginning at Zero" 144). Since all of Rocha's characters, consequently, tend to travel on foot, this is a key indication that the horses in *Antônio das Mortes* constitute overt allusions to the Western. At the same time, they act as implicit foils to derivative Nordesterns that borrow the "structure of American cinema, grounded in anti-dialectical thought" (Rocha, *On Cinema* 50, emphasis removed).

The teleological march of modernization implicit in Manifest Destiny finds no parallel in Brazil, creating a strange dissonance within the confrontation between Galdino and the surveyor. The Hegelian dialectic of Frederick Jackson Turner's "frontier thesis," which posits the emergence of a new form of humanity as the synthesis of the collision between civilization and wilderness, is entirely inappropriate to the historical trajectory of the *sertão*. Rocha's rejoinder to Vera Cruz's attempt at assimilation to the US-American model takes the form of a nondeterministic, antiteleological dialectic. Rocha's theoretical writings make clear that his heterodox conception of Marxist dialectics owes more to Eisenstein and Brecht than to Hegel. In 1967, Rocha called for an "epic/didactic cinema," a synthesis of poetry and science that would arise from "the violent dialectical process of information, analysis and rejection" (Rocha, *On Cinema* 47). This theory clearly echoes Eisenstein's notion that "*art is always conflict*" (47) and his anticipation of a "*synthesis of art and science*" (63). Rocha likewise draws from Brecht's theory of "epic theatre" and its integral concern with spectatorial address (37–38). All three of these artists overtly reject "vulgar Marxist" dialectical materialism and its belief in the inevitability of the "dictatorship of the proletariat." Rather, each of them sees dialectics as a continual creative process rather than a march toward a predetermined historical end point.[5]

With this in mind, it is curious that Ismael Xavier's otherwise brilliant *Allegories of Underdevelopment* identifies revolutionary teleology as the touchstone of Cinema Novo. Xavier attempts "to correlate ... structural variations—narrative teleology or its denial—with the different diagnoses of the human experience in time: historical teleology or its denial" (17). This either/or model and its focus on narrative structure elide Rocha's radical implementations of dialectic form. George Ciccariello-Maher has recently argued that decolonial dialecticians like Frantz Fanon, who greatly influenced Rocha's theories on political cinema, "resist all teleology, determinism, linearity, refuse all comforting promises of inherent progress. ... Their horizon remains a horizon" (7). It is precisely Rocha's rejection of teleology that allows him to mobilize Western conventions for decolonizing purposes, in contradistinction to *O Cangaceiro*.

The absence of a plausible teleology of progress in the Northeast prompted Vera Cruz to adopt an ahistorical approach, evident in the opening title card: "TIME: vague, when there were still cangaceiros. Any similarity with facts, incidents or persons alive or dead is mere coincidence" [1:53]. According to Sarah Sarzynski, Nordesterns often "start with voice-overs explaining the social and political history of Northeastern Brazil" (95). A similar Western conceit is an opening caption that situates the audience within the historical setting. It may simply state the time and place, as in *The Searchers* ("TEXAS 1868"), but often there is a longer text framing the sociohistorical scene. Anthony Mann was particularly fond of this type of caption, for instance, in *The Furies* (1950), which opens with the statement: "This is a story of the 1870s. . . . In the New Mexico Territory . . . when men created kingdoms out of land and cattle . . . and ruled their empires like feudal lords." Compare Billy Jaynes Chandler's description of the *sertão*'s social structure: "The cattle baron [or *coronel*], who owned the land, was a backlands potentate equal in his own world to the sugar plantation lord of the coast. He ruled his world almost at will, often giving short shrift to the few officials sent to impose larger law and discipline" (122). While the reign of the ranchers in the West is, at least theoretically, a bygone era, Brazil's quasi-feudal system of *coronelismo* continued throughout the time of the cangaceiro (ca. 1870–1940) and, in some remote areas, survives essentially unchanged today. This goes some way to explaining why no historical data are provided in *O Cangaceiro*'s opening caption.

This text was not included in director Lima Barreto's screenplay, which begins with a montage of exterior shots of present-day São Paulo, eventually arriving at the entrance to the state penitentiary. On his release from prison after thirty years inside, a former cangaceiro recounts his exploits in a flashback frame narrative (Barreto 39–45). The bulk of the action would thus have taken place around 1920, when there were still cangaceiros indeed. Hence, the odd contrast between the first half of the caption, which places the action in a remote mythical past, and the accompanying disclaimer, which clearly indicates that the *cangaço* (banditry) was within living memory. The elided contradiction between the two exemplifies Vera Cruz's self-consciousness regarding the image of the nation it was projecting to the world. *O Cangaceiro*'s opportunistic mimicry of the Western appealed to global audiences, but it also risked exposing socioeconomic similarities between the nineteenth-century West and the twentieth-century Northeast that could paint the latter as retrograde to foreign eyes. The studio's desire to make world-class films does not reflect an impartial regard for cinematic aesthetics, but rather its founders' material interest in disseminating an ideological vision of Brazil as a fully modernized nation. Reassuring foreign investors that Brazil was economically modern required the disavowal that the *cangaço* was a recent phenomenon.

Borrowing from the Western invoked the desired measure of historical distance, placing the narrative in what Mikhail Bakhtin called the "epic past." The temporal setting of the classical epic, he writes, "lacks any relativity, that is, any gradual, purely temporal progressions that might connect it with the present. It is walled off absolutely from all subsequent times, and above all those times in which the singer and his listeners are located" (15–16). This is perfectly in line with classical Hollywood's mode of spectator address, which presents a diegetic totality that is a plausible facsimile of the material world and yet is wholly separate from it. It also accords with Rocha's maxim, "For the European [or North American] observer, the process of artistic creation in the underdeveloped world is of interest only insofar as it satisfies a nostalgia for primitivism" ("Esthetic of Hunger" 69). By exiling the *cangaço* to the epic past, Vera Cruz achieved two apparently contradictory goals: appealing to this "nostalgia for primitivism," while also displaying an aesthetic and technical sophistication that would signal Brazil's modernity and its capacity as an international market.

A naive belief in the persuasive power of production values and the meritocratic nature of the global cinematic economy doomed Vera Cruz from the start. By the time *O Cangaceiro* won two prizes at the 1953 Cannes Film Festival (for best adventure film and best music), Vera Cruz was already going bankrupt (Galvão 277; Johnson 62–63). Nonetheless, their attempt to integrate Brazilian semantics and Hollywood syntax produced some instructive dissonances that would ultimately influence Rocha's subsequent engagement with the Western. His radical departure from the Vera Cruz method exemplifies Linda Lewin's argument that, "in the second half of the twentieth century," the cangaceiro was "adopted as a national figure of protest against what an earlier 'modernizing' generation defined as an economically backward and lawless past" (117). Whereas Vera Cruz wanted to drive a temporal wedge between the *cangaço* and the contemporary, Rocha revives the cangaceiro as a popular icon.

DRIVING INTO THE SUNSET: THE ELEGIAC
WESTERN AND GENERIC SUBVERSION

To this end, Rocha "instrumentalizes" the Western as a readily available model for holding popular myth and official history in tension (Rocha, *On*

Cinema 56–57). This approach is established by the inclusion of Lampião's demise among the foundational events of national history in the first scene of *Antônio das Mortes*. Rejecting epic temporality, Rocha presents the *cangaço* as a material historical phenomenon that continues to resonate in the present. At the same time, the film's temporal setting remains somewhat ambiguous, mirroring the context of uneven economic development that complicates the translatability of Western conventions in a Latin American context. Unlike *O Cangaceiro*, Rocha's 1969 film directly engages these temporal dislocations through an unorthodox manipulation of generic semiotics.

The vehicle for this dialectical exercise is the horse, a Western icon that appears on three discrete and quite specific occasions in *Antônio das Mortes* [1:36–2:28, 9:14–9:47, 1:29:14–1:32:39]. By alternately activating, subverting, and superseding generic expectations through juxtaposition with local traditions, Rocha aims to speak equally to Brazilian and transnational audiences.[6] Associating horses with classical Westerns and derivative Nordesterns in his opening sequence allows Rocha to mobilize Western tropes for antithetical purposes later on. Where the first appearance of horses evokes canonical conventions, the second alludes to the revisionist Westerns of the 1960s while also drawing clear connections between past and present. When a peasant uprising led by a cangaceiro occupies the village, the local *coronel* sends his political functionary, Matos—a variation on the corrupt sheriff—to town to bring the gunslinger Antônio out of retirement. Thinking he had killed the last cangaceiro at the end of *Black God, White Devil*, Antônio agrees out of sheer curiosity and tells his woman to pack his rifle and hat. Cut to a high-angle extreme long shot that pans across the mountainous countryside, stopping at the village square, which we recognize from the opening scene, now with two riders entering from the left. This is followed by a full shot of a large blue jeep pulling up in front of the Sudoeste Bar. Out step Matos and Antônio, the two equestrians nowhere to be seen [6:29–10:17]. Here Rocha juxtaposes two versions of "riding into town": the Western convention of two men on horseback, and its generic subversion in Antônio's arrival in an automobile.

This sequence is reminiscent of the opening scene of Sam Peckinpah's *Ride the High Country* (1962), in which aging Western fixture Joel McCrea, dazed by the sight of a camel racing down the main street of a typical Western town, is nearly run over by a fin-de-siècle motorcar. Edward Buscombe succinctly describes the import of this scene: "Significantly, the camel is racing against a horse; such a grotesque juxtaposition is painful. A horse in a Western is not just an animal but a symbol of dignity, grace, and power. These qualities are mocked by having it compete with a camel; and to add insult to injury, the camel wins"

("Idea of Genre" 23). Such overt reversals of generic expectations are a common factor between Rocha's Nordesterns and a roughly contemporary cycle of US-American Westerns that pushed the temporal boundaries of the genre past its conventional end point, the "closing of the frontier" in 1890 (Turner 1). A triptych of films released in 1962—*Ride the High Country, The Man Who Shot Liberty Valance* (John Ford), and *Lonely Are the Brave* (David Miller)— instantiated the "elegiac Western," which alternately problematized and reified the genre's intrinsic tendency toward nostalgia (Marsden and Nachbar 1273–74; Lusted 205–30). All three present parallels with *Antônio das Mortes*: *The Man Who Shot Liberty Valance* revolves around the tenuous alliance between a gunfighter and an intellectual, and *Lonely Are the Brave* concerns an anachronistic cowboy in a contemporary setting. The latter likewise juxtaposes the generic horse with the extrageneric automobile; the skittishness of the protagonist's horse as they cross a busy highway in the opening scene foreshadows their ultimate demise after being struck by a tractor trailer in the final reel.

The elegiac Western hypostatizes a generic convention identified by Robert Warshow: the temporal setting is often precisely "as the reign of law settles over the West and [the hero] is forced to see that his day is over; those are the pictures that end with his death or with his departure for some more remote frontier" (140). Nordesterns similarly tend to be set during the decline of the *cangaço* (ca. 1940), which supposedly signaled a new modernizing order in the *sertão* (Sarzynski 83). As we have seen, however, the Brazilian dialectic of modernization and underdevelopment persists. Antônio das Mortes does, indeed, leave town at the end of the film, but the final shot shows him walking away along a highway, cars blaring their horns as he passes underneath a Shell gas station sign [92:39–93:33].

Courtney Fellion sees this image as signaling Antônio's obsolescence, as he "walks off as though defeated by the presence of the modern world" (49). This reading tends to assimilate Rocha's film to the elegiac subgenre of the US Western, but his ending rejects the maudlin nostalgia that characterizes that cycle. I am inclined to agree with Chelsea Wessels that "the film avoids creating a solution or offering closure, keeping the ending in line with the openness of Third Cinema" (194). If this shot visually echoes the tragic roadside ending of *Lonely Are the Brave*, Rocha jettisons the earlier film's nostalgic lament by stressing Antônio's survival rather than his disappearance. The reclamation of residual folk forms in aid of an emergent radical politics denies Vera Cruz's rigid separation between a mythological past and a modernized present.[7] Instead, it exploits the radical potential of anachronism to evoke the dialectical relationship between the past and the present.

Rocha's nonlinear historiography is made manifest in the third and final appearance of a horse in *Antônio das Mortes*. While the first had established a link with the Western genre through allusion, and the second had subverted those links by invoking the elegiac mode, the third acts as the dialectic synthesis and supersession of the first two. In his comments about Brazilian cinema "lack[ing] an established grammar," Rocha recognizes the impracticality of completely ignoring Hollywood formulas. That would amount to a bad-faith disavowal of Brazilian cinema's underdevelopment, of the kind practiced by Vera Cruz. The question remains, how does one forge an anti-imperialist aesthetics using the semiotic tools disseminated by empire? The elegiac mode is insufficient to this task since it merely presents the dialectical antithesis to the Western. Rocha thus mobilizes the classical and the elegiac to produce their mutually negating synthesis. The horses of *Antônio das Mortes* turn the Western genre's iconography against itself to produce a positive negation that opens a space for new modes of expression.

THE WARRIOR SAINT: THE SYNTHESIS OF THE LOCAL/TRANSNATIONAL DIALECTIC

Standard historical narratives of Cinema Novo frame the adoption of Tropicalist bricolage and aesthetic excess as completely supplanting the bare, stark style of earlier films like *Black God, White Devil* (Johnson and Stam 30–40; Xavier 155). This usually goes hand in hand with a national frame of reference in which Tropicalism would be a response to increasing repression by the military dictatorship that had taken power in 1964 and the subsequent failure of the left to mount an effective resistance. This mode of analysis tends to follow Fredric Jameson's controversial postulate that all Third World narratives take the form of national allegory (69). Zooming out from a national scale to the global context of Brazilian film production and distribution, the continuities between the various "phases" of Cinema Novo become more apparent. Rocha's deployment of Western tropes is less a kitsch reaction to the contemporary political impasse than a strategy to triangulate geographically and socioeconomically diverse audiences, who had internalized generic expectations through continual exposure to Hollywood fare.

The culmination of Rocha's complex engagement with the Western is (as one might expect) a final showdown, in which Rocha characteristically hybridizes mass culture and folk forms [85:18–89:37]. By the end of the film, Antônio has turned against his former employer, joining forces with the history professor on the side of the rebellion. Rocha acknowledged that the image of Antônio and the professor firing side by side was inspired by *Ride the High Country*, and the highly theatrical shoot-out has been compared to the final gunfight in another Peckinpah film, *The Wild Bunch* (1969) (Buscombe, *100 Westerns* 4). Yet Rocha's antinaturalistic staging diverges drastically from Peckinpah's tendency to revel in slow-motion carnage. "When violence is presented in a descriptive manner," Rocha argued in a 1967 interview, "it pleases the audience because it stimulates their sadomasochistic instincts. What I want to present is the *idea* of violence and at the same time a certain frustration with violence. We need to reflect on violence and not make a spectacle of it" (*Revolução* 92, my translation).

For Rocha, violence finds meaning through its motivation in the liberatory aspirations of the colonized. His 1965 manifesto, "An Esthetic of Hunger," declares that "the most noble cultural manifestation of hunger is violence. Cinema Novo shows that the normal behavior of the starving is violence; and the violence of the starving is not primitive" (70). While Rocha invokes literal revolutionary violence, he was not a guerilla but a filmmaker. Accordingly, the primary connotation here is *cinematic* violence, not only in content but in form. In this sense, Rocha's films commit aesthetic violence on the spectator; for example, in cinematographer Waldemar Lima's intentional overexposure of *Black God, White Devil*'s exterior footage, which may initially read as a technical error. The blinding brightness of the earlier film, in which a peasant murders the *coronel* who exploits his labor—thus, quite literally enacting the progression from hunger to violence—is clearly echoed in the climax of its sequel, *Antônio das Mortes*.

Once Antônio and the professor have slaughtered the *jagunços*, Antão, an Afro-Brazilian leader of the uprising, unexpectedly rides in on a white horse to impale the *coronel* with a lance. The staging echoes iconic images of St. George slaying the dragon, a legend referenced in the original Portuguese title of the film, *The Dragon of Evil vs. the Warrior Saint*. São Jorge, the patron saint of Portugal, has a devoted following in Brazil, not only among Catholics but also in the syncretic Afro-Brazilian Candomblé religion (Walker 111). Antão's horse, as opposed to those that have appeared earlier in the film, does not invoke the Western. Rocha's establishment of the generic connotations of horses paves the ground for this anti-imperialist image, which now poses its horse in contradistinction to the earlier generic examples. It is also the most literal implementation of Eisensteinian cinematic dialectics. The image of Antão slaying the *coronel* is composed of three shots from the same angle, connected by jump cuts. The first two shots maintain the film's richly saturated color palette, but the third suddenly replicates the overexposure characteristic of *Black God, White Devil* and Rocha's aesthetics of hunger (fig. 11.2).[8]

Fig. 11.2 Antão as São Jorge in *Antônio das Mortes* [89:34].

Rocha offers the Brazilian public the iconography of São Jorge as an alternative to US cultural imperialism, of which the Western is a prevalent manifestation. At the same time, his aggressive visual style commits symbolic violence on the generic expectations of spectators in the Global North. Rocha's practice exemplifies Janet Staiger's argument, glossing Homi Bhabha, that transnational and minoritarian genre filmmaking troubles notions of generic stability: "To recognize a hybrid forces the dominant culture to look back at itself and see its presumption of universality. Hybridity always opens up the discriminatory presumptions of purity, authenticity, and originality from which this textual hybrid is declared to be a deviation, a bastard, a corruption" (214). This uncannily echoes a passage from "An Esthetic of Hunger": "From Cinema Novo it should be learned that an aesthetic of violence, before being primitive, is revolutionary. It is the initial moment when the colonizer becomes aware of the colonized. Only when confronted with violence does the colonizer understand, through horror, the strength of the culture he exploits" (70). Rocha's manifesto is a treatise on spectatorial positionality as much as it is the delineation of a certain Third Worldist approach to film art. The urgency of forging a form outside of institutional economic structures also calls for a decolonizing mode of spectatorial address that can reach both local and global audiences, as demonstrated in Rocha's hybrid aesthetic.

NOTES

1. On the history of US imperialism in Latin America, see Galeano.

2. The concept of textual poaching derives from de Certeau.

3. For an overview of "The Tropicalist Movement" across cinema, theater, literature, popular music, and the fine arts, see Dunn 73–121.

4. On social banditry, see Hobsbawm. For an opposing view of cangaceiros as a socially conservative phenomenon, see Lewin.

5. For a concise overview of the variants of dialectics in Marxist thought, see the introduction to Ollman and Smith (1–7).

6. *Supersession* here approximates the more precise but obscure term *sublation*, the common translation of Hegel's *Aufhebung*. Sublation is "the simultaneous abolition and retention of the elements of the old within the new" (Foley 11).

7. See the chapter entitled, "Dominant, Residual, and Emergent," in Williams (121–27).

8. The use of color in this scene also integrates modern technology (Eastmancolor film stock) with traditional art forms, as Solomon argues.

WORKS CITED

Bakhtin, Mikhail. *The Dialogic Imagination.* Edited by Michael Holquist, translated by Caryl Emerson and Michael Holquist, University of Texas Press, 1981.

Barreto, Lima. *O Cangaceiro.* Edições Universidade Federal do Ceará, 1984.

Bernardet, Lucila Ribeiro, and Francisco Ramalho, Jr. "Cangaço—Da Vontade de se Sentir Enquadrado." *Cangaço: O nordestern no cinema brasileiro,* edited by Maria do Rosário Caetano, Avathar Soluções Gráficas, 2005, pp. 33–54.

Brecht, Bertolt. *Brecht on Theatre.* Translated by John Willett, Hill and Wang, 1964.

Buscombe, Edward. "The Idea of Genre in the American Cinema." *Film Genre Reader IV,* edited by Barry Keith Grant, University of Texas Press, 2012, pp. 12–26.

———. *100 Westerns.* British Film Institute, 2006.

Certeau, Michel de. *The Practice of Everyday Life.* Translated by Steven Rendall, University of California Press, 1984.

Chandler, Billy Jaynes. *The Bandit King: Lampião of Brazil.* Texas A&M University Press, 1978.

Ciccariello-Maher, George. *Decolonizing Dialectics.* Duke University Press, 2017.

Delahaye, Michel, Pierre Kast, and Jean Narboni. "*Antônio das Mortes*: An Interview with Glauber Rocha." Translated by Helen R. Lane, *Grove Press Film Festival Book*, Grove, 1970, pp. 35–37, 81–85.

Dunn, Christopher. *Brutality Garden: Tropicália and the Emergence of a Brazilian Counterculture*. University of North Carolina Press, 2001.

Eisenstein, Sergei. *Film Form: Essays in Film Theory*. Edited and translated by Jay Leyda, Harcourt, 1949.

Fellion, Courtney. "Third Cinema Goes West: Common Ground for Film and Literary Theory in Postregional Discourse." *Western American Literature*, vol. 48, nos. 1–2, Spring–Summer 2013, pp. 41–55.

Foley, Barbara. *Marxist Literary Criticism Today*. Pluto, 2019.

The Furies. Directed by Anthony Mann, performances by Barbara Stanwyck, Wendell Corey, and Walter Huston. Paramount, 1950.

Galeano, Eduardo. *Open Veins of Latin America: Five Centuries of the Pillage of a Continent*. Monthly Review, 1997.

Galvão, Maria Rita. "Vera Cruz: A Brazilian Hollywood." *Brazilian Cinema*, edited by Randal Johnson and Robert Stam, Columbia University Press, 1995, pp. 270–80.

Hobsbawm, Eric. *Bandits*. Delacorte, 1969.

Jameson, Fredric. "Third-World Literature in an Era of Multinational Capitalism." *Social Text*, no. 15, Autumn 1986, pp. 65–88.

Johnson, Randal. *The Film Industry in Brazil: Culture and the State*. University of Pittsburgh Press, 1987.

Johnson, Randal, and Robert Stam, editors. *Brazilian Cinema*. Columbia University Press, 1995.

Klein, Christina. "Why American Studies Needs to Think about Korean Cinema, or, Transnational Genres in the Films of Bong Joon-ho." *American Quarterly*, vol. 60, no. 4, Dec. 2008, pp. 871–98.

Lewin, Linda. "The Oligarchical Limitations of Social Banditry in Brazil: The Case of the 'Good' Thief Antônio Silvino." *Past and Present*, vol. 82, no. 1, Feb. 1979, pp. 116–46.

Lonely Are the Brave. Directed by David Miller, performances by Kirk Douglas, Gena Rowlands, and Walter Matthau. Universal, 1962.

Lusted, David. *The Western*. Routledge, 2003.

The Man Who Shot Liberty Valance. Directed by John Ford, performances by James Stewart and John Wayne. Paramount, 1962.

Marsden, Michael T., and Jack Nachbar. "The Modern Popular Western: Radio, Television, Film and Print." *A Literary History of the American West*, Texas Christian University Press, 1987, pp. 1263–82.

O Cangaceiro. Directed by Lima Barreto, performances by Alberto Ruschel, Marisa Prado, and Milton Ribeiro. Vera Cruz, 1953.

Ollman, Bertell, and Tony Smith, editors. *Dialectics for the New Century*. Palgrave Macmillan, 2008.

Phillips, W. D. "*O Cangaceiro* (1953) and the Brazilian Northeastern: The Western 'in the Land of the Sun.'" *International Westerns: Re-locating the Frontier*, edited by Cynthia J. Miller and Bowdoin Van Riper, Scarecrow, 2014, pp. 243–62.

Richie, Donald. *The Films of Akira Kurosawa*. University of California Press, 1998.

Ride the High Country. Directed by Sam Peckinpah, performances by Joel McCrea, Randolph Scott, and Mariette Hartley. MGM, 1962.

Rocha, Glauber, director. *Antônio das Mortes* [*O Dragão da Maldade contra o Santo Guerreiro*], performances by Maurício do Valle, Odete Lara, and Othon Bastos. Claude-Antoine, 1969.

———. "Beginning at Zero: Notes on Cinema and Society." Translated by Joanne Pottlitzer, *The Drama Review: TDR*, vol. 14, no. 2, Winter 1970, pp. 144–49.

———, director. *Black God, White Devil* [*Deus e o Diabo na Terra do Sol*], performances by Geraldo Del Rey, Yoná Magalhães, Othon Bastos, and Maurício do Valle. Copacabana Filmes, 1964.

———. *Deus e o Diabo na Terra do Sol*. Editôra Civilização Brasileira, 1965.

———. "An Esthetic of Hunger." Translated by Randal Johnson and Burnes Hollyman, *Brazilian Cinema*, edited by Randal Johnson and Robert Stam, Columbia University Press, 1995, pp. 68–71.

———. *On Cinema*. Edited by Ismail Xavier, translated by Stephanie Dennison and Charlotte Smith, I. B. Tauris, 2019.

———. *Revolução de Cinema Novo*. Alhambra/Embrafilme, 1981.

Sarzynski, Sarah. "The Popular, the Political, and the Ugly: Brazilian *Nordesterns* in a Comparative Cold War Context, 1960–1975." *Rethinking Third Cinema: The Role of Anti-Colonial Media and Aesthetics in Postmodernity*, edited by Frieda Ekotto and Adeline Koh, Transaction, 2009, pp. 81–105.

Solomon, Stefan. "'The Cloak of Technicolor': Intermedial Colour in *Antônio das Mortes*." *Screen*, vol. 60, no. 1, 2019, pp. 137–47.

Staiger, Janet. "Hybrid or Inbred: The Purity Hypothesis and Hollywood Genre History." *Film Genre Reader IV*, edited by Barry Keith Grant, University of Texas Press, 2012, pp. 203–17.

Turner, Frederick Jackson. *The Frontier in American History*. Holt, Rinehart, and Winston, 1962.

Walker, Sheila S. "Everyday and Esoteric Reality in the Afro-Brazilian Candomblé." *History of Religions*, vol. 30, no. 2, 1990, pp. 103–28.

Warshow, Robert. "Movie Chronicle: The Westerner." *The Immediate Experience: Movies, Comics, Theatre and Other Aspects of Popular Culture*, Atheneum, 1972, pp. 135–54.

Wessels, Chelsea. "An 'Imperfect' Genre: Rethinking Politics in Latin American Westerns." *The Western in the Global South*, edited by MaryEllen Higgins, Rita Keresztesi, and Dayna Oscherwitz, Routledge, 2015, pp. 183–97.

Williams, Raymond. *Marxism and Literature*. Oxford University Press, 1977.

Xavier, Ismael. *Allegories of Underdevelopment: Aesthetics and Politics in Modern Brazilian Cinema*. University of Minnesota Press, 1997.

MIKE PHILLIPS is Clinical Assistant Professor of Cinema and Photography at Southern Illinois University Carbondale.

TWELVE

(NOT) JOHN WAYNE AND (NOT) THE US-AMERICAN WEST

Jauja (Lisandro Alonso, 2014)

JENNY BARRETT

UNTIL *JAUJA* (2014), ARGENTINE DIRECTOR Lisandro Alonso had only filmed contemporary stories of isolated men (played by nonprofessional actors), which were said, by critic James Quandt, to center on men who "ride lonesome." Set in 1880s Argentina, *Jauja* follows the story of Danish captain Gunnar Dinesen, a man who rides lonesome after his daughter has eloped into the wilderness and, ultimately, fails in his search for her. *Jauja* stars Viggo Mortensen, who is half Danish, was partly raised in Argentina, and contributed to the film's narrative and music. In keeping with the long history of Argentine cinema being dependent on both state subsidy and international funding (Falicov 55), *Jauja* is a transnational production, with funding from companies and bodies in Denmark, Argentina, Mexico, France, and the Netherlands; languages spoken in the film include Danish, French, Spanish, and Danish-accented Spanish. It was written by the Argentine screenwriter Fabían Casas and filmed by Finnish cinematographer Timo Salminen, known for his award-winning films with director Aki Kaurismäki.

The input of Mortensen, Casas, and Salminen, as the film festival interviews suggest (Diestro-Dópido, "Paradise" and "Living"; Porton), led to narrative and stylistic allusions to the classical Hollywood Western, and yet, despite his focus on "men who ride lonesome," Alonso's art cinema direction resists many of the genre's iconic and affirmatory conventions, creating an apparent tension between auteur and genre expectations. This chapter observes *Jauja* in the context of Argentine cinema and in relation to Hollywood Westerns. This particular Latin American cinema has an ongoing and complex relationship with Hollywood, described by Tamara Leah Falicov as "a complicated tango"

(5), and, since the 1980s at least, has had a significant presence at leading European film festivals (48). Taking these contexts into account and observing some of the statements made by Alonso and Mortensen in interviews, this chapter identifies stylistic and narrative elements that may seem incongruous but that build up a coherent discourse. *Jauja* makes use both of conventions familiar from the New Independent Argentine Cinema and of intertextual references to classical Hollywood. Their interaction works to create two possible readings of a highly reflective film that is critical of colonialism, both historically and culturally: one that encourages reflection on Argentina's history as a Spanish colony and one that, subsequently, draws attention to the colonizing nature of Hollywood cinema.

If conventional views of the Western define it as "a series of visual and thematic tropes that . . . came to 'speak' a nation's history, advancing a 'national iconography' and work to construct American national identity" (Carter, "Crossing" 30), Susan Kollin reminds us that it was "never a quintessential or uniquely American form" (Kollin 35). Kollin points to the early influences of colonial adventure stories, romantic attitudes toward the man of the desert gained from trips to the Middle East by Theodore Roosevelt and others, and the regularity of Westerns produced outside of the US; she also prompts a recognition of *West* and *Western* as part of a nineteenth-century Eurocentric colonial discourse that existed within "an ongoing transnational history of settler colonialism" (24). Whereas Western stories were initially labeled as such "as a way of narrating a certain type of American settler colonial activity" (23), the genre exists globally with expressions found in multiple nations where a postcolonial consciousness resides. Comparisons between the colonial histories of the US and Argentina can be made while keeping in mind their singularities. In both nations, settlers of European descent established their own "new society" through violent conflict and the forced migration of thousands of people from their lands, a form of "settler colonialism" made possible, in Lorenzo Veracini's words, through "controlling and dominating indigenous peoples" (314). Kollin's and Veracini's perspectives help us understand the Western as a genre that can both reinforce and challenge conventional constructions of US national identity, "progress," and colonial guilt or postcolonial expression. We will see how *Jauja* reprises a range of classical Western conventions to explore the period immediately after the Argentine military campaign to "conquer" the Indigenous people of the Pampas. In particular, I argue that Alonso's stylistic approach draws a strong link to Hollywood's cultural control and domination over national cinemas.

NEW ARGENTINE CINEMA

Alonso tends to be discussed critically as part of the New Argentine Cinema, a generation of young filmmakers who emerged from film schools in the late 1990s, work with low budgets, and resist genre formulas. Their work has had less commercial appeal than films such as *Comodines* (*Cops*, Jorge Nisco, 1997), one of Argentina's most successful homemade blockbusters that follows a Hollywood action movie format but has performed well at international film festivals. Falicov explains that, unlike a film movement, these filmmakers have no common purpose but, stylistically at least, appear to share a realist aesthetic referred to by some as "neo-neorealism" (121): a documentary look, minimal dialogue, and an emphasis on Argentine space. Narratively, they tend to tell stories of marginalized characters, Indigenous people, and immigrants, helping "expand the notion of Argentine citizenship to include subjects and characters who have traditionally been invisible or excluded from Argentine screens" (130). In contrast to the New Latin American Cinema of the 1960s and 1970s and the so-called "guerilla" cinema or "Third Cinema" of filmmakers such as Fernando Solanas and Octavio Getino, the New Argentine Cinema resists overt political moralizing, but its realist style and attention to the lives of those living in the margins harks back to their predecessors' determination to make Argentine films about Argentina. In the late 1960s and 1970s, Solanas and Getino sought to "'decolonise' the spectator from the dominant ideology of imperialism" by making films about a "real" Argentina, not least a cinema that rejected Hollywood glossiness, escapism, and optimism (4). The "subtle mechanisms of colonialism," Sergio Roncallo and Juan Arias-Herrera explain, "were not political interventions or state matters, but a problem of representation" (97); in other words, the realist cinema of South America in the 1960s and 1970s sought to create a new platform for Latin American representation that resisted the othering they had been subjected to through mainstream Hollywood cinema. Such a resistance was deemed a political act; as Roncallo and Arias-Herrera write, "to rebel against Hollywood was the equivalent to rebel against colonization in a broader political sense" (97). The New Argentine Cinema of the 1990s and early 2000s seemed to demonstrate a similar impulse but without the overt political discourse of films such as Solanas and Getino's *La hora de los hornos* (*Hour of the Furnaces*, 1968), with its subsections, political captions on screen, and interspersing of found footage with their own documentary images of the "real" Argentina.

Because the films of the New Argentine Cinema in the late 1990s had less domestic commercial appeal than popular genre films, funding from the

Argentine National Film Institute (INCAA) had, and continues, to be supplemented with other sources, typically from grants and coproduction opportunities with companies outside of Argentina. It is from this particular production context that the New Argentine Cinema can be understood as a transnational cinema. Its critical popularity, too, owes more to its international than its domestic box office success. Alonso's first feature film, *La libertad* (*Freedom*, 2001), for example, premiered in the Un Certain Regard section at the Cannes Film Festival in 2001. The director then moved on to collect a series of awards for his films at leading festivals in Europe. *Jauja* won the FIPRESCI Award at Cannes in 2014. Recently, Alonso became a jury member for Un Certain Regard. In a number of ways, however, *Jauja* contrasts with Alonso's earlier films, not least by featuring a non-Argentine protagonist, having a historical context for its narrative, and casting a Hollywood A-lister, Viggo Mortensen. The impact of these is discussed below, but what follows first is a summary of the film's narrative.

JAUJA AND ITS SLOW CINEMA AESTHETICS

An opening title at the film's beginning explains that *jauja* refers to a "land of abundant happiness" that is never found since those who seek it become lost on the way. Captain Dinesen, a Danish military engineer, is temporarily living in a tent near the coast of Patagonia, Argentina, with his fourteen-year-old daughter, Ingeborg. As dialogue between Dinesen and the military personnel reveals, the plot opens not long after the Conquest of the Desert, the Argentine military invasion that drew on international allies to clear the "wild" desert of Patagonia of its indigenous population and opened the way for white European settlement. One of the most highly respected officers, a man named Zuluaga, has deserted; he has a mystical reputation and is believed to be able to disappear into the desert and travel at the speed of light, or so the tales tell. Zuluaga is traveling with a band of thieves and is disguised as a woman. Conscious that the soldiers are attracted to his daughter, Dinesen attempts to control her contact with them, concluding that he and she do not belong there and will soon return to Denmark. Ingeborg, however, is in love with the desert and is secretly meeting a scout named Corto. At night, Corto and Ingeborg steal away in the dark, taking a horse and Dinesen's compass. Although Dinesen notices that his daughter is gone when it is still dark, he takes time to dress in his military uniform and waits until dawn before departing. For a number of days, Dinesen searches for his daughter without success. He follows a tall gray dog to a cave up in the rocks where he finds an elderly woman. Their conversation suggests that this woman could be Ingeborg, with her alternately referring to Ingeborg as both "she" and "I," but Dinesen leaves to continue his search for his daughter, and he falls to his knees in despair.

The film then shifts time and location to current-day Denmark where the same actress who plays Ingeborg wakes up and wanders around a palatial building and its gardens. A dog that appears to be the same one that guided Dinesen to the cave has patchy fur, and a man tells her that this is because it cannot understand why she is staying away so long. The comment remains unexplained. She walks the dog and happens upon a toy soldier that, as Ingeborg, she had found by the sea in Argentina, which she then throws into a pond. It lands in the shallow waters of what seems to be the Argentine coast, although the time cannot be ascertained; perhaps it is current day, but more likely it is back in the nineteenth century again.

Typical of art cinema, a number of devices in *Jauja* draw attention to the narration, and these devices are reminiscent of the cinema of the past. The conspicuous use of a mask with curved corners, constricting the image within a narrow ratio, recalls early presound cinema. There are points in the film when diegetic sounds are so scarce it even seems silent. For the first half of the film, the images of the coast saturate the mise-en-scène with an emerald green color bringing to mind the vibrant hues of Natalie Kalmus's Technicolor of the classical Hollywood era. The seaweed on the seashore, the grass at the encampment, and the vegetation of the wilderness are so vividly green that their loss is viscerally felt when replaced by the dry yellow of pampas grass, and the gray and black of the rocks.

Jauja conforms to a number of expectations of Alonso's work: stories about solitary men who are separated from their families and living a marginalized existence either economically or geographically, or both. *La libertad* in 2001, *Los muertos* (*The Dead*) in 2004, and *Liverpool* in 2008—each use the same slow observational cinematography and pace. Of his many stylistic nuances, the long take or sequence shot is perhaps Alonso's most characteristic, often allowing the camera to gaze at the action—or the lack thereof—for far longer than mainstream conventions would allow. Whether it is Dinesen riding across the wilderness or a soldier masturbating in a shallow pool, shots in *Jauja* may last as long as three minutes. Dennis and Joan M. West's interview with Alonso posits that the combination of a slow cinema style with narratives about men who ride lonesome elicits an active viewer, writing that his films "summon viewers to actively sift through the evidence in constant search for clues as to what made these men what they are or what they appear to be" (30). Alonso professes that he wishes for the spectator to "grasp the appropriate elements and make up his or her own world" (35), and this accounts for some of the ambiguity of his films. He would like the viewer to have "time to ponder" (37) and to become conscious of the camera and the director. In essence, this is the kind of art cinema that causes the viewer to consider a film in the light of their cinematic knowledge and to regard the film in contrast to the mainstream. Alonso's slow colonial adventure story allows for "time to ponder" at least two interrelated readings.

THE COLONIZER AND THE WESTERNER

Alonso's earlier films are set in contemporary locations atypical of popular Argentine cinema, which tends to situate itself in urban centers such as Buenos Aires. As a historical narrative set in nineteenth-century Argentina in the unsettled Pampas region to the south, *Jauja* stands out from both contemporary Argentine cinema and Alonso's previous films. Jens Anderman's exploration of New Argentine Cinema describes Alonso's films as having a "radical exclusion of any direct reference to politics and history" (85), but this was written before the release of *Jauja*. Of course, *Jauja*'s "anticolonial resonance" might originate more in the screenwriter than in the director, as Mortensen suggested: "I don't think he [Alonso] set out to do that. That might have been more Fabián's intention" (Porton 37).

The film's retrospective focus on an era of settling wild spaces, with the resultant conflict between Indigenous people, Spanish settlers, and immigrants, causes the film to become quite conspicuous in Alonso's oeuvre and encourages an active interpretation to be sought. The film's historical context is thus intriguing. *Jauja* is set after the Conquest of the Desert, the significant military sweep across the southern wilderness to force Indigenous tribes onto reservations, first, as a retaliation for attacks on settled areas by the tribes, and, second, to occupy and colonize the Pampas region (Rock 152–55). Alonso's earlier films might have led us to expect the story to present the perspective of the Indigenous people of the Pampas. However, the film follows the colonizers rather than the colonized, initially observing their mundane behaviors and eventually revealing their extraneous presence, as epitomized by Dinesen's endless, fruitless searching. The scene of the soldier masturbating in a rock pool [04:06–05:01] is indicative of a lack of respect for the environment; it is a symbolic, exploitative act by a man likely to have been involved in the military conquest of this wilderness and who speaks disparagingly of the native tribes. Dinesen's behavior, such as his excessively slow preparation to begin the hunt for his daughter, shows how ill-prepared he is, as a Danish man who, like all the military characters, does not belong here at all. Certainly, scenes such as these do advocate an anticolonial reading of the film.

As noted above, Alonso has established a reputation for casting nonactors, often using their own names, in films that have been received as a blend of documentary and narrative filmmaking (West and West 30). Casting a famous star makes the film even more conspicuous. Seeing Mortensen as a failing male, a father who cannot save his daughter, forces us to consider the role in the light of dozens of the actor's heroic, successful characters in US-American movies. Yet Mortensen's star persona is, in effect, as transnational and unconventional as *Jauja*—a Danish-American polyglot, with a well-established star profile but also an attraction to independent films and non-English-speaking roles. His enthusiasm for the collaboration with Alonso is clear from the festival interviews, which also suggest varied intentions among the film's key personnel. In his interview with *Cineaste* reviewer Richard Porton, Mortensen said that he was attracted to the film partially because the Argentine location and era "sounded like a classic Western story" (36), and he confirms that the experience of working on location brought to mind the Westerns he saw as a child. He refers to the ditch that is being dug by local men for Dinesen's engineers as "something out of a John Ford movie," designed to keep the natives away from the "civilized" area (37). Cinematographer Salminen stated that he "wanted a John Ford look" in his lighting and compositions (Diestro-Dópido, "Paradise" 20), and the script by Fabían Casas, Mortensen suggests, also reminded him of a Hollywood Western (Porton 37). All this suggests that the input of an international cast and crew may have emphasized both its anticolonial message and its Western characteristics.

Alonso's professed influence in devising the story was the death of a friend and imagining how her parents would have felt (Diestro-Dópido, "Paradise" 18). He has denied making deliberate allusions in his work to other films or filmmakers (Diestro-Dópido, "Living" 22). He resists, he says, using cinema as a political "pamphlet" and is intent only on telling stories (West and West 35), but his manner of telling those stories, like the New Latin American Cinema, is one that usually resists Hollywood convention. And yet, what is so unusual about *Jauja* is that, unlike his earlier films, it does not resist Hollywood conventions outright but makes use of particular devices that bring Hollywood cinema to mind. Whatever the festival interviews assert, and regardless of to whom we can attribute aspects of its authorship, *Jauja* invites, as *Sight and Sound* critic Adrian Martin puts it, a "dialogue with certain key forms and traditions in cinema history" (Martin 67), and its resemblances to the Hollywood Western require consideration. While *Jauja* tells the intimate, localized story of a father's loss, it is also a story of a white colonizer in the guise of a Westerner who fails to achieve his goal. Mortensen is, and is not, John Wayne, and the Argentine landscape is, and is not, the US-American West.

(NOT) THE US-AMERICAN WEST

Jauja shares much with Lucrecia Martel's 2017 film *Zama*, an adaptation of the 1956 Argentine novel by Antonio di Benetto. *Zama*, as critics Gerd Gemünden and Silvia Spitta put it, "pushes traditional notions of a colonial adventure tale to its parodic limits" (33), with the central protagonist as a colonial figure who consistently fails to prosper. Although *Jauja* is set after Argentina won its independence in the late eighteenth century, it remained a Latin country and was governed by people of Spanish descent who sought to exploit the land occupied by Indigenous peoples. So the films *Zama* and *Jauja* can be said to have a colonial setting and yet to resist colonial heroism; both end in hopelessness and ambiguity, and both present the central male figure as a man out of place in the colonized space. However, while the last section of *Zama* particularly emphasizes the civilization versus wilderness binary, it does not allude to the Hollywood Western narratively or iconographically. In contrast, consistently woven into *Jauja*'s tale of a Danish man in Argentina are Western characteristics that resolutely refuse to conform to the affirmatory narrative conventions to which they repeatedly refer: the solitary figure who is pitched against the savage in a frontier setting and, ultimately, saves the community, the Westerner who knows and understands the savage, and the violent resolution that affirms the Westerner's moral superiority. In *Jauja*, the solitary man, the savage, and the wilderness are all present, but the capable and experienced Westerner and the orthodox resolution are not.

The frontier myth is at the core of *Jauja*'s terror that is inherent in Dinesen's endless wandering in the wilderness and the likely loss of his daughter to the "savage" presence there. The myth, as Matthew Carter writes, is founded on an ideology of white (European) supremacy: "The source of the Frontier myth itself was a political discourse informed by notions of Anglo-Saxon racial superiority, American exceptionalism and of imperialism justified through divine sanction" ("Myth" 89). The white male protagonist tends to demonstrate his superiority through the completion of various goals. Challenging the mythical figure thus means challenging the political discourse based on an ideology of US-American global superiority. This is not unique; the Western genre has a long history of unconventional and unsuccessful protagonists and ambiguous resolutions—Jim Jarmusch's *Dead Man* (1995) comes to mind, with Johnny

Depp as William Blake, an accountant who is victimized, shot twice, and dies (or is reborn) having achieved virtually nothing since his arrival in the West. Recent slow Westerns, with which *Jauja* shares an unconventional slow pace and observational style, also demonstrate a similar failing male presence: in *Meek's Cutoff* (Kelly Reichardt, 2010), the scout, Meek, gets the settlers lost in the wilderness, where they remain indefinitely, and in *Slow West* (John Maclean, 2015), the youthful protagonist is shot dead by the very woman he loves when she fails to recognize him.

Marek Paryż and Sławomier Bobowski write: "The Western has developed cinematic paradigms of representing hegemony, subjugation and resistance to which contemporary audiences in former colonizing nations as well as in former colonized nations can relate. Given the international popularity of the Western, what is also at stake is the hegemony of the US in the realm of popular culture" (11). The writers remind us, here, that the contemporary Western may expose the supremacist, racist, or sexist ideologies with which the genre is often associated, and multiple audiences may read the Western from a position of postcolonial awareness. *Slow West* and *The Salvation* (Kristian Levring, 2015), for example, both made outside of the US, replace the US-American hero with an immigrant, foregrounding him as an "Other" who is out of place. As I have argued elsewhere, the consequences of such a replacement, paired with the protagonist's morally good behavior among corrupt US-Americans, exposes the ultimate failure of the American Dream (Barrett 186–203). Typically, however, these films are set in the US-American West, while *Jauja* is not. Although the wild space is beyond a frontier and sometimes resembles the US-American wilderness, it is conspicuously different with its vivid green coastline and rocky Pampas region. This is Argentina, not Arizona. Consequently, historical Argentina is drawn into a relationship with the US-American West that infers a shared condition: colonized spaces occupied by white men of European descent. To consider the implications of this relationship, it is important to analyze this particular white man in more detail.

Critic James Quandt's comment about men who ride lonesome in Alonso's films is a specific reference to Budd Boetticher's 1959 film *Ride Lonesome* starring Randolph Scott. He writes, "Alonso's men are separated, estranged, or sundered from their families," a plot device found in the Ranown Cycle collaborations between Boetticher, Scott, and writer Burt Kennedy, such as *7 Men from Now* (1956). The comparison with Boetticher, interviews with *Jauja*'s cast and crew suggest, bears less fruit than with the Westerns of John Ford. Despite Boetticher's attention to the harshness of the wilderness, as opposed to the sheer grandeur of Ford's landscapes, it is with the latter director's work that *Jauja* demonstrates the most vivid allusions, specifically to *She Wore a Yellow Ribbon* (1950) and *The Searchers* (1956), and even more so to the films' star, John Wayne.

It should be said that this is not simply submitting to the temptation of regarding *Jauja* as a straightforward take on the captivity narrative that *The Searchers* is modeled on, with Zuluaga and his followers, as bandits, simply replacing Scar and his tribe's raiding parties. Cynthia J. Miller and A. Bowdoin van Riper acknowledge the presence of bandit characters in Westerns made outside of the US, writing that they can be found "everywhere that scattered settlements grade into untamed wilderness" (3). Yet despite being analogous to the Hollywood Western's "Indian" raiding party, they have their own unique political meaning within their own production context, whether it be in Brazil, Hungary, or South Asia. Argentina is no exception. Consistently popular in commercial Argentine cinema has been the romantic figure of the gaucho, often found valiantly fighting for Argentine independence against the Spanish in films such as the hugely successful epic drama, *La guerra gaucha* (*The Gaucho War*, Lucas Memare, 1942). Gauchos were often represented in Hollywood as both cowboy types and racialized Others who could be "good" or "bad"; this is the case in the 20th Century Fox production *Way of a Gaucho* (Jacques Tourneur, 1952), where they belong to a romanticized, vanishing race of horsemen of mixed racial heritage, typically with Indigenous mothers and fathers of Spanish descent.

This othering of Indigenous or biracial characters in mainstream Hollywood films is exactly what New Latin American Cinema attempted to resist. Argentine Westerns with stereotyped Indigenous characters can be found throughout the nation's history, such as the ill-educated, sexually predatory patriarchs of *Los afincaos* (*Sons of the Earth*, Leónidas Barletta, 1941) in which a young female teacher perishes at the hands of the tribe leader because she refuses to marry him. The Argentine/Spanish/US joint production, *Savage Pampas* (Hugo Freganese, 1966), starring Robert Taylor as the military captain attempting to tame the people of the Pampas, dresses its Indigenous tribe in Native American costume (Taylor was "brownfaced" to imply his character's mixed racial heritage). Although the captain dies in the final combat, he remains a heroic symbol of the civilizing of the Pampas. Set in Argentina, the Spanish/Italian Spaghetti Western comedy *Arriva Sabata!* (*Sabata the Killer*, Tulio Demicheli, 1970) exploits Indigenous characters as comic players, such as the illiterate outlaw Mangosta, with his brownface makeup, beads, and bandolier. Whether tales of tragedy or comic outlaw escapades, Argentine Westerns have followed Hollywood custom with affirmatory resolutions that discriminate against "savagery" and reward honor, duty, and courage.

Jauja, like the rest of Alonso's films, "rides lonesome" among Argentina's Westerns. Zuluaga, the renegade who leads his own band of gauchos and fraternizes with natives, is never seen on screen, never caught, and never punished. Like the guerilla character Vicuña Porto in Martel's *Zama*, he owes more, perhaps, to Joseph Conrad's Kurtz in *Heart of Darkness* (1899) than to a gaucho, a comic native, or any Hollywood Westerner. Similarly, Dinesen is not rewarded for his efforts, and there is no heroic conflict leading to a resolution; he is instead an isolated and ill-prepared colonizer who does not belong.

(NOT) JOHN WAYNE

Critic Quintín's review of *Jauja* claimed "that Mortensen's presence is as powerful as John Wayne's" (33), suggesting that Mortensen's performance brings the Western star to mind. Although they do not look like each other, there is a certain familiarity in how Mortensen is costumed, made up, framed, and filmed. When Dinesen sits astride his horse in a low-angle long shot that takes in a moody sky and an artificially yellow glow from a campfire [33:50], there is a strong visual similarity to the expressionist color choices of the graveyard scenes at dusk in *She Wore a Yellow Ribbon*. The earlier film repeatedly returns to Captain Brittles dressing, or, rather, finishing getting dressed, on each day before his retirement. These short moments when Wayne finishes buttoning a shirt or tying a scarf are extended in two lengthy dressing scenes in *Jauja*: first, when Dinesen discusses Zuluaga with Lieutenant Pittaluga, and he takes a number of minutes to put on his socks and boots [08:09–12:08], and, second, when he lays out his uniform and starts to dress before beginning his search for Ingeborg [31:36–33:44]. As well as the obvious absurdity of this "civilized" man insisting on his own well-turned-out uniform at such a critical moment, the attention given to such mundane activities is typical of Alonso; we watch the woodcutter of *La libertad*, for instance, chopping and preparing logs in real time for over seventeen minutes without dialogue [04:18–21:42]. Dinesen's extended preparation scene in *Jauja* draws the eye to the items of clothing, particularly the military uniform and saber, which are uncannily similar to those of Captain Brittles in *She Wore a Yellow Ribbon*. Even Dinesen's graying hair and mustache have a passing resemblance to Brittles, in a film where Wayne at the age of forty-two is made to look like an older man about to retire (fig. 12.1).

Perhaps more noticeably, Dinesen's search for his daughter can be said to parallel Ethan Edwards's quest to find his niece Debbie in *The Searchers*. Although at first Ingeborg leaves of her own volition, it is later implied by a dying Corto that she has been taken by Zuluaga, the film's savage character. If

Fig. 12.1 Captain Dinesan in Timo Salminen's expressive lighting of the Argentine wilderness [33:50].

Zuluaga is *The Searchers'* Scar in all but name, Ingeborg's fate is to become one of his wives. There are also conspicuous moments when Ford's film is brought to mind through striking shot compositions, which encourage the viewer to regard Dinesen's search as a failure in contrast to Edwards's (relative) success of bringing the lost girl home. As Dinesen is about to leave the cave where he has met the elderly woman who may be Ingeborg, the medium long shot of him standing at the cave's mouth emphasizes his isolation in the wilderness [87:56]; it is strongly reminiscent of the cave where Edwards lifts Debbie up, the critical moment of the film when it is unclear whether he will kill his niece, before cradling her in his arms and saying, "Let's go home, Debbie," thus making the white settler-family whole again. Instinctively, on lifting the young woman up, he remembers doing the same when she was a child, and he instantly chooses to save her. In contrast, Dinesen's decision to leave the cave and continue his search leaves the family fragmented. The elderly woman in *Jauja* could be the lost relative, now found, but the man walks away with her left in the cave because his European, rational mind cannot believe his instinct that she could be his daughter. Shortly after, Dinesen falls to his knees in hopelessness and his

Fig. 12.2 Dinesan stands at the mouth of the cave, which recalls *The Searchers* (1956) [87:56].

head drops [90:51]. Here Mortensen's performance seems to cite John Wayne's in *The Searchers* again: Edwards's discovery of Martha's body leads to this same kneeling position, with his head falling down in utter despair. It is hard to say whether the allusion is deliberate (the festival interviews do not confirm it), but Edwards and Dinesen both meet overwhelming loss with the same pose (fig. 12.2).

Mortensen's Dinesen, in his visual and narrative similarities to Wayne's characters, draws attention to their differences. Dinesen is not the sort of character we would find as a protagonist in a classical Hollywood Western. He is not a cavalryman or an enigmatic frontiersman; he is an engineer with a limited understanding of the wilderness and its native people. Dinesen never meets Zuluaga, and there are no action sequences or shoot-outs. The strange lunar-like surface of the wild space that Dinesen stumbles through is not the yellow desert of Arizona and not the familiar panorama of Monument Valley. This is also not Hollywood's conventional US-American West because, here, the problems of the male protagonist are not resolved. This is not John Wayne because this Western hero fails to find the child. In this film, the "savage" kidnaps the vulnerable female, and she is never seen again. The savage is not defeated, nor even located. The masculine father figure is not affirmed through success; he is a resounding failure. The affirmatory closure of many Hollywood Westerns never comes, and the protagonist fails to achieve his primary goal. Ethan Edwards does not find Debbie. Captain Brittles fails to protect Miss Dandridge.

CONCLUSION

If Ford's Westerns were not as phenomenally well known, the comparisons I have made could be disregarded as the nonsense of another Ford enthusiast. However, the films mentioned in this analysis have dominated the canon of quality Westerns in discourse on the genre for more than half a century. Individual shots are celebrated to such a degree that they have become emblematic of the classical Western, referred to in countless films both in and out of Hollywood. So if the references and allusions that I have indicated can be said to be present in *Jauja*, in excess of the anticolonial story of a Danish man in Argentina, then this encourages a reading of the film in relation to Hollywood.

As West and West's interview with Alonso records, the director prefers to avoid overt politicizing and, instead, offers the viewer "time to ponder" (37). There is much that is ambiguous in *Jauja*, and the festival interviews do not necessarily cohere, but there is plenty in the film on which to ponder. Although Quintín wrote of the film's ending in his review, "neither the director, nor the lead actor, nor the screenwriter necessarily understand it any more clearly than viewers or critics will" (35), there are, at the least, two coherent readings of *Jauja* that can be made with the aforementioned contexts and references in mind and that lead to a conclusion about the film's function. *Jauja* exploits the colonizer's discourse, both the colonial adventure story and the Hollywood Western, to accuse the colonizer in the broadest sense, whether that be white settlers or the Hollywood film industry. It criticizes the Hollywood Western's proclivity to assert the superiority of the white male Westerner and, consequently, creates a cinematic space that points to the colonizing of cinema by mainstream Hollywood convention, implying a shared colonial past between the US and Latin America. The subtext, thus, emphasizes a shared colonial guilt by critiquing and aligning European imperialism and Hollywood as a cultural "empire." This might even aid us as we attempt to understand the film's final scene in contemporary Denmark. The abrupt, alienating departure from the film's central time and place and the sudden halt to Hollywood Western references could imply that cinemas outside of Hollywood have "stayed too long" under its thrall, just as the Danish girl is told that she has stayed away from home too long. The sudden wrench away from colonial critique and Western genre iconoclasm functions as a petition to acknowledge the hegemonic nature of Hollywood's style and representations. Ultimately, *Jauja* exposes colonial guilt in Argentine history and offers a critique of the colonizing nature of mainstream, commercial US-American cinema that is convinced of the significance, even the superiority, of its male subject, the Hollywood Western, and the US in a global context. Despite its differences from the New Latin American Cinema, not least the telling of a historical tale from the perspective of a European, it works, therefore, to achieve what Solanas and Getino once hoped for Argentine film: to decolonize the spectator.

WORKS CITED

Anderman, Jens. *New Argentine Cinema.* I. B. Tauris, 2012.
Barrett, Jenny. "Stranger and Friend: Non-American Westerns and the Immigrant in the Twenty-First Century." *Reframing Cult Westerns: From "The Magnificent Seven" to "The Hateful Eight,"* edited by Lee Broughton, Bloomsbury Academic, 2020, pp. 186–203.
Carter, Matthew. "'Crossing the Beast': American Identity and Frontier Mythology in *Sin Nombre*." *The Post-2000 Film Western: Contexts, Transnationality, Hybridity,* edited by Marek Paryż and John R. Leo, Palgrave Macmillan, 2015, pp. 89–105.
———. *Myth of the Western: New Perspectives on Hollywood's Frontier Perspective.* Edinburgh University Press, 2015.
Di Benetto, Antonio. *Zama.* 1956. New York Review of Books, 2016.
Diestro-Dópido, Mar. "Living the Dream." *Sight and Sound,* vol. 25, no. 5, 2015, p. 22.
———. "Paradise Lost." *Sight and Sound,* vol. 25, no. 5, 2015, pp. 18–21.
Falicov, Tamara Leah. *The Cinematic Tango: Contemporary Argentine Film.* Wallflower, 2007.
Gemünden, Gerd, and Silvia Spitta. "'I Was Never Afraid': An Interview with Lucrecia Martel." *Film Quarterly,* vol. 71, no. 4, 2017, pp. 33–40.
Jauja. Directed by Lisandro Alonso, performances by Viggo Mortensen and Viilbjørk Malling Agger, NDM, 2014. DVD Soda Pictures, 2015.
Kollin, Susan. *Captivating Westerns: The Middle East in the American West.* University of Nebraska Press, 2015.
La libertad/Freedom. Directed by Lisandro Alonso, performance by Misael Saavedra, 2001. DVD Intermedia, 2009.
Martin, Adrian. "Review of *Jauja.*" *Sight and Sound,* vol. 25, no. 5, 2015, pp. 66–67.
Miller, Cynthia J., and A. Bowdoin van Riper, eds. *International Westerns: Re-Locating the Frontier.* Scarecrow, 2014.
Paryż, Marek, and Sławomier Bobowski, editors. *Contemporary Transnational Westerns Themes and Variations since 2000.* Wydawnetwo Uniwersytetu Wrocławkiego, 2019.

Porton, Richard. "The Actor as Citizen of the World: An Interview with Viggo Mortensen." *Cineaste*, Summer 2015, pp. 36–38.

Quandt, James. "Ride Lonesome: James on the Films of Lisandro Alonso." *Artforum International*, 25 Nov. 2009, https://www.artforum.com/film/james -quandt-on-the-films-of-lisandro-alonso-24258. Accessed 7 September 2021.

Quintín. "Into the Unknown." *Film Comment*, Sept.–Oct. 2014, pp. 30–35.

Rock, David. *Argentina 1516–1987: From Spanish Colonization to the Falklands War and Alfonsín*, I. B. Tauris, 1987.

Roncallo, Sergio, and Juan Carlos Arias-Herrera. "Cinema and/as Revolution: The New Latin American Cinema." *Observatorio Journal*, vol. 7, no. 3, 2013, pp. 93–114.

The Searchers. Directed by John Ford, performances by John Wayne, Jeffrey Hunter and Vera Miles, Warner Bros., 1956.

She Wore a Yellow Ribbon. Directed by John Ford, performances by John Wayne, Joanne Dru and John Agar, RKO, 1950.

Turner, Frederick Jackson. "The Significance of the Frontier in American History." *The Frontier in American History*, 1893. University of Arizona Press, 1986, pp. 1–38.

Veracini, Lorenzo. "'Settler Colonialism': Career of a Concept." *Journal of Imperial and Commonwealth History*, vol. 41, no. 2, pp. 313–33.

West, Dennis, and Joan M. West. "Cinema beyond Words: An Interview with Lisandro Alonso." *Cineaste*, Spring 2011, pp. 30–38.

Zama. Directed by Lucrecia Martel, performance by Daniel Giménez Cacho, Bananeira Films, Rei Cinev, 2017.

JENNY BARRETT is Senior Lecturer in Film Studies at Edge Hill University. She is author of *Shooting the Civil War: Cinema, History and American National Identity*.

THIRTEEN

—ፙ—

REMAKING THE WESTERN IN
JAPANESE CINEMA

East Meets West (Kihachi Okamoto, 1995),
Sukiyaki Western Django (Takashi Miike, 2007),
and *Unforgiven* (Sang-il Lee, 2013)

VIVIAN P. Y. LEE

TRADITIONALLY CONSIDERED TO BE A Hollywood and Italian film genre, the Western has had a long history of intercultural dialogue that stretches far beyond its native soils. In Asia, "Western" films have established their own generic pedigree through direct and indirect dialogues, so much so that local-ized genre labels such as "Asian Westerns" and "Easterns" have come to repre-sent a homegrown genre in the region's film culture. By virtue of its naming, the Eastern as a generic label encapsulates the complex geocultural politics against which non-Western cinemas' encounters with the West were plotted. Since the 1960s, a two-way traffic between Japanese cinema and Hollywood has developed through mutual adaptations between the Western and the samurai film (or *chanbara*), a subgenre of the *jidaigeki* (period film) that went through a cycle of revision in the post–World War II era in the hands of rising new au-teurs, including Akira Kurosawa, Kihachi Okamoto, Hideo Gosha, and Kenji Misumi. These new voices would redefine Japanese cinema to both domestic and international audiences in the 1960s and 1970s. In Japan, the reinvention of the samurai film coincided with the postwar effort of modern nation-building under the patronage of the US, who was eager to enlist Japan as an ally to consolidate its sphere of influence in Asia. Japan's defeat in the Pacific War and its US-sponsored modernization project in the postwar decades not only demanded society-wide psychological adjustments to the dire consequences of war, but also gave rise to a crisis of subjectivity when conventional values supported by a rigid social hierarchy came into conflict with an increasing interest in the "self" as the primary agent of individual and social renewal (Yoshimoto 107).

Against this context, Japanese filmmakers' interest in the Western as an "imperialist" genre stemming from nowhere else other than the US cannot be taken simply as colonial mimicry or mere imitations of a Eurocentric master text. In this chapter, Japanese Easterns are understood as ideologically complex and self-consciously hybridized cinematic works that engage with the imperialist impulses of the West(ern) while maintaining a problematic relationship to their Japanese roots. This understanding can be applied to both the earlier classics of the 1960s, most of which belong to the samurai/chanbara subgenre, and the more recent works that more explicitly pay tribute to the Western film tradition in setting, visual motifs, and characterization. Critical reception of the Japanese Eastern, especially Akira Kurosawa's samurai films, has focused on the subtle and recontextualized evocation of Western motifs that mostly serve to interrogate the existential condition of the postwar Japanese society (Desser, "Kurosawa"; Richie; Burch and Michelson). Comparatively, less attention has been paid to later films that are *visibly* different from their predecessors. Undoubtedly, Kurosawa's adaptation and reworking of the Western has matured into an aesthetic form in itself that is well-reflected in existing literature. The discussion below begins with an overview of the critical reception of Japanese Easterns from the 1960s to establish points of departure for the analysis of more recent works, namely *East Meets West* (Kihachi Okamoto, 1995), *Sukiyaki Western Django* (Takashi Miike, 2007), and *Unforgiven* (Sang-il Lee, 2013). In addition to addressing a critical imbalance, the focus on later works serves to illuminate the changing practices and politics of transnational filmmaking at a time when genres, nations, cultures, and identities are set afloat by accelerated digital traffic. Among the three films, Miike's *Sukiyaki Western Django* is arguably the most controversial and provocative reworking of the Western by an Asian director so far, which explains its greater critical spotlight in its overseas reception, while Lee's remake of Clint Eastwood's Academy Award–winning film has received a warm reception at international film festivals. Comparatively, Okamoto's *East Meets West* is, like its director, a lesser-known member of its kind despite the domestic status of its director. Oscillating between familiarity and estrangement, the formal and thematic renegotiation in *Sukiyaki Western Django*, *East Meets West*, and *Unforgiven* reveals an inherent eclecticism that characterizes the form, content, and ideological outlook of contemporary Japanese Easterns.

THE WEST AND THE REST: ORIGINATING
THE "EASTERN" GENRE

So far, the Asian Western as a film genre has remained an underresearched subject. Stephen Teo's book-length study, *Eastern Westerns: Film and Genre Outside and Inside Hollywood,* can be seen as a breakthrough to remedy this critical lacuna.[1] It is, therefore, useful to begin with a critical mapping of Asian Westerns in film criticism to shed light on the critical reception of this hybrid genre, and no less to identify aspects of immediate concern to the film analyses that follow. Like the martial arts film in Chinese cinema, the Western connotes specific historical and geocultural parameters that might not be conducive to cross-cultural adaptation other than playful mimicry, even though Thomas Schatz has once argued that it is the "most flexible *narrative* formula" (Schatz qtd. in Teo 1, my italics). The trajectory of the Western in Asian cinemas that goes beyond the "poor copy" formula to qualify as what Teo calls a local genre in its own right, therefore, deserves special attention (Teo 2). While Asian Westerns are susceptible to Hollywood's global hegemony due to their formal affiliation to the "master genre," dynamic intergenericity in the process of mutual adaptation and cross-fertilization has engendered a two-way traffic on equal terms across film cultures. Two often cited examples are Akira Kurosawa's *Seven Samurai* (1954) and *Yojimbo* (1961), which are known to have inspired remakes and adaptations such as John Sturges's *The Magnificent Seven* (1960, readapted under the same title in 2016 by Antoine Fuqua), Sergio Leone's *A Fistful of Dollars* (1964), and Walter Hill's *Last Man Standing* (1996); Martin Ritt's *The Outrage* (1964) another, albeit less successful attempt to recast the Kurosawa classic *Rashomon* (1950) in a Western setting.[2] Ranked among the most influential directors in Japanese cinema, Kurosawa is also indebted to Western sources not limited to the cinematic, from *Shane* (in *Sanjuro*, 1962) to Shakespeare's *Macbeth* (in *A Throne of Blood*, 1957), *King Lear* (in *Ran*, 1985), and *Hamlet* (in *The Bad Sleep Well*, 1960). Teo's study reveals a more protracted, and generically specific, lineage of Easterns that display distinctive formal attributes to qualify as an Asian genre. According to Teo, an Eastern film employs a set of codes universal to the Western, such as characters in cowboy outfits, gunfights, outlaws, sheriffs, saloon whores, sidekicks, horses, chases, trains, and the landscape space. Drawing on Christopher Frayling's work on the Italian Western, and on Sergio Leone in particular, Teo approaches the Eastern by affirming it as "being a type of genre that is both derivative of the American Western but yet departing from it in significant ways." By extending and manipulating the "clichés of the equivalent Hollywood genre," the Eastern or Asian Western attempts to "criticize and redefine the 'rules' of the Hollywood Western genre" (Teo 5–8). Teo's generic mapping with reference to conformity to "universal (formal) elements" and critical efficacy founded on historical and cultural specificity makes a case for the Asian Western as a "genre entity in itself." Asian Westerns, from this perspective, are close to the concept of the "post-Western" or "Revisionist Western," which posits a more complex moral universe where good and evil are less readily distinguishable. This subgenre serves as a model of "how the Western has moved beyond the 'familiar frontier narratives that circumscribe "Westness" within a national interpretive horizon'" (A. T. Young qtd. in Teo 2). What needs to be stressed here is that, apart from being a complexly hybridized film genre, the Asian Western, as illustrated by the films discussed below, is by necessity a self-reflexive, if not self-questioning, genre shaped by its dual/multiple origins, which, in turn, give it its singular form and substance.

As far as Japanese cinema is concerned, Kurosawa's Easterns are the most frequently cited examples in comparative studies. David Desser's close analysis of the seven-part structure in *Seven Samurai* and its character types offers a point-to-point comparative analysis of the remaking of this masterpiece (or is it a master text?) in world cinema that goes beyond the East-West framework ("Remaking Seven"). Taking its points of departure from Donald Richie and Noël Burch's diverging views on *Sanjuro*, Desser's earlier essay on Kurosawa's film unravels a more complex engagement with the Western genre ("Kurosawa").[3] On the one hand, *Sanjuro* is a remake of *Shane* in terms of the characterization of the hero and the use of binary pairs such as wilderness and civilization, the good and the bad, and the strong and the weak to drive the main action. On the other hand, the film is "not a Western" by appearance: it has forsaken the landscape space intrinsic to the genre's identity and draws on expressively Japanese visual and spatial coordinates as the primary means of metaphorical and aesthetic evocations (58–60). In so doing, *Sanjuro* frustrates the normative expectations of the Western form and turns it into a vehicle for critical reflection on both its US-American and Japanese sources.

In US-American and Japanese film cultures, there exists a distant echo between the figure of the lone cowboy hero and the samurai, who usually is an outcast, long past his days of glory. Commenting on this affinity, Aaron Gerow observes that the samurai movie's central motif of "a lone hero dueling with villains to restore order to a lawless situation" makes it easier for "Japanese Easterns" to access the Western market (16). As products of two completely different historical and cultural contexts, the samurai and the cowboy figure are social outcasts, sometimes fugitives of their respective penal regimes. Each shouldering his own moral baggage, both the samurai and the cowboy are loyal to their respective codes of conduct that turn them into recalcitrant noncon-formists and/or defenders of the weak, whether volitionally or incidentally. What distinguishes the Western cowboy from the Japanese samurai most is the moral universe in which their character-driven drama of honor and chiv-alry plays out. The Wild West in the cowboy movie is a frontier town where law and order are less judicially defined than contingent on *how* disputes are settled between two parties in conflict. In revisionist and Spaghetti Westerns, the frontier myth of the white cowboy hero and the racial and gender politics associated with this genre are self-reflexively deconstructed to accommodate more complex visions of US-American and European history with allegorical allusions to the present. The samurai, on the other hand, is caught in a more confined—and visibly codified in terms of social etiquette and body gestures—hierarchical system that dictates the terms of personal honor and loyalty. Un-der the restrictive code of *bushido* (the "way" of the Japanese warrior), *being* a samurai is a collective identity, if not an existential condition, determined by political, social, and familial lineage rather than free will or personal choice. Similarly, relinquishing or losing such an identity could lead to condemnation, disgrace, deracination, and expulsion from one's clan.

In Japan, the samurai film—also known as chanbara or sword-fighting films—entered a new phase in the post–World War II era, when younger dir-ectors began to reflect on their wartime experience through the cinematic medium. Okamoto was among those young and aspiring filmmakers returning from military service, an experience that would have a deep impact on his war and samurai films. It is, therefore, no coincidence that the samurai films of this period display a self-conscious allegorical impulse in their contemplation of the moral consequences of war and violence. This also explains why postwar samurai films tend to be set during the late Tokugawa era or the early Meiji period (mid- to late nineteenth century), a time of unprecedented change and chaos, featuring the masterless samurai (*ronin*, literally a wandering person) as loners trying to come to terms with the loss of their privileged position in society and group identity. As numerous critics have noted, the post–World War II samurai film displays a noticeable difference from its predecessors in its foregrounding of violence and death to express antiwar sentiments.[4] Un-derstandably, the existential anxiety and identity crisis in times of great un-certainty where one has to redefine the self as both an individual and a social entity is a defining characteristic of this new phase of the samurai film.[5] This existential crisis applies to both the historical samurai and the postwar battle-field returnees, if not Japanese society as a whole. It is also where the samurai and the lone cowboy hero cross paths in the Japanese cinematic imagination.

Speaking to their distinctive cultural and political milieus, both are conceived as cultural metaphors to reexamine the ideological and ethical foundations of the prevailing social order with allegorical allusions to contemporary society. This intersection makes ample room for an intercultural dialogue that soon made its way to other film traditions, including but not limited to Hollywood. It is in this light that the three films in question will be discussed below.

SUKIYAKI WESTERN DJANGO: TRANSGRESSION, OTHERNESS, AND THE "BAD FILM"

As a complexly parodic "bad film" (Khoo; Stadler), *Sukiyaki Western Django* (hereafter *Sukiyaki*) has succeeded in problematizing and uprooting the ontology of the Asian Western as a genre entity of multiple origins. Oscillating between homage and pastiche, *Sukiyaki* stands out as one of the most "neurotic" films in an "Asian Western cycle" (Teo 36) that raises controversial questions about genre form and the limits of genre hybridization and subversion. The film's disorientingly complex intertextual fabric and indulgence in visual excesses at the expense of narrative intelligibility are behind its mixed critical reception. Reviewers' opinions are divided between appreciation of the director's mastery of film styles and conventions, and skepticism toward the apparently random and undisciplined use of quotations from myriad sources, including but not limited to the genre's best-known masters such as Leone, Corbucci, and Kurosawa. Miike's fondness of his cult-auteur status is certainly an impetus behind the casting of Quentin Tarantino as the narrator of a tale of revenge triggered by interclan conflicts. Critics who find themselves less than impressed by Miike's ultradeconstructive aesthetics question whether such visual overload serves any purpose other than asserting the director's status as cult-auteur.[6] Indeed, cult and auteurism combined give poetic license to the film's irreverent code-mixing and self- and interreferentiality that are prioritized over storytelling and stylistic and structural coherence. Here lies the more nuanced implications of *Sukiyaki*'s engagement with the genre's iconographies: the film's intensely hybridized form bespeaks its ambition not only to deconstruct the Western, but also to problematize its own identity as an Asian Western. What results is a meta-(con)textual dis/reassembling of the genre's definitive components. More importantly, by questioning the ontology of the (Asian) Western, the film performs transgressive acts of deterritorializing the genre through a strategy of multiple "othering," a strategy that deploys whatever "bad film" elements are deemed necessary and desirable in the making of a cult movie (fig. 13.1).

Fig. 13.1 Intertextual references in *Sukiyaki Western Django* (2007) [2:00].

From casting, set design, and dialogue to character symbolism and narrative, *Sukiyaki* is a collage of visual and verbal citations that go beyond the clever copy or even mocking tribute: it subjects the Western to a meticulous demystification by distorting and displacing every genre signifier it manages to lift from the source text. The story of a lone gunman (Hideki Ito) arriving in a frontier town who soon gets engrossed in a bloody conflict between two rival clans is a familiar plot device that recalls Leone's *A Fistful of Dollars* and Kurosawa's *Yojimbo* (the *kanji* title of the film is shown in a brief shot to announce a fight scene). Allegedly set in Nevada, the mythical quality of the Western is dramatized by the film's ambivalent historical setting: the war between two clans, the red-clad Heike and the white-clad Genji, could be an out-of-context allusion to the War of the Roses in Britain in the fifteenth century, but the opening scene introduces a middle-aged cowboy called Pei Mai (Quentin Tarantino) enjoying a *sukiyaki* (Japanese beef stew) hot pot as he narrates a longer history of the warring clans dating back to the battle of Dannoura in twelfth-century Japan. After proving his worth to both clans, the gunman's attention turns to an old woman Ruriko (Kaori Momoi), her widowed daughter-in-law and town prostitute Shizuka (Yoshino Kimura), and her grandson, a traumatized teenage boy who became mute after witnessing his father's death (the father, we are told, is none other than Pei Mai himself). What begins as a mini–gold rush among rival clans evolves into an outlaw hero's courageous defense of the defenseless. The film's arbitrary alignment of distant times, spaces, and personae that lack any putative connection intensifies the sense of exotic estrangement, which is far from compensated by the ubiquitous presence of overused clichés and quotations from well-known sources. The accented "bad English" dialogue further intensifies the multiple occurrences of *othering* sustained throughout the film.

Commenting on the politics of the "bad film" and auteurship as a tool to unsettle stereotypical notions of Asian cinema, Olivia Khoo uses Miike's deconstructive approach to the Western as a medium to construct an ontology of Asian cinema, which has remained an area studies offshoot within film studies (80–95). Against the diversity of film cultures and practices in the region, the existence of an Asian cinema has been assumed and held as a (self-) differentiating identity, often in relation to Hollywood. To Khoo, *Sukiyaki* illuminates the politics of reception of atypical cultural products that frustrate conventional (Orientalist) expectations. In Khoo's account, Miike's self-cultivated public persona as a cult film icon, irreverent citations of Western motifs using Japanese-accented English, and deconstructive maneuvering of intertextual/ metatextual references are contributing factors to the unwelcoming responses from critics educated in US-American Western conventions. Like the director's cult persona, *Sukiyaki*'s multiple impurities and transgressions account as much for its critical potential as for the critical negligence of film scholarship devoted to it. Khoo stresses the necessity to rethink Asian cinema as a "legitimate object of enquiry," with its own internal logic, methodologies, and frameworks, rather than to reduce it to "an alternative to Hollywood filmmaking and to Euro-American film studies critiques" (82–83). Khoo's use of *Sukiyaki* as an anomaly of Asian cinema, that is, as a film that resists being seen as either "Japanese" or "Asian," reintroduces the film as an exemplary case of Asian cinema as a critical category in its own right. Indeed, the film's nonconformist genre politics work like a double-edged sword that cuts through the histories of Japanese and US-American cinema. Rather than asserting an alternative genre/national/cultural identity, it is the self-conscious critique and othering of ready-made categories of identity that distinguishes *Sukiyaki*'s provocation. The complex fabric of the film's hybridization, proliferation, and denial of identification dramatizes the tension between the copy and the original, to the extent that they are as much deconstructed as mutually imbricated.

As a cinematic hybrid, *Sukiyaki* pushes the generic, cultural, and linguistic boundaries of both the Western and the Asian Western to their (il)logical extremes, and poses as many questions on the phenomenon of the Asian Western as it does on what it means to be (not) "Asian." The film's hybrid formal system is characterized by Jane Stadler as a celebration of cinematic form that "engages the audiences in an intense and aesthetic rapport" (688). According to Stadler, a phenomenological analysis seeks to equalize contrastive categories such as mainstream genre/exploitative "bad film," national/global, or Hollywood/Asia, not so much "to signify spectatorial perversion" as to reappraise the film as a celebration of genre conventions and cultural differences (689). Both Khoo and Stadler refer to Pierre Bourdieu's theory of taste and cultural consumption in his seminal work, *Distinction: A Social Critique of the Judgement of Taste*, and Jeffrey Sconce's influential essay on the "bad film" to put forward their respective arguments. Khoo is more in favor of Sconce's deconstructive revaluation of the bad film as a critical and subversive practice vis-à-vis the mainstream, an argument that facilitates a critique of Western film studies' use of authorship as a marker of Asian cinema to distinguish its otherness. Stadler suggests that phenomenology's emphasis on the equal value of all categories can shed alternative insights into the transnational circulation and permutations of popular genres. It is interesting to note that, for their different critical purposes, Khoo and Stadler have chosen the same film as an exemplary case in point, and both make reference to the bad film as a point of departure. As an outrageously self-reflexive bad film, *Sukiyaki* resists critical closure whether as a subversive or celebratory Asian Western. The irreverent cross-fertilization of cultural references, the use of an all-Japanese cast (except the cameo appearance of Quentin Tarantino) speaking in heavily accented English, and their outlandish body language operate like a double-edged sword: on the one hand, it denaturalizes "Asianness" through a denial of any claim to authenticity, which amounts to a mockery of its own intent; on the other hand, it plays up the artificiality and constructedness of the Western as the originating text of a universal myth by diegetically accentuating the genre's otherness through an awkward mix of linguistic and ethnic Others. Miike's playful and no less critical engagement with the Western as a master text does not lose sight of the gender politics that characteristically downplay female agency in both samurai and cowboy movies. *Sukiyaki* alters this gender deficit by introducing a strong woman character, Ruriko (Kaori Momori), who jumps into the role of a charismatic gun lady in one of the film's most spectacular action sequences. As a self-consciously hybridized tribute to its multiple sources, *Sukiyaki* lavishly employs and juxtaposes the "Asian" and the "Western" as an odd couple hung together in the form of a bad film. Perhaps this is the lesson to be learned from Miike's experiment with the Asian Western: it exploits the ideologically bounded binarisms between East and West, male and female, "good" and "bad" English to debunk stereotypes founded on misconceived notions of culture, ethnicity, and identity.

EAST MEETS WEST: COMIC FANTASY AND/ AS GENERIC SUBCONSCIOUS

Ten years junior to Kurosawa by age, Okamoto belonged to the postwar generation of Japanese directors who brought their political and philosophical reflections on their wartime experience to filmmaking. Compared to Kurosawa,

Okamoto was more a domestic celebrity, which is very much an outcome of an eclectic output that did not immediately appeal to the Western art film institution or academic critics. In 2007, Okamoto was featured among a selection of "unsung talents" in Japanese cinema by the Tokyo FILMeX festival. As Tom Mes observes, limited access to films by "pioneering Western historians of Japanese cinema" has been a reason behind the critical imbalance in the reception of directors like Okamoto outside Japan ("In No Man's Land" 64–66). Another explanation of this critical neglect has to do with Okamoto's relative disinterest in seeking Western distribution or recognition through festival circuits (Bergen). A director known for his fondness for US-American Westerns, Okamoto blended elements of the genre in his war and action films. Taking the cowboy-and-Indian formula of the Western out of its original context, however, Okamoto's chanbara films shed critical light on the tradition of bushido and the samurai with contemporary resonances. As Mes remarks, Okamoto had, since the 1960s, been a proponent of the new chanbara film, which shifted its emphasis from honor and heroism to "the death and misery that inevitably follow those who live by the sword and those who cross their paths" ("Tribute"). Toward the latter phase of his career, Okamoto's output took a more diverse turn that displayed a growing interest in satire and comedy, in which the director's perennial themes of conflicting loyalties and the morality of war continued to inform the portrayal of the world of gangsters and outlaws (*Boss of the Underworld*, 1959; *The Last Gunfight*, 1960; *Samurai Assassin*, 1965). *East Meets West* can be regarded as the result of the director's attempt to further "hybridize" his favorite film genres in an Eastern film package.

Set during the late Tokugawa period (1860), the film begins with a Japanese delegation to San Francisco, where the emperor's officials are supposed to negotiate the terms of a trade deal with the US government. Besieged by unprecedented changes brought on by the gold rush, San Francisco is the perfect setting for a multicultural drama of hit-and-run action, political intrigues, heroic duels, and intergeneric dialogues on social, ethnic, and gender identities. As the narrative unfolds, the Japanese delegation is infiltrated by an assassin from the revolutionaries targeting the life of the head of the delegation, Katsu. A bank robbery leading to the loss of a cache of gold brought along by the diplomats triggers a manhunt that drives the remainder of the main action. Tamajiro, a ninja hired by the delegation, is sent to track down Kamijo, a samurai-interpreter accompanying the Japanese mission and Katsu's wrongly identified culprit. The plot revolves around Kamijo and Tamajiro's adventures across the Wild West, mixing cross-purposes with sword fights, ninja stunts, gunshots, and a romantic subplot involving Tamajiro (who picked up the English name "Tommy" soon after his arrival in San Francisco) and a Native American

princess, Nantai (Angelique Roehm). Kamijo (also known by his English name
"Joe") remains the uncontested cowboy-like samurai hero in the film: he becomes a father figure to Sam, a little boy whose father was killed in the robbery,
as both embark on a journey of revenge and knight-errantry. However, much
spotlight is stolen by Tamajiro's subplot: his marriage with Nantai turns him
into a true boundary crosser as he discovers newfound freedom in the apparently unrestricted Native American territory. Back in Japan, Tamajiro was a
struggling ninja troubled by his unfulfilled aspirations to become a samurai.
His admiration for Kamijo gradually gives way to his love for Nantai, as the relationship frees him from the repressive code of conduct of the Japanese social
hierarchy. In the end, Tamajiro abandons his Japanese roots in full embrace
of the US-American West (which, of course, is an idealized vision stripped of
sociopolitical complexities). His final encounter with Kamijo shows the fork-
ing paths of the two main characters: waving goodbye to his encumbered past
on his carriage with Nantai, Tommy leaves behind the quest for honor that
Kamijo would continue, even though Kamijo, too, has loosened up his samurai
protocols that used to define his Japanese identity. In an unexpected, and a little
awkward, twist, the final scene shows Tommy, now a Native American chief,
looking over the vast wilderness of his tribal "homeland" before his death, aged
one hundred and four.

As a comic Eastern, *East Meets West* received mixed reviews due to its care-
free referencing of generic clichés and overexerted tributes to classical Western
scenes, most noticeably of John Ford's movies. Critics who are familiar with
Okamoto's more piercing social critique in his earlier films have expressed
slight disappointment in the film's comic nonchalance (Gerow 16). While
"kitsch" may not be an inappropriate description of the director's indulgence
in code-mixing, it is the gender politics of the film that makes a case for cross-
cultural reflection. The metaphorical overlap between the cowboy hero and the
samurai in the film leaves a lot of space for contemplation in regard to the codes
of honor and heroism in their respective (film) cultures, but the characterization of Nantai remains a missed opportunity to question established assumptions about the gendered and ethnic Other in the imagination and practices
of both cinematic traditions. A female warrior-like persona, Nantai is situated
on the margin of the masculinist discourse of power and honor typical of the
Western genre.[7] Her first appearance as a rebel against the encroaching white
settlers is confined to a prison cell, which effectively subjects her to the voyeuristic gaze of Tommy. True love develops, but only to elevate Tommy from
being an enslaved subject in the Japanese social hierarchy to a free and independent subject in the Wild West. Previously, Tommy's underdeveloped sense

of manhood was seen through his frustrated attempts to act like a womanizer. The role of Nantai in the film, therefore, is to heal this much battered and insulted male ego by providing him, first, sexual comfort and, at a deeper level, psychological consolation and social recognition. After their marriage, it is not so much sexual pleasure as the socialization and naturalization of Tommy in his newfound "homeland" that grants Tommy his long-lost agency and manhood. As a comic character bordering on the grotesque, Tommy is an oddity in the eyes of both his fellow Japanese and the white settler communities in the US. As a social misfit and cultural Other, Tommy finds in Nantai, a colonized subject no less alien to both worlds, a bond that transcends language and racial barriers. To Tommy, Nantai resembles the Amazonian goddess through whom he recovers his lost (or systemically castrated) manhood and acquires a new identity as both husband and tribal head. Tommy's transformation from a lowly ninja to a native lord amounts to a caricature of the colonial conquest of the Wild West, albeit by a would-be samurai from Japan.

The technical flaws of Okamoto's most daunting appropriation of the cowboy movie notwithstanding, the gendered and racialized subplot that creates the film's most outrageous and least expected "accidental hero" is ripe with symbolic and allegorical potential. If Tommy's double otherness enables him to break out of the moral universes of both the samurai and the cowboy, it is nonetheless reabsorbed into the frontier myth of the Western through a romanticized identification with an idealized Native American homeland. Okamoto himself might not have intended to interrogate the "colonial complex" of either the US-American Western or the Japanese samurai film in this comic fantasy of the East-West encounter, but the characterizations of Tommy and Nantai speak volumes about the film's ideological complicity with its dual origins. *East Meets West*, after all, is an in-between film that does not sit well as either an arthouse-cult movie, like *Sukiyaki*, or a formal tribute and remake, such as *Unforgiven* (discussed below). It is a different kind of "bad film" whose in-betweenness mirrors the deliberately clichéd title of the film itself. The most intriguing quality of the film lies in its bizarreness, most provocatively expressed in the figure of Tamajiro/Tommy as an embarrassing social type from Japan and a satirical twist on the (Asian) cowboy character and its geopolitical underpinnings.

UNFORGIVEN: REEXAMINING THE "MECHANISMS OF VIOLENCE"

A remake of Clint Eastwood's 1992 *Unforgiven*, Lee Sang-il's film presents an interesting counterexample to Miike and Okamoto's appropriations of the

Western. Mixing homage, satire, and self-reflexive hybridization, *Sukiyaki* and *East Meets West* exhibit a self-conscious otherness in recycling and reworking their "oater sources." In both cases, playfulness both sustains and disrupts coherence of plot and action. By overdoing weirdness in mimicry, the two films draw attention to the complex workings of the latent tensions and contradictions within both the Western genre itself and its cross-cultural translation in Japanese cinema, albeit in hyperbolic proportions. If Miike and Okamoto have gone down the road of the "bad film," Lee's more recent attempt exemplifies the other end of the spectrum: a faithful yet contextually sensitive remake of a contemporary Western masterpiece that has earned critical respect in its overseas circulation. Apart from the film's impressive cinematography that rivals its Western inspirations, Lee's remake reveals a perceptive grasp of Eastwood's original in terms of character psychology, moral conflicts, and, most of all, its critique of the ideological ambivalences of the US-American Western, or what Allen Redmon calls the "mechanisms of violence," prevalent not only in Western films but also in US-American culture itself (315–28). For the purposes of the analysis here, the discussion below focuses on the remake's engagement with Eastwood's critique of violence and how the recontextualization of the setting in a Japanese frontier town in the tumultuous early Meiji era opens up a space for a critical dialogue with both Eastwood's intervention in the Western (and US-American culture itself) and the Japanese cultural milieu.

Before he became an outlaw in hiding, Jubei Kamata, better known as "Jubei the Killer" (Ken Watanabe) was a samurai in the service of the Edo Shogunate. The opening scene sees Jubei fleeing armed police of the Meiji government. As Jubei tackles and kills his pursuers in a combat on the frozen grounds of Hokkaido (Northern Japan), a voice-over (apparently a projection of Jubei's internal monologue) ponders on how humans, like animals, would kill when their lives are at stake. This opening scene offers important contextual clues to Lee's recasting of Eastwood's characters and motifs in mid-nineteenth-century Japan. Like his predecessors, Lee creates a near-parallel to Eastwood's William Munny, a retired gunfighter, in the character of Jubei, an ex-samurai confronted by external enemies as well as his own inner devils. Like Munny, Jubei is convinced by a close friend, Kingo, to join him in a bounty hunt for two brothers who have disfigured a prostitute. The duo soon turns into a trio, when Goro, a young man eager to prove himself, joins the manhunt. The interactions between the three men recall much of Eastwood's film: the reformed gunfighters are unable to perform the fatal act, and Goro appears to be traumatized when he is ordered by Jubei to kill his target. The archenemy, Ichizo Oishi (Koichi Sato), is Gene Hackman's Little Bill whose propensity for peace and brutality oscillates whimsically up to the moment of his murder by Jubei in revenge for the death of Kingo. In Eastwood's film, neither Munny's nor Little Bill's inconsistent conduct is fully explained and justified, as each repeatedly shows genuine repentance for their bloodstained track records. Little Bill's more frequent outbursts of uncontrollable rage draw the wrath of Munny after Ned's death, but Munny's cold-blooded shootings inside the tavern suggest a more violent personality behind his deadpan appearance. By comparison, Lee's Oishi, the melancholy law enforcer, offers a more nuanced interpretation of his "Little Bill" incarnate: a fellow ex-samurai, Oishi's capriciousness and unpredictability is accompanied by subtle hints of a deeply troubled soul. His violent outbursts, therefore, are signs of his self-abandonment, if not self-destructiveness. As in Eastwood's original, Oishi and Jubei are less opposites than alter egos, for they are fellow prisoners of their own past in full awareness of their hidden killer instincts. If we recall the voice-over at the beginning, it becomes clear that Lee's interpretation of the "mechanisms of violence" has a stronger existential bent. What Redmon calls "redemptive violence" (315–16), repeatedly questioned in Eastwood's film, becomes an interrogation of the human instinct—which now goes beyond mere survival to encompass hatred, revenge, and reflex.[8] One can say that the voice-over and the opening scene in Lee's film are the director's "answer" to the questions posed by Eastwood's (anti)Western: the myth of redemptive violence is dismantled by returning violence to its source—the human instinct to kill, which over time becomes an instrument of power legitimized by the codes of honor, loyalty, and justice.

In Eastwood's film, however, the exposure of the inherent contradictions and ambivalence of redemptive violence is short-circuited in the ending, when we are told that Munny is able to move on to a new beginning as a successful merchant in San Francisco with the money he earned from his killings. Film scholars expressed mixed responses to this "happy ending," which not only is achieved at the expense of a dozen lives (including his best friend's) but also flattens the complex psychological and moral drama of the film. Whether the confused messages at the close of the narrative are meant to reinstate the grand myth of the US-American Western or to sabotage it by stirring up uneasiness toward this metanarrative remains a matter of debate.[9] The Japanese remake offers a very different conclusion: Jubei gives the bounty to Goro and Natsume (the disfigured prostitute) and asks them to take care of his two children whom he has left alone at the farm (fig. 13.2). In an ending shot, Jubei is seen wandering alone on the frozen land of Hokkaido. Probably Lee was aware of the potentially problematic nature of the original ending of *Unforgiven* when he adopted a more ambiguous finale: Jubei chooses to continue his

Fig. 13.2 Jubei's (*center*) farewell to Natsume (*front left*) and Goro (*far right*) in *Unforgiven* (2013) [110:48].

self-imposed exile instead of buying his place in respectable society. One can say that both Eastwood and Lee are questioning the frontier myth in their own ways. Munny's pragmatic choice may have compromised the film's foray into the imperialist unconscious of the US-American Western. Yet Munny's social redemption may also be read as the film's continued questioning of a genuine *moral* redemption. In this light, Jubei's generosity and self-imposed exile could well be the director's attempt to probe into the moral question left behind by Munny: by rejecting the temptation of the bounty, Jubei's repentance is more aligned with the moral character of the samurai. In this respect, Lee's remake has opted out of the ambivalent self-subversion to embrace a more "Japanese" resolution to the moral question at the center of Eastwood's film.

It is worth mentioning that Lee's film has inserted a plot detail that insinuates Japanese racial politics during the Meiji era. In one episode, Goro reveals his identity as a half-Ainu when he feels enraged by a group of Japanese policemen abusing Ainu villagers. Soon we learn that Jubei's deceased wife is also an Ainu, which explains his trust and brotherly care for Goro. The inclusion of this footnote on racial politics in Meiji Japan aligns the film with pro-Native American Westerns.[10] Goro's character could be a substitute for Ned (Morgan Freeman), whose black male body "becomes an object lesson on which [Little Bill] enforces the authority of his particular brand of White Western masculine law" (Alexander 477).

If Eastwood's film deromanticized the frontier myth by diminishing the heroic stature of its cowboy heroes (recall Munny's cold-shoulder response to the Schofield Kid's teenage fantasy of "real life" and Little Bill's capricious and random violence on his weaker rivals), Lee's rendition of the Japanese Eastern lays bare the troubled psyche of the ex-samurai to whom the previous codes of honor and heroism are no longer relevant, if they ever were. Goro and Jubei's affiliation with the Ainu minority, too, further complicates their otherness as outlaws under the new regime, whose imperialist ambitions would only surface decades later, when Japan extended its military stretch in Asia. To the extent that Jubei remains a drifting ronin in self-imposed exile, he has projected his hope for a better life in Goro and Natsume, who will be the surrogate parents of his children. The ending of Lee's remake is probably more forgiving of Jubei, hence less problematic, than Eastwood's treatment of Munny, who takes advantage of the blood money to become a "prosperous merchant" in San Francisco. Jubei's more "samurai-like" decision in the end puts him closer to the lone hero prototype in both the chanbara and the Western film. Munny, on the other hand, is the expression of a deeply cynical view of the US-American West, if not US-American history, that the Western has come to represent.

CONCLUSION

Since the post–World War II era, the Western has been a medium of intercultural dialogue between Hollywood and Japanese cinema. Beginning with an overview of well-known precedents of mutual inflections in the case of post–World War II chanbara films, this chapter has drawn attention to more recent efforts by Japanese filmmakers in engaging with the Western genre. By no means an exhaustive account, the three films discussed above shed light on how the formal and ideological motifs of the Western have been reworked in contemporary Japanese cinema, whether as kitsch, parody, tribute, or self-reflexive critique. Sukiyaki's radical deconstruction and displacement of the Western offers an opportunity to rethink the ontology of not only the Western genre but also "Asian cinema" itself as a critical category. What connects Miike's film to Okamoto's less ambitious project is the foregrounding of extreme otherness, especially through socially and politically disempowered characters, who in both films exist as linguistic-ethnic-psychosocial oddities. East Meets West is neither the best nor the most serious work by Okamoto, whose earlier works are known for their more poignant critique of war and violence. As suggested above, East Meets West can be seen as a playful adaptation of the Western by displacing the chanbara film onto US-American soil. While the film does not seriously question the frontier myth, its romantic subplot reveals interesting gender politics that both perpetuate the stereotype of the Native Indian woman and resist the repressive social and political hierarchy represented by the samurai class. These contradictory impulses are the result of a "taken for grantedness" toward female agency and subjectivity in both the chanbara and Western film traditions. Compared to his more senior peers, Lee Sang-il has seized on the moral ambivalence toward "redemptive violence" at the core of Clint Eastwood's *Unforgiven* to recast the same story in his remake. What differentiates Lee's film most from Eastwood's original is a more explicit disavowal of violence's redemptive potential while displacing Kingo's subplot in the figure of Goro, whose half-Ainu identity serves as a reminder of Japan's racist past. The three films, together with their more distant predecessors, offer glimpses into the way in which filmmakers in Japan have participated in the making and remaking of "Asian Westerns" by fulfilling, frustrating, and questioning the ideological and formal expectations of the genre. Such an undertaking cannot be accomplished without a self-reflexive critique from within the Japanese cultural tradition itself.

NOTES

1. On Asian Westerns, see also Fried, Khoo, Desser, and Lee.

2. For adaptations of Kurosawa's films in Hollywood and elsewhere, see, for example, Desser and Teo.

3. While Burch dismissed the film "with an annoying condescension," Donald Richie "has nothing but praise" for *Sanjuro*.

4. For a discussion on Okamoto and his generation of avant-garde directors who challenged the established war film conventions in Japan, see, for example, Standish (256–57, 331–32).

5. At the same time, film companies had maintained a steady supply of ideologically conservative chanbara films as a form of popular entertainment.

6. Having noted the use of "phonetic English for unneeded additional derangement" and "the stretches of tedium between outrages," Jim Ridley credits the film as "one of Miike's most visually impressive features." James Mudge hails it as "a vibrant cross cultural exercise" where "style reigns supreme over substance." Mark Schilling is disappointed by the film's "strenuously embellishing by-now familiar themes with ever more convoluted arabesques of cinematic referencing and auteurist posturing."

7. Feminist scholars have pointed out how masculinist discourse and prerogatives dominate the plot and action of Western films. See, for example, Annete Kuhn (11–12), Jane Tomkins (38–39), and Maureen T. Schwarz (45–71).

8. Redmon develops his analysis of the film from anthropologist René Girard's notion of "scapegoat violence" and, in particular, theologist Walter Wink's "myth of redemptive violence," which "relies on the emergence of a

stronger hero who is able, through surpassing violent force, to annihilate the powerful evil that threatens human existence." This myth, Redmon notes, runs through US history books, in which "each war is championed as a march to greater freedoms" (315–16).

    9. See, for example, Clay Motley; Joseph H. Kupfer (103–14).

    10. For readers unfamiliar with the modern history of Japan, the Meiji period saw the rise of Japan to a formidable imperial power in Asia and the militarist regime's territorial conquests in the region before the outbreak of World War II.

WORKS CITED

Alexander, Bryant Keith. "Morgan Freeman's Black Male Body as Unforgiven." *Cultural Studies/Critical Methodologies*, vol. 12, no. 6, Dec. 2012, pp. 476–78.

Bergen, Ronald. "Kihachi Okamoto." *The Guardian*, 18 Mar. 2005, https://www.theguardian.com/news/2005/mar/18/guardianobituaries.artsobituaries. Accessed 5 September 2021.

Burch, Noël, and Annette Michelson. *To the Distant Observer: Form and Meaning in the Japanese Cinema*. Scolar, 1979.

Desser, David. "Kurosawa's Eastern 'Western': 'Sanjuro' and the Influence of 'Shane.'" *Film Criticism*, vol. 8, no. 1, 1983, pp. 54–65.

———. "Remaking Seven Samurai in World Cinema." *East Asian Cinemas: Exploring Transnational Connections on Film*, edited by Leon Hunt and Leung Wing-fai, I. B. Tauris, 2008.

Fried, Daniel. "Riding Off into the Sunrise: Genre Contingency and the Origin of the Chinese Western." *Publications of the Modern Language Association*, vol. 122, no. 5, 2007, pp. 1482–98.

Gerow, Aaron. "When the East Fails to Meet the West." *Daily Yomiuri*, 8 Aug. 1995, p. 16.

Khoo, Olivia. "Bad Jokes, Bad English, Good Copy: *Sukiyaki Western Django*, or How the West Was Won." *Asian Studies Review*, vol. 37, no. 1, 2013, pp. 80–95.

Kuhn, Annete. *Women's Pictures: Feminism and Cinema*. Verso, 1994.

Kupfer, Joseph H. "The Seductive and Subversive Meta-Narrative of *Unforgiven*." *Journal of Film and Video*, vol. 60, nos. 3–4, 2008, pp. 103–14.

Lee, Vivian P. Y. "J-horror and Kimchi Western: Mobile Genres in East Asian Cinemas." *East Asian Cinemas: Regional Flows and Global Transformations*, edited by Vivian P. Y. Lee, Palgrave Macmillan, 2011, pp. 118–41.

Mes, Tom. "In No Man's Land." *Film Comment*, Sept.–Oct. 2007, pp. 64–66.

———. "A Tribute to Kihachi Okamoto." *Midnight Eye*, 12 Apr. 2005, http://www.midnighteye.com/features/a-tribute-to-kihachi-okamoto/. Accessed 5 September 2021.

Motley, Clay. "'It's a Hell of a Thing to Kill a Man': Western Manhood in Clint Eastwood's *Unforgiven*." *Americana: Journal of American Popular Culture (1900-present)*, vol. 3, no. 1, Spring 2004, https://www.americanpopularculture .com/journal/articles/spring_2004/motley.htm. Accessed 5 September 2021.

Mudge, James. "*Sukiyaki Western Django* (2007) Movie Review." *Beyond Hollywood*, 2009, http://www.beyondhollywood.com/sukiyaki -western-django-2007-movie-review/.

Redmon, Allen. "Mechanisms of Violence in Clint Eastwood's *Unforgiven* and *Mystic River*." *Journal of American Culture*, vol. 27, no. 3, Sept. 2004, pp. 315–28.

Richie, Donald. *The Films of Akira Kurosawa*. University of California Press, 1996.

Ridley, Jim. "The Absurdist Bloodshed of Takashi Miike's Sukiyaki Western Django." *Village Voice*, 27 Aug. 2008, https://www.villagevoice.com/2008/08/27 /the-absurdist-bloodshed-of-takashi-miikes-sukiyaki-western-django/. Accessed 5 September 2021.

Schilling, Mark. "'Sukiyaki Western Django' Spaghetti Western Served Up in Japan." *Japan Times*, 14 Sept. 2007, https://www.japantimes.co.jp /culture/2007/09/14/culture/sukiyaki-western-django/.

Schwarz, Maureen T. "Searching for a Feminist Western: *The Searchers, The Hired Hand*, and *The Missing*." *Visual Anthropology*, vol. 27, 2014, pp. 45–71.

Stadler, Jane. "Cultural Value and Viscerality in *Sukiyaki Western Django*: Towards a Phenomenology of Bad Film." *Continuum: Journal of Media and Cultural Studies*, vol. 24, no. 5, 2010, pp. 679–91.

Standish, Isolde. *New History of Japanese Cinema: A Century of Narrative Film*. Continuum, 2005.

Teo, Stephen. *Eastern Westerns: Film and Genre Outside and Inside Hollywood*. Routledge, 2017.

Tomkins, Jane. *West of Everything: The Inner Life of Westerns*. Oxford University Press, 1992.

Yoshimoto, Mitsuhiro, "Melodrama, Postmodernism, and Japanese Cinema." *Melodrama and Asian Cinema*, edited by Wimal Dissanayake, Cambridge University Press, 1993, pp. 101–26.

VIVIAN P. Y. LEE is Associate Professor in the Department of Chinese and History at the City University of Hong Kong. She is author of *The Other Side of Glamour: The Left-Wing Studio Network in Hong Kong Cinema in the Cold War Era and Beyond*.

THE SOUTH AFRICAN FRONTIER IN *FIVE FINGERS FOR MARSEILLES* (MICHAEL MATTHEWS, 2017)

CLAIRE DUTRIAUX AND ANNAEL LE POULLENNEC

US-AMERICAN WESTERNS INFLUENCED THE WAY international audiences viewed the US-American West in the twentieth century, and Westerns quickly came to be identified with a specific period in US-American history, in which the binary opposition of civilization versus the wilderness, inherited from Frederick Jackson Turner's frontier thesis, would play out. However, film historians and critics have pointed out that Westerns are far more complex and can offer discourses about cross-border issues[1] or about the US at the time of their production (Corkin) and that the earliest Hollywood Westerns can be read transnationally—opening up many other avenues of investigation than the construction of white masculinity through the confrontation with the US-American wilderness. Today, scores of Westerns set in other regions of the world are distributed and seen by viewers globally via festivals and various media platforms. *Five Fingers for Marseilles* (Michael Matthews, 2017) is undoubtedly transnational, according to the definition of transnational cinema given by Elizabeth Ezra and Terry Rowden: "Transnational cinema imagines its audiences as consisting of viewers who have expectations and types of cinematic literacy that go beyond the desire for and mindlessly appreciative consumption of national narratives that audiences can identify as their 'own'" (3).

Although the postapartheid film industry has jointly targeted national and international audiences, particularly from the 2000s onward, a sense of national narrative has infused numerous fiction and documentary films of the postapartheid era (Le Poullennec "The Township"). Among those, Matthews's feature film was intended for world audiences from the start; it was released in South Africa on April 6, 2018, after having traveled the world's festivals.[2] *Five Fingers for Marseilles* premiered at the forty-second Toronto International

Film Festival, in 2017, and was then screened at Austin's Fantastic Fest, BFI London Film Festival, and Palm Springs International Film Festival. The film was sold to The Jokers for distribution in France, NonStop Entertainment for Scandinavia, The Kloxworx Co. for Japan, and Uncork'd Entertainment for North America. It was then made available on Netflix, Amazon, and Apple iTunes platforms in 2018. Yet, if it is transnational in its distribution and use of an increasingly transnational genre, it also carries a deep sense of the national, as it appropriates the genre to retell (a) South African (hi)story. Consequently, it represents an immediately recognizable and yet profoundly unfamiliar object for viewers of US-American Westerns.

Hailed as "the first South African Western" by movie critics upon its release, *Five Fingers for Marseilles* actually emerged from fertile ground. Few Westerns were filmed and produced in apartheid and postapartheid South Africa, though a few "Boerewors Westerns" were made (Ritzer), but the country's love of cowboys and cowboy movies throughout the twentieth century, especially among black mining communities, has been largely documented.[3] The use of the genre, familiar to local as well as international audiences, is envisaged as a means to broach complex social issues through easily identified archetypes, themes, and conventions.[4] The use of US-American genres is not a new phenomenon in South African cinema, and the cultural exchanges between the two countries have been examined at length (notably in Nixon, partially in Balseiro and Masilela, and Saks). However, *Five Fingers for Marseilles* proposes, in many respects, to reverse and subvert the genre's conventions in order to position the film in South African space and history, making it a revisionist— and, more specifically, postcolonial—Western, which interrogates the legacies of colonialism and the damages caused by the appropriation of land and territory by white settlers, particularly among what screenwriter and producer Sean Drummond calls "those who were 'pioneered upon,' the recipients of the conquest," (Le Poullennec "Interview") that is, black South Africans.

This Western tells the story of the Five Fingers, five childhood friends who live in Railway, the impoverished township attached to Marseilles, a South African town developed at the time of colonial expansion for the purpose of housing black workers who built the railway system.[5] When the film opens, Marseilles is an apartheid-era town whose inhabitants are terrorized and racketeered by white policemen. The Fingers are children fighting for the town's freedom: Tau ("Lion" in Sesotho), the fierce one; his brother Zulu (the brave leader); Bongani ("Pockets"), the richer one; Unathi ("Shepherd"), the storyteller; Luyanda ("Cockroach"), the poor one; there is an additional sixth Finger (Lerato), just like there was a fourth musketeer, the only girl and Zulu and

Tau's love interest (as well as Bongani's). As Tau kills two racketeering police-men, falsely believing they killed Lerato, he becomes a freedom fighter turned criminal, devotes his life to crime, and spends twenty years in prison. When he gets out, Tau returns to Marseilles unbeknownst to his former friends and finds Marseilles rid of white police, but pervaded by corruption and violence. The town's major threat is Sepoko, a terrifying gang leader, who introduces himself as a peacemaker and judge, and whose mystical characterization evokes a villain straight out of Shakespeare.[6] Tau reluctantly becomes the hero who will bring the Fingers, and other companions, together again to face Sepoko, their pasts, and each other.

WESTERN ICONOGRAPHY GROUNDED IN SOUTH AFRICA

Five Fingers for Marseilles uses the genre of the Western to allow for the expres-sion of a South African story. If the film uses iconic imagery that harks back to the most famous Hollywood Westerns, as we shall see, the filmmakers have made a point of avoiding "gimmicks" by anchoring the story in South African landscapes, culture(s), and history.

The opening sequence is composed of extreme long shots of empty land-scapes and rock formations that are reminiscent of the opening shots of most US-American Westerns, and the land features prominently in the rest of the film (as in the films of John Ford, who elevated Monument Valley to the status of iconic Western landscape). The film's plot articulates four types of conflict that, according to Drummond, are characteristic of the Western: "Man against man (and community), man against himself (his nature, his past), man against the land (and the question of ownership), man versus time and the forces of history" (Le Poullennec "Interview"). Regarding the third conflict, the film revolves around the familiar binary oppositions of the wilderness versus civi-lization and dramatizes the issues of expansion and settlement much like the US-American Western. Some of the characters adopt the attire of Western heroes—Tau dons a Stetson hat from the moment he decides to settle in New Marseilles for good. The film echoes major US-American Western films, among which *Shane* (George Stevens, 1953) presents the clearest parallels to *Five Fingers*. The conflict between civilization and savagery, the difficulty of estab-lishing law and order in the wilderness, and the question of what kind of mascu-linity best applies to a frontier environment are classical US-American tropes, which the director Michael Matthews and Sean Drummond ground in a South African setting. Like Shane, Tau is a reluctant outlaw hero, who decides to reclaim his role as protector by defending his community (in Railway) against Sepoko's Night Runners gang, whose aggressiveness and demeanor in the bar, the Grey Lady, match the Rykers' in the 1953 film. As in *Shane*, the main confrontations between the outlaw hero and Sepoko's evil gunmen take place in the bar that belongs to Jonah and Lerato, where the community of Railway gathers to socialize. The confrontations between Tau and the gang revolve around similar issues, pertaining to the leadership of the community and how best to free the community from corruption—making the community free means that the reluctant outlaw hero will need to take action.

But unlike Shane who has no background and remains mysterious throughout the movie, Tau's past is shown in a long introductory sequence, which allows the film to depart from the traditional structure of the Western. In this apartheid-era sequence, which is undated, Tau is introduced as the Western's "good bad" boy, soon to become "good bad man" (see Bloom). It anchors him in South Africa, even though he later carefully introduces himself as "Nobody" to Sepoko and his gang in the Grey Lady (which, of course, evokes Tonino Valerii's 1973 Western *My Name Is Nobody*, but could also be a reference to Jim Jarmusch's 1995 *Dead Man*). We never know what crimes Shane committed in the past, but in *Five Fingers* we are shown that Tau killed two white policemen in retaliation for what he believed to be the death of his childhood sweetheart, Lerato, at the hands of the white police. The introductory sequence juxtaposes images of South African landscapes that are eerily reminiscent of the US-American West (extreme long shots of the wilderness interspersed with shots of train tracks) with more recognizably South African characters, costumes, and motifs. The children are shown to use slingshots and rocks instead of guns; they ride bikes in the wilderness instead of horses, which allows the film to depart even further from US-American Westerns set after the Civil War. The landscape shots may be unsettling for viewers used to watching US-American Westerns, due to the visual resemblance between the landscapes of the Northeastern Cape and those of the West as pictured in US-American Westerns. However, one must not mistake the filmmakers' use of visual references for an attempt to make a US-American-style Western transported into a South African context.

The irruption of Sesotho into images characteristic of the genre immediately grounds the film in a South African context, positioning it between transnational tropes and national concerns. If the choice of a black language is a recurring feature in postapartheid fiction films, Drummond insisted on authenticity, working closely with the Sesotho translator and Sesotho-speaking actors to adapt the script, originally written in English, and work it into character development.[7] The aim was for the language to be recognized as rich and culturally accurate by Sesotho-speaking audiences. For the rest of the film, the dialogues and the voice-over are mainly in Sesotho as well as IsiXhosa, the main languages of the area where the film was shot, which further anchors the film in a specific locale.[8] The costumes are also designed to fit those of the region, referencing "the unique costume pieces of the Basotho—the worn thin blankets, the restored balaclavas, the extraordinary masks, [and] the hats" (Vienings 15), all of which construct the balance between local authenticity and global recognition of cowboy attire. Horse riding, which is what Sizwe, Lerato's son does, is also at once a defining feature of the genre, fitting expectations, and customary in the area and neighboring Lesotho, notably for shepherding purposes.

In another parallel with Shane, Tau becomes a father figure for his brother's son, Sizwe, whose name means "nation" in IsiZulu and IsiXhosa. He shields him from violence and prevents him from taking part in the fight, thus symbolically protecting the young South African nation, very much like Shane who warns Joey, the symbol of America's future, about the power of guns in the valley. Such similarities between *Five Fingers for Marseilles* and Stevens's classic "super Western," in the terms of André Bazin, that is, a self-conscious Western that "looks for some additional interest to justify its existence," invite the viewer to consider *Five Fingers* as a "super Western" as well, revolving around South African history and myth rather than the myth of the US-American West.

THE WESTERN IS SOUTH AFRICAN HISTORY: REVISING COLONIAL AND APARTHEID LEGACIES

The filmmakers did not approach the Western as an exclusively US-American genre but as one that is already transnational. Rather than merely using a US-American framework to tell a South African story, it emphasizes the endogenous nature of the genre to the South African context. The appropriation of the Western and its grounding in the South African context function especially well, as the genre's conventions (structured according to the four conflicts mentioned above) also resonate with South African history and historiography. This might be somewhat facilitated by the Western's own borrowings from colonial adventure narratives (both in literature and film), sometimes set on the African continent (see, for instance, Davis on the representation of Zulus). The Turnerian concept of the frontier has been used by South African historians (Mostert), notably in a comparative perspective putting forth similarities and ruptures with the US-American context (Lamar and Thompson), and frontier(s) have been analyzed as background and motifs in the context of South African literary works (Rogez).

In *Five Fingers for Marseilles*, the concept of the frontier, as the line that marked the advancement of white settlement (and civilization) in the US-American wilderness in most classic Westerns from *The Covered Wagon* (James Cruze, 1923) to *Shane*, is adapted to the South African setting. In early South African cinema, epic films such as *De Voortrekkers* (Harold Shaw, 1916) or *Die bou van 'n nasie* (*They Built a Nation*, Joseph Albrecht, 1938) served to construct a national myth based on Afrikaner-centered white colonial identities. These works proposed representations of the Great Trek that would distill images of frontier life and conquest mythologies in South African cinema and film culture as early as the preapartheid period. There are similarities between these films and the Western, as they focus on white settlement and conflict with native tribes and associate the conquest of the land with racial issues. As in most US-American Westerns, the preferred mode of transportation of settler families is the covered wagon. Frontier mythology (as a zone of conflict between civilization and savagery, an area of conquest, a space for national construction) is also part and parcel of South African history, as related from the white settlers' perspective, particularly regarding Afrikaner historiography, which could arguably posit the Western as relatively endogenous to the South African context. The use of the frontier trope, and the conflicts of ownership and self-reinvention it comes with, is grounded in local history rather than merely imported. It might be argued, from a film history perspective, that early South African films focused on the frontier contribute to the impression of adequation between genre and context. However, Tau and his friends' story is one of resistance to colonization and injustice, constructing the film as a revisionist Western. At the beginning of the film, the children portray themselves as the only ones left standing in a town oppressed by the corruption of white policemen.

This perspective is clearly established in the opening sequence. As the images shift from open landscapes to settlement, the voice-over states: "First came the trains, and with them came the settlers. English, Dutch, German, and French, bringing their towns with them: Paris, Roma, Barcelona . . . and Marseilles. And they called it their land and decided they could do with it as they pleased. And for us who'd been there before, they put us on top of the hill, out of sight, and they called it Railway, because most of us were working on the train lines" [01:10–01:55]. In opening thus, the film posits an "us" and a "them" that distinguishes the main characters, and central point of view in the film, from the settlers. The voice-over asserts the latter's presence in the territory as secondary, reversing the classical Western trope of a virgin land open for conquest and edging the film closer to the revisionist Western of the 1970s. The process described here is evidently that of colonization, envisaged as an intrusion followed by an appropriation of land and an expropriation of the "us," who we understand to be black populations, used as a workforce for the construction of the train line. This suggests a postcolonial take on South African history, reinforced by the children's resistance against the white police, and their remark that land is their religion and freedom their common fight. In the context of South African history, this brings to mind the anti-apartheid struggle, particularly the role of the youth and student movements, often including teenagers (Diseko), notably, but not exclusively, in the 1970s.

As a revisionist Western, *Five Fingers* uses the town of Marseilles as an allegory for South Africa in another respect: to examine the construction of another frontier, this time in the sense of a dividing line, which separates Marseilles, the town, from Railway, a township. Apartheid was, of course, fundamentally spatial in nature (Christopher), although as a system it concomitantly engineered the exploitation of black labor to the benefit of the white minority. By representing the division between (New) Marseilles and Railway, which persists even after the apartheid-era flashback into the present of New Marseilles, the filmmakers interrogate the legacy and persistence of apartheid space, a question that has been largely studied since the 2000s (Judin and Vladislavić; Murray et al., among many others). The *Five Fingers* production notes underscore how the director and screenwriter aimed to show this enduring division as a "new" South African frontier, separating Railway from New Marseilles: "The death of these settler towns began long before the fall of Apartheid, with the train lines becoming obsolete, replaced with highways and a bigger focus on city living. After the advent of the new South Africa, many of those towns completely faded away, and in their place the townships began to rise up. The result is something much more proudly South African, and Matthews and Drummond made a commitment to travel the country, visiting these towns for inspiration. They found it akin to a new frontier, and in that was the parallel with the Western" (4).

This frontier is "new" in the sense that it is no longer the frontier described by Turner's discourse, but also because the film represents the challenges of the new South Africa. *Five Fingers* repurposes the concept of frontier, using it at once in a historical sense—to refer to colonial expansion (from the seventeenth to the nineteenth century)—and in the wider sense of a "new frontier," embodied by the postapartheid town of New Marseilles. The second (and main) part of the film, which follows an adult Tau, turns to the question of the legacy of the colonial past and the cycles of violence it engenders in individuals and communities. Tau, the hero, straddles two worlds, that of New Marseilles, the new town that has seemingly managed to prosper, and Railway, the township that has been left behind by town authorities but remains a site of community, as symbolized mainly by the tavern and the church. Here again, the clear-cut division of Western space becomes an apt expression of apartheid policies of strict nationwide segregation, and of its persistence in postapartheid South Africa. Tau, who has left as a child and returned as an adult, acts as the outsider hero who is not quite part of those worlds, and, as such, is able to bring them together. In its interrogation of the legacy of violence—the violence of conquest and settlement, that of appropriation and expropriation—in every character and in the town itself, the film jointly examines how collective identities are fashioned and questions the national. In postapartheid New Marseilles, colonial legacies persist, in effect, not only in space but in the trauma and violence endured and exerted by characters.

NEW MARSEILLES, RAILWAY, AND THE "NEW" SOUTH AFRICA: THE POSTAPARTHEID PARADOX

As an allegory of South Africa, Marseilles undergoes political transformation similar to that of the country. In the opening sequence, we learn from the radio that the locale is South Africa and that it is caught in an internal conflict: "The change that is going to happen is an escalation of the internal conflict in South Africa, and it will come because instead of changing the constitution so as to accommodate the legitimate demands of the majority of the people, they are changing the constitution to perpetuate the status quo. The resulting development from that is of course the continuation of the armed struggle in South Africa. It's going to be as violent . . . [*the radio is turned off*]" [04:26–05:19].

This contextualization is reminiscent of anti-apartheid armed struggle, but also of the violence enacted during the South African transition between the end of apartheid (which can be considered to have been legally dismantled in 1991) and the installment of a democratic regime (from 1994 onward). Indeed, an important plot point is the shift from white imperialist oppression, when the protagonists were children during the last days of apartheid, to strife in the postapartheid era. This participates in the contemporary critical take on the Rainbow Nation narrative in South African films and society at large, suggesting that overcoming the legacy of colonization and apartheid is an ongoing process.[9] *Five Fingers* was, indeed, developed and shot during the Zuma presidency, a period marked by numerous corruption scandals and a disillusion in government, although emanating from the former liberation's movement, to participate in the emancipation of the black working class.[10] However, the liberators-turned-oppressors framework does not fully encapsulate what is

Fig. 14.1 The not-so-new town of Marseilles.

wrong with New Marseilles. The film's focus on the Fingers and their personal trauma (a few scenes show Tau, Cockroach, and Pockets in front of a mirror, for instance), indeed, suggests that violence, which can be interpreted as a colonial legacy, keeps resurfacing in the present, thus continuing to cause damage even through the behavior of those who were "pioneered upon," in Drummond's words. In this sense, New Marseilles (and, by extension, South Africa) is not, and cannot be, new as long as internal conflicts and trauma have not been dealt with (fig. 14.1). This resonates with Lorenzo Veracini's concept of settler colonialism insofar as European settlement, in South Africa as in the US, persists beyond the colonial (and, in the South African context, apartheid) era. By shifting its attention to the permanence of trauma and violence after the democratic transition, *Five Fingers to Marseilles* can be viewed as interrogating settler colonial modes of domination.

Tau's return operates as the moment when a collusion appears between past and present. Tau works as the viewer's entry point to understand what is going wrong with New Marseilles, which initially appears as a town whose infrastructures are in development. As Tau walks along the train tracks that lead him back to his childhood home, the camera gradually reveals a fading billboard stating that Marseilles is now New Marseilles (a reference to post-apartheid South Africa being labeled "new"), with the letters "NEW" having obviously been added on the old billboard [23:48]. Tau then sees a budding town that is starkly different from the one he left as a child. Instead of a few haphazardly constructed homes, the town is now developing in a grid pattern of small houses, replete with garden patches and fences. Tau sees that the township is now under development, as the camera focuses on the Chinese store and the people walking purposefully down the main street. The mayor's speech, which Tau listens to on the next day, after a nightly visit to Railway, the adjacent township situated on the mountain, underlines the much hoped for economic boom of the town. Bongani, now the town mayor, vows to lead New Marseilles into an era of security and economic prosperity, with drinking water made accessible to all its inhabitants. However, this veneer quickly cracks. Tau witnesses the police, including his old friend Luyanda who has now become the police chief, terrorize the Chinese store's owner and his children to get their hands on their money [36:19–36:52]. The scene not only recalls the introductory sequence, when the white policemen terrorized Marseilles's inhabitants for the same purpose; it also hints at anti-immigrant sentiment and violence in South Africa, since the police chief treats the Chinese South African character as an outsider to the community, and foreign shop owners have been largely targeted in real-life xenophobic violence. This new police force, composed of black officers, participates in the film's direct attack on corruption within the lines of postapartheid governing instances. Indeed, the mayor's speech, in which he calls the townspeople "comrades," is reminiscent of the language used in the struggle against apartheid. Here, it is employed to denounce the contrast between official solidarity and the corruption that characterizes the mayor, who is mostly interested in personal gain. Tau and the viewer realize simultaneously that the city is pervaded by crime and corruption; it has nothing of the success emphasized by Bongani. This is evidenced by the fact that when Tau tries to use a tap, no drinking water flows from it [57:45–58:00]. Railway, the township on the hill, is not depicted as an appeased space in contrast either—it is also pervaded by crime and corruption, as Sepoko's gang rules over its mostly deserted dwellings. The mayor has made a deal with the ghostly gangster, allowing him to rule over Railway in exchange for Sepoko's promise not to invade New Marseilles, a reference to the perceived neglect of certain urban areas by public authorities, and yet another means to characterize Bongani as a figure of corruption. The film thus embraces the current critical take on the Rainbow Nation narrative, a term coined by Archbishop Desmond Tutu to describe postapartheid South Africa as the bringing together of people from different nations and cultures, generally framed as both a political and an economic miracle. *Five Fingers for Marseilles* focuses on the remnants of structural divisions and the oppression of the town in another form, liberated from apartheid but still plagued by inherited poverty as well as the neglect and corruption of public authorities.

A superficial resolution is found in the destruction of Sepoko and his gang by Tau, with the help of the Chinese store owner, his former partners in crime, and some of the Five Fingers. In so doing, the heroes bridge the gap between

Fig. 14.2 Sizwe and the priest walking away together.

insiders and outsiders, New Marseilles and Railway, past and present. However, Tau's objective remains to free the town, which had been the Fingers' mission all along, even if it meant, in the dead Zulu's words, "from each other." Hence, in a final circle, the remaining four Fingers shoot one another, symbolically wiping the slate clean [1:49:17–1:50:41]. Due to the other characters (notably his mother Lerato and his new father figure Tau) preventing Sizwe from committing violence and becoming part of the vicious circle of violence, the latter is preserved from most of what ailed Tau and his childhood friends and impeded them from building a new South Africa from the ashes of their struggle for freedom. The film's last shot shows Sizwe riding his horse away from the Five Fingers' shoot-out, accompanied by the priest, the only Finger to escape the massacre as he kept his vow to protect the town [1:51:57–1:52:18] (fig. 14.2). Sizwe, we have mentioned, means "nation" in isiZulu. Thus, with the older generation settling the score horizontally, the young generation, symbolized by Sizwe, and thus the town itself, might be exempted from the legacy of violence and its inhabitants might finally be free.

The movie ends like a classical Western by constructing Sizwe as a true Western hero. Not only is he repeatedly shown riding a horse or shooting a rifle to perfection, but, as a symbol for "nation," his presence at the very end might signify that this South African Western has symbolically created a new model for the South African man, a model of masculinity without the legacy of violence, a modern all South-African hero. As Sizwe walks off with the priest, a duo departing from the lone cowboy trope, the South African frontier and its inherited divisions give way to a space full of potential, where conflicts are resolved and past violence might not have such an effect, where a new South Africa could potentially be reborn, for good this time.

CONCLUSION

Five Fingers for Marseilles uses the conventions of the classical and revisionist Westerns as a framework to translate specific South African concerns, while also making them relatable to non–South African audiences who may not be informed of the country's history and culture. At the same time, the South African Western is transnational in nature, as it tells a story of the legacy of colonial era violence, and of what is left of communities once the colonizers have left, which viewers worldwide can relate to. The film definitely illustrates that following the conventions of a Western does not ultimately imply that the Western is informed by US-American history and culture. By renewing tropes and conventions, and by anchoring the film's visuals, characters, and story within South African history and postapartheid preoccupations, it appropriates the Western as South African. If elements of the narrative of imperialism remain, particularly in the first part of the film, where the black townsmen are pitted against the white colonial police force, the notion of imperialism is more pervasive and latent in the film's interest in long-term consequences, not on the colonizers but on those who were "pioneered upon," and the cycles of violence that colonial imperialism sets into motion, through time. Moreover, if the film clearly proposes a distinction between apartheid and postapartheid eras, the remnants of colonial violence through its legacy on individual characters clearly begs the question of whether postapartheid South Africa is, indeed, postcolonial or if the figure of Sizwe, finally emancipated from reproducing violence, becomes a template for a utopian South Africa, truly emancipated from layers of colonial violence. In this respect, the end of the film proposes to answer positively the question of the possibility of freedom, which was the children's main driving force in fighting the apartheid regime.

NOTES

1. In the preface to the collection of essays *Back in the Saddle Again* (6–7), Edward Buscombe remarked that some of John Ford's films leave a great amount of space to Hispanic identity, including the films that outwardly seem to be concerned with US-American history, for instance, in *My Darling Clementine* (1946).

2. This was underlined by Sean Drummond, the movie's screenwriter, in a *Variety* piece: "We've been conscious from the start of developing this film for an international audience as well as a South African one" (Vourlias).

3. This love for cowboy movies that extolled US-American imperialism and, particularly, the genocide of Native Americans in the name of white identity

is examined in Burns as well as Reynolds, and less recently by anthropologist Hortense Powdermaker, who argued in *Copper Town* that in a context of colonialism, white cowboys were not viewed by black South African audiences as European but as American, which meant these audiences could paradoxically side with the cowboy across racial boundaries.

4. "Genre is an interesting means to explore real topics, because it's accessible to people. You can make something very political or challenging, but if you situate it within genre, you give people themes and conventions they are familiar with. The mayor and the chief of police, the returning outlaw, these things have connotations and meaning attached to them. You can get more detailed in the characters as the base level is already explained to people. And this is also accessible internationally" (Le Poullennec "Interview").

5. Townships, in a South African context, are racially segregated areas of settlement, generally located at the periphery of a city or town. Most South African townships were established under apartheid to accommodate the black and colored workforce, thus also contributing to the control of their residents' movements. Although segregation was abolished in 1991, with the repeal of the Group Areas Act (1950), townships themselves persist in the South African geography and social fabric, accommodating a large part of the population.

Although Marseilles is an actual town in South Africa, situated near the northwestern border of Lesotho, the film was shot in and around Lady Grey, also close to Lesotho but near the southern border.

The construction of the railway system was initiated in the second half of the nineteenth century, by the then British provinces and independent Boer republics, and was merged into a national system as the Union was formed in 1910.

6. "Sepoko, the Ghost, is a catalyst. Almost like an Iago, a Shakespearean tragic character, his role is to push characters to accomplish their fate or destiny." Sean Drummond in interview conducted with Le Poullennec.

7. For instance, Sepoko (Ghost) speaks what Drummond characterizes as an older, more traditional, or more formal form of Sesotho, from the mountain area, which contributes to constructing the mythical nature of the character (Le Poullennec "Interview").

8. Originally written in English, the script is, indeed, delivered in Sesotho, with a sprinkling of English, Afrikaans, and IsiXhosa.

9. See, for instance, the films of Jenna Bass, particularly *High Fantasy* (2017).

10. Former South African president (2009–2018) Jacob Zuma was charged with corruption in 2007 and 2019, and implicated in other corruption affairs such as the Schabir Shaik trial and the State capture accusations.

WORKS CITED

Balseiro, Isabel, and Masilela, Ntongela, editors. *To Change Reels: Film and Culture in South Africa*. Wayne State University Press, 2003.

Bazin, André. *Qu'est-ce que le cinéma?* Éditions du Cerf, 1962.

Bloom, Peter J. "Beyond the Western Frontier: Reappropriations of the 'Good Bad-Man' in France, the French Colonies, and Contemporary Algeria." *Westerns: Films through History*, edited by Janet Walker, Routledge, 2001, pp. 197–218.

Burns, James. "The Western in Colonial Southern Africa." *The Western in the Global South*, edited by MaryEllen Higgins, Rita Keresztesi, and Dayna Oscherwitz, Routledge, 2015, pp. 11–23.

Christopher, A. J. *The Atlas of Apartheid*. Routledge, 1993.

Davis, Peter. *In Darkest Hollywood: Exploring the Jungles of Cinema's South Africa*. Ohio University Press, 1996.

Diseko, Nozipho J. "The Origins and Development of the South African Student's Movement (SASM): 1968–1976." *Journal of Southern African Studies*, vol. 18, no. 1, 1 Mar. 1992, pp. 40–62.

Ezra, Elizabeth, and Terry Rowden, editors. *Transnational Cinema: The Film Reader*. Taylor and Francis, 2006.

Five Fingers for Marseilles. Directed by Michael Matthews, performances by Vuyo Dabula and Zethu Dlomo, Indigenous Film, 2017.

———. Production Notes, Indigenous Film Distribution, 2018, http://indigenousfilm.co.za. Accessed 22 May 2019.

Higgins, MaryEllen, Rita Keresztesi, and Dayna Oscherwitz. *The Western in the Global South*. Routledge, 2015.

Lamar, Howard, and Leonard Thompson. *The Frontier in History: North America and Southern Africa Compared*. Yale University Press, 1981.

Le Poullennec, Annael. Interview. Conducted by Sean Drummond, July 2018 and December 2019.

———. "The Township and the Gangster in 'Tsotsi': Local and Global Aspirations of the New South African Cinema." *Cultures of the Commonwealth*, no. 18, Autumn 2012, pp. 103–20.

Mostert, Noël. *Frontiers: The Epic of South Africa's Creation and the Tragedy of the Xhosa People*. Knopf, 1992.

Murray, Noëleen, Nick Shepherd, and Martin Hall. *Desire Lines: Space, Memory and Identity in the Post-Apartheid City*. Routledge, 2007.

Nixon, Robert. *Homelands, Harlem and Hollywood: South African Culture and the World Beyond*. Routledge, 1994.

Powdermaker, Hortense. *Copper Town: Changing Africa—The Human Situation on the Rhodesian Copperbelt*. Harper and Row, 1962.

Reynolds, Glenn. *Colonial Cinema in Africa: Origins, Images, Audiences.* McFarland, 2015.

Ritzer, Ivo. "Locating the Boerewors Western in Southern Africa." *Critical Perspectives on the Western: From* A Fistful of Dollars *to* Django Unchained, edited by Lee Broughton, Rowman and Littlefield, 2016, pp. 41–56.

Rogez, Mathilde. "La Frontière dans les romans de Mark Behr et de J. M. Coetzee." Dissertation, Université Paris 10, 2008.

Saks, Lucia. *Cinema in a Democratic South Africa: The Race for Representation.* Indiana University Press, 2010.

Veracini, Lorenzo. *Settler Colonialism: A Theoretical Overview.* Palgrave Macmillan, 2010.

Vienings, Pierre. "Costumes." *Five Fingers for Marseilles* Production Notes, Indigenous Film Distribution, 2018, http://indigenousfilm.co.za. Accessed 22 May 2019.

Vourlias, Christopher. "South African Thriller 'Five Fingers' Launches Production with All-Star Cast," *Variety,* 16 June 2016, https://variety.com/2016/film/festivals/five-fingers-for-marseilles-south-africa-sean-drummond-michael-matthews-1201796380/. Accessed 3 Sept. 2021.

CLAIRE DUTRIAUX is Associate Professor in American Studies and Cinema at Sorbonne University.

ANNAEL LE POULLENNEC is Associate Researcher at Institut des Mondes Africains. She is author, with Marie-Claude Mosimann-Barbier and Michel Prum, of *Race, identité et mondialisation en Afrique australe.*

"THEY LIKE ALL PICTURES WHICH REMIND THEM OF THEIR OWN"

The "Entangled" Development of Australian Westerns

EMMA HAMILTON

TRADITIONAL UNDERSTANDINGS OF THE AUSTRALIAN Western genre tend toward a bifurcation emphasizing either the distinctiveness of Australian filmmaking or its derivativeness. On the one hand, some posit that, while Australia may have developed cycles of bushranging and other "Western-like" films, these products are distinct from the US-American genre. Following this argument, and despite the remarkable parallels in the historical experiences of Australian and US-American frontierism, colonialism, and displacement, and the development of a national cinema that focused on that frontier experience at the same time, the Australian genre of outlaw/bushranger films should be considered as a separate genre, unrelated to the US-American Western whose worldwide popularity would come to dwarf it. For example, as Ben Goldsmith asserts in his introduction to the *Directory of World Cinema: Australia and New Zealand* edition, "The bushranger film and the Western developed separately and should be considered as distinct" (11). On the other hand, there are those who may argue that, although audiences may receive cultural products in various and diverse ways (see, e.g., Pearson), the Australian Western could only ever be derivative of (and, therefore, also less than) its US-American counterpart given the ubiquity of the US-American genre and the size and scale of Hollywood's economic and cultural power. Thus, for André Bazin, in his discussion of the Australian film *Overlanders* (1946), "A Western theme is borrowed . . . [and the film's] success was due to an unusual combination of circumstances" (131) (see also, e.g., Cooke; Lewis). These bifurcated perspectives, however, rejoin at a similar conclusion: the Western was/is/cannot be Australian. One may have either the "Australian" or the "Western" film but not both at the same time.

This bifurcation—a quest for distinctiveness pulling against a fear of derivativeness—is not necessarily restricted to questions regarding the existence of the Australian Western, or even to Australian cinema as a form of cultural expression generally. As Sarwal and Sarwal acknowledge, since the continent was colonized by the British in 1788, questions of national identity and culture have preoccupied white Australia with two generally conflicting views: that white Australia has no culture (or at least no culture that rivals Britain), a view that clearly omits Aboriginal peoples' cultures, or that a wholly unique culture has emerged from its historical experiences of convictism, frontier violence, and its geographic location in the Asia Pacific region (xxxv). It is no wonder, then, that debates occur about the existence of the Australian Western, as such conversations reflect on larger questions of white Australia's quest to understand its own history, identity, independence, and place in the world. This is, perhaps, exacerbated in discussions about the Western genre because of the very fact that Westerns are such an important vehicle for exploring those very same concepts. Indeed, as Goldsmith reminds us, "The cinematic origins of the nation have ensured that film in Australia can never simply be approached as entertainment. From its earliest days, Australian cinema has been infused with a national imperative" ("Settings" 25). This is particularly evident in attempts to understand the Western Down Under.

Current international Western scholarship and scholars of the Australian Western are increasingly turning to methods that seek to reconcile such dichotomous understandings. Recent work on the transnational and intertextual Western, such as, for example, Cynthia Miller and A. Bowdoin van Riper's edited collection, *International Westerns*, has pointed to the transcendental qualities of the Western that allow it to speak across time and place, and to its transferability to other international contexts experiencing similar issues and histories (vix). For Peter Limbrick, the Australian Western can be understood as a form of settler cinema: "As transnational constructions forged through histories of imperial and colonial rule, by mutually formative encounters between settler and indigenous cultures, and, crucially by ideological and material traffic between and across settler societies themselves . . . industries, authors, actors, viewers, and film narratives have collided, colluded, and made conflict with the complexities of settler coloniality" (*Making Settler Cinemas* 3–4; see also, "Australian Western"). That is, understanding the Australian contribution to the Western as either distinctive or derivative reduces more complex and transnational interplays of processes, products, and ideologies of production. As I have argued elsewhere, the Western is a historical genre, too, and considering the historical parallels between US-American and Australian experiences in terms of both nations' contested settlement, their renegotiated meanings of a violent "frontier experience," and their attempt to weave a cohesive national identity from the disparate threads of ethnicity, experience, and displacement have led to the development of films that are distinctly Western (Hamilton, "Such Is" 32; also "Australia").

In this way, the Western genre becomes a metadiscourse through which to explore concepts of violence, identity, land, and belonging within "othered" spaces, regardless of whether they are situated within or outside of the US, and these stories contribute to an understanding of what the Western genre is actually about. Such a perspective has increasingly been used by scholars to (re)define the Western film genre and conceptualize settler colonial theory. For example, as Neil Campbell asserts, "the Western has always had a global dimension. . . . To examine the West in the twenty-first century is to think of it as always already transnational . . . [a genre] whose meanings move between cultures, crossing, bridging, and intruding simultaneously" (3–4).

This chapter contributes to this scholarship by examining not the either/ or of the local or the international, or of the distinctive or the derivative development of the Australian Western film genre, but rather the inevitability that local and international perspectives would be mutually informing. It does so by using the theoretical perspective of "entanglement" to examine how the Australian "bushranging" film cycle developed hand in hand with the influence of US-American media and genre structures as well as other international and British developments in film technology and exhibition. In 2017, the *Entangled Media Histories* network published its first research report outlining the significance of "entanglements" as an analytical lens through which to examine media. "Entangled" media historians use the concept of "entanglements" to examine the ways in which media transcends national contexts; rather, entangled histories focus on the transnational, intertextual, interdisciplinary, and, ultimately, interconnected nature of media. As Marie Cronqvist and Christoph Hilgert argue ("Entangled Media Histories" 134), media "entanglement can be defined as intended or unintended, obvious or hidden, structured or chaotic interaction(s) in space, knowledge or time. Various forms or modes of entanglement are imaginable—reciprocal, symmetrical or asymmetrical. Interesting concepts and metaphors to work with may be: overlapping, convergence, divergence, dissemination, transfer, imperialism, adoption, resistance, adaption, encounters, hubs, crossovers, interference, translation, and hybridization." Such a perspective, they argue, sees that "nations are not, and have never been, discrete and self-contained spaces . . . [and yet] a transnational perspective does not dispense with the study of nations, but it does problematize the analytical frame" within which media have often been examined (132). Indeed, it also acknowledges that terms like *national* may give the impression of coherence and uniformity, when actually there exists messiness and multiplicity (and, in Australia's case, no nationhood at all until the federation of Australian colonies became one nation in 1901) (Moran and O'Regan xiv). It also, necessarily, positions media itself as an important agent of historical entanglement; that is, media itself proactively entangles the histories of nations across time and place by allowing national cinemas to speak to and make meaning of shared concerns across national boundaries in dialogue with one another. In the case of the Western genre, for example, transnational histories of imperialism, colonization, displacement, and a search for home are "entangled" using many of the metaphors listed above, or, as Limbrick suggests, "colonial histories have been shaped through encounter, exchange, and mutual entanglement rather than binaristic certainties" (*Making Settler Cinemas*, 11).

Current research in the field of media entanglement includes studies of specific individuals, agencies, and networks on creating media that transcend nation-states, with various impacts on notions of nationhood, and media's roles in developing and challenging social, cultural, and political values. Entangled media histories also challenge us to consider economic implications of entanglement and, socially, the ways to make often marginalized perspectives seen and heard (see also, e.g., Hilmes; Griffen-Foley; Cronqvist and Hilgert, "Response"). Yet one aspect of media entanglement that has been sidelined in this discussion is the impact of genre entanglement. One could argue that genre entanglements are particularly significant precisely because they are largely invisible compared to the entanglements of media corporations, actors, or filmmaking personnel, despite the fact that most genres are transnational, yet often uniquely interpreted for national conditions. Thus, for example, French noir, Bollywood musicals, and English comedies speak to, yet are different from, their US-American counterparts in reflecting particular local contexts, ideologies, and histories. In this sense, one could argue that genre becomes a transnational metadiscourse through which different national cinemas speak to local issues and also contribute to the broader transnational dialogue occurring about that genre and its inherent ideological assumptions. Furthermore, national cinematic interpretations of genre films speak back, reciprocally, to the international interpretations of that genre, and, in doing so, breathe new life and meaning into it as one part of a broader transnational (his)story. This point is especially important: understanding the entanglement of the Western allows us, then, to understand the conceptualizations of colonialism, for example, transnationally, while also accounting for regional dialects: differences in representing and understanding the colonization process in distinct localities or national contexts. This entanglement also allows us to invert the question, so that it reads not, "Is there such a thing as an Australian Western?" but, rather, "Is there such a thing as the US-American Western without its international counterparts?"

"Entanglement," then, is used conceptually to examine the emergence of the Western film genre in Australia in the early 1900s, when the production of the "bushranging" film cycle was at its peak. It does so by exploring the social landscape and media context in Australia at the turn of the twentieth century and its relationship to the US-American context. It suggests that historical and ideological parallels were important in making Australian audiences amenable to both Western and bushranging narratives, but, more so even, that these historical experiences were mutually reinforcing and supplemented by the exchange of media forms, narratives, and other points of cultural crossover. It also suggests, therefore, that the attempts to distinguish between a uniquely Australian or US-American product in the Australian viewing context misses a larger and more profound cocreation of genre and genre tropes over time as history, ideology, viewer expectations, gender norms, and production processes themselves were transnationally constructed rather than confined within the borders of the nation-state. Understanding the entangled nature of media structures and the genre itself allows us to better grapple with both the universal themes of the genre and their local inflections.

It could be argued that the development of the Australian film industry broadly, and the Australian Western in particular, have been entangled with Hollywood virtually since its inception. A filmmaking industry was present in Australia from the late 1880s, which was based largely on the production of short documentary or factual releases, and background screenings for stage plays (Australian Film Commission). Australian film is widely considered to have "arrived" in 1906 when, three years after the release of the silent short film and first US-American Western, *The Great Train Robbery* (Edwin S. Porter, 1903), Charles Tait released Australia's (and the world's) first feature-length narrative film, *The Story of the Kelly Gang* (1906; see Walsh). It was not, however, Australia's first bushranger film and it certainly would not be the last. Films in this cycle portrayed some of Australia's most (in)famous outlaws and include but are not limited to: *Bushranging in Northern Queensland* (Joseph Perry, Limelight, 1904), *The Bushranger* (Fitzgerald Family, 1904), *Robbery under Arms* (Charles MacMahon, MacMahon's Exquisite Pictures, 1907), *The Squatter's Daughter, or Land of the Wattle* (Bert Bailey, 1910), *Thunderbolt* (John Gavin, Southern Cross Motion Pictures/West's Pictures, 1910), *A Tale of the*

Australian Bush (Gaston Mervale, Australian Biograph Company, 1911), and *Attack on the Gold Escort* (Pathe Frere, 1911) (see, for a full overview of this cycle and film list, Routt).

Andrew Couzens points out that the films in the bushranger cycle are, on the whole, characterized by a number of similar techniques and scenes. For example, he establishes that in this film cycle, the notion of spectacle is centrally important. By this he means: physical spectacle and remarkable feats of physicality, wherein films that were often "filled with sensation" and scenes such as "the horseback cliff plunges of bushrangers in *Captain Midnight, the Bush King* [Alfred Rolfe, 1911], and *Frank Gardiner, King of the Road* [John Gavin, 1911]" (92) were heavily promoted; the spectacle of realism, a concern for the perception of authenticity, for example, in the use of costumes, props, setting, and in the retelling of "real stories" of historical personages (not so far in the past), like in *The Story of the Kelly Gang*; and the spectacle of the everyday, or the portrayal of recognizable scenes of Australian life, such as long shots of pastoral scenes, which situate the film within the landscape and are "transgressive because they depict outlaws reappropriating the land for the working poor" (97). Scenes within these films are also characterized by: archetypal representations of the "gentleman bushranger" such as in *Robbery under Arms*, or the "heroes of the poor" such as in *The Kelly Gang* (Harry Southwell, 1920) (93); and scenes of their emergence from the bush, where the boundaries of the bush itself create a natural stage for performers, both reassuring viewers that they are watching a story set in the bush without obscuring the performers or incurring technical difficulties in moving equipment. He demonstrates, then, that there are points of significant overlap between bushranger films, generally, and in the techniques, stories, and archetypes told in literature, and filmic and theatrical performances in Britain and the US, "but the deviations are even more interesting" (89).

Overall, bushranging films formed the cornerstone of the Australian market for local productions in Australian cinema's formative years, constituting a quarter of all films made in Australia between 1906 and 1912 (Goldsmith 19). The year 1911 marked the peak production year for Australian-made films, and bushranging was the most popular Australian product; at the same time, US-American Westerns emerged for the first time as popular imports (Collins 51). Just as they reached the zenith of their popularity, however, this cycle of bushranging films faced serious obstacles in its ongoing development, stymied by state censorship laws and morality campaigns concerned that films portraying such characters in a largely sympathetic light would spark a rash of imitations, increase and romanticize criminality and lawlessness, and offend the living victims and families of the outlaws they portrayed (Eisenberg 147; Bertrand 15). World War I acted to further solidify US-American dominance in the Australian film market, resulting in US-American films constituting "94 percent of all overseas features shown in Australia" by the mid-1920s (Lewis 8). As the US-American market share increased, audiences also became more likely to expect imports and, therefore, the US-American conventions of the Western genre. The overall impact of these factors caused the virtual elimination of this cycle—although, of course, the Western is always declared dead only to ride again and the continual reinvention of Ned Kelly in cinema certainly attests to this (Hamilton, "Such Is"). That said, it is impossible to ignore the reality that, if only for a short period, the Australian Western, made manifest in bushranging narratives, was more popular and profitable with local audiences than their US-American counterparts (Collins 62, 50).

There can be little argument that Australian cinema has been saturated with US-American products virtually from its inception. However, to focus on this saturation is also to ignore the genuine processes of "encounter, exchange, and mutual entanglement" occurring structurally, historically, and culturally in this period (Limbrick, *Making Settler Cinemas* 11). Structurally, it is important to point out that, when the feature-length film emerged, film production was a truly global phenomenon, and there is an element of anachronism to approaching its development as anything other than deeply entangled with the histories of other nations (Bertrand and Routt 4). As Bertrand and Routt assert, "Films and personnel circulated from country to country" with "ease" (6). In Australia, movie attendance rapidly increased; indeed, as Diane Collins asserts, in her study of film's emergence in Australia from 1896, "nowhere was [film's popularity] more pronounced than Australia," and the domestic market, though relatively small, was from the outset considered potentially lucrative for investors (3). British and US-American exhibitors established screening facilities throughout Australia, but the superior production values and technological proficiency of US-American films meant that "people were already showing a partiality not for British but American films" and for US-American methods of film exhibition (Collins 46). This was no small shift, considering that the white population was overwhelmingly of British extraction; indeed, many continued to conceptualize themselves as Australian-Britons, and films featuring British landscapes were as close as many "Australian-Britons" would ever get to visiting the "home country" (Collins 37, 46).

This is an important acknowledgment: an examination of the contributions of the Australian Western must correspondingly recognize that for many white Australians at the turn of the century their national allegiance was not neatly categorized, with many primarily identifying themselves based on cultural heritage (e.g., as Australian-Britons) or based on their State of residency (e.g., as a New South Welshman) or based on religion or class, before identifying as "Australian." Certainly, nationalist sentiment existed, but it did so in an environment of empire loyalty that renders the concept of "Australianness" itself as complex (for a critical examination of the concept of nationalism in Australia, see Meaney). Thus, in the 1920s, when the oversaturation of the Australian market by US-American products became such a cause of concern for the federal government that it launched a Royal Commission into the state of film in 1927, the commission's recommendations related to mechanisms intended not just to protect the Australian industry but also to support British ambitions to "create an empire market to challenge American hegemony" (Bertrand and Routt 23).

In early Australian cinema, more British cinematic products were shown in Australia than in Britain itself; in 1909–1910, 23.6 percent of films exhibited were British, compared to 15 percent in the British market, which was dominated more by French and US-American films than homegrown products (Megaw 29). Stuart Doyle, "the most powerful and flamboyant of early Australian film men" (see Graham), noted in his evidence before the Royal Commission that Union Theatres and Australasian Films, companies responsible for exhibition and distribution, respectively, in Australia, being "all-Australian, with Australian directors, staff, and shareholders, [have] a natural inclination and leaning towards British and Australian pictures" (45). He thereby indicated that he recognized that Australian and British imperial interests were linked and that British films culturally aligned with "our natural sentimental Australian outlook"; he defended the declining amount of British content exhibited in Australia since the early years of cinema by suggesting that only pictures of "good average standard merit" were shown in order to protect the public perception of the "prestige" of British production (45–46). Underpinning Doyle's evidence, though, are also pragmatic and other concerns: he recognizes that a higher standard of British films will "give us a lever to purchase American-produced pictures on more advantageous terms" (46); he calls himself "an Australian, born in Sydney," discusses the need for Australian companies to be "entirely independent" (45), and discusses cinema in terms of developing and protecting Australian jobs and interests; he suggests that the success or failure of a picture is entirely dependent on international markets; and he notes that it is "insulting" to viewing audiences to consider that exposure to any media—film, literature, or theater—will have the effect of "Americanising" them (47). In sum, Doyle's evidence reflects the complex web of identification and interests wrapped up in early Australian cinema, and the focus on the Australian market as a pawn in larger US-American or British imperial interests is to presuppose that audiences possessed a unity of nationhood and identification that did not necessarily exist in the early 1900s. Rather, what we can see is that media structures were, from the outset, deeply entangled throughout the globe, and methods of identification were equally deeply entangled so that neat national-ist ideas of cinema are complicated. White Australia was developing a national culture that was influenced by, and that informed other, cultures, particularly the UK and US.

This entanglement is reflected in the features and content of the films them-selves. Australian bushranging films, as William D. Routt asserts in his study of the cycle, share important similarities with their Western counterparts at this time (although, he ultimately argues that "this type of film is likely to have played a key role in Australian film history even in the [unimaginable] absence of the American cinema"). In particular, both sets of films focus on a narrative located in a "timeless" frontier setting, within a distinct historical period, and with plots focused on historical (or semihistorical) personages that "borrow extensively from local popular and folk traditions." They also draw from a deep well of transnational archetypes of the outlaw hero, common not only to the US but to Britain as well; they allowed an emergent nation to acknowledge concepts, ideas, and characters that were part of a shared cultural understand-ing while playing with elements of these narratives that may be distinct (Seal; see also Dixon's analysis of colonial adventure narratives). As discussed earlier, Andrew Couzens (91) established, for example, the substantial overlap in nar-ratives and techniques between Australian early cinema, transnational theater, and live amusements. He also discusses this in relation to personnel using one of the most prolific bushranger directors, John F. Gavin, as an example. Gavin had a ten-year theatrical and vaudeville career and toured with Buffalo Bill's Wild West show throughout the US before turning to bushranger pictures. His films, like others in the genre, drew on the storytelling formulas and the stage setups familiar to audiences internationally and, indeed, did so inevitably due to these overlaps in his personal experience of these professional contexts. Interestingly, the effect of governmental censorship in stymying the develop-ment of bushranger stories in Australia meant that Gavin returned to the US to appear in B-Westerns (Goldsmith 91).

These portrayals, though, are not just archetypal but deeply reflective of entangled historical and cultural contexts: "The 'bush' films appealed to Aus-tralians caught up in an increasingly urbanised and industrialised society. They were full of movement, space and unfettered individual action" that played on transnational themes of outlaw, civilization, and a conquered frontier, but with Australian inflections that saw outlaws as more civilized than upholders of the law, and that explored histories of class, convictism, and English-Irish animus (Collins 50). Likewise, US-American Western imports held a similar appeal, enacting and legitimizing frontier conflict in sweeping, open landscapes that reflected Australian's cultural concerns and geographic landscape. For example, the British vice consul in Sydney noted the popularity of US-American Westerns for Australian audiences: "Australian audiences are very fond of scenes illuminating incidents in American cowboy and Indian life, and they like all pictures which remind them of their own" (qtd. in Collins 46). Such a perspective illustrates that, at the time, the bushranging cycle in Australia was not perceived as threatened by US-American imports and their impact on the genre but, rather, that these narratives were mutually informing.

Culturally and historically, when filmmaking first arrived in Australia, it did so in the context of a rapidly closing frontier, much like the US's. The economic boom occasioned by the gold rush had dwindled, and Australian colonies were facing economic depression and social upheaval in the 1890s. The traumatic legacies of frontier conflict and the violent dispossession of Aboriginal peoples continued, and the Australian colonies' desire for federation owed, in large part, to a push toward a uniform and nationally enforceable form of immigration control to maintain a "White Australia" (a push that absents Aboriginal peoples, nonwhite migrants already in the country, and the wide diversity in the colonies' "white" populations based on heritage, religion, class, and a history of convictism). Australia's separate colonies formed a federated nation only in 1901, and, in the years preceding and immediately following federation, Australia was, scholars widely consider, preoccupied with the search for a national identity; indeed, some scholars would argue that this has been Australia's primary preoccupation since its colonization (for a general history of Australia in this period, see Macintyre). For some, the answer to this quest could be found in the bush, where the unique landscape brought about a "new man," distinct from his British ancestors. Such a view was promoted widely via the so-called "Bard of Bush," such as "Banjo" Paterson, John Furphy, and Henry Lawson. Their work and other Bush Bards was also disseminated via Australia's *Bulletin* magazine, which published works of bush poetry and fiction, along with political commentary, and was read widely, especially as literacy rates in the colonies continued to improve (see, e.g., Davison; Waterhouse). At the same time, the majority of the Australian population were urban dwellers. The bounty of the bush may have been witnessed on kitchen tables, made ever more convenient by improvements to the railways and telegraph, but the realities of the hardships of bush living were not evident to the vast majority of white Australia (for seminal works regarding Australian identity, see Ward; White). Indeed, Collins suggests that, in doing so, the *Bulletin* writing of the 1890s performed a societal function that would be echoed by bushranger films in the 1900s and 1910s (50). Thus, the bush, and the legend that emerged from it of a white, taciturn, egalitarian, and antiauthoritarian man, existed for most not necessarily in actuality but, rather, in the Australian imaginary, propagated by media forms including literature, theater, and cinema.

If this story sounds familiar it should: the frontier and the mythologized (white) man who emerges from it are seminal to US-American identity and Western film representations. From Fredrick Jackson Turner's "frontier thesis" to Richard Slotkin's *Gunfighter Nation*, the frontier—its wilderness and its wildness—has been conceptualized as central to the formulations of masculine white US-American cultural identity. Moreover, the development of the Australian legend founded in the experience of a mythologized white frontiersman did not simply develop and become propagated in parallel to the US-American tradition; rather, they were reciprocal and overlapping in their development. This has been examined by Marilyn Lake, who asserts that while histories of nationalist sentiment focus on the local, it is more telling to focus on how the policies, attitudes, and mythologized masculinities of countries like the US, Canada, New Zealand, South Africa, and Australia were "dynamically interconnected and, most significantly, mutually formative" (281). Indeed, such were the similarities in national identifications and mythologies that marketing the Australian bush legend "posed a challenge to *Bulletin* writers whose ideas were predicated on the uniqueness of Australia's experience"; their concern to emphasize Australia's distinctiveness arose more from the interests of those attempting to sell cultural products than from the preferences of the consumers who purchased them (Couzens 55). Such attitudes and ideologies were not simply political or policy driven, but also disseminated in popular media forms that crisscrossed the globe in the form of stage shows, literature such as dimestore novels, and other exhibitions, and the marketing that accompanied them; this dissemination helped lay the foundation for the international emergence of the cinematic Western.

This is patent, for example, in Andrew James Couzens's analysis of US-American *Wild West* shows in Australia. He acknowledges that the very idea for the shows, which became widely popular in the US and contributed to the development of US-American Western genre tropes, was conceptualized while cofounder, Nate Salsbury, was returning to America from Australia and reflecting on his experiences there (54–55). US-American performers collaborated and competed with their Australian counterparts throughout Wild West tours in Australia, and Australians adapted their own versions for local touring, playing on themes that would become ubiquitous to the US-American Western but with Australian flair and variation, including placing a greater emphasis on bushranger characters, and heroes who were more likely to be egalitarian and antiauthoritarian, like other populist (anti)heroes of the US Western such as Jesse James (Slotkin 127–28). The contextual and historical transformations taking place in Australian society at the time, and the influence of preexisting media forms including popular magazines and shows, such as *Wild West* performances and their various iterations, prove that tropes that would later come to be associated with the US-American Western already had currency in Australia and fed directly into the bushranger film cycle. This is the result not simply of historical coincidence but, rather, of cultural exchanges among Western nations and across media forms. Such developments meant that the US's and Australia's releasing two films centered on outlaws within three years of each other and helping birth a genre of Western films was inevitable.

Stefan Zimmermann would write about the development of the Australian Western that, while US-American Westerns valorized the outlaw to "mythologize the West," in Australia, bushranger films were instead used in a particular postcolonial context "to prepare in a way the long path to Australian autonomy and the overcoming of the British" (145). When we examine the development of the Australian Western via the bushranger cycle through the lens of entanglement, however, a different, much messier and convoluted, and less valiant, narrative emerges. In this alternative narrative, this cycle is less about the push and pull of Australia being similar or different, derivative or unique, but, rather, about deconstructing those binaries to see how manifestations of the Western were the result of exchange, dialogue, and mutually reinforcing cultural ideologies and (trans)national histories. These cultural ideologies and histories largely rested on exclusionary gender and racial representations, and were propagated in media forms and structures across time and place. When we deconstruct these binaries, Australian nationhood emerges as a more tenuous and fractured concept, and less about a restless campaign for autonomy from either the British Empire or the hegemony of US-American cultural and economic imperialism. But there is also a particular freedom in this, where audiences are less concerned with nationalism and more concerned to see stories that "remind them of their own," to see similarities across transnational experiences, not just the parochial, and to see "movement *between* sites not just the effect of one national cinema on another national cinema"

(Limbrick, *Making Settler Cinemas* 5). This is a freedom for the US-American genre, too, in that entanglement helps us conceptualize it not just as a form of representation imposed on, and then imitated by, "others" but, instead, as always alive, always impacted by the international, and always in the process of becoming.

WORKS CITED

Australian Film Commission. "The Australian Cinema—An Overview." *Australian Bureau of Statistics*, 22 Nov. 2012, https://www.abs.gov.au /AUSSTATS/abs@.nsf/featurearticlesbyReleaseDate/C83EBE935009D14CCA 2569DE0025C18A?OpenDocument. Accessed 6 September 2021.

Bazin, André. "The Western: Or the American Film Par Excellence." *Film Theory: Critical Concepts in Media and Cultural Studies*, edited by Philip Simpson, Andrew Utterson, and Karen J. Stephenson, Routledge, 2004, pp. 130–36.

Bertrand, Ina. "The Essential Cinematic Ned." *Metro Magazine* vol. 52, 1980, pp. 14–17.

Bertrand, Ina, and William D. Routt. "The Big Bad Combine: Some Aspects of National Aspirations and International Constraints in the Australian Cinema, 1896–1929." *Australian Screen*, edited by Albert Moran and Tom O'Regan, Penguin, 1989, pp. 3–27.

Campbell, Neil. *The Rhizomatic West: Representing the American West in a Transnational, Global, Media Age.* University of Nebraska Press, 2008.

Collins, Diane. *Hollywood Down Under: Australians at the Movies—1896 to the Present Day.* Angus and Robertson, 1987.

Cooke, Grayson. "Whither the Australian Western? Performing Genre and the Archive in Outback and Beyond." *Transformations*, vol. 24, 2014, pp. 1–20.

Couzens, Andrew James. *A Cultural History of the Bushranger Legend in Theatres and Cinemas, 1828–2017.* Anthem, 2019.

Cronqvist, Marie, and Christoph Hilgert. "Entangled Media Histories: Response to the Responses." *Media History*, vol. 23, no. 1, 2017, pp. 148–49.

———. "Entangled Media Histories: The Value of Transnational and Transmedial Approaches in Media Historiography." *Media History*, vol. 23, no. 1, 2017, pp. 130–41.

Davison, Graeme. "Sydney and the Bush: An Urban Context for the Australian Legend." *Intruders in the Bush: The Australian Quest for Identity*, edited by John Carroll, 2nd ed., Oxford University Press, 1992.

Dixon, Robert. *Writing the Colonial Adventure: Race, Gender and Nation in Anglo-Australian Popular Fiction.* Cambridge University Press, 1995.

Doyle, Stuart. "A Trade Viewpoint." *An Australian Film Reader*, edited by Albert Moran and Tom O'Regan, Currency, 1985, pp. 45–47.

Eisenberg, Daniel. "'You Got the Wrong F***in' Black Man!' The Indigenous Experience in the Australian Western." *International Westerns: Re-Locating the Frontier*, edited by Cynthia Miller and A. Bowdoin Van Riper, Scarecrow, 2014, pp. 202–19.

Goldsmith, Ben. "Introduction: Australian Cinema." *Directory of World Cinema: Australia and New Zealand*, edited by Ben Goldsmith and Geoff Lealand, Intellect Books, 2010, pp. 9–21.

———. "Settings, Subjects and Stories: Creating Australian Cinema." *Creative Nation: Australian Cinema and Cultural Studies Reader*, edited by Amit Sarwal and Reema Sarwal, SSS Publications, 2009, pp. 13–26.

Graham Shirley, "Doyle, Stuart Frank (1887–1945)," *Australian Dictionary of Biography*, National Centre of Biography, Australian National University, http://adb.anu.edu.au/biography/doyle-stuart-frank-6012/text10273, published first in hardcopy, 1981. Accessed 26 Feb. 2020.

Griffen-Foley, Bridget. "Entangled Media Histories: A Response." *Media History*, vol. 23, no. 1, 2017, pp. 145–47.

Hamilton, Emma. "'Australia. What Fresh Hell Is This?' Conceptualizing the Australian Western in *The Proposition*." *The Post-2000 Film Western: Contexts, Transnationality, Hybridity*, edited by Marek Paryż and John R. Leo, Palgrave Macmillan, 2015, pp. 131–46.

———. "Such Is Western: An Overview of the Australian Western via Ned Kelly Films." *Contemporary Transnational Westerns: Themes and Variations*, vol. 38, 2017, pp. 31–44.

Hilmes, Michele. "Entangled Media Histories: A Response." *Media History*, vol. 23, no. 1, 2017, pp. 142–44.

Lake, Marilyn. "White Man's Country: Locating Australia in the World." *Making Australian History: Perspectives on the Past since 1788*, edited by Deborah Gare and David Ritter, Cengage, 2008, pp. 280–86.

Lewis, Glen. *Australian Movies and the American Dream*. Praegar, 1987.

Limbrick, Peter. "The Australian Western, or a Settler Colonial Cinema Par Excellence." *Cinema Journal*, vol. 46, no. 4, 2007, pp. 68–95.

———. *Making Settler Cinemas: Film and Colonial Encounters in the United States, Australia and New Zealand*. Palgrave Macmillan, 2010.

Macintyre, Stuart. *A Concise History of Australia*. Cambridge University Press, 2009.

Meaney, Neville. "Britishness and Australian Identity: The Problem of Nationalism in Australian History and Historiography." *Australian Historical Studies*, vol. 32, no. 116, 2001, pp. 76–90.

Megaw, Ruth. "American Influence on Australian Cinema Management, 1893–1923." *An Australian Film Reader*, edited by Albert Moran and Tom O'Regan, Currency, 1985, pp. 24–33.

Miller, Cynthia J., and A. Bowdoin Van Riper, editors. *International Westerns: Re-Locating the Frontier*. Scarecrow, 2014.

Moran, Albert, and Tom O'Regan. "Introduction." *Australian Screen*, edited by Albert Moran and Tom O'Regan, Penguin, 1989, pp. ix–xvi.

The Overlanders. Directed by Harry Watt, performances by Chips Rafferty, John Nugent Hayward, and Daphne Campbell, Ealing Studios, 1946.

Pearson, Sarina. "Cowboy Contradictions: Westerns in the Postcolonial Pacific." *Studies in Australasian Cinema*, vol. 7, nos. 2–3, 2013, pp. 153–64.

Routt, William D. "More Australian than Aristotelian: The Australian Bushranger Film, 1904–1914." *Senses of Cinema*, vol. 18, no. 1, 2001, pp. 1–19.

Sarwal, Amit, and Reema Sarwal. "Creative Nation: Approaching Australian Cinema and Cultural Studies—Introductory Chapter." *Creative Nation: Australian Cinema and Cultural Studies Reader*, edited by Amit Sarwal and Reema Sarwal, SSS Publications, 2009, pp. xxvi–xlix.

Seal, Graham. *The Outlaw Legend: A Cultural Tradition in Britain, America and Australia*. Cambridge University Press, 1996.

Slotkin, Richard. *Gunfighter Nation: The Myth of the Frontier in Twentieth-Century America*. HarperPerennial, 1993.

The Story of the Kelly Gang. Directed by Charles Tait, performances by John Forde and Elizabeth Tait, J. and N. Tait, 1906.

Walsh, Mike. "The Picture That Might Have Been: The Story of the Kelly Gang." *Metro Magazine*, vol. 153, 2007, pp. 102–5.

Ward, Russel. *The Australian Legend*. Oxford University Press, 1958.

Waterhouse, Richard. "Australian Legends: Representations of the Bush, 1813–1913." *Australian Historical Studies*, vol. 31, no. 115, 2000, pp. 201–21.

White, Richard. *Inventing Australia*. Allen and Unwin, 1981.

Zimmermann, Stefan. "I Suppose It Had to Come to This . . . How a Western Shaped Australia's Identity." *Crossing Frontiers: Intercultural Perspectives on the Western*, edited by Thomas Klein, Ivo Ritzer, and Peter W. Schulze, Schuren, 2012, pp. 134–48.

EMMA HAMILTON is Senior Lecturer of History at the University of Newcastle. She is author of *Masculinities in American Western Films: A Hyper-Linear History* and editor with Alistair Rolls of *Unbridling the Western Film Auteur: Contemporary, Transnational and Intertextual Explorations*.

SIXTEEN

WESTERNS FROM AN ABORIGINAL POINT OF VIEW OR WHY THE AUSTRALIAN WESTERN (STILL) MATTERS

The Tracker (Rolf de Heer, 2002) and
Sweet Country (Warwick Thornton, 2017)

DAVID ROCHE

GENRE FILMS HAVE LONG BEEN suspected of catering to the norm, and, if genre theorists are keen to remind us that a given genre is not governed by a given ideology, the assumption that such films tend to be reactionary, more often than not, persists. Recent Australian productions like *The Tracker* (2002), *The Proposition* (John Hillcoat, 2005), and *Sweet Country* (2017) explore the possibility of decentering the genre's ideology of conquest. They position themselves within a specifically Australian tradition of the Western as one of the dominant national genres ever since the first Australian feature film, Charles Tait's 1906 *The Story of the Kelly Gang* (O'Regan 7, 168; see Hamilton in this volume)—*Sweet Country* even depicts a screening of the film [73:54–76:33]. These films also participate in a transnational effort of revising the revisionist Western and its tendency to reinstate the frontier myth via a "counter-myth" that reproduces "the standard Western mythology of captivities, rescues, and regenerative violence," while reversing the "'normal' racial referents" (Slotkin 590).

Yet *The Tracker* and *Sweet Country* do more than just side with Indigenous peoples—as was the case of the Hollywood cycle of pro-Indian films of the 1950s that partly influenced the Australian classic *Jedda* (Charles Chauvel, 1955)—or deconstruct the classical Western through parody as *Little Big Man* (Arthur Penn, 1970) and *Buffalo Bill and the Indians* (Robert Altman, 1976) tried to do; they seek to revise not just the master narrative—the hero-centered narrative through which the imperialist myth is conveyed—but the modes of narration that deliver it and that ensure its imaginative power. More than mere deconstruction of classical paradigms, it is the expression of other experiences of the sensible that, I argue, is the ambition of such films. The political endeavor to decenter and decolonize the genre and its myths is an attempt to both reveal and counter what Gayatri Chakravorty Spivak identified as the "epistemic violence" of Western imperialism—that is, the imperialist discourses that aimed to "constitute the colonial subject as Other" (280–81), "as the Self's shadow" (280) existing solely in relation to the colonizer. It is also a resolutely aesthetic endeavor, one that finds echoes in Jacques Rancière's contention that "there is a politics of aesthetics in the sense that new forms of circulation of speech, of displays of the visible and of production of affects determine new capacities that break with older configurations of the possible" (70, my translation). The attempt to revise the revisionist Western is not condescending to the past but, rather, acknowledging that the revisionist enterprise was problematic from the start while remaining ethically and politically valuable.

I have chosen to focus solely on *The Tracker* and *Sweet Country* because not only are these productions centered on an Aboriginal man accused of committing a crime against a white person, when the real crimes turn out to be directed against Aboriginal peoples, but they are efforts in which Aboriginal and white Australians collaborate in the negotiation of national history. As such, they suggest that the genre still matters as a historiographical discourse to interrogate this history and its representations.

NATIONAL AND INTERNATIONAL TRADITIONS

In an Australian Western tradition dominated by white bushrangers, with feature films about Ned Kelly coming out on a regular basis—I count at least nine (1906, 1920, 1934, 1951, 1970, 1980, two in 2003, 2019)—and very few dealing with Indigenous peoples (Hamilton, "Australia What Fresh" 132–33), the Aboriginal fugitive plot is a fairly recent development in Australian cinema. It can be traced to *The Chant of Jimmie Blacksmith* (Fred Schepisi, 1978), whose eponymous hero, played by Aboriginal actor Tommy Lewis, gets harassed by white people after marrying a white woman and ends up murdering several white women before going on a killing spree. *The Tracker* expands the second half of the 1978 film by making the chase the core of the narrative, shifts the point of view to the pursuers, and inverts the finale, with the Aboriginal characters ordaining and enacting the law on Aboriginal and white people alike. *Sweet Country*, on the other hand, quite provocatively renders explicit what was implicit in the 1978 film, where a parallel is drawn between Jimmie Blacksmith and Ned Kelly; by naming the Aboriginal fugitive Sam Kelly, *Sweet Country* merges the traditional bushranger plot with the more revisionist Aboriginal fugitive plot, with Sam's trial taking place in the exact same spot as the screening of Tait's 1906 film.

Both *The Tracker* and *Sweet Country* feature a staple secondary character of Australian Westerns and outback narratives, the Aboriginal tracker, who becomes the protagonist of the 2002 film and an important character (Archy) in the 2017 film, while Sam Kelly is also shown keeping track of those following in his own. Although the Aboriginal tracker has a North American equivalent, the Native American scout is far less present in classical Hollywood Westerns (with rare instances in John Ford's 1924 *The Iron Horse* and 1939 *Stagecoach*) than in literature, travel writing, or contemporary Westerns. By comparison, the Aboriginal tracker is an essential figure of Australian culture (Hamilton, "Probably a White" 68), with famous instances in *Robbery Under Arms* (1907) and Harry Watt's 1946 film *The Overlanders*, Patrick White's 1957 novel *Voss*, *The Chant of Jimmie Blacksmith*, and, more recently, *The Proposition*. Aboriginals are employed to help navigate the land, track down fugitives, and also find white people who got lost in the bush (in Joan Lindsay's 1967 novel *Picnic at Hanging Rock* and Rachel Perkins's 2001 film *One Night the Moon*).

And yet, though both *The Tracker* and *Sweet Country* wear their Australian credentials on their sleeves (the title of the 2017 film refers to the Aboriginal notion of *country*), they evoke international cinema to inscribe themselves within a transnational cultural history of the representation of Western colonization. The premises of both films clearly recall *The Searchers*: an indigenous character is pursued for committing a crime (kidnapping, rape, and/or murder) against white people. It is *The Tracker* that most directly plays against the 1956 classic by framing a fairly similar plot with a fairly similar title. The 2002 film changes, however, the perspective from the white men to the Aboriginal, from those who pursue the racial Other in search of their kin to he who has been commissioned to track down a member of his race but not of the same country (a distinction that is lost on the white characters), and who is treated like a slave instead of an employee (he is put in chains a third of the way through the film [34:12]). The title's switch from the plural to the singular is particularly significant. Whereas *The Searchers* insists on the commonality of purpose uniting Ethan Edwards and Martin Pawley in spite of the tensions between them (i.e., Edwards' racism), *The Tracker* has a figure usually relegated to the role of helper immediately take charge of the plot. The singular is not so much the mark of heroism as of alienation and oppression; the protagonist is enrolled to traverse a country that is not his own because, in the eyes of his white employers, black people—and their environment—are all the same. The title thus refers to a function and an ideology (based on racism and individualism) imposed on the Aboriginal protagonist, both of which will be called into question by the narration through the play on point of view.

In *Sweet Country*, the Fordian hypotext is also a visual model. The use of frame-within-the-frame compositions—of Harry March [29:24, 30:25], Fletcher and Minty [37:45], Philomac and Archy [70:19], Lucy and Sam [77:30]—are not mere homage; their repeated use highlights the political implications of the figures they decenter from the actual frame to recenter in the diegetic one, constituted by the doorway or window. It is the political and reflexive potential of the device that Thornton borrows from *The Searchers*. Such shots call on the memory of the hypotext to reprise the racial drama— the savagery common to both indigenous and white men—while drawing attention to certain narrative and cultural differences. If Ethan Edwards finds a fairly logical counterpart in Fletcher, Scar makes way for an abject white criminal (Harry March), Debbie for an Aboriginal woman (Lizzie), who manages to convince the Aboriginal outlaw to trust the law and, thus, generally speaking, to renounce his similarity to the white bushranger (Ned Kelly was captured and hanged) or the typical US-American Western hero, and Martin for another "half-caste" (Philomac), who will ultimately abandon white culture.

Sweet Country also calls on a more unexpected hypotext. Fletcher's crossing the white desert only to be saved by Sam, who, like Moses in *Exodus* 17:6, provides him with water [59:52–65:15], is an inversion of the famous scene in which Lawrence soon-to-be of Arabia saves an Arab named Gasim in the Saudi Arabian desert in David Lean's 1962 epic [65:57–71:39]. Both scenes are crucial turning points. Fletcher, whose motives are arguably less noble than Lawrence's, nonetheless matches his predecessor's arrogance when he ignores a native's (Archy's) admonition not to enter the barren white expanse. Thornton recycles many of Lean's devices—the 2.35:1 ratio emphasizing the flatness of the land, low-angle shots combined with lens flares mimicking the force of the scorching sun, dissolves evoking mirages—but later resorts to jump cuts (instead of Lean's cuts) and abrupt changes in angles to express the white man's dazed condition. As it becomes increasingly clear that Fletcher is a failed Lawrence, the "real" master of the desert will, like Lawrence, appear ghostlike, while being visually and racially marked as unlike Lawrence (and Fletcher): Sam Kelly resembles a dark specter not so much because of the color of his skin, hat, and pants, but because he stands in the back light of a blinding sun (fig. 16.1). The reprisal of this famous scene aims to set the score straight not just vis-à-vis *Lawrence of Arabia* and other empire movies where white British officers successfully go native—such as *The Four Feathers* (Zoltan Korda, 1939)

Fig. 16.1 The inversion of *Lawrence of Arabia*'s famous desert scene serves to debunk the white savior figure and the ideology it carries.

and its remakes of the 1950s (Chapman and Cull 15–32)—but, rather, in relation to the colonial master narrative in general, of which the Western is certainly the most enduring variant. Debunking the sense of racial superiority inherent in the White Savior figure equally debunks the US-American Western figure of the "man who knows Indians," of whom Ethan Edwards is a prime example (Slotkin 461).

By referring to these seminal hypotexts (*The Story of the Kelly Gang, The Searchers, Lawrence of Arabia*), *The Tracker*, and even more so *Sweet Country*, ask that they—and, perhaps, the Western, in general—be considered as both specific of a given culture, that of Australia, and especially of its Indigenous peoples, and characteristic of the global effects of Western colonialism. This is furthered in *The Tracker* by the invocation of conflicting traditions of landscape painting. Many static establishing shots of the pursuers advancing reprise traditional Western iconography—the riders crossing a hilltop [19:58, 45:50, 65:51] or a flat rocky expanse [36:23], skirting a mountainside [22:46, 42:51] or a cliff [55:06], emerging from the bush [59:49], setting up camp [66:04], and, finally, the Aboriginal hero riding off across the plain [90:09]—but the images lack perspective. Cinematographer Ian Jones's utilization of a long lens flattens the terrain in spite of the mountains and crevices; this is enhanced by the desaturated colors that envelop both characters and environment in a predominantly yellowish gray mineral hue. A particularly salient variation of such shots involves zooming out from long shot to establishing shot [8:39, 53:29, 81:19]; the radical shift in shot size strains our eye to keep the characters in view, but the distance ultimately erases them, rendering their movements futile given the immensity of the land.

Not only are the landscapes made to resemble the paintings of Australian artist Peter Coad that open and frame the film (the radiant colors of which the film also desaturates), as the initial and final dissolves insist [0:15, 90:30], but the reduction of perspective expresses a form of resistance to the teleological discourse of progress (physical, technological, moral) that underpins the imperialist ideology of the Western and the empire film. Armando José Prats, in particular, related the use of perspective in landscape images of the West to the ideology of conquest and the commodification of the West: "Perspective already possesses the spaces of the Other, for it claims them, in consequence of the distance and the demurral, for civilization" (84). *The Tracker's* approach to landscape thus further contributes to positioning the film in a dialogue that is simultaneously national and transnational, that is, that has its own national singularities while sharing commonalities with a transnational master narrative of Western imperialism.[1]

VISUALIZING AND VISIBILIZING VIOLENCE

Perhaps the references to films like *The Searchers* and *Lawrence of Arabia* that have also been read as critiques of white male heroism (Slotkin 470; Chapman and Cull 100, 103) should also be seen as invitations to attend to the ambiguities that inhabit(ed) both Western and empire films. One of these ambiguities concerns both genres' problematic relation to violence: that is, their reliance on the narrative, dramatic, and spectacular potential of violence, and, ideologically speaking, its celebration of regeneration through violence in a less than palatable context of violent conquest. Violence, whether verbal, physical, psychological, social, or all of the above, is at once the instrument of Western imperialist ideology and its most visible manifestation. It is this foundational violence that revisionist Westerns—and precursors like *The Ox-Bow Incident* (William A. Wellman, 1942)—bring to the fore, without necessarily abandoning the regenerative (*Little Big Man* [Arthur Penn, 1970]), redemptive (*The Outlaw Jose Wales* [Clint Eastwood, 1976]), cathartic (*The Wild Bunch* [Sam Peckinpah, 1969]), and/or poetic (*Dead Man* [Jim Jarmusch, 1995]) functions of violence.

The specificity of the Australian Western's relationship to violence is grounded in its material: the nation's history. With no equivalent of the North American Indian Wars or the New Zealand Wars (Connor), a state of affairs the kidnapped teacher mentions to the 1978 Jimmie Blacksmith, the physical violence of the Australian Western has long been coded as white, notably in the bushranger films. The history of the conquest of Australia and popular representations such as *The Overlanders* tend to ignore acts of persecution of, and rebellion by, Indigenous peoples; they are portrayed, instead, as utterly subjected to the system of oppression. The violence is primarily social, systemic, epistemic, and invisible.

It is this that the premises of *The Tracker* and *Sweet Country*—and their precursor *The Chant of Jimmie Blacksmith*—put into relief (social and systemic violence) and contest (the lack of physical and psychological violence and rebellion). The plots are premised on the Aboriginal characters' inferior social status; the 2002 tracker's position is subordinate to that of the white people who command him, and the majority of the white characters of *Sweet Country* see the Aboriginal employees as quasi-slaves (March asks Fred Smith where he "got his black stock from" [3:55] and later chains Philomac to a rock [24:57]). These power dynamics make the Aboriginal characters the habitual targets of verbal and physical abuse, and it is this that the films contextualize in relation to both national history and the history of the genre. By portraying a racist and vindictive white frontier community, *Sweet Country* gives the lie to Australian representations of cordial relations between Aboriginal peoples and their employers, as depicted in *The Overlanders*, and debunks the myth of the natural morality of the Westerner (Slotkin 133, 176), Sam's killer remaining invisible in the wilderness like a devious Hollywood Indian.

The Tracker attacks the federal government metonymically through its fanatical embodiment, an excessive version of the prejudiced Fordian antiheroes of *Fort Apache* (1948) and *The Searchers*, but the finale, which sees Aboriginals deliver justice onto white and Aboriginal people alike, is directed at the systemic injustice that deprived Aboriginal peoples of rights for so long, and, notably "the founding doctrine of *terra nullius* (i.e., land belonging to no one)" that was only overturned by the Mabo decision of 1992 (Collins and Davis 3). The film's conclusion not only inverts the end of *Walkabout* (Nicolas Roeg, 1971) in which Gulpilil's character hangs himself; it "subverts many Australian (and US-American, for that matter) Westerns by privileging Aboriginal justice over that of the white man" (Eisenberg 214–15).

While the obvious targets of each film are complementary (federal in *The Tracker*, local in *Sweet Country*), both treat racism as an ideology and a pathology—again much like *The Searchers* (Slotkin 470) or, more recently, *Django Unchained* (Quentin Tarantino, 2012)—one to which all the white characters are, at least to some degree, subjected. In *The Tracker*, the Follower is momentarily contaminated by the Fanatic's bloodlust, while in *Sweet Country*, Fletcher's lover, Nell, is so appalled by the judge's decision to release Sam Kelly that she quits the audience, debunking the pro-Indian Western conceit promoted in films like *Devil's Doorway* (Anthony Mann, 1950), *Cheyenne Autumn* (Ford, 1964), and *Soldier Blue* (Ralph Nelson, 1970) that women would be, essentially, more sensitive to the plight of indigenous populations. Even the religious Smith, who describes Sam, Lizzie, and Lucy as "equals" and has dinner with them, gives in to the dominant system by allowing March to borrow them—granted because March manipulates Smith by calling on his Christian generosity—and is thus indirectly responsible for putting them in harm's way.

The physical acts of violence function as catalysts for the plot, triggering singular acts of violence on the part of the Aboriginal characters: Jimmie Blacksmith's crimes, the 2002 Tracker's revenge, Sam Kelly's act of self-defense. Unlike its US-American counterpart the pro-Indian movie, then, the "pro-Aboriginal" Western frames indigenous violence as a negation of the noble savage figure's innocence and as a signifier of agency. The outcomes suggest little hope of escaping the cycle of violence at the heart of imperialist ideology. If Sam Kelly renounces violence only to be shot in the back after having been found not guilty, the 2002 Tracker ultimately condemns the Fanatic, knowing full well that the Australian judicial system would never condemn the white man. The plots recognize the impasse of either outcome: there will be blood in the end. And it is here where *The Tracker* and *Sweet Country* rejoin the global concerns of contemporary Westerns that violence only leads to more violence, which makes for compelling drama but is problematic ethically and politically.

Both films are particularly sensitive to the intertwining of the ethics and politics of violence with its aesthetics, and resort to specific strategies to set certain acts of violence at a distance. An array of well-worn filmic devices that self-censor the more disturbing images are employed in *The Tracker*: the Fanatic and the Follower's harassing of a group of Aboriginal people is narrated in a music video sequence, the upbeat music almost drowning out the aural violence, while jump cuts mimic the Fanatic's madness and contest any moral logic in his behavior [15:51–17:22]; the murder of the Veteran occurs during his sleep at night [49:36–52:05]; that of an elderly Aboriginal man is shown in a very long shot [60:30]; the Fanatic's hanging is metonymically represented via his booted feet [76:31], and the result is portrayed in a backlit establishing shot of the Fanatic hanging from a tree against the rising sun [77:16], before his dead body is finally revealed [79:09].

If we are allowed a modicum of vengeful satisfaction in the fact that the Fanatic gets his comeuppance (Hamilton, "Probably a White" 78), *The Tracker* mostly refuses to indulge in violence regardless of race and even species (the horse). The acts of violence the film chooses not to show are depicted in Coad's paintings (that is, in fact, the paintings' primary function) [17:23, 19:34, 22:07,

39:21, 41:17, 51:24, 60:31, 76:40, 86:20], which sometimes anticipate them [14:34] or their possibility [10:21]. The distancing of violence is, thus, furthered through an intermedial disruption whereby painting makes way for photography, moving images for still ones, depth for flatness (the characters may be recognizable, but Coad's style is by no means realistic). The paintings are also, Emma Hamilton argues, "symptomatic of a desire to act on and subvert traditional notions of history and how historical knowledge is validly conveyed" ("Probably a White" 73); they serve to establish a distance not only with the violence depicted, but with the historical account of violence or lack thereof.

In *Sweet Country*, the degree of graphic violence is somewhat correlated to the character's guilt. The rapist March's choking on his own blood as it spurts out his jugular is depicted in a sixteen-second-long extreme close-up [31:52], and the soldier who pulled his gun out at the sight of a group of Aboriginal warriors gets a brief close-up as he lays dying from a blow [54:01]. Sam's death, by comparison, is depicted in a medium close-up that includes the characters (Smith, Lizzie) who grieve him [106:16]. Other acts of violence are depicted in a less grotesque fashion. The punches traded between Mick Kennedy, Sam, and Barney are, for instance, depicted in a series of muted flashbacks [23:14]. The scene in which March rapes Lucy occurs in complete darkness, sparing us the sight of her ordeal, and the young woman's body is only revealed after the fact as she lays in shock on the bed in a forty-five-second-long medium shot meant to express her trauma [14:45–17:49].

Yet the aesthetics of restraint is only skin deep. Not only does the rape scene remain quite brutal aurally speaking, the sound design lending depth to the flatness of the dark screen, but the fact that the darkness is justified diegetically by March's shutting the door and shutters is in itself indicative of his abject racism: he is not only endeavoring to muffle the sounds of the act, but erasing the sight of the Aboriginal woman, denying her humanity and subjectivity, and thus the contradiction inherent in his desire for her. The darkness is eminently brutal because it is the mark of the dehumanizing effect of his racism and functions as a sort of surplus to the dehumanization rape inevitably entails. And the act itself is symptomatic of March's perception of the Aboriginal bodies as interchangeable and exchangeable—he does not even assault the woman he intended to in the first place (Lucy).

Contemporary Australian Westerns dealing with the oppression of Aboriginal peoples follow the revisionist tendency of depicting the various forms of violence inflicted on indigenous peoples as well as the complicity of government and individuals, while expressing an awareness of the pitfalls of relying on violence as a narrative and dramatic conceit (the perpetuation of violence) and/or an aesthetic motif (the potential sadism of graphic depictions). This is complicated by the fact that, in an Australian context, the violence committed by Aboriginals is meant to insist on the agency and capacity to resist of Aboriginal peoples that Australian cultural history has glossed over, as Warwick Thornton points out (Johnston 31). Both films' endings express this unease. While *Sweet Country* violently rejects a happy ending that would seem to forgive the federal government, represented by the honorable Judge Taylor, and, in so doing, express concerns about the situation of Aboriginal peoples today (for instance, that the Mabo decision has not resolved issues of systemic racism and racist attitudes), *The Tracker*'s embarrassment regarding its concluding images of its eponymous hero as a Western righter-of-wrongs is patent in Gulpilil's wry humor, as if the actor were poking fun at the icons (the tracker, the cowboy, the movie Indian) he is problematically embodying.

MANY OTHER POINTS OF VIEW

The Tracker and *Sweet Country* aim to further decolonize the Western narrative—and counter a more diffuse form of violence, namely, "epistemic violence," in the process—by placing Aboriginal peoples at the center not just of the narrative but of the narration. The Aboriginal protagonists are the first characters we see, and in *The Tracker*, the first voice we hear is that of Aboriginal singer Archie Roach. The introductory shots are strikingly similar: the camera tracks slowly in on the Tracker's [0:25–1:29] and Sam's [1:04–2:12] faces, which occupy the center of the frame, relegating the white characters (and white star Sam Neill in the 2017 film) to the blurry background. Each man is presented as a face, which, for Béla Balázs, was a cinematic expression of subjectivity (60). The narration thus endows them with a value that is at once aesthetic (the face in close-up) and ethical—the Levinassian face of the Other as "the corporeal emblem of the other's otherness" through which "the whole of humanity . . . looks at us" (Waldenfels 63)—and that counters the lack of value (other than utilitarian) they hold in the racist world of the diegesis.[2]

In terms of focalization, here understood as the "cognitive point of view of the story" (Gaudreault and Jost 130), *The Tracker*, as the title indicates, primarily aligns us with the character portrayed by the film's star. Three strategies, in particular, are employed to construct David Gulpilil's character as its cognitive, emotional, and narrative center:

1. Scenes in which he is the undisputed focalizer, most notably the sequence showing him gathering herbs and receiving an unknown Aboriginal's aid [67:14–67:46];

2. Close-ups of the Tracker that allow us to gauge reactions the white characters fail to see, whether his fear for the Aboriginals they come across early on [13:20], his amusement when the three white men shave [7:32], or his sorrow and anger after the death of an elderly Aboriginal man [64:42];

3. Eyeline matches that show us what he actually sees, sometimes combined with zoom-ins or -outs that simultaneously insist on his reaction and single out the detail he has picked up; these occur on a regular basis, notably when he notices Aboriginal peoples on the canyons cliffs [10:18, 58:14] or the Fanatic's future victims [13:13, 63:37], foresees an attack on his group's horses [21:56], or witnesses the Fanatic murder the Veteran [51:30].

The film avoids the revisionist trappings of merely inverting the racial terms of the imperialist master narrative, and thus maintaining the ideology of male individualism at the heart of the Western, by multiplying subjectivities—and this in spite of its one-track title. The Fanatic's victims are presented in a close-up that slowly pans over their faces immediately after their tormentors charge [14:41–15:19]. The Fugitive is introduced when an establishing shot of his pursuers zooms out to an over-the-shoulder shot of him observing them, revealing that all along we were aligned with his gaze (it is followed by a reverse close-up of his face) [3:13–3:44]. Occurring as early as the presentation of the main characters, this high-angle establishing shot of the pursuers endows all subsequent similar shots with the potential of being POV shots or over-the-shoulder shots from the Fugitive's or another Aboriginal person's perspective—in effect, two are [55:17, 80:59], but most are not [8:31, 9:56, 10:46, 19:58, 42:51, 53:29, 58:06, 59:49, 65:37, 81:20, 82:07] (fig. 16.2).

The narration allows us access to the subjectivities of the white characters as well. The Fanatic, the Veteran, and the Follower are, like the Tracker, presented in shots that track in to close-ups, the duration of each shot (roughly two times shorter than that of the Tracker) emphasizing their subordinate status on the narrative level [1:30–2:58]. The point is driven in, yet again, during a music video sequence in which the close-ups of the Aboriginal faces (the Fugitive and the Tracker) bookend those of the white ones (the Veteran, the Follower, the Fanatic) [24:22–27:35]. Visual point of view is occasionally aligned with one of the white characters, for instance, a series of two lateral tracking shots that reproduce the Follower's and the Veteran's points of view [12:53–13:05], or the Veteran's contorted features as he suffers from a spear wound and the shot/reverse shots depicting the Follower's concern over the latter's health [43:31–44:06]. On several particularly dramatic occasions, focalization even aligns us with the Follower instead of the Tracker, notably when the former silently rejects his complicity in the Fanatic's doings [23:04], realizes the Tracker has disappeared

Fig. 16.2 *The Tracker*: The camera zooms out to reveal the Fugitive looking at his pursuers who have disappeared into the bush [3:39].

under his watch [31:02–33:49], finds the Fanatic's hanging body [78:56], and, finally, watches the Tracker ride off into the bush [89:36].

The film's distribution of point of view has implications that are aesthetic, ethical, and political. First, it does not seek to erase the colonizing gaze but quite deliberately turns it into the minority one, positioning the white man's (the Follower's) redemption as a subplot. Not only does it decenter the thrust of many pro-Indian Westerns from *Broken Arrow* (Daves, 1950) to *Dances with Wolves* (Costner, 1990), but it casts a cloak of mystery over the Tracker by encouraging us to view him occasionally as both strange and admirable in the eyes of the Follower. Unlike the pro-Indian Westerns mentioned above, *The Tracker* does not invite us to follow the Follower's "innocent" discovery of the white man's cruelty and the native man's qualities; it is, rather, the Follower who follows us by coming to see the Tracker as we saw him all along: as a charismatic force embodied by a major Australian film star.

The multiplication of points of view also turns filmic space—the space of the diegesis but also the plasticity of the medium itself—into a form of borderland inhabited by a variety of subjectivities (the Aboriginal victims' pain, the Veteran's melancholy disenchantment, the Follower's guilt and empathy, the Fanatic's righteousness), an audiovisual expression of Gloria Anzaldúa's (1987) *frontera* as a culturally hybrid space rather than a demarcation line. The country-western songs composed by Graham Tardiff and performed by Archie Roach are instrumental in voicing a sort of idea(l) of the frontier as borderland. The songs are endowed with an authority akin to that of an Aboriginal storyteller or, in film, a narrative voice-over. Roach's voice, the lyrics, and the cuing of the music initially seem to be culturally, racially, narratively, and aesthetically on the side of the Aboriginal characters. The music fulfills a narrative function that is akin to the Tracker's own as focalizer, providing the narration with a backbone in keeping with its revisionist approach. Yet, like the eponymous character, it also connects the different characters and resonates with the white characters' inner lives (something the protagonist achieves by token of his social and narrative function). Given the hybridity of the music and the film as a whole, it would be mistaken to see this as a form of inverted appropriation, with the Aboriginal voice appropriating white experience; rather, it is an attempt to seek, through artistic collaboration, a degree of universalism beyond race. This is evidenced in the abovementioned music video sequence, in which each face in close-up is accompanied by a verse of a tune titled, "All Men Choose the Path They Walk." The music does more than invite connections through its lyrics; it envelops the characters and the space-time they inhabit in the same soundscape.

The Western ideology of white male individualism is, in a sense, easier to circumvent for *Sweet Country* because of its multiprotagonist narrative. The 2017 film, as its title indicates, focuses on a specific area and cuts between various groups of characters in specific settings. The first act centers on three farms: Smith's, Kennedy's, and March's [2:20–35:11]. In the second act [38:06–73:53], the use of intercutting becomes even more dynamic: the manhunt is narrated in a series of sequences depicting Sam and Lucy in one environment (the bush), Archy, Fletcher, Kennedy, Smith, and Minty in another (the town and the bush), Barney and Philomac in a third (the Kennedy farm and the bush), until Sam and Fletcher briefly meet up, and the characters are split up into smaller units. In the final act [73:54–104:51], the narration operates on a similar mode in spite of the more restricted setting (the frontier town and one scene at Kennedy's), allowing us to spend time with the various characters.

If Aboriginal peoples and whites are allowed screen time, Sam unquestionably becomes the heart and lungs of the narrative from the moment he kills March, the white man who imposed an economic logic on the land, and a narrative one on the film, based on the exchange of black bodies—the first shot following the title shows March's riding onto Smith's land [2:20]. After March's death, each transition is determined by Sam's movements, yet, even prior to that, the camerawork positioned us on Sam's side. When March questions Sam about his niece Lucy, Sam turns around to pick up a wooden post, momentarily facing the camera in medium shot and relegating March to the left midground [12:27–13:07]. If Sam remains silent throughout the scene, it is his physical force that directs the composition; his movement (he steps forward) and the movements he causes (he picks up the post before letting it go and setting March off-balance) occurring along the same oblique axis (from upper-right foreground to lower-left background), allow Sam to stand tall and occupy the center of the frame, and force March to reintegrate the center of the composition in a subsequent shot. The camerawork (the camera tilts) is, thus, energized by Sam's silent act of resistance.

The film's second main focalizer is the boy Philomac. Unlike the other characters, his action and movements are not determined by those of Sam Kelly—the boy runs off on his own three times [8:40, 26:08, 33:57]—making him an agent unto himself who takes charge of a subplot that points to the continuation of Aboriginal resistance—he grins when he finds out that Sam Kelly has evaded the party [65:54]. The film's epilogue, a flashback in which Philomac takes Barney's advice and gives up the watch he had stolen off March's corpse, suggests that the character might resist the lure of white Anglo culture, in spite of Kennedy's recognizing him as his son [109:07], and retain the memory that was orally passed on to him by Barney [45:47–47:32] and Archy [70:19–71:44].

The multiplication of point of view is cognitive; it is also emotional, psychological, and cosmic. The narration resorts to the close-up and medium close-up to express the Aboriginal characters' emotions, particularly during the harrowing trial scene [86:49–99:29]. The content of the mental images we are shown is likewise diverse, and their sources and even nature are often uncertain—Thornton describes them as "the character's memories, dreams and nightmares" (qtd. in Johnston 31). If the handling of space reproduces the seductive landscapes of the classical Western or empire movie, with references to Ford, Lean, and Sergio Leone, it is the genres' teleological narrative that the film proposes to reconfigure through its handling of narrative time. Not only is the film organized according to a flashback structure, something which was quite a rarity until *The Man Who Shot Liberty Valance* (Ford, 1962) and *Lawrence of Arabia*, but the flashback structure itself is framed by two other space-times. The proleptic shot of Sam awaiting his trial [1:44, 86:59] is preceded by a close-up of coffee being heated over a fire while shouting can be heard off-screen (mental scene 0) [0:35], a scene that is later revealed to have occurred prior to the events depicted in the film, while the concluding images show a grown-up Philomac abandoning March's watch at an indeterminate point in time [109:07]. The logic of the flashback structure—which is in itself not enough to call into question the teleological logic of the Western (e.g., *The Man Who Shot Liberty Valance*)—is, thus, compromised by the prologue and epilogue, in which the origin of the subjectivity is either unknown (is it Sam's, Archy's, Barney's, Kennedy's, or Philomac's memory?) or different from the hero's.

The narration is further disrupted by the mental scenes that punctuate the film. Expectations based on traditional Western schemes—and I am using

Western in terms of both genre and culture here—lead us to identify the first such disruption (mental scene 1 of a drunken March) as a flashback [4:43].

Mental scenes 2 and 3—Archy fighting against Sam [6:59], Philomac eating a watermelon [8:17]—seem to confirm this flashback logic. Subsequently, a scene reminiscent of mental scene 1—March loading his bayonet in front of the fire [10:36]—indicates that the latter was actually a flashforward. And, subsequently, narrative disruptions are repeated without ever becoming systematic.

Mental scene 4—Lucy all bloody and leaning back against a carriage [21:08]—resembles, in context, a projection of Sam's fears for her in light of March's inquiries and is only revealed to be a flashforward at the end of the film [108:27].

Mental scene 5 turns out to be a flashback that explicates mental scenes 0 (the opening image) and 2, since we see the same close-up of the pot and Archy getting beaten up by Kennedy [23:11].

Mental scene 6 likewise adds to previous images, as we see March praying to his rifle at night [30:38]. By this stage, we have come to understand that the nature of these images is unstable.

Mental scene 7—Fletcher and Nell in bed [36:08]—appears as a likely flashback but is recast as a flashforward a minute later when they are shown in bed [37:02].

Mental scene 8—Constable Minty lying dead on the ground [37:34]—could very well relay Fletcher's concerns about his subordinate officer but, like the image of Lucy, later turns out to be a flashforward [54:01].

Mental scene 9 juxtaposes what are presumably a happy and an unhappy memory, an image of Lizzie and Sam sitting happily together with one of March getting shot [38:57].

Mental scene 10—a recap of the dramatic events on the Kennedy farm—depicts what Philomac witnessed and withholds from Kennedy [40:03].

The status of mental scenes 11, 12, and 13—Archy cleaning a pair of shoes [66:33], Sam aiming his rifle at Lizzie [67:37], Nell waiting in the door of her pub [69:43]—is unclear, as they may be flashforwards, flashbacks, or (Philomac's, Sam's, and Fletcher's) fantasies.

In context, mental image 14—a white man pulling on a rope [85:29]—seems to foreshadow Sam's likely hanging but ends up being proleptic of Smith's building of the church, also depicted in a flashforward (mental scene 15) [117:17].

Mental image 16—Lizzie and Sam running off—is an obvious flashback repeating a familiar image [106:09].

If the nature of most mental scenes is, ultimately, resolved by the narration, with eight flashbacks, six flashforwards, and only three indeterminate images, their source is often enigmatic. The first shot of the film immediately sets the tone, as the absence of a human subject in the close-up leaves the question of origin in suspense. Mental scene 1 provides hardly more clarity [4:43–4:51]. The most logical explanation is that March himself is the origin of such images, but because it is preceded by Smith's looking his new neighbor up and down, doubt persists as to whether it depicts what Smith is imagining. Sam's presence points to a third potential origin, especially in view of the flashback structure, which suggests he is the core subjectivity. The source of mental scene 2 is equally uncertain, since it is framed by a medium close-up of Kennedy and Archy together. Yet even if the source of the flashbacks (0, 2, 3, 5, 6, 9, 10, 15) and even some of the flashforwards (1, 4, 7, 8, 14, 15) or possible fantasies (11, 12, 13) could originate from the subjectivity of a given character, the flashforwards that refer to events that lie beyond the scope of the flashback structure (4, 14, 15) can only originate from the narration.

In fact, the reliability of the flashback structure as a point of reference is itself questionable: Sam simply does not have the same authority over the story as Ramsom Stoddard in Ford's 1962 film—he is not in the know when it comes to Philomac's adventures and Fletcher's love life. Access to such images thus originates from the narration itself; their source is more cosmic than psychological. The narration subordinates the teleological narrative of Western imperialism to a different conception of space-time, one that I believe is inspired from the Aboriginal notion of the Dreaming. Anthropologist Philippe Descola describes the Dreaming as "neither a remembered past nor a retroactive present, but an expression and an acknowledgement of the eternal in space, an invisible cosmic framework that ensures the continued existence of ontological subdivisions" (259). It is this, I believe, that the narration of Sweet Country strives to express cinematically, and it is through it that Australian history is told and, more broadly, that the imperialist master narrative is called into question.

VARIETIES OF COUNTRY

The Australian Western matters, The Tracker and Sweet Country suggest through their intertexts, because the native genre provides a template for exploring the singularity of the nation's history while situating the latter in the more global context of Western imperialism. The films' critiques of violence—notably the insistence on the cyclical nature of violence—resonate with the revisionist attitudes of Western productions worldwide, while asserting that the violence peculiar to the relations between colonizers and Aboriginal peoples should be considered as an instrument of both oppression and resistance. Both films test-ify to an awareness that a mere revising of the narrative is not radical enough: the modes of narration must also be reconfigured to do justice to the complex-ity and diversity of the borderland, and the cultural clashes and exchanges that took place there. In this respect, the films integrate a transnational revision of the notion of the frontier as a *frontera*—which also informs *The Proposition* (Hamilton, "Australia What Fresh" 145)—while endeavoring to aesthetically express its singularity. This is especially the case of the films' handling of space, which they engage through the figure of the Aboriginal tracker and the Aborig-inal notion of country.

Subjected to a Western economic understanding of the land, the two track-ers (and Sam Kelly) do not so much lose the white characters—as the latter sometimes suspect [*The Tracker* 36:53; *Sweet Country* 54:41]—as lead them into another cultural landscape, one that is not governed by the same laws (of jus-tice, time, space, etc.). Felicity Collins and Therese Davis argue that "the Track-er's hospitality extends to a willingness to share cultural knowledge, opening the eyes of The Follower and the spectator to his cultural understanding of the land as 'country'" (16). The trackers' informing their "bosses" that the fugi-tives are "a day . . . maybe half a day" [*Sweet Country* 51:03] and "half-a-day" or "maybe a couple of hours" [*The Tracker* 11:13, 36:39] ahead of them encapsulates this hesitation, especially in the 2002 film: Are their answers mockery or ac-counted for by cultural differences? Tracking, initially a sign of the imposition of a Western imperialist system onto indigenous peoples, is thus resignified as an act of resistance, an occupation that reveals the differences between Aborig-inal and Western cultures, and notably between two different conceptions of space-time that involve both the realms of the sensible (how you experience it) and of ideology (how you fit in a given system of ideas). The teleological view of time and progress that the ideology of conquest is grounded in is, thus, upset by a view in which time is not a one-track line but a multifarious plane. The Westerner's dream of life on the frontier is called into question by the memory of the land of Aboriginal peoples, a transcendent view by a more immanent one.

This distinction is particularly evidenced in the 2017 film's play on the word *country*. The word is used three times, with three different meanings, by four different people and in two different languages. Barney and Archy want to convince Philomac of the importance of "country" [46:54, 70:49], that is, "a tract of land, or sometimes a set of sites, to which an individual has strong spiritual and historic connections that are recognised and given some legit-imacy by the rest of their community" (Clarke 38). Fletcher's, "There's some sweet country out there. Cattle country," echoes Bret McBain's "Sweetwater" in *Once Upon a Time in the West* (Leone, 1968) in his attempt to sell his lover Nell the Turnerian pastoral ideal [75:41]. Smith laments the nation's future in the film's final words, "What chance has this country got?" [108:49]. These instances seem to reinstate the teleological force of progress—from Aboriginal culture (the past) to frontier culture (the present) to nationhood (the future). Yet the film ends on an act of resistance—Philomac's giving up March's watch—that points us back to the manhunt. Because the manhunt scenes did not celebrate the "cattle country" Fletcher speaks of; instead, they offered a singular experience of space-time.

In effect, disruptions do not just occur during the white desert scenes. At the very moment when Archy explains they are riding into "tribal land," the iconic Western image of the riders crossing the plains is intercut by medium full shots of Fletcher and Fred on horseback at a standstill looking around as if lost, images whose nature is uncertain [51:02–51:32]. The handling of space-time is just as uncertain when Fletcher makes it out of the white sandy hell and floats in a pool of water [68:01–70:18], the shots of Sam and his rifle recalling mental image 12 but foreshadowing the subsequent assault of Lizzie by three Aboriginal men in a similar location [71:45–73:03]. The radicalization of the narration was announced in the early stages of the manhunt when the white officer's voice-over—Fletcher's obituary in honor of a fellow soldier (March) who "fought for king and country" [41:48–42:43]—made way for another longer tirade: Barney's account of local colonization (how Kennedy's father stole their land) and of the centrality of "dreamtime stories," which frames Sam's and Philomac's story in the broader context of the colonization of Australia. A Western from an Aboriginal perspective, *Sweet Country* suggests, should not just be a way to lament the past. As a genre defined by history and geography, it may offer the aesthetic means of reclaiming agency through the remembrance and perpetuation of an idea: country.

NOTES

1. One online bio describes Coad's work as testifying to an "awareness of the indigenous myths and legends of the land." See http://www.manyunggallery .com.au/Artist-Detail.cfm?ArtistsID=802. Accessed on 21 Apr. 2020.

2. Bernhard Waldenfels is here citing *Totality and Infinity*.

WORKS CITED

Anzaldúa, Gloria. *Borderlands—La Frontera: The New Mestiza*. Spinsters, Aunt Lute Books, 1987.

Balázs, Béla. *Theory of the Film: Character and Growth of a New Art*. Dennis Dobson, 1952.

Chapman, James, and Nicholas J. Cull. *Projecting Empire: Imperialism and Popular Cinema*. I. B. Tauris, 2009.

Clarke, Philip. *Where the Ancestors Walked: Australia as an Aboriginal Landscape*. Allen and Unwin, 2003.

Collins, Felicity, and Therese Davis. *Australian Cinema after Mabo*. Cambridge University Press, 2004.

Connor, John. *The Australian Frontier Wars, 1788–1838*. University of New South Wales Press, 2002.

Descola, Philippe. *Beyond Nature and Culture*. 2005. University of Chicago Press, 2013.

Eisenberg, Daniel. "'You Got the Wrong F***in' Black Man!' The Indigenous Experience in the Australian Western." *International Westerns: Re-locating the Frontier*, edited by Cynthia J. Miller and A. Bowdoin Van Riper, Scarecrow, 2014, pp. 202–19.

Gaudreault, André, and François Jost. *Le Récit filmique: Cinéma et récit II*. Nathan, 1990.

Hamilton, Emma. "'Australia What Fresh Hell Is This?' Conceptualizing the Australian Western in *The Proposition*." *The Post-2000 Film Western: Contexts, Transnationality, Hybridity*, edited by Marek Paryż and Jorn R. Leo, Palgrave Macmillan, 2015, pp. 131–46.

———. "'Probably a White Fella': Rolf de Heer, *The Tracker* and the Limits of Auteurism." *Unbridling the Western Film Auteur: Contemporary, Transnational and Intertextual Explorations*, edited by Emma Hamilton and Alistair Rolls, Peter Lang, 2018, pp. 65–84.

Johnston, Trevor. "Red Earth." *Sight and Sound*, vol. 28, no. 4, April 2018, pp. 29–31.

O'Regan, Tom. *Australian National Cinema*. Routledge, 1996.

Prats, Armando José. *Invisible Natives: Myth and Identity in the American Western*. Cornell University Press, 2002.

Rancière, Jacques. *Le Spectateur émancipé*. La Fabrique, 2008.

Slotkin, Richard. *Gunfighter Nation: The Myth of the Frontier in Twentieth-Century America*. 1992. University of Oklahoma Press, 1998.

Spivak, Gayatri Chakravorty. "Can the Subaltern Speak?" *Marxism and the Interpretation of Culture*, edited by Cary Nelson and Lawrence Grossberg, Macmillan Education, 1988, pp. 271–313.

Sweet Country. Directed by Warwick Thornton, performances by Hamilton Morris, Natassia Gorey Furber, Ewen Leslie, Sam Neill, Thomas M. Wright, Gibson John, Tremayne Doolan, Shanika Cole, Bryan Brown, Anni Finsterer, Matt Day, and Tom Willoughby, Bunya Productions/Sweet Country Films, 2017.

The Tracker. Written and directed by Rolf de Heer, performances by David Gulpilil, Gary Sweet, Damon Gameau, Grant Page, and Noel Wilton, Adelaide Festival of Arts/SBS Independent/Vertigo, 2002.

Waldenfels, Bernhard. "Levinas and the Face of the Other." *The Cambridge Companion to Levinas*, edited by Simon Critchley and Robert Bernasconi, Cambridge University Press, 2002, pp. 63–81.

DAVID ROCHE is Professor of Film Studies at Université Paul Valéry Montpellier 3. He is author of *Making and Remaking Horror in the 1970s and 2000s: Why Don't They Do It Like They Used To?* and of *Quentin Tarantino: Poetics and Politics of Cinematic Metafiction.*

CODA

We Will Not Ride Off into the Sunset

HERVÉ MAYER AND DAVID ROCHE

IT IS THE DESTINY OF any scholarly adventure that it will fail to fully exhaust its topic and inevitably raise yet more questions. This sense of perpetual to-be-continuedness is one of the things that make research so exciting, frustrating, and gratifying—it can never be over, and new discoveries often end up being old ones seen from a new perspective. It is a particularly apt feeling when reaching the end of a book that has attempted to explain the endurance of the global Western by emphasizing not only the capacity of a genre and myth to circulate and mutate, but also the ideological core that has allowed it to travel around the world and resonate in a wide variety of cultural environments. We have argued that the Western is the site of an ongoing and dynamic interrogation of imperialism in its many forms, from colonization to economic and cultural imperialism. The openness of this book reflects the fact that this interrogation remains relevant today because of the presence of imperialist structures worldwide; it also works to counter the forward-marching teleology of progress by acknowledging the impossibility—nay, the undesirability—of closing off the meaning of cultural history and shutting the door on the participation of others in its construction and deconstruction.

It strikes us that the scholarly adventure pursued in this book begs to be carried on in terms of the corpora explored and the methodology employed. The Western is such a global phenomenon that the theses argued herein would need to be verified in a range of national cinemas that are barely or not at all touched on in this book—British Westerns, German Westerns, Indian Westerns, Russian Westerns, Thai Westerns, Turkish Westerns, the list goes on. Analyses of specific corpora are paramount because, if we insisted on the transnational trajectory of the Western, one of the central conclusions of this book is that national and historical contexts always matter in the end. The transnational does not constitute a denial of the national but, rather, a recognition of the flow between nations; it does not transcend the national but posits a dynamic relation between territories, and considers borders not as impassable barriers but as spaces of tension both conflictual and creative.

Another corpus of Westerns that warrants study from a transnational perspective would be composed of works directed, produced, and/or written by minorities and women. Much of the genre's endurance has to do with the decentering perspectives the material has been approached with, and, in recent years, much of this decentering and decolonizing has been the work of women and minority directors, as the analyses of *Tejano* (Garcia, 2018), *Adieu Gary* (Amaouche, 2009), and *Sweet Country* (Thornton, 2017) in chapters 4, 8, and 16, respectively, have shown. More research could be carried out on the work of Australian writer/director Ivan Sen; his post-Western films and series—*Mystery Road* (2013), *Goldstone* (2016), and *Mystery Road* (ABC, 2018–)—follow an Aboriginal detective, Jay Swan, whose investigations in the Australian outback lead him to explore crimes that are tributary to the nation's imperialist past and racist present, and celebrate the Aboriginal hero's "quiet strength" (Teo 209). The films of Kelly Reichardt and Chloé Zhao would also represent a vital part of this corpus. In fact, as we are writing this coda in January 2021, Reichardt's and Zhao's most recent forays into the genre—the Western *First Cow* and the post-Western *Nomadland* starring Francis McDormand—have just received awards from the New York Film Critics Circle (for Best Film and Director, respectively), and *Nomadland* has won Best Picture, Best Director, and Best Actress at the Oscars.

First Cow pursues Reichardt's revisionist project, initiated in *Meek's Cutoff* (2010), this time by exploring the relationship between two men, a traveled Chinese man named King-Lu and a cook named Cookie, who come together out of basic humanity but also because of a common economic enterprise, which may have led to their demise (the film leaves the question dangling). In a nod to both Raymond Carver and Marcel Proust, Cookie's homemade hotcakes are small, good things that bring solace and a sense of home to the settlers as well as more down-to-earth versions of the natural resources they have come to exploit; the cow milk evoked in the title thus comes to encapsulate the intermeshed stakes of frontier life—survival, economy, loneliness, and companionship—forces that are both positive and negative. *Nomadland*, on the other hand, expands on Zhao's exploration of the contemporary West as a *frontera* (Ben-Youssef; Mayer). If the characters of *Songs My Brother Taught Me* (2015) and *The Rider* (2017) demonstrate the hybridity of contemporary

Native American and cowboy culture, those of *Nomadland* draw comfort from the power of the contemporary West as a natural and social space. Portrayed as a viable alternative to capitalism, which, as the Amazon factory suggests, demands that workers lead static lives in order for goods to circulate, nomad life derives its rhythms from one's encounters with the natural world and with people whose backgrounds and experiences are varied.

One set of multiple frontiers that requires prime attention concerns the international circulation not so much of Western movies as such, but of the myth of the West. Such research would pursue the work carried out by Emily C. Burns in *Transnational Frontiers: The American West in France*, and chapters 1, 9, and 15 of the present volume. They show that the production of silent Westerns owed less to the development of the US-American Western movie as to other influences, including the popularity of Pathé Western-themed productions, Buffalo Bill's Wild West Show, and, even earlier and more generally, a fascination for the US-American West that had grown since the Paris exposition of 1867. Thus, a more complete view of the transnational history of the Western will need to answer such questions: Did the myth of the West circulate broadly before the emergence of cinema? And how was it articulated with local cultures of imperialism? It is well known, for instance, that James Fenimore Cooper's Leatherstocking tales were translated in French only a couple of years after their publication in the US, that George Catlin's "Indian gallery" was enthusiastically received in Europe in the 1840s, and that Buffalo Bill's Wild West Show toured Western and Eastern Europe in 1905–1906. But less clear are how these texts and spectacles resonated with local myths of empire, and how their reception abroad came to shape, in turn, the production of the myth of the West in the US.

Another path that needs further trailblazing involves the variety of media and practices that sustained the global circulation of the Western. Once cinema had become a popular art, did it become the dominant purveyor of the myth or did other media play a significant role? Comics published in Belgium and France (*Lucky Luke*, 1946–), Switzerland (*Yakari*, 1969–), Italy (*Il Grande Blek*, 1954–1967; *Tex Willer*, 1948–), and Yugoslavia (the original and translated series of Dnevnik's *Zlatna serija*, 1968–1992) come to mind but, as Emily Burns noted of the impact of the US-American West on France's creative production in the late nineteenth century, art forms and artefacts such as "illustration, painting, sculpture, photography, literature, posters, caricature, toys, ceramics, metalwork, film, cartography, collecting, and live performance" must be explored as well (3). The pervasiveness of the Western and the myth of the West in all areas of cultural production is also manifest at the level of cultural practices. Square dancing and country singing formations, rodeo clubs, and

Western-themed festivals and events appear on the municipal billboards of the remotest towns from Japan to Poland, where audiences appropriate the folklore of the US West and articulate it to local popular arts. Closer to film, television is another important medium in the production of the global Western. Children around the world have grown up watching Western-themed Japanese anime such as *Monarch: The Big Bear of Tallach* (TV Asahi, 1977) and *Tom Sawyer* (Fuji TV, 1980). More recently, television has participated in the global surge of interest for the Western genre, with productions such as *Tierra de lobos* in Spain (Telecinco, 2010–2014), *Templeton* in France (OCS, 2015), and *Mystery Road* in Australia—although to this day very few Western TV series produced outside the US seem to have garnered a resonant success and influence beyond their national borders.

The venues of exploration raised by this book have convinced us that it is by no means time to ride off into the sunset alone. On the contrary, it is time to pursue the adventure collectively and, like Zhao's nomads, to pay careful attention to the vital forces of the West and the Western.

WORKS CITED

Ben-Youssef, Fareed. "Just Make Me Look Good: The Duel against Mythic Representation in the Transnational Western Films of Chloé Zhao." Paper presented at the conference "Transnationalism and Imperialism: New Perspectives on the Western." Université Paul Valéry Montpellier 3, 16 Nov. 2018.

Burns, Emily C. *Transnational Frontiers: The American West in France.* University of Oklahoma Press, 2018.

Mayer, Hervé. "Neo Frontier Cinema: Rewriting the Frontier Narrative from the Margins in *Meek's Cutoff* (Kelly Reichardt, 2010), *Songs My Brother Taught Me* (Chloé Zhao, 2015) and *The Rider* (Chloé Zhao, 2017)." *Miranda*, vol. 18, 2019, https://journals.openedition.org/miranda/16672. Accessed 19 Jan. 2021.

Teo, Stephen. *Eastern Westerns: Film and Genre Outside and Inside Hollywood.* Routledge, 2017.

HERVÉ MAYER is Assistant Professor of American Studies at Université Paul Valéry Montpellier 3. He is author of *Guerre sauvage & empire de la liberté* and *La Construction de l'Ouest américain dans le cinéma hollywoodien.*

DAVID ROCHE is Professor of Film Studies at Université Paul Valéry Montpellier 3. He is author of *Making and Remaking Horror in the 1970s and 2000s: Why Don't They Do It Like They Used To?* and of *Quentin Tarantino: Poetics and Politics of Cinematic Metafiction.*

INDEX

CPSIA information can be obtained
at www.ICGtesting.com
Printed in the USA
JSHW050542200422
25100JS00001BA/51